CompTIA Server+
Study Guide

CompTIA Server+®
Study Guide

Troy McMillan

Senior Acquisitions Editor: Kenyon Brown
Development Editor: David Clark
Technical Editors: Robin Abernathy and Quentin Docter
Production Editor: Christine O'Connor
Copy Editor: Elizabeth Welch
Editorial Manager: Mary Beth Wakefield
Production Manager: Kathleen Wisor
Executive Editor: Jim Minatel
Book Designers: Judy Fung and Bill Gibson
Proofreader: Rebecca Rider
Indexer: John Sleeva
Project Coordinator, Cover: Brent Savage
Cover Designer: Wiley
Cover Image: Getty Images Inc./Jeremy Woodhouse

Copyright © 2016 by John Wiley & Sons, Inc., Indianapolis, Indiana

Published simultaneously in Canada

ISBN: 978-1-119-13782-5
ISBN: 978-1-119-13784-9 (ebk.)
ISBN: 978-1-119-13783-2 (ebk.)

Manufactured in the United States of America

For general information on our other products and services or to obtain technical support, please contact our Customer Care Department within the U.S. at (877) 762-2974, outside the U.S. at (317) 572-3993 or fax (317) 572-4002.

Wiley publishes in a variety of print and electronic formats and by print-on-demand. Some material included with standard print versions of this book may not be included in e-books or in print-on-demand. If this book refers to media such as a CD or DVD that is not included in the version you purchased, you may download this material at http://booksupport.wiley.com. For more information about Wiley products, visit www.wiley.com.

Library of Congress Control Number: 2016940086

For my wife Heike, who makes the hard work all worth it

Acknowledgments

Special thanks go to David Clark for keeping me on schedule and ensuring all the details are correct. Also I'd like to thank Robin Abernathy and Quentin Docter for the excellent technical edit that saved me from myself at times. Finally, as always I'd like to acknowledge Kenyon Brown for his continued support of all my writing efforts.

About the Author

Troy McMillan writes practice tests, study guides, and online course materials for Kaplan IT Cert Prep, while also running his own consulting and training business. He holds over 30 industry certifications. Troy can be reached at mcmillantroy@hotmail.com.

Contents at a Glance

Contents

Table of Exercises

CompTIA.

Becoming a
CompTIA Certified
IT Professional is Easy

It's also the best way to reach greater
professional opportunities and rewards.

Why Get CompTIA Certified?

Growing Demand

Labor estimates predict some
technology fields will
experience growth of over 20%
by the year 2020.* CompTIA
certification qualifies the skills
required to join this workforce.

Higher Salaries

IT professionals with
certifications on their resume
command better jobs, earn
higher salaries and have more
doors open to new multiindustry
opportunities.

Verified Strengths

91% of hiring managers
indicate CompTIA certifications
are valuable in validating IT
expertise, making certification
the best way to demonstrate
your competency and
knowledge to employers.**

Universal Skills

CompTIA certifications are
vendor neutral—which means
that certified professionals can
proficiently work with an
extensive variety of hardware
and software found in most
organizations.

 **Learn** > **Certify** > **Work**

Learn more about what
the exam covers by
reviewing the following:

- Exam objectives for
  key study points.

- Sample questions for a general
  overview of what to expect
  on the exam and examples
  of question format.

- Visit online forums, like LinkedIn,
  to see what other IT professionals
  say about CompTIA exams.

Purchase a voucher at a
Pearson VUE testing center
or at CompTIAstore.com.

- Register for your exam at a
  Pearson VUE testing center.

- Visit pearsonvue.com/CompTIA to
  find the closest testing center to you.

- Schedule the exam online. You will
  be required to enter your voucher
  number or provide payment
  information at registration.

- Take your certification exam.

Congratulations on your
CompTIA certification!

- Make sure to add your
  certification to your resume.

- Check out the CompTIA
  Certification Roadmap to plan
  your next career move.

Learn more: Certification.CompTIA.org/serverplus

Introduction

The Server+ certification program was developed by the Computing Technology Industry Association (CompTIA) to provide an industry-wide means of certifying the competency of computer server technicians. The Server+ certification, which is granted to those who have attained the level of knowledge and troubleshooting skills that are needed to provide capable support to the most commonly used server and storage systems, is similar to other certifications in the computer industry. The theory behind these certifications is that if you needed to have service performed on any of their products, you would sooner call a technician who has been certified in one of the appropriate programs than you would just call the first so-called "expert" in the phone book.

CompTIA's Server+ exam objectives are periodically updated to keep the certification applicable to the most recent hardware and software. This is necessary because a technician must be able to work on the latest equipment. The most recent revisions to the objectives—and to the whole program—were introduced in 2015 and are reflected in this book.

This book and Sybex's *CompTIA Server+ Complete Study Guide* (both the Standard and Deluxe Editions) are tools to help you prepare for this certification—and for the new areas of focus of a modern server technician's job.

What Is Server+ Certification?

The Server+ certification program was created to offer a wide-ranging certification, in the sense that it's intended to certify competence with servers from many different makers/vendors. Everyone must take and pass one exam: SK0-004.

The Server+ certification isn't awarded until you've passed the test. For the latest pricing on the exams and updates to the registration procedures, call Pearson VUE at (877) 551-7587. You can also go to the website, www.vue.com, for additional information or to register online. If you have further questions about the scope of the exams or related CompTIA programs, refer to the CompTIA website at www.comptia.org.

Who Should Buy This Book?

If you want to acquire a solid foundation in servers and the storage systems they use, and your goal is to prepare for the exams by filling in any gaps in your knowledge, this book is for you. You'll find clear explanations of the concepts you need to grasp and plenty of help to achieve the high level of professional competency you need in order to succeed in your chosen field.

If you want to become certified as a Server+ holder, this book is definitely what you need. However, if you just want to attempt to pass the exam without really understanding the basics of personal computers, this guide isn't for you. It's written for people who want to acquire skills and knowledge of servers and storage systems.

What Does This Book Cover?

This book covers everything you need to know to pass the CompTIA Server+ exam.

What's Included in the Book

We've included several learning tools throughout the book:

Objective map and opening list of objectives   We have included a detailed exam objective map showing you where each of the exam objectives is covered. In addition, each chapter opens with a list of the exam objectives it covers. Use these resources to see exactly where each of the exam topics is covered.

Assessment test   We have provided an assessment test that you can use to check your readiness for the exam at the end of this Introduction. Take this test before you start reading the book; it will help you determine the areas on which you might need to brush up. The answers to the assessment test questions appear on a separate page after the last question of the test. Each answer includes an explanation and a note telling you the chapter in which the material appears.

Exam essentials   Each chapter, just before the summary, includes a number of exam essentials. These are the key topics that you should take from the chapter in terms of areas on which you should focus when preparing for the exam.

Chapter Review Questions   To test your knowledge as you progress through the book, there are review questions at the end of each chapter. As you finish each chapter, answer the review questions and then check your answers—the correct answers appear in the Appendix. You can go back to reread the section that deals with each question you got wrong to ensure that you answer correctly the next time you're tested on the material.

Interactive Online Learning Environment and Test Bank

The interactive online learning environment that accompanies CompTIA Server+ Exam SK0-004 provides a test bank with study tools to help you prepare for the certification exams and increase your chances of passing them the first time! The test bank includes the following elements:

Sample tests   All of the questions in this book are provided, including the assessment test, which you'll find at the end of this introduction, and the chapter tests that include the review questions at the end of each chapter. In addition, there are two practice exams. Use these questions to test your knowledge of the study guide material. The online test bank runs on multiple devices.

Flashcards   One set of questions is provided in digital flashcard format (a question followed by a single correct answer). You can use the flashcards to reinforce your learning and provide last-minute test prep before the exam.

Glossary   The key terms from this book and their definitions are available as a fully searchable PDF.

 Go to http://sybextestbanks.wiley.com to register and gain access to this interactive online learning environment and test bank with study tools.

How to Use This Book

If you want a solid foundation for preparing for the Server+ exam, this is the book for you. I've spent countless hours putting together this book with the sole intention of helping you prepare for the exams.

This book is loaded with valuable information, and you will get the most out of your study time if you understand how we put the book together. Here's a list that describes how to approach studying:

1. Take the assessment test immediately following this introduction. It's okay if you don't know any of the answers—that's what this book is for. Carefully read over the explanations for any question you get wrong, and make note of the chapters where that material is covered.

2. Study each chapter carefully, making sure you fully understand the information and the exam objectives listed at the beginning of each one. Again, pay extra-close attention to any chapter that includes material covered in questions you missed on the assessment test.

3. Read over the summary and exam essentials. These will highlight the sections from the chapter with which you need to be familiar before sitting for the exam.

4. Answer all of the review questions at the end of each chapter. Specifically note any questions that confuse you, and study the corresponding sections of the book again. Don't just skim these questions! Make sure that you understand each answer completely.

5. Go over the electronic flashcards. These help you prepare for the latest Server+ exam, and they're really great study tools.

6. Take the practice exam.

Performance-Based Questions

CompTIA includes performance-based questions on the Server+ exams. These are not the traditional multiple-choice questions with which you're probably familiar. These questions require the candidate to know how to perform a specific task or series of tasks. The candidate will be presented with a scenario and will be asked to complete a task. They will be taken to a simulated environment where they will have to perform a series of steps and will be graded on how well they complete the task.

Tips for Taking the Server+ Exam

Here are some general tips for taking your exams successfully:

- Bring two forms of ID with you. One must be a photo ID, such as a driver's license. The other can be a major credit card or a passport. Both forms must include a signature.

- Arrive early at the exam center so you can relax and review your study materials, particularly tables and lists of exam-related information.

- Read the questions carefully. Don't be tempted to jump to an early conclusion. Make sure you know exactly what the question is asking.

- Don't leave any unanswered questions. Unanswered questions are scored against you.

- There will be questions with multiple correct responses. When there is more than one correct answer, a message at the bottom of the screen will prompt you to either "Choose two" or "Choose all that apply." Be sure to read the messages displayed to know how many correct answers you must choose.

- When answering multiple-choice questions you're not sure about, use a process of elimination to get rid of the obviously incorrect answers first. Doing so will improve your odds if you need to make an educated guess.

- On form-based tests (nonadaptive), because the hard questions will eat up the most time, save them for last. You can move forward and backward through the exam.

- For the latest pricing on the exams and updates to the registration procedures, visit CompTIA's website at www.comptia.org.

The CompTIA Server+ Exam Objectives

CompTIA goes to great lengths to ensure that its certification programs accurately reflect the IT industry's best practices. The company does this by establishing Cornerstone Committees for each of its exam programs. Each committee consists of a small group of IT professionals, training providers, and publishers who are responsible for establishing the exam's baseline competency level and who determine the appropriate target audience level.

Once these factors are determined, CompTIA shares this information with a group of hand-selected Subject Matter Experts (SMEs). These folks are the true brainpower behind the certification program. They review the committee's findings, refine them, and shape them into the objectives you see before you. CompTIA calls this process a Job Task Analysis (JTA).

Finally, CompTIA conducts a survey to ensure that the objectives and weightings truly reflect the job requirements. Only then can the SMEs go to work writing the hundreds of questions needed for the exam. And, in many cases, they have to go back to the drawing board for further refinements before the exam is ready to go live in its final state. So, rest assured, the content you're about to learn will serve you long after you take the exam.

Exam objectives are subject to change at any time without prior notice and at CompTIA's sole discretion. Please visit the certification page of CompTIA's website at www.comptia.org for the most current listing of exam objectives.

CompTIA also publishes relative weightings for each of the exam's objectives. The following tables list the objective domains and the extent to which they're represented on each exam.

SK0-004 Exam Domains	% of Exam
1.0 Server Architecture	12%
2.0 Server Administration	24%
3.0 Storage	12%
4.0 Security	13%
5.0 Networking	10%
6.0 Disaster Recovery	9%
7.0 Troubleshooting	20%
Total	100%

The following sections look at the objectives beneath each of these domains in more detail.

CompTIA SK0-004 Exam

1.1 Explain the purpose and function of server form factors

- Rack mount
  - Dimensions
    - 1U, 2U, 4U
  - Cable management arms
  - Rail kits

- Tower
- Blade technology
  - Blade enclosure
- Backplane/Midplane
- Power supply sockets
- Network modules/switches
- Management modules
  - Blade server

1.2 Given a scenario, install, configure and maintain server components

- CPU
  - Multiprocessor vs. multicore
  - Socket type
  - Cache levels: L1, L2, L3
  - Speeds
- Core
- Bus
- Multiplier
  - CPU stepping
  - Architecture
- x86
- x64
- ARM
- RAM
  - ECC vs. non-ECC
  - DDR2, DDR3
  - Number of pins
  - Static vs. dynamic
  - Module placement
  - CAS latency
  - Timing
  - Memory pairing

- Bus types, bus channels, and expansion slots
    - Height differences and bit rate differences
    - PCI
    - PCIe
    - PCI-X
- NICs
- Hard drives
- Riser cards
- RAID controllers
- BIOS/UEFI
    - CMOS battery
- Firmware
- USB interface/port
- Hotswap vs. non-hotswap components

1.3 Compare and contrast power and cooling components

- Power
    - Voltage
- 110v vs. 220v vs. −48v
- 208v vs. 440v/460v/480v
- Wattage
    - Consumption
    - Redundancy
    - 1-phase vs. 3-phase power
    - Plug types
- NEMA
- Edison
- Twist lock
- Cooling
    - Airflow
    - Thermal dissipation
    - Baffles/shrouds

- Fans
- Liquid cooling

2.1 Install and configure server operating systems

- Determine server role/purpose
- Update firmware
- BIOS/UEFI configuration
    - Boot order
- Disk preparation
    - RAID setup
    - Partitioning
    - Formatting
    - File system type
        - Ext 2, 3, 4
        - NTFS
        - FAT32
        - ReiserFS
        - UFS
        - VMFS
        - ZFS
    - Swap
- Configure host name
- Local account setup
- Connect to network
- Join domain/directory
- Address security concerns
    - Patching
    - OS hardening
    - Compliance to company procedures/standards
- Enable services
- Install features/roles/applications/drivers
- Performance baseline
    - Server optimization
    - Swap or pagefile optimization

- Unattended/remote installations
  - Deploying images and cloning
  - Scripted installs
    - PXE boot
    - TFTP

2.2 Compare and contrast server roles and requirements for each

- Web server
- Application server
- Directory server
- Database server
- File server
- Print server
- Messaging server
- Mail server
- Routing and remote access server
- Network services server
  - DHCP
  - DNS/WINS
  - NTP

2.3 Given a scenario, use access and control methods to administer a server

- Local hardware administration
  - KVM
  - Serial
  - Virtual Administration console
- Network-based hardware administration
  - KVM over IP
  - ILO
  - iDRAC

- Network-based operating system administration
    - RDP
    - SSH
    - VNC
    - Command line/shell

2.4 Given a scenario, perform proper server maintenance techniques

- Change management
- Patch management
    - Operating System updates
    - Application updates
    - Security software updates
    - Firmware updates
    - Device drivers updates
    - Compatibility lists
- Operating systems
- Hardware
- Applications
    - Testing and validation
- Outages and service level agreements
    - Scheduled downtime
    - Unscheduled downtime
    - Impact analysis
    - Client notification
    - MTTR
- Performance monitoring
    - CPU utilization
    - Memory utilization
    - Network utilization
    - Disk utilization
        - Disk IOPS
        - Storage capacity

- Comparison against performance baseline
- Processes and services monitoring
- Log monitoring
- Hardware maintenance
  - Check system health indicators
    - LEDs
    - Error codes
    - Beep codes
    - LCD messages
  - Replace failed components
    - Fans
    - Hard drives
    - RAM
    - Backplanes
    - Batteries
  - Preventative maintenance
    - Clearing dust
    - Check proper air flow
  - Proper shut down procedures
- Fault tolerance and high availability techniques
  - Clustering
    - Active/active
    - Active/passive
  - Load balancing
    - Round robin
    - Heartbeat

2.5 Explain the importance of asset management and documentation

- Asset management
  - Licensing
  - Labeling
  - Warranty

- Life cycle management
  - Procurement
  - Usage
  - End of life
  - Disposal/recycling
- Inventory
  - Make
  - Model
  - Serial number
  - Asset tag
- Documentation
  - Service manuals
  - Network diagrams
  - Architecture diagrams
  - Dataflow diagrams
  - Recovery documentation
  - Baseline documentation
  - Change management policies
  - Service Level Agreement
  - Server configuration
- Secure storage of sensitive documentation

2.6 Explain the purpose and operation of virtualization components

- Hosts and guests
- Management interface for virtual machines
- Hypervisor
  - Type I
  - Type II
  - Hybrid
- Hardware compatibility list
  - BIOS/UEFI compatibility and support
  - CPU compatibility support
  - AMD-V/Intel VT

- Resource allocation between Guest and Host
  - CPU
  - Storage
  - Memory
  - Network connectivity
    - Direct Access (Bridging) vs. NAT
    - Virtual NICs
    - Virtual switches
  - Video

3.1 Given a scenario, install and deploy primary storage devices based on given specifications and interfaces

- Disk specifications
  - RPM
  - Dimensions/form factor
  - Capacity
  - Bus width
  - IOPS
  - Seek time and latency
  - Hotswap vs. non-hotswap components
- Interfaces
  - SAS
  - SATA
  - SCSI
  - USB
  - Fibre Channel
- Hard drive vs. SSD

3.2 Given a scenario, configure RAID using best practices

- RAID levels and performance considerations
  - 0

- 1
- 5
- 6
- 10
- Software vs. hardware RAID
  - Performance considerations
- Configuration specifications
  - Capacity
  - Bus types
  - Drive RPM
- Hotswap support and ramifications
- Hot spare vs. cold spare
- Array controller
  - Memory
  - Battery backed cache
  - Redundant controller

3.3 Summarize hardware and features of various storage technologies

- DAS
- NAS
  - iSCSI
  - FCoE
- SAN
  - Fibre Channel
  - LUN and LUN masking
  - HBAs and fabric switches
- JBOD
- Tape
  - Drive
  - Libraries
- Optical drive
- Flash, Compact Flash, and USB drive

3.4 Given a scenario, calculate appropriate storage capacity and plan for future growth

- Base10 vs. Base2 disk size calculation (1000 vs. 1024)
- Disk quotas
- Compression
- Capacity planning considerations:
    - Operating system growth
        - Patches
        - Service packs
        - Log files
    - Temporary directories
    - Databases
    - Application servers
    - File servers
    - Archival

4.1 Compare and contrast physical security methods and concepts

- Multifactor Authentication
    - Something you have
    - Something you know
    - Something you are
- Security concepts
    - Mantrap
    - RFID chip
    - ID card
    - Biometric
    - Keypad
    - Access list
    - Security guard
    - Security camera

- Keys & Locks
  - Cabinet
  - Rack mount
  - Server
- Safe

4.2 Given a scenario, apply server hardening techniques

- OS hardening
  - Stopping unneeded services/closing unneeded ports
  - Install only required software
  - Install latest operating system patches
- Application hardening
  - Install latest patches
  - Disabling unneeded services/roles/features
- Endpoint security
  - HIDS
  - Anti-malware
- Remediate security issues based on a vulnerability scan
- Hardware hardening
  - Disabling unneeded hardware and physical ports/devices
  - BIOS password
  - Disable WOL (Wake on LAN)
  - Set up boot order
  - Chassis locks/intrusion detection

4.3 Explain basic network security systems and protocols

- Firewall
  - Network-based
  - Host-based
- Port security/802.1x/NAC
- Router access list
- NIDS

- Authentication protocols
  - LDAP
  - RADIUS
  - TACACS
  - TACACS+
- PKI
  - Private key
  - Public key
  - Certificate authority
  - SSL/TLS
- VPN
- IPSEC
- VLAN
- Security zones
  - DMZ
  - Public and private
  - Intranet and extranet

4.4 Implement logical access control methods based on company policy

- Access control lists
  - Users
  - Groups
    - Roles
  - Resources
    - File system
    - Network ACLs
    - Peripheral devices
    - Administrative rights
    - Distribution lists
  - Permissions
    - Read
    - Write/Modify
    - Execute

- Delete
- Full control/Superuser
- File vs. share

4.5 Implement data security methods and secure storage disposal techniques

- Storage encryption
  - File-level encryption
  - Disk encryption
  - Tape encryption
- Storage media
  - Soft wipe
    - File deletion
  - Hard wipe
    - Zero out all sectors
  - Physical destruction
  - Remote wipe

4.6 Given a scenario, implement proper environmental controls and techniques

- Power concepts and best practices
  - UPS
    - Runtime vs. capacity
    - Automated graceful shutdown of attached devices
    - Periodic testing of batteries
    - Maximum load
    - Bypass procedures
    - Remote management
  - PDU
    - Connect redundant rack PDUs to separate circuits
  - Capacity planning
    - PDU ratings
    - UPS ratings
    - Total potential power draw

- Multiple circuits
    - Connect redundant power supplies to separate PDUs
- Safety
    - ESD procedures
    - Fire suppression
    - Proper lifting techniques
    - Rack stability
    - Floor load limitations
    - Sharp edges and pinch points
- HVAC
    - Room and rack temperature and humidity
        - Monitoring and alert notifications
    - Air flow
        - Rack filler/baffle/blanking panels
    - Hot aisle and cold aisle

5.1 Given a scenario, configure servers to use IP addressing and network infrastructure services

- IPv4 vs. IPv6
- Default gateway
- CIDR notation and subnetting
- Public and private IP addressing
- Static IP assignment vs. DHCP
- DNS
    - FQDN
    - Default domain suffix/search domain
- WINS
- NetBIOS
- NAT/PAT
- MAC addresses
- Network Interface Card configuration
    - NIC teaming
    - Duplexing
        - Full

- Half
- Auto
- Speeds
  - 10/100/1000 Mbps
  - 10 Gbps

5.2 Compare and contrast various ports and protocols

- TCP vs. UDP
- SNMP 161
- SMTP 25
- FTP 20/21
- SFTP 22
- SSH 22
- SCP 22
- NTP 123
- HTTP 80
- HTTPS 443
- TELNET 23
- IMAP 143
- POP3 110
- RDP 3389
- FTPS 989/990
- LDAP 389/3268
- DNS 53
- DHCP 68

5.3 Given a scenario, install cables and implement proper cable management procedures

- Copper
  - Patch cables
    - Crossover
    - Straight through
    - Rollover

- CAT5
- CAT5e
- CAT6
- Fiber
  - Singlemode
  - Multimode
- Connectors
  - ST
  - LC
  - SC
  - SFP
  - RJ-45
  - RJ-11
- Cable placement and routing
  - Cable channels
  - Cable management trays
    - Vertical
    - Horizontal
- Labeling
- Bend radius
- Cable ties

6.1 Explain the importance of disaster recovery principles

- Site types
  - Hot site
  - Cold site
  - Warm site
- Replication methods
  - Disk to disk
  - Server to server
  - Site to site
- Continuity of Operations
  - Disaster recovery plan
  - Business continuity plan

- Business impact analysis
    - Who is affected
    - What is affected
    - Severity of impact

6.2 Given a scenario, implement appropriate backup techniques

- Methodology
    - Full/Normal
        - Copy
    - Incremental
    - Differential
    - Snapshot
    - Selective
    - Bare metal
    - Open file
    - Data vs. OS restore
- Backup media
    - Linear Access
        - Tape
    - Random Access
        - Disk
        - Removable media
        - Optical media
- Media and restore best practices
    - Labeling
    - Integrity verification
    - Test restorability
    - Tape rotation and retention
- Media storage location
    - Offsite
    - Onsite
    - Security considerations
    - Environmental considerations

7.1 Explain troubleshooting theory and methodologies

- Identify the problem and determine the scope
  - Question users/stakeholders and identify changes to the server/environment
  - Collect additional documentation/logs
  - If possible, replicate the problem as appropriate
  - If possible, perform backups before making changes
- Establish a theory of probable cause (question the obvious)
  - Determine whether there is a common element of symptom causing multiple problems
- Test the theory to determine cause
  - Once theory is confirmed, determine next steps to resolve problem
  - If theory is not confirmed, establish new theory or escalate
- Establish a plan of action to resolve the problem and notify impacted users
- Implement the solution or escalate as appropriate
  - Make one change at a time and test/confirm the change has resolved the problem
  - If the problem is not resolved, reverse the change if appropriate and implement a new change
- Verify full system functionality and if applicable implement preventative measures
- Perform a root cause analysis
- Document findings, actions and outcomes throughout the process

7.2 Given a scenario, effectively troubleshoot hardware problems, selecting the appropriate tools and methods

- Common problems
  - Failed POST
  - Overheating
  - Memory failure
  - Onboard component failure
  - Processor failure
  - Incorrect boot sequence
  - Expansion card failure
  - Operating system not found
  - Drive failure

- Power supply failure
- I/O failure
- Causes of common problems
  - Third-party components or incompatible components
  - Incompatible or incorrect BIOS
  - Cooling failure
  - Mismatched components
  - Backplane failure
- Environmental issues
  - Dust
  - Humidity
  - Temperature
  - Power surge/failure
- Hardware tools
  - Power supply tester (multimeter)
  - Hardware diagnostics
  - Compressed air
  - ESD equipment

7.3 Given a scenario, effectively troubleshoot software problems, selecting the appropriate tools and methods

- Common problems
  - User unable to logon
  - User cannot access resources
  - Memory leak
  - BSOD/stop
  - OS boot failure
  - Driver issues
  - Runaway process
  - Cannot mount drive
  - Cannot write to system log
  - Slow OS performance
  - Patch update failure

- Service failure
- Hangs on shut down
- Users cannot print
- Cause of common problems
  - User Account Control (UAC/SUDO)
  - Corrupted files
  - Lack of hard drive space
  - Lack of system resources
  - Virtual memory (misconfigured, corrupt)
  - Fragmentation
  - Print server drivers/services
  - Print spooler
- Software tools
  - System logs
  - Monitoring tools (resource monitor, performance monitor)
  - Defragmentation tools
  - Disk property tools (usage, free space, volume, or drive mapping)

7.4 Given a scenario, effectively diagnose network problems, selecting the appropriate tools and methods

- Common problems
  - Internet connectivity failure
  - Email failure
  - Resource unavailable
  - DHCP server mis-configured
  - Non-functional or unreachable
  - Destination host unreachable
  - Unknown host
  - Default gateway mis-configured
  - Failure of service provider
  - Cannot reach by host name/FQDN
- Causes of common problems
  - Improper IP configuration
  - VLAN configuration

- Port security
- Improper subnetting
- Component failure
- Incorrect OS route tables
- Bad cables
- Firewall (mis-configuration, hardware failure, software failure)
- Mis-configured NIC, routing/switch issues
- DNS and/or DHCP failure
- Mis-configured hosts file
- IPv4 vs. IPv6 misconfigurations
- Networking tools
  - ping
  - tracert/traceroute
  - ipconfig/ifconfig
  - nslookup
  - net use/mount
  - route
  - nbtstat
  - netstat

7.5 Given a scenario, effectively troubleshoot storage problems, selecting the appropriate tools and methods

- Common problems
  - Slow file access
  - OS not found
  - Data not available
  - Unsuccessful backup
  - Error lights
  - Unable to mount the device
  - Drive not available
  - Cannot access logical drive
  - Data corruption

- Slow I/O performance
- Restore failure
- Cache failure
- Multiple drive failure
- Causes of common problems
  - Media failure
  - Drive failure
  - Controller failure
  - HBA failure
  - Loose connectors
  - Cable problems
  - Mis-configuration
  - Improper termination
  - Corrupt boot sector
  - Corrupt file system table
  - Array rebuild
  - Improper disk partition
  - Bad sectors
  - Cache battery failure
  - Cache turned off
  - Insufficient space
  - Improper RAID configuration
  - Mis-matched drives
  - Backplane failure
- Storage tools
  - Partitioning tools
  - Disk management
  - RAID array management
  - Array management
  - System logs
  - Net use/mount command
  - Monitoring tools

7.6 Given a scenario, effectively diagnose security issues, selecting the appropriate tools and methods

- Common problems
    - File integrity issue
    - Privilege escalation
    - Applications will not load
    - Can't access network file/shares
    - Unable to open files
    - Excessive access
    - Excessive memory utilization
- Causes of common problems
    - Open ports
    - Active services
    - Inactive services
    - Intrusion detection configurations
    - Anti-malware configurations
    - Local/group policies
    - Firewall rules
    - Misconfigured permissions
    - Virus infection
    - Rogue processes/services
- Security tools
    - Port scanners
    - Sniffers
    - Cipher
    - Checksums
    - Telnet client
    - Anti-malware

Objective Map

The following objective map shows you where the exam objectives are covered in the chapters. Use it as a reference to find the information you're looking for.

CompTIA Server + Study Guide

SK0-004 Exam Objectives

Exam specifications and content are subject to change at any time without prior notice and at CompTIA's sole discretion. Please visit CompTIA's website (www.comptia.org) for the most current information on the exam content.

Assessment Test

1. Which of the following is *not* part of the form factor of a server?
   A. Size
   B. Appearance
   C. Dimensions
   D. Security

2. Which function is made easier when a server has a rail kit?
   A. Installation
   B. Maintenance
   C. Configuration
   D. Accessing

3. Which of the following is the unit of measurement when discussing rack components?
   A. M
   B. I
   C. U
   D. C

4. Which of the following is another term for RAID 1?
   A. Duplicating
   B. Doubling
   C. Duplexing
   D. Mirroring

5. What is the primary function of PXE?
   A. Remote booting
   B. Secure routing
   C. Remote administration
   D. Redundant connections

6. Shares are used to allocate which of the following to VMs?
   A. ROM
   B. CPU
   C. NVRAM
   D. L2 cache

7. What is the most common protocol a SAN uses?

    A. IPX

    B. IP

    C. Ethernet

    D. Fibre Channel

8. Which of the following is true of a NAS?

    A. A NAS has lower latency and higher reliability than a SAN.

    B. A NAS typically supports only RAID 5.

    C. A NAS does not support high throughput.

    D. Implementing a NAS is inexpensive.

9. To which protocol is the term LUN related?

    A. SCSI

    B. IP

    C. SSL

    D. FDDI

10. What is the role of a DHCP server in a network?

    A. Issues IP configurations

    B. Translates private to public addresses

    C. Authenticates users

    D. Resolves IP addresses to hostnames

11. The metric IOPS is used to describe the performance of which resource?

    A. Memory

    B. Disk

    C. CPU

    D. Network

12. As the number of users assigned to a printer increases, which resource should be increased?

    A. Disk

    B. Metwork

    C. CPU

    D. Memory

13. What is the function of the command-line utility wevtutil?

    A. Manages log files

    B. Manages network connections

    C. Manages memory issues

    D. Manages CPU affinity

14. Which of the following is deleted when you execute Disk Cleanup?

 A. Temp files

 B. Memory

 C. Routing tables

 D. Pagefile

15. Which RAID version requires at least three drives?

 A. RAID 0

 B. RAID 1

 C. RAID 5

 D. RAID 10

16. Which of the following statements is true with respect to safes?

 A. No safes are fireproof.

 B. Consumer Reports assigns ratings to safes that you can use to assess the suitability of the safe.

 C. Those that are fire resistant will protect a backup tape from being damaged.

 D. When considering a safe, you should focus on two items: the cost and the size.

17. Which of the following is true of an HIDS?

 A. A high number of false negatives can cause a lax attitude on the part of the security team.

 B. An HIDS cannot address authentication issues.

 C. Encrypted packets can be analyzed.

 D. An HIDS monitors only traffic destined for the machine on which it is installed.

18. The MBSA vulnerability scanner works on which operating system only?

 A. Linux

 B. Windows

 C. Unix

 D. Mac

19. Which of the following would Joe use to digitally sign a document so that Sally can verify his signature?

 A. Joe's private key

 B. Sally's private key

 C. Joe's public key

 D. Sally's public key

20. Which authentication mechanism is an example of something you are?

   A. Password

   B. Username

   C. Smartcard

   D. Retina scan

21. What is a common host-based firewall on Linux-based systems?

   A. iptables

   B. nessus

   C. tripwire

   D. scannow

22. Which of the following can be accomplished using port security?

   A. Set the minimum number of MAC addresses that can be seen on a port

   B. Set the maximum number of IP addresses that can be seen on a port

   C. Define exactly which MAC addresses are not allowed on the port

   D. Set the maximum number of MAC addresses that can be seen on a port

23. When discussing 802.1x, which of the following roles is played by the user's computer?

   A. Supplicant

   B. Authenticator

   C. Authentication server

   D. Imperative

24. Which is the minimum category of cable required for 100 Mbps transmissions?

   A. CAT3

   B. CAT5

   C. CAT5e

   D. CAT6

25. Which of the following services uses port number 443?

   A. SFTP

   B. NTP

   C. HTTP

   D. HTTPS

26. What issue does the 802.1ax-2008 standard address?

   A. NIC teaming

   B. Deterministic routing

   C. Secure DNS

   D. MIMO

27. Which of the following parts of a MAC address is unique for each interface made by a vendor?

    A. UAA

    B. BAA

    C. OUI

    D. EUI-64

28. How many sets of backup tapes are used in the GFS system?

    A. 2

    B. 3

    C. 4

    D. 5

29. When creating a backup, what function can be used to verify the integrity of the results?

    A. Checksums

    B. Encryption

    C. Digital signatures

    D. Transaction logs

30. If you perform a full backup once a week and use a differential backup scheme the rest of the week, how many tapes are required for a restore four days after the Full backup is taken?

    A. 1

    B. 2

    C. 3

    D. 4

31. Which of the following components is the one you *most* likely would measure with a multimeter?

    A. NIC

    B. Hard drive

    C. Power supply

    D. CPU

32. What can be the result of high humidity?

    A. Corrosion

    B. ESD

    C. RFI

    D. EMI

33. Which of the following is not true about server backplanes?

    A. They can be a single point of failure.

    B. They provide data and control signal connectors for CPU.

    C. Backplane failures are uncommon.

    D. You should implement redundant backplanes.

34. Which of the following steps in the CompTIA troubleshooting method come first?

    A. Verify full system functionality and, if applicable, implement preventive measures.

    B. Document findings, actions, and outcomes throughout the process.

    C. Identify the problem and determine the scope.

    D. Perform a root cause analysis.

35. Which command is used on a Windows computer to identify the path taken to a destination network?

    A. `traceroute`

    B. `tracert`

    C. `ipconfig/trace`

    D. `trace`

36. On which type of device is port security used?

    A. Hub

    B. Switch

    C. Router

    D. Multiplexer

37. You receive a destination unreachable message with a source IP address. Where is it coming from?

    A. A remote router

    B. A remote DNS server

    C. A local DNS server

    D. The local router

38. The `sudo fdisk -l` command lists the partitions on what type of system?

    A. Windows

    B. Mac

    C. Novell

    D. Linux

39. In Linux, what is `fstab` used for?

   A. To mount partitions in boot

   B. To create partitions

   C. To format a partition

   D. To defragment a drive

40. What component locates the operating system in Linux?

   A. NTLDR

   B. GRUB

   C. Bootmgr

   D. boot.ini

Answers to Assessment Test

1. **D.** Form factor refers to the physical appearance and dimensions of the server.

2. **B.** Rail kits, when implemented, allow for the server to be slid out of the rack for maintenance.

3. **C.** Each U is 1.75 inches (4.445 cm) high.

4. **D.** RAID 1 is also known as disk mirroring. This is a method of producing fault tolerance by writing all data simultaneously to two separate drives.

5. **A.** The Preboot Execution Environment (PXE) is an industry standard client/server interface that allows networked computers that are not yet loaded with an operating system to be configured and booted remotely by an administrator.

6. **B.** There are three ways the allocation of the use of the physical CPU(s) can be controlled. These methods are as follows:
   - Shares: Using values such as Low, Normal, High, and Custom (in VMWare, for example), these values are compared to the sum of all shares of all virtual machines on the server. Therefore, they define the relative percentage each VM can use.
   - Reservation: Guaranteed CPU allocation for a VM.
   - Limit: Upper limit for a VM's CPU allocation.

7. **D.** In a classic SAN, devices communicate using the Fibre Channel protocol over a fiber network of storage devices typically connected to a Fibre Channel switch.

8. **D.** Implementing a NAS is inexpensive when compared to implementing a SAN.

9. **A.** A logical unit number (LUN) identifies a device addressed by the SCSI protocol or protocols that encapsulate SCSI, such as Fibre Channel or iSCSI.

10. **A.** DHCP servers are used to automate the process of providing an IP configuration to devices in the network. These servers respond to broadcast-based requests for a configuration by offering an IP address, subnet mask, and default gateway to the DHCP client.

11. **B.** IOPS (Input/Output Operations per Second, pronounced eye-ops) is a common disk metric that describes how fast the disk subsystem is able to read and write to the drive. Therefore, the higher this value, the better.

12. **D.** Print servers need lots of memory to hold the print jobs waiting in the print queue. The exact amount will depend on the number of users assigned to the printers being managed by this print server.

13. **A.** Managing log files can be done at the command line using the following command, inserting the name of log file and the maximum size in bytes:

```
wevtutil sl <LogName> /ms:<MaxSizeInBytes>
```

14. A. Manually performing a disk cleanup will allow you to get rid of these files (and many other useless files as well), but if you would like to create a batch file, you can automate the process.

15. C. A minimum of three drives is required for RAID 5.

16. A. With respect to fire, no safe is fireproof. Many are fire resistant and will protect a document from being destroyed, which occurs at a much higher temperature than many of the other items (such as backup tapes and CDs) can tolerate without damage. For these reasons, items such as backup tapes should be stored offsite.

17. D. A host-based system is installed on the device (for purposes of our discussion, a server) and the system focuses solely on identifying attacks on that device only.

18. B. For your Windows servers, an excellent tool is the Microsoft Baseline Security Analyzer (MBSA). This tool can identify missing security patches, weak passwords, and other security issues that are specific to installed products.

19. A. Since Sally will use Joe's public key to verify the signature, he must sign it with his private key.

20. D. While passwords and usernames are examples of something you know and a smartcard is an example of something you possess, a retina scan provides something you are.

21. A. On Linux-based systems a common host-based firewall is iptables, which replaces a previous package called ipchains. It has the ability to accept or drop packets.

22. D. It is possible to specify a maximum number of MAC addresses allowed on a port.

23. A. The user's computer is the supplicant, the access device (WAP, Dial in the server or VPN server) is the authenticator, and the RADIUS or TACACs + server is the authentication server.

24. B. CAT5 transmits data at speed up to 100 Mbps and specifies cable lengths up to 100 meters.

25. D. HTTPS is a secure form of HTTP that uses port 443.

26. A. Combining physical links can be done using proprietary methods, and there is also an IEEE standard for the process called 802.3ad, later replaced by 802.1ax-2008.

27. A. Each part of this address communicates information. The left half of the address is called the Organizationally Unique Identifier (OUI). It identifies the vendor who made the interface. The right half is called the Universally Administered Address (UAA). It will be unique for each interface made by the vendor. Together they make a globally unique MAC address.

28. B. In the Grandfather-Father-Son (GFS) backup scheme, three sets of backups are defined. Most often these three definitions are daily, weekly, and monthly.

29. A. If you create the backup using checksums (which is an option with many utilities), it will allow you to check that the data has not changed since it was made or that it has been corrupted or damaged.

30. B. You will need the last full backup tape and the last differential tape. Each differential tape contains all changes that occurred since the last full backup.

31. C. With a multimeter you can measure voltage, current, and resistance.

32. A. It is a balancing act to keep humidity at the right level since low humidity causes ESD and high humidity causes moisture condensation.

33. B. Backplanes are advantageous in that they provide data and control signal connectors for the hard drives. They also provide the interconnection for the front I/O board, power and locator buttons, and system/component status LEDs. Unfortunately, this creates a serious single point of failure because if the backplane fails, we lose communication with the servers to which it is connected.

34. C. The steps in order are

- Identify the problem and determine the scope.
- Establish a theory of probable cause.
- Test the theory to determine the cause.
- Establish a plan of action to resolve the problem and notify impacted users.
- Implement the solution or escalate as appropriate.
- Verify full system functionality and, if applicable, implement preventive measures.
- Perform a root cause analysis.
- Document findings, actions, and outcomes throughout the process.

35. B. The tracert command (traceroute in Linux and Unix) is used to trace the path of a packet through the network on routers.

36. B. Some of the things you can specify using this feature are the only MAC address or addresses allowed to send traffic in the port, the total number of MAC addresses that can transmit on the port, and an action to be taken when a violation occurs (either shut the port down or prevent transmissions by the guilty MAC address).

37. A. If the message comes with no source IP address, that means the message is coming from the local router (the default gateway of the sender). If it has a source IP address of the sender, then it is another router in the path.

38. D. The sudo fdisk -l command lists the partitions on a Linux system.

39. A. fstab (File System Table) is a file used by Linux operating systems to mount partitions on boot.

40. B. In Linux this handled by GRUB.

Chapter

1

Server Hardware

COMPTIA SERVER+ EXAM OBJECTIVES COVERED IN THIS CHAPTER:

✓ **1.1 Explain the purpose and function of server form factors**

- Rack mount (dimensions [1U, 2U, 4U], cable management arms, rail kits)

- Tower

- Blade technology (blade enclosure [backplane/midplane, power supply sockets, network modules/switches, management modules], blade server)

✓ **1.2 Given a scenario, install, configure and maintain server components**

- CPU (Multiprocessor vs. multicore, socket type, cache levels: L1, L2, L3, speeds [core, bus, multiplier], CPU stepping, architecture [x86, x64, ARM])

- RAM (ECC vs. non-ECC, DDR2, DDR3, number of pins, static vs. dynamic, module placement, CAS latency, timing, memory pairing)

- Bus types, bus channels and expansion slots (height differences and bit rate differences, PCI, PCIe, PCI-X)

- NICs

- Hard drives

- Riser cards

- RAID controllers

- BIOS/UEFI (CMOS battery)

- Firmware

- USB interface/port

- Hotswap vs. non-hotswap components

✓ 1.3 Compare and contrast power and cooling components

- Power (voltage [110V vs. 220V vs. -48V, 208V vs. 440V/460V/480V], wattage, consumption, redundancy, 1-phase vs. 3-phase power, plug types [NEMA, Edison, twist lock])

- Cooling (airflow, thermal dissipation, baffles/shrouds, fans, liquid cooling)

While servers and workstations have many of the same hardware components and in many cases use the same or similar operating systems, their roles in the network and therefore the requirements placed upon them are quite different. For this reason, CompTIA has developed the Server+ certification to validate the skills and knowledge required to design, install, and maintain server systems in the enterprise. Although many of the skills required to maintain workstations are transferable to maintaining servers, there are certainly enough differences both in the devices themselves and in the environment in which they operate to warrant such a certification. This book is designed to prepare you for the SK0-004 exam, otherwise known as the CompTIA Server+ exam.

Server Form Factors

When we use the term *form factor* when discussing any computing device or component, we are talking about its size, appearance, or dimensions. Form factor is typically used to differentiate one physical implementation of the same device or component from another. In the case of servers, we are talking about the size and dimensions of the enclosure in which the server exists.

In this section we'll look at the major server form factors: the rack mount, the tower, and the blade. Each has its own unique characteristics and considerations you need to take into account when deploying.

Rack Mount

Rack mount servers are those that are designed to be bolted into a framework called a rack and thus are designed to fit one of several standard size rack slots, or *bays*. They also require *rail kits*, which when implemented allow you to slide the server out of the rack for maintenance. One of the benefits of using racks to hold servers, routers, switches, and other hardware appliances is that a rack gets the equipment off the floor, while also making more efficient use of the space in the server room and maintaining good air circulation. A rack with a server and other devices installed is shown in Figure 1.1.

FIGURE 1.1   Server in a rack

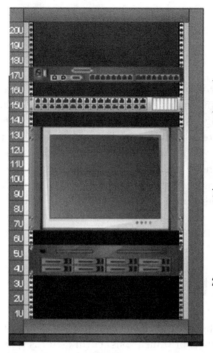

1U KVM Switch

1U Ethernet Switch/Hub

7U LCD

2U Server

20U Rack

Dimensions

As you may have noticed in Figure 1.1, there are several items in the rack and they take up various amounts of space in the rack. While both 19 and 23 inch wide racks are used, this is a 19 inch wide rack. Each module has a front panel that is 19 inches (482.6 mm) wide. The dimension where the devices or modules differ is in their height. This dimension is measured in *rack units*, or U for short. Each U is 1.75 inches (44.45 mm) high. While in the diagram the Liquid Crystal Display (LCD) takes up 7U, there are four standard sizes for servers:

1U   These are for very small appliances or servers that are only 1.75 inches high. In the diagram, there is a KVM switch (which provides a common keyboard, mouse, and monitor to use for all devices in the rack) and an Ethernet switch or hub that uses a 1U bay.

2U   This is the middle of the most common sizes. In the diagram there is a server in the bottom of the rack that is using a 2U bay.

3U   While not as common, 3U servers are also available.

4U   Although there are no devices in the rack shown in Figure 1.1 that use 4U, this is a common bay size for servers. A 4U server is shown in Figure 1.2. For comparison, this server has twice the height of the 2U server in Figure 1.1.

FIGURE 1.2   A 4U server

It is also worth knowing that there are enclosures for blade servers that can be 10U in size. The typical rack provides 42U of space.

Cable Management Arms

One of the challenges in the server room is to keep control of all the cables. When you consider the fact that servers use rail kits to allow you to slide the servers out for maintenance, there must be enough slack in both the power cable and the data cable(s) to permit this. On the other hand, you don't want a bunch of slack hanging down on the back of the rack for each device. To provide the slack required and to keep the cables from blanketing the back of the rack and causing overheating, you can use *cable management arms* (see Figure 1.3). These arms contain the slack and are designed to follow the server when you slide it out of the bay.

FIGURE 1.3   Cable management arm

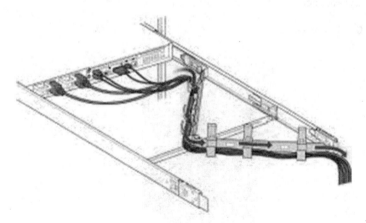

Rail Kits

You already know that rail kits are used to provide a mechanism for sliding the server out of the rack. The rail kits have an inner rack and an outer rack. The inner rack attaches to the server, whereas the outer one attaches to the rack. The inner rack is designed to fit inside the outer rack and then it "rides" or slides on the outer rack. The installation steps are shown in Figure 1.4.

FIGURE 1.4   Rail kit installation

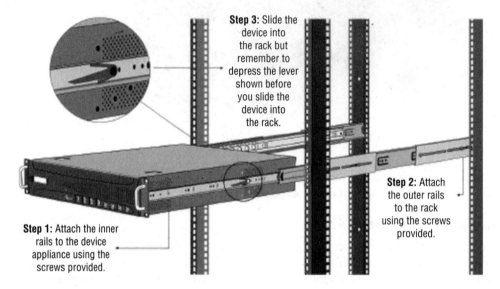

Step 3: Slide the device into the rack but remember to depress the lever shown before you slide the device into the rack.

Step 2: Attach the outer rails to the rack using the screws provided.

Step 1: Attach the inner rails to the device appliance using the screws provided.

Tower

A second form factor with which you are likely to be familiar is the *tower server*. This type bears the most resemblance to the workstations you are used to working with. When many of these devices are used in a server room, they reside not in the rack but on shelves. They are upright in appearance, as shown in Figure 1.5.

FIGURE 1.5   Tower server

It is also possible to place a tower server in a rack by using a conversion kit. The issue with this approach is that it wastes some space in the rack. A tower server using a conversion kit is shown in Figure 1.6.

FIGURE 1.6   Tower server in a rack

Blade Technology

Finally, servers may also come in blade form. This technology consists of a server chassis housing multiple thin, modular circuit boards, known as *server blades*. Each blade (or card) contains processors, memory, integrated network controllers, and other input/output (I/O) ports. Servers can experience as much as an 85 percent reduction in cabling for blade installations over conventional 1U or tower servers. Blade technology also uses much less space, as shown in a comparison of a blade system and a rack system in Figure 1.7.

FIGURE 1.7   Rack vs. blade

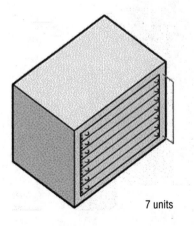

7 units

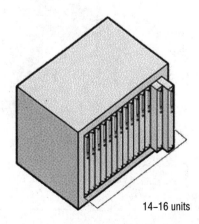

14–16 units

Blade Enclosure

A blade enclosure is a system that houses multiple blade servers. The chassis of the enclosure provides power and cooling to the blade servers. In Figure 1.8, a blade server is shown being inserted into an enclosure.

FIGURE 1.8   Blade enclosure

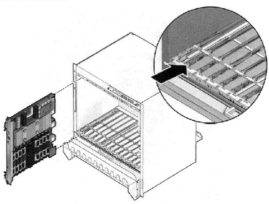

Backplane/Midplane

The backplane provides a connection point for the blade servers in the blade enclosure. Some backplanes are constructed with slots on both sides, and in that case, they are located in the middle of the enclosure and are called *midplanes*. In other cases, servers will be connected on one side, and power supplies and cooling might be connected on the other side. This arrangement is shown in Figure 1.9. The component labeled 3 is the midplane.

FIGURE 1.9   Midplane

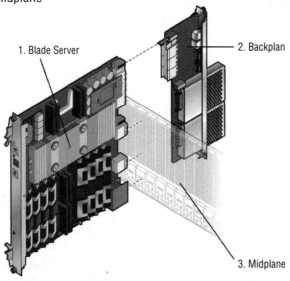

Power Supply Sockets

The midplane or backplane also supplies power connections to various components. When a midplane is in use, connections are provided on the back side for power modules. The power connectors on an IBM midplane are shown in Figure 1.10. The blade power connector is where the blade servers get their power and the power module connector is for the cable that plugs into the power sockets.

FIGURE 1.10   Midplane power

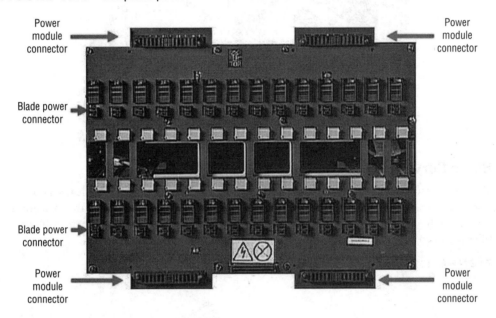

Network Modules/Switches

Blade enclosures can accept several types of modules in addition to blade servers. At least one and probably two switch modules will be present to provide networking for the servers. This switch module is typically Ethernet but not always.

Management Modules

Finally, there will be a management module that allows for configuring and managing the entire enclosure of blade servers. This includes things like the IP addresses of the individual blade servers and connecting to and managing the storage. For redundancy's sake, there may be multiple management modules. The typical location of the management module is shown in Figure 1.11.

FIGURE 1.11   Advanced management module

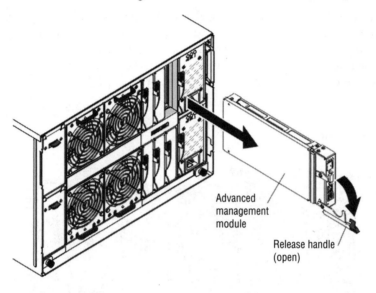

Blade Server

The blade servers are individual cards, each of which acts as a separate physical server. There will be a number of these—for example, 8, 16, or 24. Any blade slots that are not in use should have the blade filler in place. The insertion of both a blade server and a blade filler is shown in Figure 1.12.

FIGURE 1.12   Inserting a blade server and filler

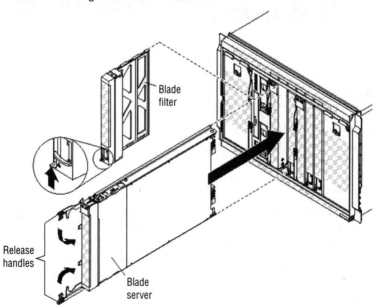

Installing and Configuring Server Components

Just as an A+ technician needs to be familiar with all of the possible components that may exist inside the box and how to install, maintain, and repair those components, as a Server + technician, you must know the same with regard to servers. Servers have all the same components that are found in workstations, but due to the high workloads they experience as a result of their roles in the network, the components must be more robust. This section explores server versions of key components.

CPU

The central processing unit (CPU) in servers must be capable of handling high workloads without overheating. In many cases, this requires the use of both multiple-core processors and multiple CPUs. A multiple-core processor is one with multiple cores, each of which can operate as a separate CPU. In this section we'll look at the types of sockets server CPUs use, the way they use memory, the possible architectures you may encounter, and the various speed values you may see and their meaning. We'll also introduce the concept of CPU stepping.

Socket Type

CPUs are connected to the motherboard via a socket on the board. The most common socket types are listed in Table 1.1.

TABLE 1.1   Server socket types

Socket name	CPU families supported	Package	Pin count	Bus speed
LGA 771/ Socket J	Intel Xeon	LGA	771	1600 MHz
LGA 1366/ Socket B	Intel Core i7 (900 series) Intel Xeon (35xx, 36xx, 55xx, 56xx series), Intel Celeron	LGA	1366	4.8–6.4 GT/s (gigatransfers per second)
LGA 1248	Intel Itanium 9300-series	LGA	1248	4.8 GT/s
LGA 1567	Intel Xeon 6500/7500-series	LGA	1567	4.8–6.4 GT/s

TABLE 1.1   Server socket types *(continued)*

Socket name	CPU families supported	Package	Pin count	Bus speed
LGA 2011/ Socket R	Intel Core i7 3xxx Sandy Bridge-E Intel Core i7 4xxx Ivy Bridge-E Intel Xeon E5 2xxx/4xxx [Sandy Bridge EP] (2/4S) Intel Xeon E5-2xxx/4xxx v2 [Ivy Bridge EP] (2/4S)	LGA	2011	4.8–6.4 GT/s
Socket F	AMD Opteron 13xs, 2200, 2300, 2400, 8200, 8300, 8400, AMD Athlon 64 FX	LGA	1207	200 MHz
Socket 940	Opteron 100, 200 and 800	PGA-ZIF	940	800 MHz
G34	AMD Opteron 6000	LGA	1974	3.2 GHz
AM3+	AMD Phenom II, Athlon 2, Sempron, Opteron 3xxx	PGA-ZIF	942	3.2 GHz

Notice in Table 1.1 that most of the processors use the land grid array (LGA) package. These types of sockets don't have pins on the chip. Instead, they have bare gold-plated copper that touches pins that protrude from the CPU that goes in the socket. The LGA 2011/ Socket R, however, uses a version of pin grid array (PGA), an alternative design in which the socket has the pins and they fit into the CPU when it is placed in the socket. A comparison of PGA (on the left) and LGA sockets is shown in Figure 1.13.

FIGURE 1.13   PGA and LGA

LGA-compatible sockets have a lid that closes over the CPU and is locked in place by an L-shaped arm that borders two of the socket's edges. The nonlocking leg of the arm has a bend in the middle that latches the lid closed when the other leg of the arm is secured.

For CPUs based on the PGA concept, zero insertion force (ZIF) sockets are used. ZIF sockets use a plastic or metal lever on one of the two lateral edges to lock or release the mechanism that secures the CPU's pins in the socket. The CPU rides on the mobile top portion of the socket, and the socket's contacts that mate with the CPU's pins are in the fixed bottom portion of the socket.

Cache Levels: L1, L2, L3

CPUs in servers use system memory in the server, but like most workstation CPUs they also contain their own memory, which is called *cache*. Using this memory to store recently acquired data allows the CPU to retrieve that data much faster in the event it is needed again. Cache memory can be located in several places, and in each instance it is used for a different purpose.

The Level 1 (L1) cache holds data that is waiting to enter the CPU. On modern systems, the L1 cache is built into the CPU. The Level 2 (L2) cache holds data that is exiting the CPU and is waiting to return to RAM. On modern systems, the L2 cache is in the same packaging as the CPU but on a separate chip. On older systems, the L2 cache was on a separate circuit board installed in the motherboard and was sometimes called cache on a stick (COASt).

On some CPUs, the L2 cache operates at the same speed as the CPU; on others, the cache speed is only half the CPU speed. Chips with full-speed L2 caches have better performance. Some newer systems also have an L3 cache, which is external to the CPU die but not necessarily the CPU package.

The distance of the cache from the CPU affects both the amount of cache and the speed with which the CPU can access the information in that cache. The order of distance, with the closet first, is L1, L2, and L3. The closer to the CPU, the smaller the cache capacity, but the faster the CPU can access that cache type.

Speeds

When measuring the speed of a CPU, the values are typically expressed in megahertz (MHz) and gigahertz (GHz). You may sometimes see it (as in Table 1.1) expressed in gigatransfers per second (GT/s). When expressed in GT/s, to calculate the data transmission rate, you must multiply the transfer rate by the bus width.

However, there are two speeds involved when comparing CPUs: core and bus.

Core   Processors can have one or more *cores*. Each core operates as an individual CPU and each has an internal speed, which is the maximum speed at which the CPU can perform its internal operations, and is expressed in either MHz or GHz.

Bus   The bus speed is the speed at which the motherboard communicates with the CPU. It's determined by the motherboard, and its cadence is set by a quartz crystal (the system crystal) that generates regular electrical pulses.

Multiplier

The internal speed may be the same as the motherboard's speed (the external or bus speed), but it's more likely to be a multiple of it. For example, a CPU may have an internal speed of 1.3 GHz but an external speed of 133 MHz. That means for every tick of the system crystal's clock, the CPU has 10 internal ticks of its own clock.

CPU Performance

CPU time refers to the amount of time the CPU takes to accomplish a task for either the operating system or for an application, and it is measured in clock *ticks* or seconds. The CPU *usage* is the total capacity of the CPU to perform work. The CPU time will be a subset of the usage and is usually represented as a percentage.

CPU usage values can be used to assess the overall workload of the server. When CPU usage is high—say 70 percent—there might be a slowing or lag in the system. CPU time values for a specific application or program, on the other hand, represent the relative amount of CPU usage attributable to the application.

We can also monitor CPU usage in terms of which component in the system is being served and in which security domain it is taking place. There are two main security domains in which the CPU operates: user mode and kernel mode. In user mode, it is working on behalf of an application and does not directly access the hardware. In kernel mode, it is working for the operating system and has more privileges.

When you are monitoring CPU performance, the following are common metrics and their meanings you'll encounter:

User Time   Time the CPU was busy executing code in user space.

System Time   Time the CPU was busy executing code in kernel space.

Idle Time   Time the CPU was not busy; measures unused CPU capacity.

Steal Time (Virtualized Hardware)   Time the operating system wanted to execute but was not allowed to by the hypervisor because it was not the CPU's turn for a time slot.

CPU Stepping

When CPUs undergo revisions, the revisions are called *stepping levels*. When a manufacturer invests money to do a stepping, that means they have found bugs in the logic or have made improvements to the design that allow for faster processing. Integrated circuits have two primary classes of *mask sets* (mask sets are used to make the changes): *base layers* that are used to build the structures that make up the logic, such as transistors, and *metal layers* that connect the logic together. A base layer update is more difficult and time consuming than one for a metal layer. Therefore, you might think of metal layer updates as software versioning. Stepping levels are indicated by an alphabetic letter followed by a numeric number—for example, C-4. Usually, the letter indicates the revision level of a chip's base layers, and the number indicates the revision level of the metal layers. As an example, the first version of a processor is always A-0.

Architecture

Some processors operate on 32 bits of information at a time, and others operate on 64 bits at a time. Operating on 64 bits of information is more efficient, but is only available in processors that support it and when coupled with operating systems that support it. A 64-bit processor can support 32-bit and 64-bit applications and operating systems, whereas a 32-bit processor can only support a 32-bit operating system and applications. This is what is being described when we discuss the *architecture* of the CPU. There are three main architectures of CPUs.

x86   Processors that operate on 32 bits of information at a time use an architecture called x86. It derives its name from the first series of CPUs for computers (8086, which was only 16 bits, 286, 386, and 486).

x64   Processors that operate on 64 bits of information at a time use an architecture called x64. It supports larger amounts of virtual memory and physical memory than is possible on its 32-bit predecessors, allowing programs to store larger amounts of data in memory.

ARM   Advanced RISC Machine (ARM) is a family of reduced instruction set computing (RISC) instruction set architectures developed by British company ARM Holdings. Since its initial development, both ARM and third parties have developed CPUs on this architecture. It is one that requires fewer resources than either x86 or x64. In that regard, ARM CPUs are suitable for tablets, smartphones, and other smaller devices.

In Exercise 1.1, you'll replace a CPU in a server.

EXERCISE 1.1

Replacing a CPU in a Server

1. Shut down and remove power from the entire system.

2. Remove the server node from the system. (Many systems have multiple servers in bays. To get to each server, you must remove the bay.)

3. Remove the server node cover (follow any instructions included with the documentation).

4. Use the proper type and size of screwdriver (usually a Number 2 Phillips-head) to loosen the screws (usually 4) holding the heatsink, and then lift it off of the CPU. (Yours may require a different type of screwdriver.)

5. Unclip the first CPU retaining latch and then unclip any remaining (usually there are two) latches.

6. Open the hinged CPU cover plate.

7. Remove the old CPU.

8. Insert the new CPU.

9. Install the heatsink (don't forget to put thermal grease between the CPU and the heatsink).

10. Replace the server node cover.

11. Reinstall the server node.

12. Replace power cords and then power on the system.

RAM

Like any computing device, servers require memory, and servers in particular require lots of it. In this section we will discuss the types of memory chips that are used in servers and describe some of the characteristics that differentiate them.

ECC vs. Non-ECC

When data is moved to and from RAM, the transfer does not always go smoothly. Memory chips have error detection features and in some cases error correction functions. A type of RAM error correction is error correction code (ECC). RAM with ECC can detect and correct errors. To achieve this, additional information needs to be stored and more processing needs to be done, making ECC RAM more expensive and a little slower than non-ECC RAM.

In ECC, an algorithm is performed on the data and its check bits whenever the memory is accessed. If the result of the algorithm is all zeroes, then the data is deemed valid and processing continues. ECC can detect single- and double-bit errors and actually correct single-bit errors. This is a now a rarely used type of parity RAM. Most RAM today is non-ECC.

DDR2 and DDR3

Double data rate (DDR) is clock-doubled SDRAM (covered later in this section). The memory chip can perform reads and writes on both sides of any clock cycle (the up, or start, and the down, or ending), thus doubling the effective memory executions per second. So, if you're using DDR SDRAM with a 100 MHz memory bus, the memory will execute reads and writes at 200 MHz and transfer the data to the processor at 100 MHz. The advantage of DDR over regular SDRAM is increased throughput and thus increased overall system speed.

DDR2

The next generation of DDR SDRAM is DDR2 (double data rate 2). This allows for two memory accesses for each rising and falling clock and effectively doubles the speed of DDR. DDR2-667 chips work with speeds of 667 MHz and PC2-5300 modules.

DDR3

The primary benefit of DDR3 over DDR2 is that it transfers data at twice the rate of DDR2 (eight times the speed of its internal memory arrays), enabling higher bandwidth or peak data rates. By performing two transfers per cycle of a quadrupled clock, a 64-bit wide DDR3 module may achieve a transfer rate of up to 64 times the memory clock speed in megabytes per second (MBps). In addition, the DDR3 standard permits chip capacities of up to 8 GB. Selected memory standards, speeds, and formats are shown in Table 1.2.

TABLE 1.2   Selected memory details

Module standard	Speed	Format
DDR-500	4000 MBps	PC4-000
DDR-533	4266 MBps	PC4-200
DDR2-667	5333 MBps	PC2-5300
DDR2-750	6000 MBps	PC2-6000
DDR2-800	6400 MBps	PC2-6400
DDR3-800	6400 MBps	PC3-6400
DDR3-1600	12,800 MBps	PC3-12800

Number of Pins

Memory modules have pins that connect them to the motherboard slot in which they reside. Dual inline memory modules (DIMMs) have two rows of pins and twice the contact with the motherboard, creating a larger interface with it and resulting in a wider data path than older single inline memory modules (SIMMs). DIMMs differ in the number of conductors, or pins, that each particular physical form factor uses. Some common examples are 168-pin (SDR RAM), 184-pin (DDR, DDR2), and 240-pin (DDR3) configurations.

Static vs. Dynamic

RAM can be either static or dynamic. Dynamic RAM requires a refresh signal whereas static RAM does not. This results in better performance for static RAM. A static RAM cell, on the other hand, requires more space on the chip than a dynamic RAM cell, resulting in less memory on the chip. This results in static RAM being more expensive when trying to provide the same number of cells.

In summary, static RAM is more expensive but faster, whereas dynamic RAM is slower but cheaper. The two types are often both used, however, due to their differing strengths and weaknesses. Static RAM is used to create the CPU's speed-sensitive cache, and dynamic RAM forms the larger system RAM space.

Module Placement

Utilizing multiple channels between the RAM and the memory controller increases the transfer speed between these two components. Single-channel RAM does not take advantage of this concept, but dual-channel memory does and creates two 64-bit data channels. Do *not* confuse this with DDR. DDR doubles the rate by accessing the memory module twice per clock cycle.

Using dual channels requires a motherboard that supports dual channels and two or more memory modules. Sometimes the modules go in separate color-coded banks, as shown in Figure 1.14, and other times they use the same colors. Consult your documentation.

FIGURE 1.14 Dual-channel memory slots

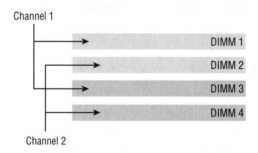

Memory runs in banks with two slots compromising a bank. The board should indicate which two slots are in the same bank by the color coding. It could be orange and yellow, or it might be some other combination of two colors. When installing the memory, install the same size modules in the same bank. If you don't, the modules will not operate in dual channel mode. This will impair the performance of the bank.

CAS Latency

Another characteristic than can be used to differentiate memory modules is their CAS latency value. Column access strobe (CAS) latency is the amount of time taken to access a memory module and make that data available on the module's pins.

The lower the CL value, the better. In asynchronous DRAM, the delay value is measured in nanoseconds and the value is constant, while in synchronous DRAM, it is measured in clock cycles and will vary based on the clock rate.

Timing

Memory timing measures the performance of RAM and consists of four components:

CAS Latency   The time to access an address column if the correct row is already open

Row Address to Column Address Delay   The time to read the first bit of memory without an active row

Row Precharge Time   The time to access an address column if the wrong row is open

Row Active Time   The time needed to internally refresh a row

Memory timings are listed in units of clock cycles; therefore, when translating these values to time, remember that for DDR memory, this will be half the speed of the transfer rate. It is also useful to note that memory timing is only part of the performance picture. The memory *bandwidth* is the throughput of the memory. Although advances in bandwidth technology (DDR2, DDR3) may have a negative effect on latency from timing, DDR2 and DDR3 can be clocked faster, resulting in a net gain in performance.

Memory Pairing

Each motherboard supports memory based on the speed of the front-side bus (FSB) and the memory's form factor. If you install memory that is rated at a lower speed than the FSB, the memory will operate at that lower speed, if it works at all. In their documentation, most motherboard manufacturers list which type(s) of memory they support as well as maximum speeds and required pairings.

With regard to adding and upgrading memory, faster memory can be added to a server with slower memory installed, but the system will operate only at the speed of the slowest module present.

Moreover, although you can mix speeds, you cannot mix memory types. For example, you cannot use SDRAM with DDR, and DDR cannot be mixed with DDR2. When looking at the name of the memory, the larger the number, the faster the speed. For example, DDR2-800 is faster than DDR2-533.

Finally, memory pairing also refers to installing matched pairs of RAM in a dual-channel memory architecture.

Bus Types, Bus Channels, and Expansion Slots

The motherboard provides the platform to which all components are attached and provides pathways for communication called *buses*. A bus is a common collection of signal pathways over which related devices communicate within the computer system. Expansion buses incorporate slots at certain points in the bus to allow insertion of external devices. In this section, we'll look at common server bus types and their characteristics.

Height Differences and Bit Rate Differences

Two major differentiating characteristics of bus types are their bit rates and the form factor of the slot and adapter to which it mates. The dominant bus types in servers are forms of the Peripheral Component Interconnect (PCI) expansion bus. In the following sections, the three major types of PCI buses are covered, with attention given to both form factor and bit rate.

PCI

The Peripheral Component Interconnect (PCI) bus is a 33 MHz wide (32-bit or 64-bit) expansion bus that was a modern standard in motherboards for general-purpose expansion devices. Its slots are typically white. You may see two PCI slots, but most motherboards have gone to newer standards. Figure 1.15 shows some PCI slots.

FIGURE 1.15 PCI slots

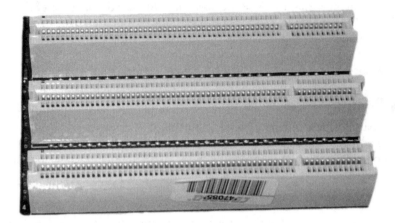

PCI cards that are 32 bit with 33 MHz operate up to 133 MBps, whereas 32-bit cards with 64 MHz operate up to 266 MBps. PCI cards that are 64 bit with 33 MHz operate up to 266 MBps, whereas 64-bit cards with 66 MHz operate up to 533 MBps.

PCI-X

PCI-eXtended (PCI-X) is a double-wide version of the 32-bit PCI local bus. It runs at up to four times the clock speed, achieving higher bandwidth, but otherwise it uses the same protocol and a similar electrical implementation. It has been replaced by the PCI Express (see the next section), which uses a different connector and a different logical design. There is also a 64-bit PCI specification that is electrically different but has the same connector as PCI-X. There are two versions of PCI-X: version 1 gets up to 1.06 GBps, and version 2 gets up to 4.26 GBps.

PCIe

PCI Express (PCIE, PCI-E, or PCIe) uses a network of serial interconnects that operate at high speed. It's based on the PCI system; you can convert a PCIe slot to PCI using an adapter plug-in card, but you cannot convert a PCI slot to PCIe. Intended as a replacement for the Advanced Graphics Processor (AGP was an interim solution for graphics) and PCI, PCIe has the capability of being faster than AGP while maintaining the flexibility of PCI. There are four versions of PCIe: version 1 is up to 8 GBps, version 2 is up to 16 GBps, version 3 is up to 32 GBps, and as of this writing final specifications for version 4 are still being developed. Figure 1.16 shows the slots discussed so far in this section. Table 1.3 lists the speeds of each. The PCIe speeds shown are per lane. So a 4-lane version of PCIe 2 would operate at 20 GBps.

FIGURE 1.16 Comparison of PCI slot types

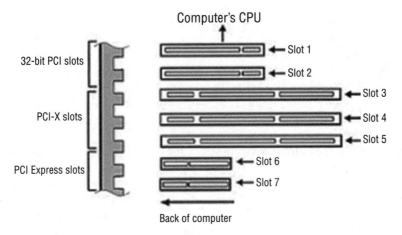

TABLE 1.3 PCI and PCIe slot speeds

Type	Data transfer rate
PCI 33, 32-bit	133 MBps
PCI 33, 64-bit	266 MBps
PCI 66, 32-bit	266 MBps
PCI 66, 64-bit	533 MBps
PCIe version 1	2 GBps
PCIe version 2	5 GBps
PCIe version 3	8 GBps
PCIe version 4	16 GBps

NICs

Network cards do exactly what you would think; they provide a connection for the server to a network. In general, network interface cards (NICs) are added via an expansion slot or they are integrated into the motherboard, but they may also be added through USB. The most common issue that prevents network connectivity is a bad or unplugged patch cable.

Network cards are made for various access methods (Ethernet, token ring) and for various media types (fiber optic, copper, wireless) connections. The network card you use must support both the access method and the media type in use.

The most obvious difference in network cards is the speed of which they are capable. Most networks today operate at 100 Mbps or 1 Gbps. Regardless of other components, the server will operate at the speed of the slowest component, so if the card is capable of 1 Gbps but the cable is only capable of 100 MBps, the server will transmit only at 100 Mbps.

Another significant feature to be aware of is the card's ability to perform auto-sensing. This feature allows the card to sense whether the connection is capable of full duplex and to operate in that manner with no action required.

There is another type of auto-sensing, in which the card is capable of detecting what type of device is on the other end and changing the use of the wire pairs accordingly. For example, normally a PC connected to another PC requires a crossover cable, but if both ends can perform this sensing, that is not required. These types of cards are called auto-MDIX.

In today's servers you will most likely be seeing 10 Gb cards and you may even see 40 Gb or 100 Gb cards. Moreover, many servers attach to storage networks and may run converged network adapters (CNAs), which act both as a host bus adapter (HBA) for the storage area network (SAN) and as the network card for the server. This concept is shown in Figure 1.17. In the graphic, FC stands for Fiber Channel and NC stands for Network Card.

FIGURE 1.17 Traditional and CNA

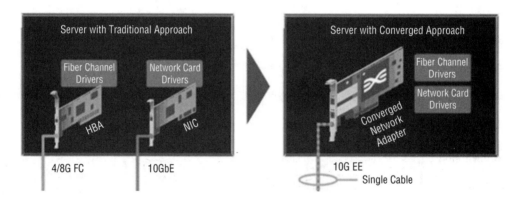

Hard Drives

Servers can contain three different types of hard drive architectures. In this section we'll look at each type.

Magnetic Hard Drives

Magnetic drives were once the main type of hard drive used. The drive itself is a mechanical device that spins a number of disks or platters and uses a magnetic head to read and write data to the surface of the disks. One of the advantages of solid-state drives (discussed in the next section) is the absence of mechanical parts that can malfunction. The parts of a magnetic hard drive are shown in Figure 1.18.

FIGURE 1.18   Magnetic hard drive

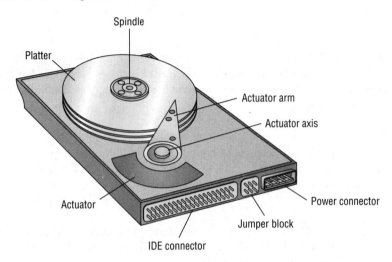

The basic hard disk geometry consists of three components: the number of sectors that each track contains, the number of read/write heads in the disk assembly, and the number of cylinders in the assembly. This set of values is known as CHS (for cylinders/heads/sectors). A *cylinder* is the set of tracks of the same number on all the writable surfaces of the assembly. It is called a cylinder because the collection of all same-number tracks on all writable surfaces of the hard disk assembly looks like a geometric cylinder when connected together vertically. Therefore, cylinder 1, for instance, on an assembly that contains three platters consists of six tracks (one on each side of each platter), each labeled track 1 on its respective surface. Figure 1.19 illustrates the key terms presented in this discussion.

FIGURE 1.19   CHS

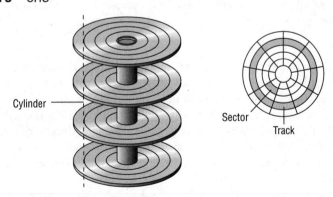

5400 rpm

The rotational speed of the disk or platter has a direct influence on how quickly the drive can locate any specific disk sector on the drive. This locational delay is called latency and is measured in milliseconds (ms). The faster the rotation, the smaller the delay will be. A drive operating at 5400 rpms will experience about 5.5 ms of this delay.

7200 rpm

Drives that operate at 7200 rpm will experience about 4.2 ms of latency. As of 2015, a typical 7200 rpm desktop hard drive has a sustained data transfer rate up to 750 Mbps. This rate depends on the track location, so it will be higher for data on the outer tracks and lower toward the inner tracks.

10,000 rpm

At 10,000 rpm, the latency will decrease to about 3 ms. Data transfer rates (about 1.5 Gb) also generally go up with a higher rotational speed but are influenced by the density of the disk (the number of tracks and sectors present in a given area).

15,000 rpm

Drives that operate at 15,000 rpm are higher-end drives and suffer only 2 ms of latency. They operate at just under 2 Gb. These drives also generate more heat, requiring more cooling to the case. They also offer faster data transfer rates for the same areal density (areal density refers to the amount of bits that can be stored in a given amount of space.).

Hot-Swappable Drives

If a drive can be attached to the server without shutting down, then it is a hot-swappable drive. Drive types that are hot-swappable include USB, FireWire, SATA, and those that connect through Ethernet. You should always check the documentation to ensure that your drive supports this feature.

Solid-State Drives

Solid-state drives (SSDs) retain data in nonvolatile memory chips and contain no moving parts. Compared to electromechanical hard disk drives (HDDs), SSDs are typically less susceptible to physical shock, are silent, have lower access time and latency, but are more expensive per gigabyte.

Hybrid Drives

A hybrid drive is one in which both technologies, solid-state and traditional mechanical drives, are combined. This is done to take advantage of the speed of solid-state drives while maintaining the cost effectiveness of mechanical drives.

There are two main approaches to this: dual-drive hybrid and solid-state hybrid. Dual-drive systems contain both types of drives in the same machine, and performance is optimized by the user placing more frequently used information on the solid-state drive and less frequently accessed data on the mechanical drive—or in some cases by the operating system creating hybrid volumes using space in both drives.

A solid-state hybrid drive (SSHD), on the other hand, is a single storage device that includes solid-state flash memory in a traditional hard drive. Data that is most related to the performance of the machine is stored in the flash memory, resulting in improved performance. Figure 1.20 shows the two approaches to hybrid drives. In the graphic mSATA refers to a smaller form of the SATA drive and NAND disk refers to a type of flash memory named after the NAND logic gate.

FIGURE 1.20 Hybrid approaches

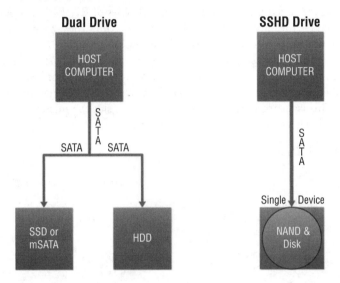

Riser Cards

Riser cards allow you to add expansion cards to a system. You may already be familiar with their use in low-profile cases where the height of the case doesn't allow for a perpendicular placement of the full-height expansion card. They are also used in rack mount and blade servers to allow you to add feature cards in a horizontal position (instead of a standard vertical position).

Typically, a 1U system uses a 1U single-slot riser card whereas a 2U system uses a 2U three-slot riser card. An example of a riser card in a rack server is shown in Figure 1.21.

FIGURE 1.21 Riser card in rack server

RAID Controllers

Redundant Array of Independent Disks (RAID) is a multiple disk technology that either increases performance or allows for the automatic recovery of data from a failed hard drive by simply replacing the failed drive. There are several types of RAID that provide varying degrees of increased performance and/or fault tolerance. All of these techniques involve two or more hard drives operating together in some fashion.

RAID can be implemented using software or hardware. The highest levels of protection are provided by using hardware RAID, which requires that the system have a RAID *controller*. This hardware device is used to manage the disks in the storage array so they work as a logical unit. This is a card that fits into a PCI express slot to which the drives in the array are connected. This concept is shown in Figure 1.22.

FIGURE 1.22   RAID controller

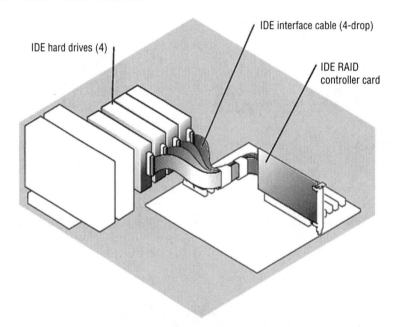

BIOS/UEFI

Servers also contain firmware that provides low-level instructions to the device even in the absence of an operating system. This firmware, called either the Basic Input/Output System (BIOS) or the Unified Extensible Firmware Interface (UEFI), contains settings that can be manipulated and diagnostic utilities that can be used to monitor the device.

UEFI is a standard firmware interface for servers and PCs designed to replace BIOS. Some advantages of UEFI firmware are

- Better security; protects the preboot process
- Faster startup times and resuming from hibernation

- Support for drives larger than 2.2 terabytes (TB)
- Support for 64-bit firmware device drivers
- Capability to use BIOS with UEFI hardware

At startup, the BIOS or UEFI will attempt to detect the devices and components at its disposal. The information that it gathers, along with the current state of the components, will be available for review in the BIOS settings. Some of the components and the types of information available with respect to these devices and components are covered in this section.

You can view and adjust a server's base-level settings through the CMOS Setup program, which you access by pressing a certain key at startup, such as F1 or Delete (depending on the system). Complementary metal oxide semiconductor (CMOS) refers to the battery type that maintains power to the BIOS settings (also referred to as BIOS Setup). The most common settings you can adjust in CMOS are port settings (parallel, serial, USB), drive types, boot sequence, date and time, and virus/security protections. The variable settings that are made through the CMOS setup program are stored in nonvolatile random access memory (NVRAM), whereas the base instructions that cannot be changed (the BIOS) are stored on an EEPROM (Electrically Erasable Programmable Read-Only Memory) chip.

CMOS Battery

The CMOS chip must have a constant source of power to keep its settings. To prevent the loss of data, motherboard manufacturers include a small battery to power the CMOS memory. On modern systems, this is a coin-style battery, about the diameter of a U.S. dime and about as thick. One of these is shown in Figure 1.23.

FIGURE 1.23   CMOS battery in a server

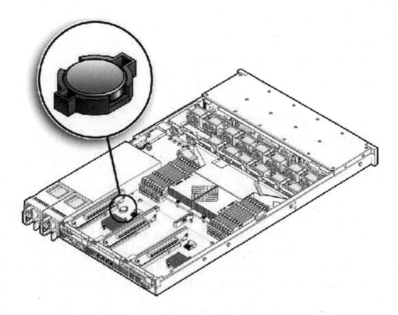

When the server is not keeping correct time or date when turned off, it is usually a CMOS battery issue and a warning that the battery is soon going to die. In the absence of the server receiving time and date updates from a time server such as a Network Time Protocol (NTP) server, the time kept in the CMOS is the time source for the computer.

Firmware

Firmware includes any type of instruction for the server that is stored in nonvolatile memory devices such as ROM, EPROM, or flash memory. BIOS and UEFI code is the most common example for firmware. Computer BIOSs don't go bad; they just become out of date or contain bugs. In the case of a bug, an upgrade will correct the problem. An upgrade may also be indicated when the BIOS doesn't support some component that you would like to install—a larger hard drive or a different type of processor, for instance.

Most of today's BIOSs are written to an EEPROM chip and can be updated through the use of software. Each manufacturer has its own method for accomplishing this. Check out the documentation for complete details. Regardless of the exact procedure, the process is referred to as *flashing* the BIOS. It means the old instructions are erased from the EEPROM chip and the new instructions are written to the chip.

Firmware can be updated by using an update utility from the motherboard vendor. In many cases, the steps are as follows:

1. Download the update file to a flash drive.
2. Insert the flash drive and reboot the machine.
3. Use the specified key sequence to enter the CMOS setup.
4. If necessary, disable Secure Boot.
5. Save the changes and reboot again.
6. Reenter the CMOS settings.
7. Choose boot options and then boot from the flash drive.
8. Follow the specific directions with the update to locate the upgrade file on the flash drive.
9. Execute the file (usually by typing **flash**).
10. While the update is completing, ensure you maintain power to the device.

USB Interface/Ports

Like other computing devices, servers will probably have USB ports. There will probably be at least two, one for a mouse and keyboard respectively (although you will probably use a KVM switch for this when the servers are rack mounted or blade). These will probably be on the front of the server, although there may be additional ones on the back of the server.

Some specialized server products are able to operate as USB servers in that they allow network devices to access shared USB devices that are attached to the server. This typically requires some sort of USB management software. In this case it may be necessary to use a USB hub connected to one of the USB ports on the server if there are not enough ports provided by the server.

Hot-Swappable Component

A hot-swappable component is one that can be changed without shutting down the server. This is a desirable feature because for many server roles, shutting down the server is something to be minimized. However, just because a component is hot swappable doesn't mean changing the component doesn't require some administrative work before you make that change.

For example, to change a hot-swappable hard drive, in most cases you must prevent any applications from accessing the hard drive and remove the logical software links. Moreover, in many cases drives cannot be hot-plugged if the hard drive provides the operating system and the operating system is not mirrored on another drive. It also cannot be done if the hard drive cannot be logically isolated from the online operations of the server module. Nevertheless, it is still a great feature. In some high-end servers, it is even possible to hot-swap memory and CPU.

Maintaining Power and Cooling Requirements

Computing equipment of any kind, including servers, require a certain level of power and an environment that is cool enough to keep the devices from overheating. In this section we'll discuss both power and cooling requirements and issues you should be aware of relating to those issues.

Power

When discussing power it is helpful to define some terms that relate to power. In this section we'll do that, and we'll also look at power consumption and power redundancy. Finally, we'll explore power plug types you may encounter when dealing with servers in the enterprise.

Voltage

Two terms that are thrown about and often confused when discussing power are voltage and amperage. *Voltage* is the pressure or force of the electricity, whereas *amperage* is the amount of electricity. They together describe the *wattage* supplied. The watts required by a device are the amps multiplied by the voltage.

Amps multiplied by the volts give you the wattage (watts), a measure of the work that electricity does per second.

Power supplies that come in servers (and in all computers for that matter) must be set to accept the voltage that is being supplied by the power outlet to which it is connected. This voltage is standardized but the standard is different in different countries. Almost all IT power supplies are now autosensing and universal voltage-capable (100-250 V) to allow the same product to operate worldwide. Those that do not will provide a switch on the outside of the case that allows you to change the type of power the supply is expecting, as shown in Figure 1.24.

FIGURE 1.24   Voltage switch

Single-Phase vs. Three-Phase Power

There are two types of power delivery systems: single-phase and three-phase. Single-phase power refers to a two-wire alternating current (AC) power circuit. Typically there is one power wire and one neutral wire. In the United States, 120V is the standard single-phase voltage, with one 120V power wire and one neutral wire. In some countries, 230V is the standard single-phase voltage, with one 230V power wire and one neutral wire. Power flows between the power wire (through the load) and the neutral wire.

Three-phase power refers to three-wire AC power circuits. Typically there are three (phase A, phase B, phase C) power wires (120 degrees out of phase with one another) and one neutral wire. For example, a three-phase, four-wire 208V/120V power circuit provides three 120V single-phase power circuits and one 208V three-phase power circuit. Installing three-phase systems in datacenters helps to consolidate the power distribution in one place, reducing the costs associated with installing multiple distribution units.

Single-phase is what most homes have whereas three-phase is more typically found in industrial settings.

110V vs. 220V vs. 48V

Although 110V is used in some parts of the world and 220V in others, the two systems have advantages and disadvantages. While 220V is more efficient in that it suffers less transmission loss (and it can use wiring rated for less current), 110V is safer if someone is electrocuted. Some datacenters deliver power to a rack at 220V and then use a transformer to step it down to 110V to the equipment if required.

Some equipment also is made for -48V DC power rather than 110/220 AC power. 48V is the common power scheme used in central offices and many datacenters. Many telcos can deliver 48V DC power to the facility and many are currently doing so. The advantage of using it is heat output. You no longer have the AC/DC conversion inside each device—just a DC/DC conversion. Less heat output means less (smaller) HVAC equipment. You will, however, need a rectifier, which is a small device that receives the 48V power and makes it -48V.

120/208V vs. 277/480V

Earlier you learned that systems can be one-phase or three-phase. Most commercial systems use one of two versions of three-phase. The first we mentioned earlier: 120/208V. To review, that power circuit provides three 120V single-phase power circuits and one 208V three-phase power circuit.

The 277/480V circuit provides two 277V single-phase power circuits and one 480V three-phase power circuit. Server power supplies that operate directly from 480/277V power distribution circuits can reduce the total cost of ownership (TCO) for a high-performance cluster by reducing both infrastructure and operating cost. The trade-off is that 277/480V systems are inherently more dangerous.

Wattage

Earlier you learned that voltage is the pressure or force of the electricity, whereas amperage is the amount of electricity. They together describe the wattage supplied. Amps multiplied by the volts give you the wattage (watts), a measure of the work that electricity does per second. The power supply must be able to provide the wattage requirements of the server and any devices that are also attached and dependent on the supply for power.

Consumption

Servers vary in their total consumption of power. However, there have been studies over the years that can give you an idea of what a server and some of its components draw in power. The following can be used as a rough guideline for planning:

- 1U rack mount x86: 300 W–350 W

- 2U rack mount, 2-socket x86: 350 W–400 W

- 4U rack mount, 4-socket x86: average 600 W, heavy configurations, 1000 W

- Blades: average chassis uses 4500 W; divide by number of blades per chassis (example: 14 per chassis, so about 320 per blade server)

Keep in mind that these are values for the server only. In a datacenter, much additional power is spent on cooling and other requirements. A value called power usage effectiveness (PUE) is used to measure the efficiency of the datacenter. It is a number that describes the relationship between the amount of power used by the entire datacenter and the power used by the server only. For example, a value of 3 means that the datacenter needs three times the power required by the servers. A lower value is better. Although this is changing, the general rule of thumb is that PUE is usually 2.0, which means a datacenter needs twice the power required by the servers.

Redundancy

Datacenters usually deploy redundant power sources to maintain constant power. Redundancy can be provided in several ways:

- Parallel redundancy or the N+1 option describes an architecture where there is always a single extra UPS available (that's the +1) and the N simply indicates the total number of UPSs required for the datacenter. Because the system runs in two feeds and there is only one redundant UPS, this system can still suffer failures.

- 2N redundancy means the datacenter provides double the power it requires. This ensures that the system is fully redundant.

Redundancy also refers to using redundant power supplies on the devices. Many servers come with two supplies, and you can buy additional power supplies as well. Always ensure that the power supply you buy can accommodate all the needs of the server. As you saw earlier in the section "Consumption," many 4U rack and blade servers use a lot of power.

Plug Types

You'll encounter several types of power plugs with servers. Let's examine each.

NEMA

Power plugs that conform to the U.S. National Electrical Manufacturers Association (NEMA) standards are called NEMA plugs. There are many types of these plugs, and they differ in the orientation of the plugs and their shape. The two basic classifications of NEMA device are straight-blade and locking.

Edison

The term *Edison plug* refers to the standard three-prong grounded or two-prong ungrounded plugs with which we are all familiar. Both are shown in Figure 1.25. Keep in mind the shape of the plug may differ somewhat.

FIGURE 1.25   Edison plug

Twist Lock

Twist-locking connectors refer to NEMA locking connectors manufactured by any company, although "Twist-Lock" remains a registered trademark of Hubbell Inc. The term is applied generically to locking connectors that use curved blades. The plug is pushed into the receptacle and turned, causing the now-rotated blades to latch.

A sample of this connector for a 6000 W power supply is shown in Figure 1.26.

FIGURE 1.26   Locking plug

Cooling

When all power considerations have been satisfied, your attention should turn to ensuring that the servers do not overheat. The CPUs in a server produce a lot of heat, and this heat needs to be dealt with. In this section, we'll look at the sources of heat in a server room or datacenter and approaches used to control this heat so it doesn't cause issues such as reboots (or worse).

Airflow

Airflow, both within the server and in the server room or datacenter in general, must be maintained and any obstructions to this flow must be eliminated if possible. Inside the server case, if you add any fans, avoid making the following common mistakes:

- Placing intake and exhaust in close proximity on the same side of the chassis, which causes exhausted warm air to flow back into the chassis, lowering overall cooling performance
- Installing panels and components in the way of airflow, such as the graphics card, motherboard, and hard drives

You must also consider the airflow around the rack of servers and, in some cases, around the rows of racks in a large datacenter. We'll look at some approaches to that in the "Baffles/Shrouds" section later in this chapter.

Thermal Dissipation

Heat is generated by electronic devices and must be dissipated. There are a number of techniques to accomplish this. Heatsinks are one approach with which you are probably already familiar. Although heatsinks may pull the heat out of the CPU or the motherboard, we still have to get the heat out of the case, and we do that with fans. Finally, we need to get the collected heat from all of the servers out of the server room, or at least create a flow in the room that keeps the hot air from reentering the devices.

One of the ways to do that is through the use of hot and cold aisle arrangements. The goal of a hot aisle/cold aisle configuration is to conserve energy and lower cooling costs by managing airflow. It involves lining up server racks in alternating rows with cold air intakes facing one way and hot air exhausts facing the other. The cold aisles face air conditioner output ducts. The hot aisles face air conditioner return ducts. This arrangement is shown in Figure 1.27.

FIGURE 1.27 Hot aisle/cold aisle configuration

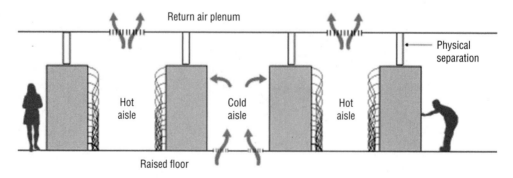

Baffles/Shrouds

Another technique used both inside the case and in the server room is deploying baffles or shrouds to direct and alter the flow of air. Inside the case they are used to channel the air in the desired direction. For example, in Figure 1.28 they are used to direct the air over components that might block the desired airflow.

FIGURE 1.28   Baffles

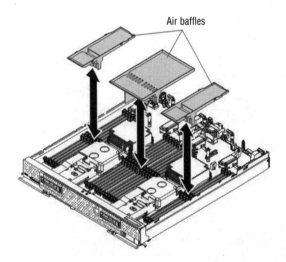

Air baffles

In the server room or datacenter, baffles may be deployed to channel the air in a desirable fashion as well. Here they are usually used to cover open rack slots, and in some cases, they are used under the raised floor to close holes there as well. Closing off these holes improves the airflow. You may have learned that open slots on the back of a tower computer should be closed with spacers. That recommendation is made for the same reason: improved airflow.

Fans

Fans are used in several places inside the server case. There may be one on top of the heatsink used to assist the heatsink in removing the heat from the CPU. However, there will also be at least one, if not two, case fans used to move the hot air out of the case.

In server rooms and datacenters, the racks in which servers reside will probably also have multiple fans to pull the air out of the rack. An example of the fans in the back of a rack system is shown in Figure 1.29. In this instance the fans are located in an external unit that can be bought and placed on the back of a rack that either has no fans or has insufficient fans.

FIGURE 1.29   Rack fans

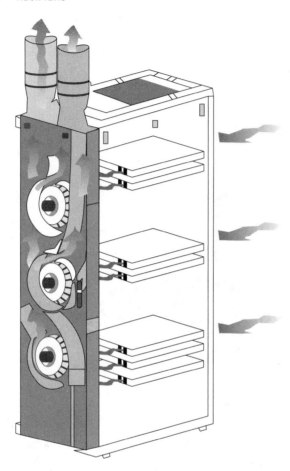

Liquid Cooling

In cases where passive heat removal is insufficient, liquid cooling may be deployed inside the case. In large datacenters this may be delivered from outside the case to the chips that need cooling. When done in this fashion, each server receives cool water from a main source, the heated water from all of the servers is returned to a central location, and then the process repeats itself. Figure 1.30 shows a server receiving liquid cooling in this way.

FIGURE 1.30   Liquid cooling

Summary

In this chapter we covered hardware in a server, including the topics in Objective 1 of the exam. This included a discussion of form factors such as the tower, rack, and blade server. We also discussed configuring and maintaining server components such as CPU, memory, NICs, hard drives, riser cards, and RAID controllers. We ended the chapter by exploring methods of satisfying the power and cooling requirements of servers and of the server rooms and datacenters in which they live.

Exam Essentials

Differentiate the server form factors.   These include tower servers; 1U, 2U, 3U, and 4U rack mount servers; and blade servers. The U in the rack server notation indicates the number of units in the rack that the servers use.

Describe the components found inside the server.   Inside the server case you will find all of the same components you might find in a workstation, but they will be more robust and there may be more of them. These include CPU, memory, NICs, hard drives, riser cards, and RAID controllers.

Understand the power requirements of servers.   Servers can require from 350 W (for a 1U rack mount) to 4500 W for a chassis with 14 blades in it.

Identity and mitigate cooling issues.   Explain how to use heatsinks, fans, and baffles inside the case to eliminate the heat created by servers. In the server room or datacenter, understand how to deploy baffles and hot/cold aisles to remove heat from the room.

Review Questions

You can find the answers in the Appendix.

1.   Which term refers to the size, appearance, or dimensions of a server?
     A.   Form factor
     B.   Footprint
     C.   Physical reference
     D.   U measure

2.   Which of the following is used to make maintenance easier with a rack server?
     A.   KVM
     B.   Rail kits
     C.   Baffles
     D.   Rack slot

3.   How large is each U in a rack?
     A.   19 inches
     B.   4.445 inches
     C.   1.75 inches
     D.   It depends on the rack.

4.   What technology consists of a server chassis housing multiple thin, modular circuit boards, each of which acts as a server?
     A.   Rack servers
     B.   Towers
     C.   KVM
     D.   Blade technology

5.   What type of CPU cache holds data that is waiting to enter the CPU?
     A.   L1
     B.   L2
     C.   L3
     D.   L4

6.   What term describes the relationship between the internal speed of the CPU and the speed of the system bus?
     A.   CPU time
     B.   Multiplier
     C.   Differential
     D.   Coefficient

7. What term describes the time the CPU was executing in kernel mode?

   A. User time

   B. Steal time

   C. System time

   D. Idle time

8. What are revisions in CPUs called?

   A. Service packs

   B. Hot fixes

   C. Base layers

   D. Stepping levels

9. Which CPU architecture was designed for a tablet?

   A. ARM

   B. x86

   C. x64

   D. LGA

10. DDR3 memory is _____ as fast as DDR2.

   A. Three times

   B. Twice

   C. Half

   D. One-third

11. True/False: DDR doubles the rate by accessing the memory module twice per clock cycle.

12. What statement is true with regard to dual-channel memory?

   A. Installing different size modules in the same bank will result in the modules operating in single-channel mode.

   B. Installing different size modules in the same bank will result in the modules operating in dual-channel mode.

   C. Installing equal size modules in the same bank will result in the modules operating in single-channel mode.

   D. Installing different size modules in the same bank will increase the performance of the bank.

13. Which if the following is the time to access a memory address column if the correct row is already open?

   A. CAS Latency

   B. Row Address to Column Address Delay

   C. Row Precharge Time

   D. Row Active Time

14. Which of the following can be mixed when installing memory? Choose two.
   - **A.** Different speeds
   - **B.** Different types
   - **C.** Different form factors
   - **D.** Different manufacturers

15. Which of the following is a double-wide version of the 32-bit PCI local bus?
   - **A.** PCI
   - **B.** PCI-X
   - **C.** PCIe
   - **D.** PCI/2

16. Which type of NIC detects the type of device on the other end and changes the use of the wire pairs accordingly?
   - **A.** Auto-MDIX
   - **B.** Full-duplex
   - **C.** Converged
   - **D.** HBA

17. What type of NIC acts as both a host bus adapter (HBA) for the SAN and also as the network card for the server?
   - **A.** Auto-MDIX
   - **B.** Full-duplex
   - **C.** Converged
   - **D.** HBA

18. What are the two implementations of hybrid drives?
   - **A.** Dual-drive
   - **B.** Single-drive
   - **C.** Solid-state
   - **D.** Dual-state

19. What is the height of a 2U system?
   - **A.** 1.75″
   - **B.** 3.5″
   - **C.** 5.25″
   - **D.** 7″

20. Which statement is false with regard to UEFI?
   - **A.** It protects the preboot process.
   - **B.** It has a slower startup time than BIOS.
   - **C.** It supports 64-bit firmware device drivers.
   - **D.** It supports drives larger than 2.2 terabytes (TB).

Chapter

2

Installing and Configuring Servers

COMPTIA SERVER+ EXAM OBJECTIVES COVERED IN THIS CHAPTER:

✓ **2.1 Install and configure server operating systems.**

- Determine server role/purpose.
- Update firmware.
- BIOS/UEFI configuration (boot order).
- Disk preparation (RAID setup, partitioning, formatting, file system type [ext 2, 3, 4, NTFS, FAT32, ReiserFS, UFS, VMFS, ZFS, Swap]).
- Configure host name.
- Local account setup.
- Connect to network.
- Join domain/directory.
- Address security concerns (Patching, OS hardening, Compliance to company procedures/standards).
- Enable services.
- Install features/roles/applications/drivers.
- Performance baseline (server optimization, swap or pagefile optimization).
- Unattended/remote installations (deploying images and cloning, scripted installs (PXE boot, TFTP).

✓ **2.3 Given a scenario, use access and control methods to administer a server.**

- Local hardware administration (KVM, serial, virtual administration console).
- Network-based hardware administration (KVM over IP, ILO, iDRAC).
- Network-based operating system administration (RDP, SSH, VNC, command line/shell).

✓ 2.6 Explain the purpose and operation of virtualization components.

- Hosts and guests.

- Management interface for virtual machines.

- Hypervisor (Type I, Type II, Hybrid).

- Hardware compatibility list (BIOS/UEFI compatibility and support, CPU compatibility support, AMD-V/Intel VT).

- Resource allocation between Guest and Host (CPU, storage, memory, network connectivity [Direct Access (Bridging) vs. NAT, Virtual NICs, Virtual switches] Video).

A server will be of no use unless it has an operating system (OS) that can be used to access and control the hardware you learned about in Chapter 1, "Server Hardware." The OS is a prerequisite to installing any software that runs on the server as well, because in modern systems, applications are not allowed to directly access the hardware and must have an underlying OS to function as a liaison between the hardware and the applications. As you may already know, this is a good thing because it prevents any single application that hangs from hanging up the entire system. In this chapter, we'll look at installing operating systems and some of the preinstallation tasks that are required, as well as securing access to the server for the purpose of managing it. Finally, since in today's networks you'll probably encounter virtualized servers, we'll explore the basics of visualization components.

Installing and Configuring Server Operating Systems

You've probably installed an operating system before if you are reading this book. If you have, then you know that the entire process goes much more smoothly when it has been planned correctly and all information required has been gathered ahead of time and all preinstallation tasks have been completed successfully. What you may not know is that when it comes to servers, the stakes are higher because of the significant role they play in the network.

In this section, we'll discuss factors in common with those that are taken into account with workstations as well as factors that are unique to servers. We'll also talk about various ways to perform the installation and tasks that should follow the successful installation. Finally, we'll discuss some methods you can use to optimize the performance of the server when it's up and running.

Determining the Server Role/Purpose

One of the first items to consider before starting an installation is the role that the server is going to play in the network. The answer to this question will impact several items. Some server roles require more memory than others, and some place more of a premium on fast disk access or multiple CPUs. In Chapter 3, "Server Maintenance," you will learn more about the major roles that servers can play in the network. For now just keep in mind that the server's role will drive some of the hardware decisions that you make.

The role of the server will also have an impact on the operating system you install and the services you will enable and configure. It may also impact the amount and type of redundancy you provide for the role the server is playing. For example, if the server will be either a domain controller or a DNS server, you will almost certainly want to have multiple servers for these roles because the loss of these functions in the network is devastating. The bottom line is that you should have a clear understanding of all the roles the server will be playing before the installation begins.

Updating Firmware

The server hardware on which you will install the operating system already has some basic instructions installed by the manufacturer called *firmware*, just as a workstation will. This firmware, stored in nonvolatile memory of some sort or on a chip, will be dated as soon as the server leaves the factory where the firmware was installed. If vendors waited until all bugs had been discovered in this firmware, the servers would never ship, so it's understandable that over time, problems are discovered and updates are issued that correct these issues.

It's also true that in some cases these updates don't correct problems—they add functionality or features. As you probably already know, in many cases where you add a new CPU to a system, a firmware update is required for the system to support the new CPU. Another example might be that the firmware update adds support for hardware virtualization.

Regardless of whether you are trying to ensure all issues or bugs have been corrected or you want to ensure all the latest features are available, you should always check for and install any firmware updates that may be available. The place to check for this is the manufacturer's website. Not only will they have the latest update, they also typically have utilities for updating the firmware.

BIOS/UEFI Configuration

For years workstations and servers have relied on the BIOS as the firmware controlling the boot process. Limitations imposed by the traditional BIOS and the need for better security that could not be provided by the BIOS led to the development of the Unified Extensible Firmware Interface (UEFI) as the new standard. UEFI specifications define an interface in which the implementation of UEFI performs the equivalent of the BIOS by initiating the platform and loading the operating system. Some of the enhancements this new interface provides are as follows:

- Protects the preboot process from bootkit attacks
- Resumes from hibernation faster and starts faster
- Supports drives larger than 2.2 TB
- Supports 64-bit firmware drivers, which can be used to access more than 17.2 GB of memory during startup
- Supports both BIOS and UEFI

Although there are a number of things you can do with either the BIOS or the UEFI interface, the one that relates directly to installing an operating system is setting the boot order.

Boot Order

In either the BIOS setup or by using the UEFI, you can influence the order of the devices where the system will search for boot files. The most common source of boot files is the hard drive, but the files can also be located on DVDs, USB drives, and external drives, or they can be accessed from network locations as well as by using a PXE boot. The system will execute the first boot files (or any executable files) that it encounters in this search. When installing the operating system, you want the system, when booted, to look first in the location where the installation files are located.

If the system already has an operating system, this becomes even more important. This is because normally the first place the system looks is the hard drive. If this order is unaltered, the system will continue to boot to the old operating system, even though you may have the installation DVD in the DVD drive or the installation files located on a USB drive.

This means you must be familiar with entering the BIOS or UEFI and changing this boot order. It also means that when you have completed the installation you need to change it back so that it boots to the operating system you just installed.

Many new servers allow you to use either UEFI or BIOS settings to manage the boot process. In the following exercises, based on a Dell PowerEdge server, you will enter both systems. In either system you can set the boot mode, which tells the server which system to use to manage the boot process.

 WARNING   The operating system that you intend to install must be one that can support UEFI if you plan to use that system. If you set the device to use the UEFI boot mode and the OS does not support that, it could prevent the operating system from booting.

In the first exercise, you will use the traditional BIOS; in the second you will use the UEFI.

EXERCISE 2.1

Changing the Boot Order Using the BIOS

1. Turn on or restart your system.

2. Press F2 after you see the following message:

   `<F2> = System Setup`

3. You will now be on the main system setup screen, as shown here.

EXERCISE 2.1 *(continued)*

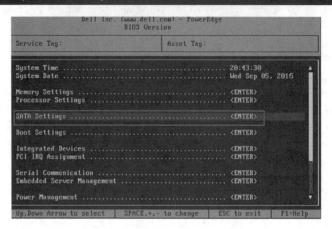

4.   Use the up and down keys to move to the Boot Settings screen.

5.   There are two settings related to the boot process on this screen. One is the Boot Mode field, which can be used to set the mode to either BIOS or UEFI, as shown here. The other is the Boot Sequence field; use the arrow keys to focus on and select that field. Then select the device from the list where the boot files are located.

6.   Exit from this screen and choose to save your settings.

7.   Reboot the server and it should boot to the installation files.

This exercise demonstrates the process on a Dell PowerEdge. Your system may be different. Consult your documentation.

EXERCISE 2.2

Changing the Boot Order Using the UEFI

1. Turn on or restart your system.

2. Press F11 after you see the following message:

`<F11> = UEFI Boot Manager`

You will now be on the UEFI Boot Manager screen.

3. Use the up and down keys to move to the UEFI Boot Settings screen.

4. Use the up and down keys to move to the Change Boot Order screen.

5. Use the arrow keys to focus on and select this field. Then select the device from the list where the boot files are located.

6. Exit from this screen and choose to save your settings.

7. Reboot the server and it should boot to the installation files.

Disk Preparation

Before you can install the operating system, prepare the disk on which you'll install it. This process includes some required tasks such as formatting the drive and creating a partition in which to install the system, and, if you are implementing RAID, the setup of the RAID array.

Once you have installed multiple drives in the server or purchased a server with multiple drives already present, you are ready to set up the drive in the desired RAID configuration. First let's review the three major types of RAID.

RAID Types

RAID stands for Redundant Array of Independent Disks. It's a way of combining the storage power of more than one hard disk for a special purpose such as increased performance or fault tolerance. RAID can be done with SCSI drives, but it is more often done with Serial Attached SCSI (SAS) drives. Several types of RAID are covered in the following sections. Due to the methods used to provide fault tolerance, the total amount of usable space in the array will vary, as discussed in each section.

RAID 0

RAID 0 is also known as *disk striping*. This is a form of RAID that doesn't provide fault tolerance. Data is written across multiple drives, so one drive can be reading or writing while the next drive's read/write head is moving. This makes for faster data access. However, if any one of the drives fails, all content is lost. In RAID 0, since there is no fault tolerance, the usable space in the drive is equal to the total space on all the drives. So if the two drives in an array have 250 GB each of space, 500 GB will be the available drive space.

RAID 1

RAID 1 is also known as *disk mirroring*. This is a method of producing fault tolerance by writing all data simultaneously to two separate drives. If one drive fails, the other drive contains all the data and may also be used as a source of that data. However, disk mirroring doesn't help access speed, and the cost is double that of a single drive. Since RAID 1 repeats the data on two drives, only one half of the total drive space is available for data. So if two 250 GB drives are used in the array, 250 GB will be the available drive space.

RAID 5

RAID 5 combines the benefits of both RAID 0 and RAID 1 and is also known as *striping with parity*. It uses a parity block distributed across all the drives in the array, in addition to striping the data across them. That way, if one drive fails, the parity information can be used to recover what was on the failed drive. A minimum of three drives is required. RAID 5 uses $1/n$ (n = the number of drives in the array) for parity information (for example, one third of the space in a three-drive array), and only $1 - (1/n)$ is available for data. So if three 250 GB drives are used in the array (for a total of 750 GB), 500 GB will be the available drive space.

RAID Setup

The management of hardware RAID is usually done through a utility that you select to access during the boot process, as you would if you were selecting to enter setup. An example of this is the PowerEdge Expandable RAID Controller BIOS Configuration Utility. When you boot the server, you press Ctrl+M to launch this utility. From a high level you will use the utility and the arrow keys to do the following:

This example uses a Dell PowerEdge. Your server may be different. Consult the documentation.

1.   Select Configure ➢ View/Add Configuration on the initial screen, as shown in Figure 2.1.

FIGURE 2.1   View/Add Configuration

2.   On the next screen (Figure 2.2), drives that are already online will show as ONLINE and any that have just been added will be shown with a status of READY. For any drives that still show as READY, select the drive and press the spacebar, which will change the status from READY to ONLINE. When you have selected the drives that will be in the array, they will be blinking. Press Enter to confirm that these drives will be members of this array.

FIGURE 2.2   Confirming the drive additions

3. Press F10 to display the Array configuration screen (Figure 2.3).

FIGURE 2.3   Array configuration screen

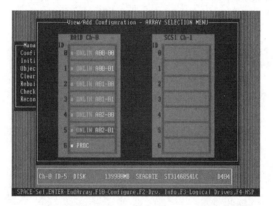

4. The array number that was assigned for the new disk drives from the previous step is displayed here. Press the spacebar to display the Span-1 message just below where the array number appears. Press F10 and you are now ready to select the RAID level, as shown in Figure 2.4.

FIGURE 2.4   Selecting the RAID level

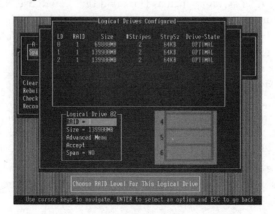

5. Select the RAID level, keeping in mind the number of drives required for each type. Finally, select the size of the array.

6. Save the configuration and reboot the system.

Partitioning

When all of the volumes have been configured as you would like them, you must create a partition on one of the volumes to contain the operating system. This can be done during the installation of the operating system using the GUI provided with the installation utility. For example, during the installation of Windows Server 2012 R2 (see Figure 2.5), you can create a partition of the desired size. Be mindful of the space required for the operating system and include some additional space.

FIGURE 2.5   Creating a partition

Where do you want to install Windows?

Name	Total size	Free space	Type
Drive 0 Unallocated Space	60.0 GB	60.0 GB	

Refresh   ✕ *Delete*   ✔ *Format*   ✳ *New*

⟲ *Load driver*   *Extend*

Next

Formatting

Once the partition has been created, it must be formatted with a filesystem. The filesystem choices will be driven by the operating system. Windows, for example, will require using either FAT or NTFS. Other systems, such as Unix and Linux, will use other filesystems. We'll look at filesystems in a bit. You can format the partition during the installation. Using the Windows Server 2012 R2 example, you'd choose the Format option shown in Figure 2.5. Similar options are provided during the installation of many forms of Linux and Unix as well.

Filesystem Type

There are many different filesystems you may encounter. In the following sections, we'll take a brief survey of these filesystem types and see where and when they are used.

ext2, ext3, and ext4

ext2, ext3, and ext4 are Linux filesystems. As you would expect, each version is more capable than the previous one. Although ext4 has the advantages listed here, it should be noted that it is not compatible with Windows. (You can, however, obtain third-party programs that will allow Windows to read ext4.) The following are the strengths of ext4:

- It supports individual file sizes up to 16 TB.

- The overall maximum ext4 filesystem size is 1 EB (exabyte). (1 EB = 1024 PB [petabyte]. 1 PB = 1024 TB [terabyte]).

- The directory can contain 64,000 subdirectories as opposed to 32,000 in ext3.

- You can mount an existing ext3 filesystem as an ext4 filesystem (without having to upgrade it).

- The performance and reliability of the filesystem is improved compared to ext3.

- In ext4, you also have the option of turning off the journaling feature. Journaling is a process where the filesystem records its intention to record a change before the change is made. Although this approach is beneficial when the system crashes before the change is committed, it does take resources.

NTFS

Introduced along with Windows NT (and available on all Windows Server and client operating systems), NTFS (NT Filesystem) is a much more advanced filesystem in almost every way than all versions of the FAT filesystem. It includes such features as individual file security and compression, RAID support, and support for extremely large file and partition sizes and disk transaction monitoring. It is the filesystem of choice for high-performance computing. Only when the volume is very small will FAT be more efficient than NTFS.

FAT32

FAT (File Allocation Table) is an acronym for the file on a filesystem used to keep track of where files are. It's also the name given to this type of filesystem, introduced in 1981. The largest FAT disk partition that could be created was approximately 2 GB for FAT16. FAT32 was introduced along with Windows 95 OEM Service Release 2 and supported partitions up to 16 MB. As disk sizes grew, so did the need to be able to format a partition larger than 2 GB. FAT32 was based more on Virtual File Allocation Table (VFAT) than on FAT16. VFAT was the filesystem developed for Windows 95 that allowed for filenames longer than 8 characters. It allowed for 32-bit cluster addressing, which in turn provided for a maximum partition size of 2 terabytes (2048 GB). It also included smaller cluster sizes to avoid wasted space (which we discuss later). FAT32 support is included in current Windows server versions.

ReiserFS

ReiserFS is a filesystem support by Linux that provides journaling and was the default system in Novell's SUSE Linux Enterprise until 2006, when ext3 was adopted. It is the default filesystem on many other Linux distributions as well. It was introduced in version 2.4.1 of the Linux kernel and is now maintained by volunteers as an open source project. It supports volumes of 16 TB (each terabyte, or TB, is 1024 GB) with a maximum file size of 1 EB. (Each exabyte, or EB, is 1 billion GB). Filenames when used with Linux can be up to 255 characters.

UFS

The Unix filesystem (UFS) is used by Unix and other Unix-like operating systems. Although Linux includes a UFS implementation for binary compatibility at the read level with other versions of Unix, it does not fully support writing to UFS. In Mac OS X, it was available as an alternative to Apple's proprietary filesystem. It has a maximum volume size of 8 ZB (each zettabyte, or ZB, is a trillion GB) and a maximum file size of 8 ZB. It allows any files sizes up to 255 bytes.

VMFS

The VMware filesystem (VMFS) is used by the VMware virtualization suite, vSphere. There are four versions of VMFS, corresponding with ESX Server product releases. Although NFS can also be used with VMware, it has some unique features that make it perfect for virtualization. It was developed to store virtual machine disk images, including snapshots. It allows for multiple servers to access the filesystem at the same time. Volumes can be expanded by spanning multiple VMFS volumes together. The maximum virtual disk size of VMFS is 64 TB, whereas each file can have a maximum size of 62 TB. It also supports long filenames.

ZFS

The Zettabyte filesystem (ZFS) is one developed by Sun Microsystems, but it is also an open source project. It is supported on many other operating systems, such as some versions of BSD (BSD, or Berkeley Software Distribution, is a version of Unix). At one point, Apple appeared to be interested in this filesystem but has since dropped that project. ZFS has a focus on integrity of data, which distinguishes it from some of the other filesystems that focus more on performance. ZFS allows for volumes up to 256 ZB and a maximum file size of 16 EB. It also supports filenames up to 255 characters.

Swap

Today's operating systems support the use of swap files. These are files located on the hard drive that are utilized temporarily to hold items moved from memory when there is a shortage of memory required for a particular function. The running programs believe that their information is still in RAM, but the OS has moved the data to the hard drive. When the application needs the information again, it is swapped back into RAM so that the processor can use it. Providing adequate space for this file is a key disk management issue. Every operating system seems to have its own recommendations as to the optimum size of this file, but in all cases the swap file should be on a different drive than the operating system if possible.

Configuring Hostnames

One of the first things you'll want to configure on a server is its hostname. This is typically done during the installation of the operating system. Although you can change the hostname later if desired, doing so could cause issues for users who have drives mapped using the old name. When you're naming servers, it is helpful to arrive at a naming convention that implies where the server is located and perhaps a code for the role the server is playing. Clearly identifying the role of the server could be a security risk. Your naming convention doesn't have to follow any standard suggestion you may find in books; it's important only that it serve these purposes and make sense to you and others working in the network. It is also important that the naming convention is followed by everyone when they are naming servers.

Some examples of server characteristics that have been used as a part of a naming convention are

- The environment in which the server operates (examples: dev for development, prd for production)
- The role of the server (examples: sql for database server, dns for name server)
- The location of the server (examples: atl for Atlanta, dal for Dallas)

Combining these, for example, might result in this name for a production SQL server located in Atlanta:

sql01-prd-atl

Local Account Setup

To manage the server, you will need a local account created on the server. A local administrator account is typically created during the process of installing the operating system, but that account will have complete access to everything (called *root access* in some systems), which may be more control than you want technicians to have.

Security best practices recommend that technicians use standard user accounts unless they need to do something that requires administrator access. They can then execute that task using admin credentials. In Windows, this is called running the task *as administrator* (you right-click the icon or app and select Run As Administrator from the context menu), as shown in Figure 2.6. The menu option has a shield next to it, and if you're at the command line, you preface the command with runas. This executes the function in an admin security context and ends that context when the process is over. Figure 2.7 shows the use of runas at the command line. Notepad opened after the execution of the command a prompt for credentials which were then provided.

FIGURE 2.6 Running an application as administrator

FIGURE 2.7   Using runas

Later, if you join the server to the domain, the domain administrator account will be added to the local administrators group, giving domain administrators full rights to the server. Keep in mind that the same recommendation to use an administrator account *only* when required applies to those in the domain administrators group as well.

Connecting to the Network

When the server is up and running, you will need to connect it to the network. This obviously includes connecting a cable to it and then connecting to a switch, but it also includes the following steps:

- Assigning an IP address, subnet mask, and (usually) default gateway. Although typically we want servers to keep the same IP address, this can be accomplished through a reservation if we want the server to participate in DHCP, which is a desirable thing. DHCP will be covered in detail in Chapter 8, "Networking."

- Assigning the server a DNS server address and allowing the server to register its IP address with the DNS server. Setting the server to DHCP to receive this from DHCP will allow the server to update with no manual intervention if the address of the DNS server changes.

- In some cases (an email server, for example), creating a DNS record manually.

Joining a Domain/Directory

Enterprise networks join servers, workstations, and other devices in security associations called *domains* or *realms*. These associations are made possible through the use of directory services such as Active Directory. Such associations are what make the concept of single sign-on possible. This means that any user can log into the network using any device that is a domain member and receive all their assigned rights and privileges by using a single logon.

You can join the server to the domain during the installation in some cases, but most administrators do this after the successful installation of the operating system. Figure 2.8 shows an example of how this is done in Windows Server 2012 R2. To navigate to System Properties in Windows Server 2012 R2, open Control Panel and select the System icon (using icon view); then select Advanced System Settings from the menu on the left side of the page. This opens the System Properties dialog box. Select the Computer Name tab and click Change to access the Computer Name/Domain Changes dialog box.

FIGURE 2.8   Joining the server to the domain

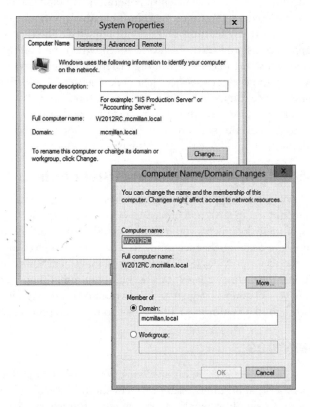

Addressing Security Concerns

After the server is securely joined to the domain, the next issue to address is security. No server should be connected to the network, especially the Internet, until the system has had all security patches installed and antivirus software has been installed and updated. Beyond that, there are several other security considerations that we will also cover in the following sections.

Patching

Just as the driver files that comes with every operating system is dated the moment that the installation DVD leaves the factory, so is the security posture of the operating system. As soon as possible after the installation, you need to apply all operating system patches and service packs. Some operating systems, such as the Windows and Linux systems, offer the ability to download and apply these updates during the installation.

OS Hardening

The next thing that should be done is harden the operating system. The goal of hardening an operating system is to reduce the attack surface. This involves disabling all services that are not used and turning off any features that are not required. The theory behind this is that all services, applications, and features have well-known vulnerabilities that hackers can leverage to compromise the machine. Although keeping up with security patches mitigates this, disabling any unnecessary services just makes sense. An additional benefit is better server performance since it must no longer allocate resources for that service.

Finally, any application not in use should be uninstalled and any ports that are unneeded should be closed. Any user accounts that may exist that are not needed should be deleted and any built-in accounts should have the default passwords changed.

Complying with Company Procedures/Standards

While applying all firmware and operating system patches is a starting baseline for securing the new server, your company's standards and procedures may require that you go further. It may be that upon review of these documents you may find that there are additional actions that you must take. For example, it could be that according to policy certain server roles require that the network service the server provides (SQL or Project Management Server, for example) be configured to run under the security context of a user account rather than under the context of the system account (a very common safeguard). The bottom line is that no new server should be released to the network until it conforms to all security policies and procedures.

Enabling Services

If you paid attention during the section on operating system hardening (let's hope you did!), you will remember that no unnecessary services should be enabled. At the same time, all *required* services should be enabled. At one point the security paradigm in place on Windows servers assigned the responsibility for managing the security of services to the administrator. What that meant was all services were enabled by default and it was the responsibility of the administrator to disable what was *not* required.

That approach led to services being left enabled mistakenly, which also led to systems being hacked through unsecured services. Now Microsoft has taken a different approach and many services are *not* enabled, which means you will need to enable all services you require while leaving disabled any you don't need.

In other operating systems, this same principle should be followed. Their security with regard to services may vary. Exercise 2.3 takes a look at disabling a service in Windows Server.

This exercise uses a Windows Server 2012 R2 operating system. Your system may have different steps.

EXERCISE 2.3

Disabling a Service in Windows Server 2012 R2

1. Open Server Manager if it isn't already open.

2. Select Tools ➤ Services to open the Services utility. All services, both running and not running, are displayed.

3. Right-click on a service.

4. Select Properties from the context menu.

5. In the Startup Type drop-down box, select Disabled, as shown here.

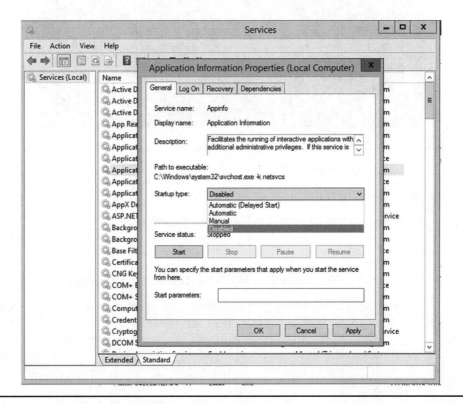

To disable a service in Linux, you must identify its process ID (PID) first; the PID will be how you specify the service when you execute the kill command. To identify the PID of the service, you must know the name of the service. For example, to disable FTP you must execute a command that displays all open ports along with the name of the service and the PID. Let's tie these things together in Exercise 2.4.

EXERCISE 2.4

Disabling a Service in Linux

1. Identity all open ports by executing the following command:

    [admin@bigco]netstat -lp

    In the output, locate FTP as shown here. It is the last program in the list before the screen cutoff.

```
Active Internet connections (only servers)
Proto Recv-Q Send-Q Local Address              Foreign Address        State      PID/P
rogram name
tcp         0      0 *:31138                    *:*                    LISTEN     1485/
rpc.statd
tcp         0      0 *:mysql                    *:*                    LISTEN     1882/
mysqld
tcp         0      0 *:sunrpc                   *:*                    LISTEN     1276/
rpcbind
tcp         0      0 *:ndmp                     *:*                    LISTEN     2375/
perl
tcp         0      0 *:webcache                 *:*                    LISTEN     2312/
monitorix-http
tcp         0      0 *:ftp                      *:*                    LISTEN     2174/
vsftpd
```

2. Locate the PID in the PID column of the output. In this case, the PID is 2174.

3. Now that you know the PID, execute the following command to kill FTP:

    [admin@bigco]kill -9 2174

The –9 parameter tells the system to kill the process without saving.

Installing Features, Roles, Applications, and Drivers

The role the server will play in the network will dictate what features and roles need to be installed or enabled. With regard to Windows, the same security paradigm that's applied to services has been applied to what are called *features* and *roles* in Microsoft. For example, if the server will be a DNS server, then you must install that role and the related features required to perform that role. This is done in Server Manager, as shown in Figure 2.9, where the FTP role has been added. To navigate to the Add Roles And Features Wizard, open Server Manager and select Manage ➢ Add Roles And Features.

Performance Baseline

When all applications have been installed and proper services enabled, you need to create what is called a *performance baseline*. This is a snapshot of the performance of key resources in the server such as the CPU, memory, disk, and network card. This snapshot should be taken during a period of normal activity.

FIGURE 2.9   Adding a role in Server Manager

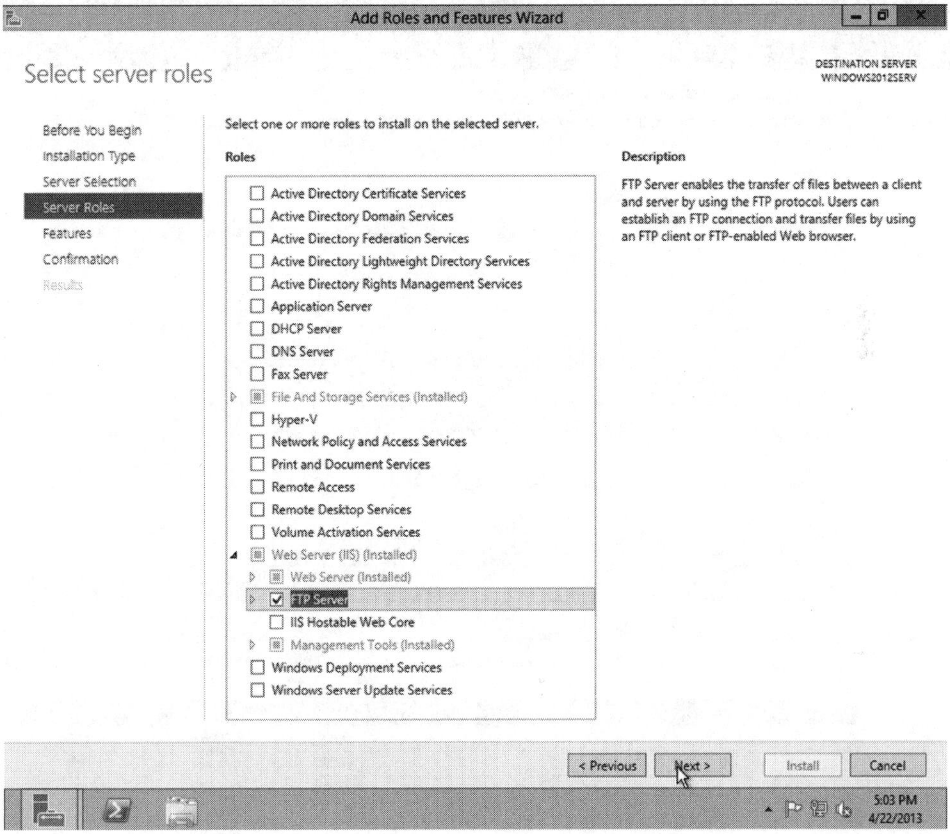

You can use third-party monitoring tools, or you can rely on some that are built into the system, such as the Performance Monitor tool in Windows Server 2012 R2. The Performance Monitor tool can be used to take these snapshots over a period of time as well, so you get a feel for the rise and fall of the workload on the server. In this way, you can better understand the times of day when a higher workload is normal. You may also want to take advantage of tools such as System Center Operations Manager, which allows you to easily do this for a number of servers from a single console. Figure 2.10 shows the seven-day Memory Pages Per Second report for a Windows Server 2012 Datacenter computer.

To navigate to the Performance Monitor in Windows Server 2012 R2, open Server Manager and select Tools ➤ Performance Monitor.

FIGURE 2.10   Seven-day Memory Pages Per Second report

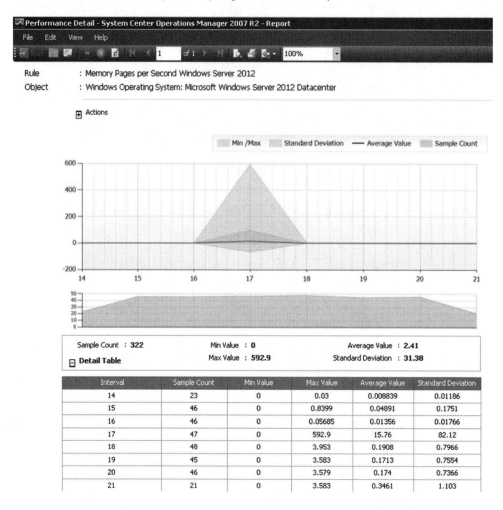

Save the performance baseline as a reference point for future readings. It is impossible to know when something abnormal is happening unless you know what normal is. That is the function of this baseline. It also helps anticipate a rise in workload over time, so you can take steps to add resources before an issue arises.

Server Optimization

The term *server optimization* refers to the proper allocation of resources to servers so that the resources are neither under- nor overutilized. In the past, this would be accomplished by examining the role of each server, attempting to anticipate the workload and then installing resources (CPU, NIC, memory, disk) to as closely as possible match the needs of the server. Invariably, no matter how much care is taken, resources still tended to be over- and under-utilized. It is simply impossible to know the future.

Today, virtualization of servers is making this task much easier. Servers deployed as virtual machines can be dynamically assigned resources in real time as the need arises. Then these resources can be dynamically reallocated and deployed elsewhere when the workload of the server drops. Virtualization will be covered later in this chapter in the section "Purpose and Operation of Virtualization Components."

Swap or Pagefile Optimization

Earlier in this chapter you were introduced to the concept of the swap file, or the *pagefile* as it is sometimes called. Optimizing this file amounts to determining the proper amount of disk space to allocate for this function. Although it is not easy to pin down some vendors on a specific recommendation, you should always start with whatever guidelines the vendor may provide. Best practices have evolved over time.

With regard to Windows servers, here are some best practices:

- Set the pagefile at 1.5 times the RAM.
- Servers hosting databases or resource-hungry applications should have the pagefile set at 3 times the RAM.
- Split the pagefile on two different drives, preferably on two different disks.
- For Windows 2008, Windows Server 2008 R2, and Windows Server 2012 R2, the C drive should have a 6 GB pagefile.

In Linux, there is a parameter called swappiness that controls how aggressively the system swaps to disk. It ranges from 0 to 100, and when swappiness=0 it tells the kernel to avoid swapping processes out of physical memory for as long as possible. When swappiness=100 it tells the kernel to aggressively swap processes out of physical memory and move them to swap cache. You may want to experiment with this setting if you find the system is swapping frequently (which hurts performance).

Regardless of the operating system, if the server is frequently swapping to the swap or pagefile, that means the server needs more physical memory. Moving data back and forth from memory to disk and having to retrieve something from disk that should have been in memory hurts performance.

Unattended/Remote Installations

There's nothing wrong with installing an operating system by inserting the DVD, booting to the DVD, and following the prompts to execute the installation manually. However, there are easier ways. In this section, we'll take a look at unattended installations of various types. Not only do they make the process somewhat more automated, it also helps to maintain a consistent process for deploying both workstations and servers in the enterprise.

Deploying Images and Cloning

One way in which operating systems can be deployed quickly and with consistency is to create images of completed installations and use disk imaging software to copy the image to a drive. Not only does this speed the deployment process, but the image can be preconfigured according to the company policy with regard to the role the server will play.

Another of the advantages of a virtualized environment is the ability to maintain an inventory of these images for quick use. Virtualization is not required, however, and there are tools provided by vendors such as Microsoft that make the creation, management, and deployment of images easier. Windows Deployment Services (WDS) in Windows Server 2012 R2 is one such tool. This tool can be used to

- Capture an image of an existing server

- Create a boot image to send down to devices with no existing operating system so they can boot up and connect to the deployment server using PXE boot (more on PXE boot in a bit)

- Create boot media containing images used to connect to the deployment server for devices that do support PXE boot

- Perform unattended installations that contain an answer file that answers all of the prompts in the installation (more on these types of installations in the next section)

Scripted Installs

Scripted installations differ from simple image deployment in one way: there is some type of file associated with the deployment that makes changes to the deployment or provides answers for the installation. In a Windows classic unattended installation, this file is called an *answer file*. When using Windows Deployment Services or any third-party deployment tool, there will be a number of script files that might be used during either an image deployment or a full installation. In an image deployment, the file makes changes to or provides drivers for the image; in a full installation, the full installation process takes place with the file providing answers to the prompts.

Regardless of which type of deployment is taking place, the new system, with no operating system, must be able to

- Boot up and get an IP configuration

- Locate the deployment server

- Download the image or installation files

- Locate and download any additional scripts that need to run

There are a couple of ways to accomplish this, and we'll look at them now.

PXE Boot and TFTP

Preboot Execution Environment (PXE) makes it possible to boot a device with no operating system present and come to a location in the network where the operating system files might be found and installed.

A device that is PXE-enabled will have an additional boot option called PXE Boot. When the device is set to boot to that option, it will attempt a PXE network boot. The process after that follows these steps:

1. The system begins by looking for a DHCP server. This is referred to as Discover.

2. The DHCP server answers with a packet called the Offer packet, indicating a willingness to supply the configuration. This step is referred to as Offer.

3. The client indicates to the DHCP server that it requires the location of the network boot program (NBP). This step is called the Request.

4. The DHCP server supplies the IP address of this location. This step is called Acknowledge.

 If you have installed Microsoft DHCP using WDS, the original Offer packet from the DHCP server already includes the location of the PXE server and the NBP.

5. The client, using Trivial File Transfer Protocol (TFTP), downloads the NBP from the network location specified by the PXE server.

6. The NBP is initialized. At this point, either the full installation occurs with an answer file or an image is deployed with or without additional script files.

Note that the process is independent of the operating system. Although we have framed this discussion in terms of Windows, the system being deployed can be any operating system. The PXE boot process is shown in Figure 2.11.

FIGURE 2.11 PXE boot process

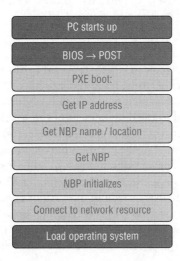

Using Access and Control Methods to Administer a Server

Although it is possible to enter your server room or datacenter and use a keyboard and mouse connected to the server to manage the server, it's unlikely that you'll manage the server in this fashion unless you are forced to do so. In this section, we'll discuss methods of managing both the hardware of the server and the operating system.

Local Hardware Administration

When I refer to managing hardware "locally," I mean that you will not be connecting to the device over the network—you will be in the server room or datacenter when you do this. The available options depend on whether the server is a physical device like a rack server, blade server, or tower server, or of it is a virtual server deployed as a virtual machine (VM) on a virtualization host. In this section, we'll explore three ways to manage hardware locally.

KVM

When working with servers locally—that is, standing in the same room with the server— one of the most common ways technicians connect to the server is through a KVM. A keyboard, video, and mouse (KVM) device allows you to plug multiple PCs (usually servers) into the device and to switch easily back and forth from system to system using the same mouse, monitor, and keyboard. The KVM is actually a switch that all of the systems plug into. There is usually no software to install. Just turn off all the systems, plug them all into the switch, and turn them back on; then you can switch from one to another using the same keyboard, monitor, and mouse device connected to the KVM switch. The way in which this switch connects to the devices is shown in Figure 2.12.

Serial

Although serial connections have been largely replaced by the use of KVM switches, it is still possible to connect to a server using a serial connection. The issue that arises is that even if a technician's laptop had a serial port (which is unlikely today), there would be at most one. This conundrum led to the development of the serial device server. It provides a number of serial ports, which are then connected to the serial ports of other equipment, such as servers, routers, or switches. The consoles of the connected devices can then be accessed by connecting to the console server over a serial link such as a modem, or over a network with terminal emulator software such as Telnet or SSH, maintaining survivable connectivity that allows remote users to log in the various consoles without being physically nearby. This arrangement is shown in Figure 2.13. One of the advantages of this is the ability to get to the servers "out of band." This means even if the network is down, servers can be reached through the serial ports either locally or through the modem.

FIGURE 2.12   Standard KVM switch

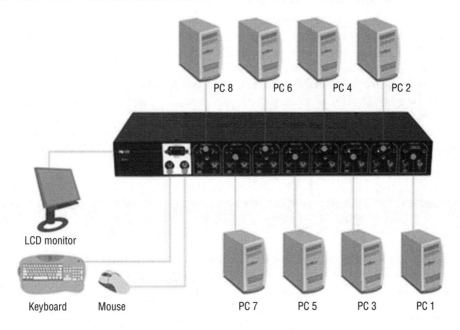

FIGURE 2.13   Serial device server

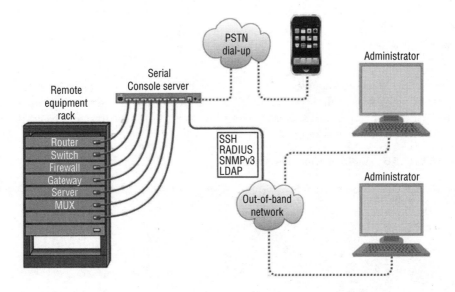

Virtual Administration Console

To manage servers in a virtual environment, vendors of virtualization software provide administration consoles that allow for one server to another for the purpose of maintenance and administration. Examples include the VMware Server Console and the Virtual Machine Manager Console in Windows Hyper-V.

In Figure 2.14, an example of the VMware Server Console is shown. Here the System Monitor page shows the workload on a specific virtualization host (more on virtualization later, but a host is a physical machine that has multiple virtual machines on it). You can see there are four VMs hosted by server, all of which are currently powered off. That would explain why only 2 percent of CPU and only 1.3 GB of memory are being used, none it by the VMs.

FIGURE 2.14 VMware Server Console

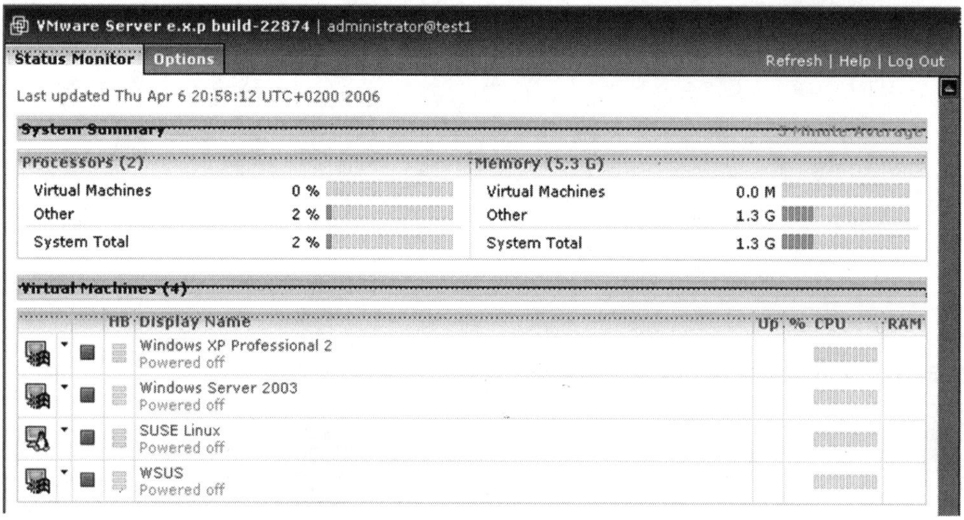

The Virtual Machine Manager (VMM) Console in Hyper-V is shown in Figure 2.15. It also allows for managing the servers centrally from this console. Here two VMs are shown on the host named Hypervisor8. One of the two VMs is 90 percent through the creation process whereas the other is stopped.

FIGURE 2.15 VMM in Windows Hyper-V

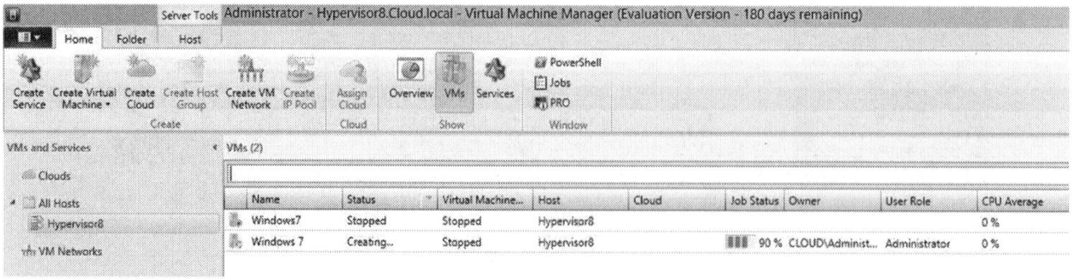

Network-Based Hardware Administration

Although some of the management of servers may occur locally, most of the time you will find yourself connecting to the servers over the IP-based network. A number of options are available to accomplish this. In this section, we'll talk about managing the hardware of the server using network-based administration.

KVM over IP

Earlier you learned about using a basic KVM switch. KVM vendors have responded to the need for a KVM switch that can be accessed over the network. The switch is like the one you saw earlier with one difference—it can be reached through the network, as shown in Figure 2.16. This means it is accessible not only from a workstation in the next room, but from anywhere. In this particular implementation (it can be done several ways), each server has a small device between it and the KVM switch that accepts the serial and keyboard/mouse connections.

FIGURE 2.16   KVM over IP

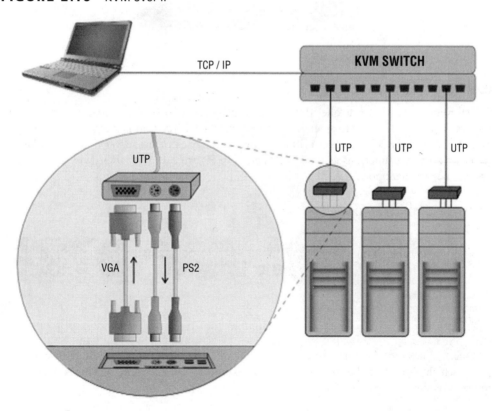

iLO

Integrated Lights-Out (iLO) is technology embedded into Hewlett-Packard (HP) servers that allows for out-of-band management of the server. Out-of-band management refers to any method of managing the server that does not use the network.

The physical connection is an Ethernet port that will be on the server and will be labeled iLO. In Figure 2.17, one of these iLO ports is shown in an HP Moonshot chassis (these hold blade servers). HP iLO functions out-of-the-box without additional software installation regardless of the server's state of operation, giving you complete access to the server from any location via a web browser or the iLO Mobile App.

FIGURE 2.17   iLO port

iDRAC

A Dell Remote Access Controller (DRAC) card provides out-of-band management for Dell servers. The iDRAC refers to a version of these interface cards that is integrated on the motherboard of the server. There will be a port on the back of the server that looks like an Ethernet port that functions as the iDRAC port. In Figure 2.18 it is labeled the designated system management port.

FIGURE 2.18   iDRAC port

Once configured, the port will present the technician with an interface on their computer, which is connected to the port when the connection is established. This console interface is shown in Figure 2.19.

FIGURE 2.19   iDRAC console

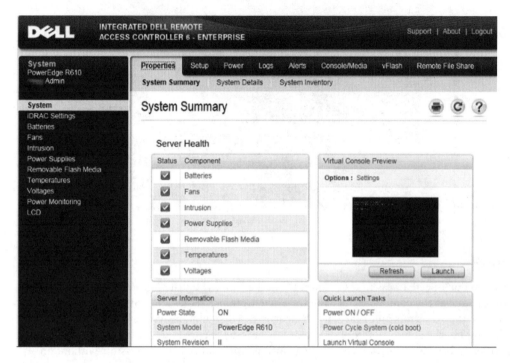

Network-Based Operating System Administration

When you need to make changes to the operating system, there are a number of ways in which you can remotely make a connection. In this section, we'll survey the most popular methods of accomplishing network-based operating system administration.

RDP

Developed by Microsoft, Remote Desktop Protocol (RDP) allows you to connect to remote computers and run programs on them. When you use RDP, you see the desktop of the computer you've signed into on your screen. The computer at which you are seated is the client and the computer you're logging into is the server. The server uses its own video driver to create video output and sends the output to the client using RDP. All keyboard and mouse input from the client is encrypted and sent to the server for processing. RDP also supports sound, drive, port, and network printer redirection.

A tool that can be used for this is the Microsoft Remote Desktop Connection Manager (RDCMan). It is a handy console, as shown in Figure 2.20. Note it is *not* limited to managing Microsoft servers and clients can be found for non-Microsoft systems.

FIGURE 2.20   RDCMan

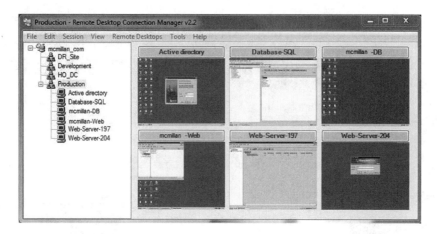

SSH

If you don't need access to the graphical interface and you just want to connect to a server to operate at the command line, you have two options: Telnet and SSH. Telnet works just fine, but it transmits all of the data in cleartext, which obviously would be a security issue. Therefore, the connection tool of choice has become Secure Shell (SSH). It's not as easy to set up because it encrypts all of the transmissions and that's not possible without an encryption key.

Although the commands will be somewhat different based on the operating system, you must generate a key, which is generated using some unique information about the server as seed information, so that the key will be unique to the server (the encryption algorithm will be well known). Once configured, the connection process will be very similar to using Telnet, with the exception, of course, that the transmissions will be protected.

VNC

Another remote administration tool that functions like RDP is Virtual Network Computing (VNC). It differs in that it uses the Remote Framebuffer (RFB) protocol. It operates like RDP with respect to the experience, but it is not a secure protocol. It doesn't transmit in cleartext, but cracking the password is possible if the encryption key and the password are captured. Therefore, strong passwords should be used, and it may be advisable to tunnel it over a VPN or SSH connection.

Command Line or Shell

A shell is a type of user interface that may or may not be graphical. In most cases shells are command-driven interfaces. There are many shells for Unix systems. They all have their own command, syntax, and capabilities. Some operating systems have a single shell—for example, the MS-DOS program. Other Windows systems have multiple shells that can be used such as PowerShell. Devices like routers and switches also have shells like the Cisco IOS. When used over the network, shells are sometimes referred to as remote shells.

Purpose and Operation of Virtualization Components

In today's networks you must understand virtualization. Organizations large and small are moving to take advantage of the benefits of this technology. They are saving power, consolidating, and downsizing (some would say right-sizing) their physical footprint and suffering far fewer bottlenecks caused by resource limitations. This section introduces you to the components that make virtualization work and the specific role each component plays in making these benefits possible.

Hosts and Guests

The foundation of virtualization is the host device, which may be a workstation or a server. This device is the physical machine that contains the software that makes virtualization possible and the containers, or *virtual machines*, for the guest operating systems. The host provides the underlying hardware and computing resources, such as processing power, memory, disk, and network I/O, to the VMs. Each guest is a completely separate and independent instance of an operating system and application software.

The host is responsible for allocating compute resources to each of the VMs as specified by the configuration. The software that manages all of this is called the *hypervisor*. Based on parameters set by the administrator, the hypervisor may take various actions to maintain the performance of each guest as specified by the administrator. Some of these actions may include

- Turning off a VM if not in use

- Taking CPU resources away from one VM and allocating them to another

- Turning on additional VMs when required to provide fault tolerance

The exact nature of the relationship between the hypervisor, the host operating system, and the guest operating systems depends on the type of hypervisor in use. Later on in this section that will be clearer when you learn about hypervisors. From a high level the relationship is shown in Figure 2.21.

FIGURE 2.21   Hosts and guest

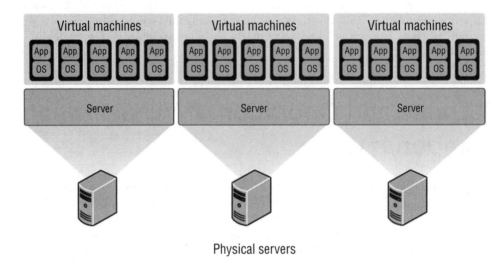

Management Interface for Virtual Machines

One of the benefits of virtualization products such as VMware vSphere, Microsoft Hyper-V, and Oracle VM VirtualBox is the management interface they provide. These interfaces allow you to create, view, and make changes to VMs. Some of these changes can be done when the device is running, and some require shutting the VM down. The VMware Server Console was shown earlier in this chapter in Figure 2.14, in the section "Virtual Administration Console." In the same section, in Figure 2.15, was the Microsoft Virtual Machine Manager (VMM) Console in Hyper-V. Figure 2.22 shows Oracle VM VirtualBox management console. In this console you can see there are three VMs. We've highlighted the VM named test2, and the details about the resources of that VM appear in the details pane.

Hypervisor

Earlier you learned that the exact nature of the relationship between the hypervisor, the host operating system, and the guest operating systems depends on the type of hypervisor in use. There are three types of hypervisors in use today. Let's review them now.

Type I

A Type I hypervisor (or native, bare-metal) runs directly on the host's hardware to control the hardware and to manage guest operating systems. A guest operating system runs on another level above the hypervisor. Examples of these are VMware vSphere and Microsoft Hyper-V.

FIGURE 2.22   Oracle VM VirtualBox

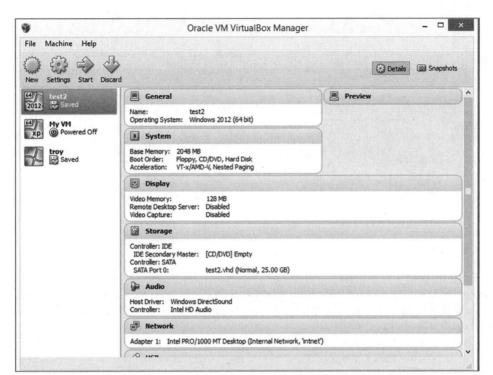

Type II

A Type II hypervisor runs within a conventional operating system environment. With the hypervisor layer as a distinct second software level, guest operating systems run at the third level above the hardware. VMware Workstation and VirtualBox exemplify Type II hypervisors. A comparison of the two approaches is shown in Figure 2.23.

Hybrid

In the datacenter you will most likely encounter Type I hypervisors, but you should be aware of an emerging type of hypervisor: the hybrid. This is basically a Type II hypervisor, but it is integrated with a cloud. The best example of this is VMware Workstation version 12. With this version, it is possible to connect to vCloud Air or to any private cloud and upload, run, and view VMs from the Workstation interface.

Another new approach that might be considered a hybrid is container-based virtualization. Container-based virtualization is also called operating system virtualization. This kind of server virtualization is a technique where the kernel allows for multiple isolated user-space instances. The instances are known as containers, virtual private servers, or virtual environments.

FIGURE 2.23   Type I and II hypervisors

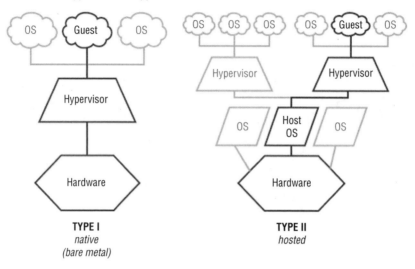

In this model, the hypervisor is replaced with operating system–level virtualization, where the kernel of an operating system allows multiple isolated user spaces or containers. A virtual machine is not a complete operating system instance but rather a partial instance of the same operating system. The containers in Figure 2.24 are the blue boxes just above the host OS level. Container-based virtualization is used mostly in Linux environments, and examples are the commercial Parallels Virtuozzo and the open source OpenVZ project.

FIGURE 2.24   Container-based virtualization

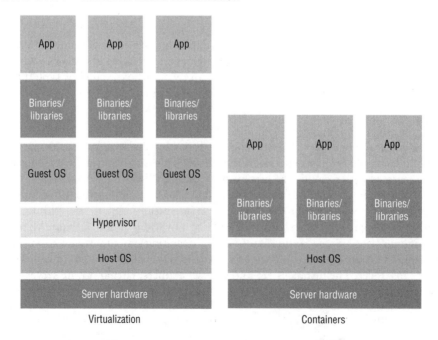

Hardware Compatibility List

When choosing the host (server) for a virtualization solution, you should consider the hardware required to achieve the most benefit from the solution. Review the compatibility guides offered by the major vendors: VMware, Citrix (XenServer), and Microsoft. These guides can offer critical guidance with respect to the hardware required by their solutions based on your specific requirements. Having said that, there are some general features and components that are worth mentioning due to their importance. The following sections cover some of these.

BIOS/UEFI Compatibility and Support

In many cases the motherboard and associated BIOS/UEFI settings need no alteration to provide services to virtual machines. However, some of the virtualization products, such as Microsoft Hyper-V, require that the motherboard support hardware-assisted virtualization. This is because in these cases the virtualization product is not installed on top of a regular operating system but instead is installed directly on bare metal—that is, as an integral part of the operating system, as in Windows Server 2012 R2.

The benefit derived from using hardware-assisted virtualization is it allows the hypervisor to dynamically allocate memory and CPU to the VMs as required. When the motherboard and the BIOS support this technology, you must ensure that it is enabled. Figure 2.25 shows an example of the settings. Although most new servers will support hardware-assisted virtualization, it is a feature and a consideration you should know about.

FIGURE 2.25   Enabling hardware-assisted virtualization

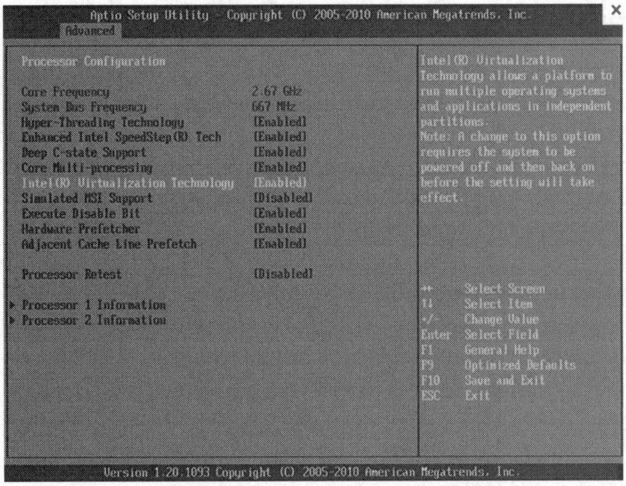

CPU Compatibility Support

One of the key issues to consider when reviewing compatibility guides is the CPU. This component plays a critical role in the overall success of the virtualization solution. You should not only ensure that the CPU you are considering or that is present in the candidate host machine is listed on the compatibly list, but you should also make every effort to use a CPU that supports instruction extensions and features designed to enhance virtualization. Let's look at two major vendors and their technologies.

AMD-V and Intel VT

CPUs come with varying abilities to support or enhance virtualization. Intel provides an entire line of processers that support what they call Intel Virtualization Technology. The benefits derived from using a CPU with this technology include

- Acceleration of fundamental virtualization processes throughout the platform

- Reduced storage and network latencies, with fewer potential bottlenecks

- The enhanced security that a solid hardware foundation provides

- Improved short- and long-term value from your software and server investments

AMD has a similar line of processors with a technology they call AMD Virtualization (AMD-V). It adds to the instruction set of the CPU and provides many of the same benefits as the Intel technology.

Although a server may fully support hardware-assisted virtualization and the CPU may support virtualization extensions to the instruction set, you may need to enable both of these in the BIOS/UEFI to obtain the benefits.

Resource Allocation Between Guest and Host

One of the issues you need to understand is how the host system and the guest operating systems share resources. Keep in mind that the host and the guests are all sharing the same physical resources (CPU, memory, disk, NIC). This is an advantage of a Type 1, or bare-metal hypervisor. There is no underlying operating system using resources. The resources that are allocated to the VMs are called virtual resources, the number of which need not match the number of physical resources in the host machine. For example, the host may have two processors, yet you could assign four virtual CPUs to the guest. Having said that, according to best practices you probably shouldn't do that. The exact manner in which the resources are assigned and the way in which the administrator uses these assignments to arbitrate use of the physical resource depends on the resources. Let's look at the way the four major resources are allocated in a virtual environment.

CPUs

You can control the allocation of physical CPU(s) use in one of three ways:

Shares   Values such as Low, Normal, High, and Custom (using VMware as an example) are compared to the sum of all shares of all VMs on the server. Therefore, they define the relative percentage each VM can use.

Reservation   Guaranteed CPU allocation for a virtual machine.

Limit   Upper limit for a virtual machine's CPU allocation.

These settings are used to ensure that the desired VMs have priority to the CPU (shares), that certain VMs are always guaranteed CPU time (reservations), and that no single VM monopolizes the CPU (limits). In Figure 2.26, you can see how this is done in Microsoft Hyper-V. Although the terminology is slightly different, the concepts are the same. As this figure shows, you can assign multiple virtual CPUs to a VM, which is another way to influence the VMs' performance.

FIGURE 2.26   Setting CPU allocations in Hyper-V

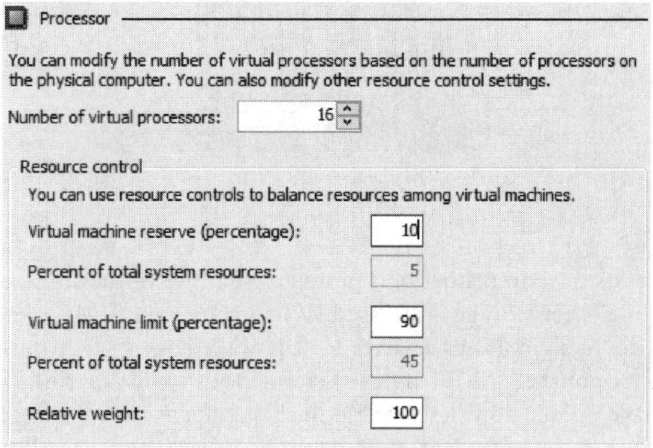

Storage

A benefit of virtualization is the ability of VMs to share storage. This storage can be located in a single storage device or appliance, or it can be located on multiple storage devices. By logically centralizing the storage and managing it centrally, you reduce the waste that formerly occurred when each server used its own storage.

Increasingly, storage is presented to the VMs as local storage but is actually located in either a storage area network (SAN) or on network-attached storage (NAS). A SAN is a high-performance data network separate from the LAN, and NAS is a storage device or appliance that resides on the LAN.

The VMs reside on the host servers and the host servers are attached to the shared storage devices, as shown in Figure 2.27. Conceptually, the shared storage could be either NAS or a SAN, the difference being that, with a SAN, the servers will need to have a host bus controller card installed that can connect the server to the fiber network that typically comprises the SAN.

FIGURE 2.27   Shared storage

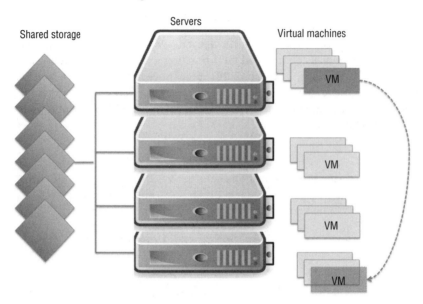

One of the benefits of shared storage is more efficient use of the storage, with less storage sitting idle while other storage is stressed. When you create VMs, one of the steps involves the creation of a virtual hard drive for the VM. This is space in the shared storage for keeping the image of the VM. There are several types of virtual disks you can create, and some types have unique abilities that aid in this efficient use of space. Every virtualization vendor attaches somewhat different names for these, but they all offer the same basic types. As an example, we'll look at the types offered by VMware, the market leader in virtualization.

Thick Provision Lazy Zeroed   This is analogous to the classic regular hard drive with one exception. Like the classic disk, space required for the virtual disk is allocated during creation. If data is present on the disk, it is not deleted until the space is needed for new data.

Thick Provision Eager Zeroed   This is like lazy zeroed but any data on the disk is zeroed out ahead of time. This means it takes longer to create one of these disks.

Thin Provision   This is where the disk efficiency comes in. At first, a thin-provisioned disk uses only as much datastore space as the disk initially needs. If the thin disk needs more space later, it can grow to the maximum capacity allocated to it.

In Figure 2.28, you can see how this is done in Hyper-V, and although the terminology is slightly different, the concepts are the same with most vendors. As this figure shows, you can create what is called a *differencing* disk. This disk type is not unique to Hyper-V. It is used to store changes made to an image when you decide to keep a copy of a previous version of the image. This is what allows for the process of rolling back an image after making changes that you would like to reverse. This makes virtualization perfect for testing changes before an enterprise rollout.

FIGURE 2.28   Creating a virtual disk in Hyper-V

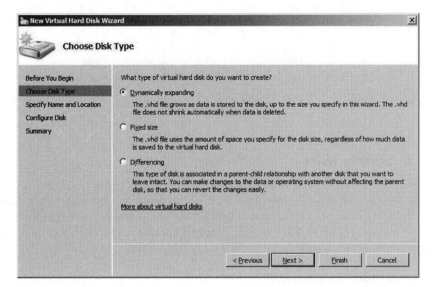

Memory

Memory resources for a virtual machine are allocated using reservations, limits, and shares, much in the same way as CPU time. A virtual machine can use three user-defined settings that affect its memory resource allocation.

Limit   Limits the consumption of memory for a virtual machine. This value is expressed in megabytes.

Reservation   Guarantees a minimum allocation for a virtual machine. The reservation is expressed in megabytes.

Shares   Represent a relative metric for allocating memory capacity. The more shares a virtual machine is assigned, the more often it gets a time slice of a memory when there is no memory idle time.

In Citrix XenServer, you can use Dynamic Memory Control, which permits the memory utilization of existing VMs to be compressed so that additional VMs can boot on the host. Once VMs on that host are later shut down or migrated to other hosts, running VMs can reclaim unused physical host memory. You enable Dynamic Memory Control by defining minimum and maximum memory settings for virtual machines, as shown in Figure 2.29. In VMware, this concept is called *overcommitting memory*.

FIGURE 2.29   Citrix dynamic memory allocation

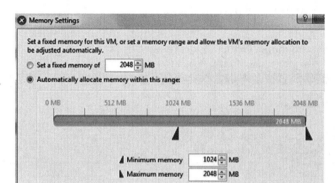

Network Connectivity

It is possible to connect VMs together in a network and that network can be the same network as the LAN or separate from the LAN. The network can have Internet access or not, depending on how you use the virtual networking components at your disposal. Some of the ways you can connect VMs to the host, to one another, and to devices "outside the box" are covered in this section.

Direct Access (Bridging) vs. NAT

There are two basic options for connecting the VM to the host machine:

- Direct access (bridging), which uses the physical NIC on the host system.

- Network Address Translation (NAT), which creates a private network on the host system, with the host system acting as a DHCP server. When access to networks beyond this private network is required, the host will perform NAT on the private IP address and use its own IP address.

The easiest configuration is to bridge the VM to use the NIC of the host and use its own IP address. But if you want the IP address of the VM to be hidden, then using NAT will ensure that all packets coming from either the VM or its host will appear to come from the host.

If you want to create a network in which the VMs can reach one another, you can use either configuration. Figure 2.30 shows that both methods can be used in the host. You see that some of the hosts are using NAT, which is why they have IP addresses that are used on the LAN, whereas one of the VMs has been bridged and thus does not have an IP address that works on the LAN.

Virtual NICs

You've probably already put this together from the our earlier discussions on virtual networking, but to enable a VM to communicate on either the LAN or a private virtual network you must assign it a virtual NIC (vNIC). Multiple vNICs can be added to the same VM for fault tolerance or not of load balancing. Once the vNIC is added, you assign it to a network.

FIGURE 2.30   NAT vs. bridged

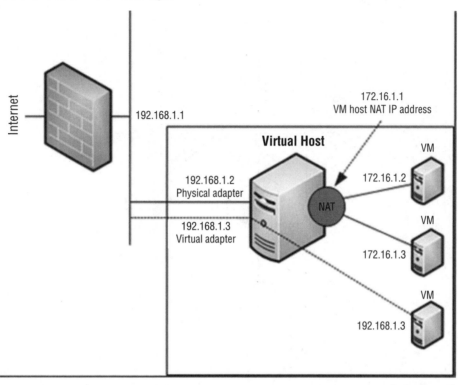

Virtual Switches

To create a virtual network as discussed in the previous section, you have to create a virtual switch that will interconnect the VMs and the host. The vNICs of the VMs are connected to the virtual switch, which in turn (if desired) is connected to the physical NIC on the host, as shown in Figure 2.31. Notice that one of the switches is connected to the LAN and other is not.

When creating a vSwitch, you can choose whether or not to connect the vSwitch to a physical NIC. In Figure 2.32, a vSwitch created in VMware indicates there are two physical adapters available to assign to this switch.

Video

In a virtual desktop infrastructure (VDI), VMs are used to house images that are used by users as their desktops. One of the pain points often experienced when implementing VMs in this fashion is poor video performance: screens that are slow to drag, changes to the display that occur slowly, and other issues that crop up.

This issue is not limited to a VDI but is common to it. Use the video adapter settings of the VM to increase the video memory of the problematic VM, as shown in Figure 2.33. In cases where this must be done to a large number of VMs, you can use a PowerShell script to change them all.

FIGURE 2.31   vSwitch

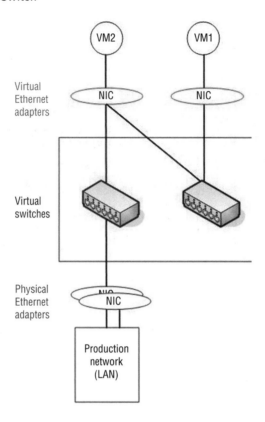

FIGURE 2.32   Assigning a vSwitch to physical adapters

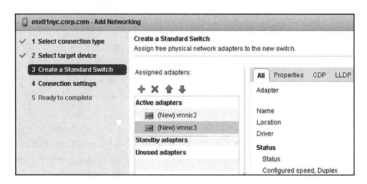

FIGURE 2.33 Increasing video memory

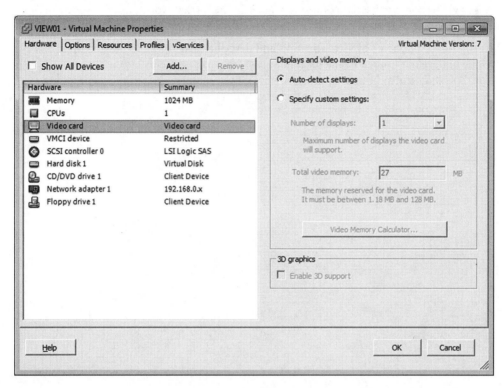

Summary

In this chapter you learned how to install and configure server operating systems, including key steps like updating firmware, configuring the BIOS/UEFI, preparing the disk, and connecting the server to the network. You also learned about the various ways you can manage the server, both locally and across the network. Finally, we covered the basics of virtualization, including the relationship between host and guest, the role of the hypervisor, the types of hypervisors, and how resources are shared by the VMs.

Exam Essentials

Install and configure a server operating system. Describe the steps in the process and identify which are required and which are optional. Understand the importance of creating a performance baseline and hardening the system.

Describe the methods available to manage the server. The local methods include using KVM switches, making serial connections, and in the virtual world, using a virtual administration console. Network methods include using KVM over IP, iLO, and iDRAC.

Identify the components of virtualization and describe their roles. These components include but are not limited to the host and guest, the management interface, and the hypervisor. You should also be able to describe how CPU, memory, and other resources are shared by the VMs.

Review Questions

You can find the answers in the Appendix.

1. Which of the following is *not* true with respect to UEFI?
    A. It provides better security by helping to protect the preboot process.
    B. It provides faster startup and resuming from hibernation times.
    C. It does not provide support for drives larger than 2.2 terabytes (TB).
    D. It supports modern, 64-bit firmware device drivers.

2. Which RAID type provides no fault tolerance?
    A. RAID 0
    B. RAID 1
    C. RAID 3
    D. RAID 5

3. Which of the following is a Microsoft filesystem?
    A. ext2
    B. NTFS
    C. ReiserFS
    D. UFS

4. Which filesystem was created by Sun Microsystems?
    A. ext2
    B. ZFS
    C. ReiserFS
    D. UFS

5. Where is the swap file located?
    A. In memory
    B. In the L1 cache
    C. On the hard drive
    D. Across the network

6. Which of the following is *not* a part of hardening the system?
    A. Disabling all unused services
    B. Uninstalling unneeded applications
    C. Ensuring all patches are installed
    D. Ensuring sufficient processing power

7. What tool is used in Windows Server 2012 R2 to create a baseline?

   A. Performance Monitor

   B. Action Center

   C. System Information

   D. Event Viewer

8. What is another term for a swap file?

   A. vDisk

   B. Pagefile

   C. Virtual RAM

   D. Checkpoint file

9. How large should the pagefile be on a Windows server that is not a database server?

   A. Half the size of RAM

   B. Equal to the size of RAM

   C. 1.5 times the size of RAM

   D. Twice the size of RAM

10. What Windows tool can be used to create and deploy images?

   A. WDS

   B. NFS

   C. PXE

   D. DAV

11. Which of the following is an industry standard client-server interface that allows networked computers that are not yet loaded with an operating system to be configured and booted remotely by an administrator?

   A. DNS

   B. PXE

   C. iDRAC

   D. NBP

12. Which device allows you to plug multiple PCs (usually servers) into the device and to switch easily back and forth from system to system using the same mouse, monitor, and keyboard?

   A. ILO

   B. iDRAC

   C. KVM

   D. vSwitch

13. Which technology is found on HP servers?

   A. iLO

   B. iDRAC

   C. vSwitch

   D. VMM

14. What Microsoft technology allows you to connect to remote computers and run programs on them?

    A. iDRAC

    B. RDP

    C. KVM

    D. SSL

15. What vendor creates iDRAC cards?

    A. EMC

    B. Dell

    C. HP

    D. Cisco

16. Which of the following uses the Remote Framebuffer (RFB) protocol?

    A. VNC

    B. RDP

    C. iDRAC

    D. ILO

17. Which remote management technology is *not* graphical in nature?

    A. VNC

    B. SSH

    C. RDP

    D. Shell

18. Which statement is true with respect to hypervisors?

    A. Type II is called native.

    B. Type II runs directly on the host's hardware.

    C. A Type II hypervisor runs within a conventional operating system environment.

    D. VMware Workstation and VirtualBox exemplify Type I hypervisors.

19. Which technique is used to allocate relative access to the CPU among VMs?

    A. Reservations

    B. Limits

    C. Shares

    D. Time slots

20. Which RAID type is also called mirroring?

    A. RAID 0

    B. RAID 1

    C. RAID 3

    D. RAID 5

Chapter

3

Server Maintenance

COMPTIA SERVER+ EXAM OBJECTIVES COVERED IN THIS CHAPTER:

✓ **2.2 Compare and contrast server roles and requirements for each**

- Web server

- Application server

- Directory server

- Database server

- File server

- Print server

- Messaging server

- Mail server

- Routing and remote access server

- Network services server (DHCP, DNS/WINS, NTP)

✓ **2.4 Given a scenario, perform proper server maintenance techniques**

- Change management

- Patch management (operating system updates, application updates, security software updates, firmware updates, device drivers updates, compatibility lists [operating systems, hardware, applications] testing and validation)

- Outages & service level agreements (scheduled downtime, unscheduled downtime, impact analysis, client notification, MTTR

- Performance monitoring (CPU utilization, memory utilization, network utilization, disk utilization [Disk IOPS, storage capacity] comparison against performance baseline, processes and services monitoring, log monitoring)

- Hardware maintenance (check system health indicators [LEDs, error codes, beep codes, LCD messages], replace failed components [fans, hard drives, RAM, backplanes, batteries], preventative maintenance [clearing dust, check proper air flow], proper shut down procedures

- Fault tolerance and high availability techniques (clustering [active/active, active/passive], load balancing [round robin, heartbeat])

✓ **2.5 Explain the importance of asset management and documentation**

- Asset management (licensing, labeling, warranty, life cycle management [procurement, usage, end of life, disposal/recycling], inventory [make, model, serial, number, asset tag])

- Documentation (service manuals, network diagrams, architecture diagrams, dataflow diagrams, recovery documentation, baseline documentation, change management policies, service level agreement, server configuration)

- Secure storage of sensitive documentation

Once you've installed your servers, you must take additional steps to enable them to perform the roles you chose for them in the network. You also need to monitor and maintain the servers so that they continue to perform well. In addition, you want to avoid security-related issues such as malware infections and data breaches by instituting and following best practices with regard to patches, updates, and data security. Finally, you must develop systems that allow you to manage these critical organizational assets in a standardized method throughout the entire asset life cycle.

Server Roles and Requirements

Servers exist to serve the network and its users in some form. Each server has a certain role to play, although in small networks a server performs multiple roles. Each of those roles places different types of demand on the hardware and software of the server. Some roles demand lots of memory, whereas others place a heavier load on that CPU. By understanding each server role, you can more appropriately ensure that the proper resources are available to enable the server to successfully serve the network with as little latency and downtime as necessary. In this section we'll explore the major server roles you are likely to encounter and the specific compute resources (CPU, memory, network, and disk) that are stressed in the process of performing those roles.

When discussing hardware requirements for a server role, we can only speak in general terms based on the typical operation of the software running on the server. The size of your network, the number of servers you have performing a role, and in some cases the exact way you deploy the server role will have a big impact on the requirements. The recommendations in this chapter are simply starting points.

Web Server

Web servers are used to provide access to information to users connecting to the server using a web browser, which is the client part of the application. A web server uses HTTP as its transfer mechanism. This server can be contained within a network and made so it is only available within the network (called an intranet server) or it can be connected to the Internet where it can be reached from anywhere. To provide security to a web server it can be configured to require and use HTTPS, which uses SSL to encrypt the connection with no effort on the part of the user, other than being aware that the URL must use https rather than http.

Here are some of the components that should be maximized to ensure good performance in a web server:

Disk Subsystem   Disk latency is one of the major causes of slow web performance. The disk system should be as fast as possible. Using high-speed solid-state drives can be beneficial, and if possible, you should deploy either a RAID 0 or RAID 5 configuration, either of which will improve the read performance. If fault tolerance is also a consideration, then go with RAID 5 since RAID 0 will give you no fault tolerance.

RAM   Memory is also critical to a web server. Eighty percent of the web requests will be for the same 20 percent of content. Therefore, plenty of memory may ensure requested pages may still be contained in memory from which access is faster. You can help this situation by deploying web caching. This can be done on the proxy server if you use one.

CPU   CPU is important but not a critical issue for a web server unless the server will be performing encryption and decryption. If that is the case, it may be advisable to use a network card with its own processor for this process.

NIC   The NIC should be at least 1 Gbps, and using multiple cards would be even better. The amount of traffic you expect will influence this.

Application Server

An application server is one that users connect to and then run their applications on. This means the server is doing all the heavy lifting while the user machine is simply sending requests to the server and displaying the output. In many cases this server is the middle tier in a three-tier architecture that accepts users' requests to its application and then communicates with a database server where content is stored, as shown in Figure 3.1.

Here are some of the components that should be maximized to ensure good performance in an application server:

CPU   This component is stressed on an application server since it is doing all of the processing on behalf of the clients. Multicore and multiple processors are advisable.

NIC   Considering the traffic the server will be handling (and that could be in two directions if the server is running middleware), the NIC(s) should be 1 Gbps at least.

Disk   The disk system should be fast but it's not the most critical part of the equation for an application server.

Memory   Application servers also require lots of memory, especially if acting as a middle tier to a backend database server.

FIGURE 3.1   Three tiers

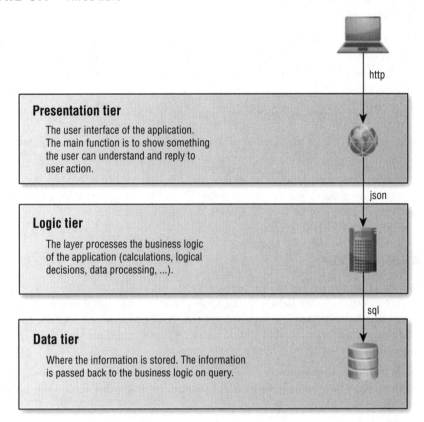

Directory Services Server

A directory services server is one that accepts and verifies the credentials of users. Typically it not only authenticates them but also provides them with access to resources using single sign-on (SSO). SSO allows users to authenticate once and *not* be required to authenticate again to access the resources to which they have been given access. Moreover, these resources may be located across the network on various devices. One of the best examples is a domain controller in a Windows Active Directory domain. These servers are the point to which all users are directed when they need to log in to the network.

Here are some of the components that should be maximized to ensure good performance in a directory services server:

Disks   Use a fast system, and since this function is so important, implement RAID 5 for fault tolerance and performance. Put the Active Directory (AD) database (ntds.dit) onto separate disk spindles. Allow at least 0.5 GB per 1,000 users when allocating disk space for the AD database.

Network Connections   Although this will probably not be the bottleneck on the system, if other resources are sufficient it could become one. Ensure you have 1 Gbps cards. If encryption will be involved (which is highly likely), consider offloading this encryption to the network card.

Processor   Multiple-core processors should be used if the server will be performing encryption. If you have not offloaded that encryption to the NIC, you should have multiple CPUs as well. Keep in mind that as the number of users goes up, you may need to add more processing power.

Memory   The memory requirements depend on the size of the AD database or the `ntds.dit` file. You should have enough memory to hold this file or file with 20 percent additional space added. The `ntds.dit` file is located at `%systemroot%\ntds\ntds.dit`.

Database Server

A database server is one that runs database software such as SQL Server or Oracle. It contains information stored in the database and users can search the database, either directly by issuing commands or by using an application that does this through a GUI. Here are some of the components that should be maximized to ensure good performance in a database server:

CPU   Your CPUs (yes, multiple) should be as fast as you can afford with multiple cores and plenty of cache. The specific number should be driven by the database software recommendations and the number of users.

Memory   With respect to memory, you should fill all available slots with the cheapest memory you can get. That means smaller DIMMs (dual in-line memory modules) but more of them. For example, rather than filling 12 slots with 64 GB of memory, save some money for very little cost in speed by installing 32 GB DIMMs.

Disk   You should use multiple disks in a RAID5 configuration so you get performance and fault tolerance. The exact number of disks depends on the features you are installing and the size of the database. Review the database software recommendations.

Network   As with all enterprise servers you should use a 1 Gbps card at a minimum. If the server is critical, use multiple cards for fault tolerance and load balancing.

File Servers

File servers are used to store files that can be accessed by the network users. Typically users are encouraged or even required to store any important data on these servers rather than on their local hard drives, because these servers are typically backed up on a regular basis, whereas the user machines typically are not. Here are some of the components that should be maximized to ensure good performance in a file server:

Disk   File servers should have significant amounts of storage space and may even have multiple hard drives configured in a RAID array to provide quicker recovery from a drive crash than could be provided by recovering with the backup.

CPU   The number of processors is driven by the number of concurrent users you expect and whether you will be doing encryption on the server. As the number of users increases, at a certain point it becomes better to use more and slower processors rather than fewer and faster ones. This is because as many concurrent requests come in, multiple slower CPUs will handle the overall load better by spreading the requests among themselves, whereas fewer faster CPUs will try to keep up with a form of multitasking that is not as efficient.

Memory   You should increase RAM in step with the increase in users accessing the file server. Start with the amount designated as a minimum for the operating system and add at least 50 percent to that.

NIC   The same recommendation I gave for all of these roles applies. Use 1 Gbps NICs, and if this server will be very busy, use more than one for fault tolerance and load balancing.

Print Server

Print servers are used to manage printers, and in cases where that is their only role, they will manage multiple printers. A print server provides the spooler service to the printers that it manages, and when you view the print queue, you are viewing it on the print server. Many enterprise printers come with a built-in print server, which makes using a dedicated machine for the role unnecessary. Here are some of the components that should be maximized to ensure good performance in a print server:

Memory   Print servers need lots of memory to hold the print jobs waiting in the print queue. The exact amount will depend on the number of users assigned to the printers being managed by this print server.

CPU   The number and type of CPUs are impacted by the amount of processing power available on the print devices the server is managing. If they are heavy-duty enterprise printers with plenty of memory and processing power, you'll need less on the server. A physical server will need less processing power than a virtual print server because the physical server can offload some of the print processing to the CPU on the graphics card whereas a virtual print server cannot.

Disk   As is the case with processing power, if there is plenty of disk space on the print device, you will need less on the print server. One thing you should do is to move the spool file to a disk other than the one where the operating system is located. If your enterprise requires that completed print jobs be stored, ensure that you periodically remove them to keep them from eating up all the space.

NIC   As always use 1 Gbps NICs, and if the server will be managing many printers and thus many users, you may want to have multiple NICs for fault tolerance and load balancing.

Messaging Server

Messaging servers run instant messaging software and allow users to collaborate in real time through either chat or video format. Here are some of the components that should be maximized to ensure good performance in a messaging server:

Memory   The amount of memory required is a function of the number of *concurrent* connections. Users have varying habits when it comes to messaging. Some never use it and others use it constantly, so this is hard to predict and you may have to monitor the server usage and adjust memory accordingly.

Disk   Include disk space for the operating system and the instant messaging software. The disk throughput of the system is critical so that the server can keep up, which means you should use faster disks.

CPU   The processing power required is a function of the types of users you have. If most of the users are inactive (that is, they are connected but not chatting), then you will need less CPU than if a high percentage of them are active.

NIC   This resource should be sized using the same guidelines as CPU. If you have many active users, you need faster and/or multiple NICs (as always, 1 Gbps).

Mail Server

Mail servers run email server software and use SMTP to send email on behalf of users who possess mailboxes on the server and to transfer emails between email servers. Those users will use a client email protocol to retrieve their email from the server. Two of the most common are POP3, which is a retrieve-only protocol, and IMAP4, which has more functionality and can be used to manage the email on the server. Here are some of the components that should be maximized to ensure good performance in a mail server:

Disk   The disk system is most often the bottleneck on an email server. It should be high speed, perhaps solid state, and it should be set up in a RAID 5 configuration unless you are using a distributed configuration and the server is not the mail server.

Memory   The amount of memory should be based not on the number of users, but rather on the amount of email they generate and receive. This is an item for which you should seek guidance from the vendor's documentation.

CPU   The amount of CPU used will be a function of the amount of email that is sent and received at a time, meaning if the email traffic is spread out evenly over the day, it will need less CPU than if the email all comes in during a 4-hour window.

Routing and Remote Access Service (RRAS) Server

A server running Windows Routing and Remote Access Service (RRAS) can act as a remote access (dial-up) and virtual private network (VPN) server, while it is also able to act as a router. In its role as a remote access or VPN server (its most common role), some of the components that should be maximized to ensure good performance are as follows:

CPU   The amount of processing power is driven by the number of users you expect to be connecting concurrently and the type of data transfer. Transfers that create smaller packets will take more processing power as will a larger number of concurrent connections.

Memory   Treat the sizing of the memory as you would CPU. As the number of concurrent users increases, memory needs will as well. Memory and CPU are the most stressed resource on this server.

Disk   The disk system is not an area where contention usually occurs with RRAS servers.

NIC   The speed and number of NICs will depend on the amount of concurrent traffic and the need for redundancy. If the VPN connection is mission critical, you should have multiple NICs.

Network Services Server

The next three server roles are critical to the functioning of the network and you should probably have more than one for redundancy. They provide automatic IP configurations to the devices, manage name resolution, and keep the devices in the network in sync from a time perspective, which is critical for the function of certain security features and for proper log analysis.

DHCP

Dynamic Host Configuration Protocol (DHCP) servers are used to automate the process of providing an IP configuration to devices in the network. These servers respond to broadcast-based requests for a configuration by offering an IP address, subnet mask, and default gateway to the DHCP client. While these options provide basic network connectivity, many other options can also be provided, such as the IP address of a Trivial File Transfer Protocol (TFTP) server that IP phones can contact to download a configuration file. Here are some of the components that should be maximized to ensure good performance:

CPU   Processing power is not one of the critical resources on a DHCP server. Ensure you have the recommended speed for the operating system with the DHCP service installed as indicated by the operating system documentation.

Memory   RAM is one of the critical components on the DHCP server. You should provide plenty of RAM. After deployment you may discover you need to add more if you find the server's usage of memory to be exceeding its capacity.

Disk   Disk is the second critical component. If you intend to host a large number of scopes (scopes are ranges of IP addresses) on the server, keep in mind that each time you add a scope you need more disk space.

NIC   Although this is not a component that's critical to the operation of DHCP, the NIC could become a bottleneck in the system if it is not capable enough or if there are not enough NICs. Use at least 1 Gbps NICs and consider the option of using multiple NICs.

DNS

Domain Name System (DNS) servers resolve device and domain names (website names) to IP addresses, and vice versa. They make it possible to connect to either without knowing the IP address of the device or the server hosting the website. Clients are configured with the IP address of a DNS server (usually through DHCP) and make requests of the server using *queries*. The organization's DNS server will be configured to perform the lookup of IP addresses for which it has no entry in its database by making requests of the DNS servers on the Internet, which are organized in a hierarchy that allows these servers to more efficiently provide the answer. When the DNS servers have completed their lookup, they return the IP address to the client so the client can make a direct connection using the IP address. Here are some of the components that should be maximized to ensure good performance:

RAM   Memory is the most important resource because the entire DNS zone file will be loaded into memory. As you add zones, or as a zone gets larger, you should add memory. If you expect the server to be answering large numbers of queries concurrently, then that will require additional memory as well.

Disk   Disk is not a critical component, but it does need to be large enough to hold all of the zones as well.

NIC   The NIC is not a critical resource unless it becomes a bottleneck during times when there is an overwhelming number of concurrent queries. If you find that to be the case often, add more NICs.

CPU   CPU is not a critical resource, but if you expect a heavy query load then you should get the fastest processor the budget allows. The CPU can become a bottleneck just as the NIC can in times of high workload.

NTP

Network Time Protocol (NTP) servers are used as a time source by the devices in the network. When the devices are configured with the address of an NTP server, they will periodically check in with the server to ensure their time is correct. This service ensures that log entries that are time stamped can be properly interpreted and that digital certificates, which depend heavily on time, continue to function correctly. NTP servers do not typically have high resource requirements, and this service is a good candidate for adding to a server already performing another role.

Proper Server Maintenance Techniques

Like all networking devices, servers need some attention from time to time. If regular maintenance procedures are followed, there will be less downtime, fewer hardware issues, and less frequent headaches for all. In this section, we'll look at what those procedures should be.

Change Management

The old saying "Too many cooks spoil the broth" applies when it comes to managing servers. When technicians make changes to the servers that are not centrally managed and planned, chaos reigns. In that environment, changes might be made that work at cross purposes. All organizations need a change management process whereby every change goes through a formal evaluation process before it is implemented.

This process ensures that all changes support the goals of the organization and that the impact of each change is anticipated before the change is made. There should be a change management board to which all changes are submitted for review. Only when the change has been approved should it be made.

Patch Management

You already know how important it is keep current on security patches, but that is not the only type of patch and update about which you should be concerned. In this section we'll identify some of the types of updates that should be a part of a formal patch management policy. This policy should be designed to ensure that none of these types of updates fall through the cracks.

Operating System Updates

All operating system vendors periodically offer updates for their systems. These updates sometimes fix bugs or issues, and sometimes they add functionality. In some cases they close security loopholes that have been discovered. Regardless of the reason for their issuance, you should obtain, test, and deploy all of these updates. Many vendors like Microsoft makes that simple by including tools such as Windows Update that allow you to automate the process. If the operating system does not provide such a utility, then you should take it upon yourself to seek it out. In Exercise 3.1 you will schedule updates using the Windows Update tool in Windows Server 2012 R2.

EXERCISE 3.1

Using Windows Update

1. On the Start screen, click Control Panel.

2. In Control Panel, open the Windows Update window.

3. Click or tap Change Settings from the left pane.

4. In the Important Updates section, in the drop-down box you'll see the following:

   - Install Updates Automatically

   - Download Updates But Let Me Choose Whether To Install Them

   - Check For Updates But Let Me Choose Whether To Download And Install Them

   - Never Check For Updates

If you want to test the updates before deploying them, select Download Updates But Let Me Choose Whether To Install Them. If you just want them installed, select Install Updates Automatically.

Application Updates

Many servers run applications and services that require updating from time to time. The server might be running a database program or email software or any of the services required for the server to perform the roles described in the earlier section "Server Roles and Requirements." Although keeping up with these updates may not be as simple as operating system updates (which in many cases can be automated), you should develop a system to keep aware of these updates when they are available. You might get on the mailing list of the application vendor so that you can be informed when updates are available. If all else fails, make it a point to visit their website from time to time and check for these updates.

Security Software Updates

These are among the most critical updates we will cover in this section. These updates include those for antivirus and antimalware. This software should be regularly updated (with particular interest paid to the definition files). While steps and options to configure these updates are unique to each product, with respect to the built-in Windows tools, such as Windows Defender, those definitions will be updated along with other updates you receive from Windows Update. Most vendors of security software provide a mechanism to download and apply these updates automatically. You should take advantage of such a mechanism if it is available. Although this software is important for users' machines, it is even more essential for servers, which are frequent targets of attacks.

Firmware Updates

Any software that is built into a hardware device is called *firmware*. Firmware is typically in flash ROM and can be updated as newer versions become available. An example of firmware is the software in a laser printer that controls it and allows you to interact with it at the console (usually through a limited menu of options). Firmware updates are often released by hardware vendors. You should routinely check their websites for updates that you need to download and install.

Device Driver Updates

Device drivers are files that allow devices to communicate with the operating system. Called drivers for short, they're used for interacting with printers, monitors, network cards, sound cards, and just about every type of hardware attached to the server. One of the most common problems associated with drivers is not having the current version—as problems are fixed, the drivers are updated. Typically driver updates don't come into the picture until something stops working. When that is the case, you should consider the possibility that a driver update for the device might solve the issue before wasting a lot of time troubleshooting.

Compatibility Lists

When deploying a new server or when adding devices and applications to a server, it can be highly beneficial to ensure compatibility between the new addition and the server before spending money. Vendors of both software and hardware create compatibility lists that can be used to ensure that a potential piece of software or hardware will work with the server. These compatibility lists fall into three categories, as covered in the following sections.

Operating Systems

Major operating system vendors issue several types of compatibility lists. Some list the hardware requirements of each operating system. Others list hardware devices that have been tested and are known to work with the operating system. Microsoft calls its list the Windows Compatible Products List. You'll find it here: `https://sysdev.microsoft.com/en-US/Hardware/lpl/`.

Hardware

Vendors of the hardware we often connect to our servers also create compatibility lists that describe the operating systems and other pieces of hardware with which their devices are compatible.

Applications

Finally, vendors of software applications also issue compatibility lists that describe the operating systems on which their software will run and the hardware requirements of the system on which the software will be installed.

Testing and Validation

We've just finished discussing all kinds of updates that you might apply to a server. Because servers are so important to the function of the network, you must treat updates for them with a dose of caution and skepticism. It is impossible for vendors to anticipate every scenario in which the server might be operating and thus impossible for them to provide assurance that the update won't break something (like a mission-critical operation). With the potential exception of security updates, you should always test the updates and validate their compatibility with your set of hardware and software.

These tests should occur in a test network and not on production servers. One of the benefits of having a virtualization environment is the ability to take images of your servers and test the updates on those images in a virtual environment. Once the updates have been validated as compatible, you can deploy them to the live servers.

Outages and Service-Level Agreements

IT support departments typically have written agreements with the customers they support called service-level agreements (SLAs). In some cases these agreements are with other departments of the same company for which they provide support. These agreements specify the type of support to be provided and the acceptable amount of time allowed to respond to support calls.

Typically these time windows are different for different types of events. For example, they may be required to respond to a server outage in 20 minutes, whereas responding to a user having problems with a browser may only require a response by the end of the day. The following sections explore some of the issues that might be covered in a formal SLA as well as other related issues.

Scheduled Downtime

An SLA might specify that taking any infrastructure equipment down for maintenance requires prior notification and that the event may only occur during the evening or on the weekend. This type of event is called *scheduled downtime*. It is important that when you schedule this event, you allow enough time in the window to accomplish what you need to, and you should always have a plan in case it becomes obvious that the maintenance cannot be completed in the scheduled downtime.

Unscheduled Downtime

Unscheduled downtime is the nightmare of any administrator. This is when a device is down or malfunctioning outside of a scheduled maintenance window. Some SLAs might include an unscheduled downtime clause that penalizes the support team in some way after the amount of unscheduled downtime exceeds a predetermined level. If the support is being provided to a customer, there might be a financial penalty. If the SLA applies to another department in the same organization, the penalty might be in a different form.

Impact Analysis

Another typical issue requirement in most SLAs is that any schedule downtime should be communicated to all users and that the communication should include the specific parties that will be affected by the downtime and exactly what the impact will be. For example, a notification email describing the scheduled downtime might include the following:

- Departments affected
- Specific applications or service impacted
- Expected length of downtime

Client Notification

SLAs should also specify events that require client notification and the time period in which that must occur. It will cover all scheduled downtime but should also address the time period in which notifications should be sent out when unscheduled events occur. It might also discuss parameters for responding to client requests.

MTTR

One of the metrics that is used in planning both SLAs and IT operations in general is mean time to repair (MTTR). This value describes the average length of time it takes a vendor to repair a device or component. By building MTTR into the SLA, IT can assure that the time taken to repair a component or device will not be a factor that causes them to violate the SLA requirements. Sometimes MTTR is considered to be from the point at which the failure is first discovered to the point at which the equipment returns to operation. In other cases it is a measure of the elapsed time between the point where repairs actually begin and the point at which the equipment returns to operation. It is important that there is a clear understanding by all parties with regard to when the clock starts and ends when calculating MTTR.

Performance Monitoring

Earlier in this chapter, we covered the resources typically required by certain server roles. As noted, those were only guidelines and starting points in the discussion based on general principles. You should monitor the servers once deployed on a regular basis to determine whether the system is indeed handling the workload. When monitoring resources, you select performance counters that represent aspects of the workload the resource is undergoing. But first you need to know what normal is for your server.

Comparison Against Performance Baseline

If you have ever tried to look up a particular performance metric on the Internet to find out what a "normal" value is, you may be quite frustrated that you can't get a straight answer. This is because you have to define what is normal for your network. This is done by creating a set of performance metrics during normal operations when all is working well. While earlier in this chapter we listed some rough guidelines about certain metrics, that is all they are: guidelines.

Only until you have created this set of values called a *performance baseline* can you say what is normal for your network. Creating the set of values should be done during regular operations, not during either times of unusual workload or times of very little workload. After this you can compare the performance metrics you generate later with this baseline. Let's look at the four main resources.

CPU Utilization

When monitoring CPU, the specific counters you use depends on the server role. Consult the vendor's documentation for information on those counters and what they mean to the performance of the service or application. Common counters monitored by server administrators are

Processor\% Processor Time   The percentage of time the CPU spends executing a non-idle thread. This should not be over 85 percent on a sustained basis.

Processor\% User Time   Represents the percentage of time the CPU spends in user mode, which means it is doing work for an application. If this value is higher than the baseline you captured during normal operation, the service or application is dominating the CPU.

Processor\% Interrupt Time   The percentage of time the CPU receives and services hardware interrupts during specific sample intervals. If this is over 15 percent, there could be a hardware issue.

System\Processor Queue Length   The number of threads (which are smaller pieces of an overall operation) in the processor queue. If this value is over 2 times the number of CPUs, the server is not keeping up with the workload.

Memory Utilization

As with CPUs, different server roles place different demands on the memory, so there may be specific counters of interest you can learn by consulting the vendor documentation. Common counters monitored by server administrators are

Memory\% Committed Bytes in Use   The amount of virtual memory in use. If this is over 80 percent, you need more memory.

Memory\Available Mbytes   The amount of physical memory (in megabytes) currently available. If this is less than 5 percent, you need more memory.

Memory\Free System Page Table Entries   The number of entries in the page table not currently in use by the system. If the number is less than 5,000, there may be a memory leak (memory leaks occur when an application is issued memory that is not returned to the system. Over time this drains the server of memory.).

Memory\Pool Non-Paged Bytes   The size, in bytes, of the non-paged pool, which contains objects that cannot be paged to the disk. If the value is greater than 175 MB, you may have a memory leak (an application is not releasing its allocated memory when it is done).

Memory\Pool Paged Bytes   The size, in bytes, of the paged pool, which contains objects that can be paged to disk. (If this value is greater than 250 MB, there may be a memory leak.)

Memory\Pages per Second   The rate at which pages are written to and read from the disk during paging. If the value is greater than 1,000 as a result of excessive paging, there may be a memory leak.

Network Utilization

As you learned in the section "Server Roles and Requirements," the NIC can become a bottleneck in the system if it cannot keep up with the traffic. Some common counters monitored by server administrators are

Network Interface\Bytes Total/Sec   The percentage of bandwidth of which the NIC is capable that is currently being used. If this value is more than 70 percent of the bandwidth of the interface, the interface is saturated or not keeping up.

Network Interface\Output Queue Length   The number of packets in the output queue. If this value is over 2, the NIC is not keeping up with the workload.

Disk Utilization

On several of the server roles we discussed, disk was the critical resource. When monitoring the disk subsystem, you must consider two issues: the speed with which the disk is being accessed and the capacity you have available. Let's examine those metrics in more detail.

Disk IOPS

Disk Input/Output Operations per Second (IOPS) represents the number of reads and writes that can be done in a second. One of the advantages of newer solid-state drives (SSDs) is that they exhibit much higher IOPS values than traditional hard disk drives. For example, a 15,000 rpm SATA drive with a 3 Gb/s interface is listed to deliver approximately 175–210 IOPS, whereas an SSD with a SATA 3 Gb/s interface is listed at approximately 8,600 IOPS (and that is one of the slower SSD drives).

Storage Capacity

The second metric of interest when designing a storage solution is capacity. When planning and managing storage capacity, consider the following questions:

- What do you presently need? Remember that this includes not only the total amount of data you have to store but also the cost to the system for fault tolerance. For example, if data is located on a RAID 1 or mirrored drive, you need twice as much space for the data. Moreover, if the data is located on a RAID 5 array, your needs will depend on the number of drives in the array. As the number of drives in the array go up, the amount of space required for the parity information goes down as a percentage of the space in the drive. For example, with three drives you are losing 33 percent of the space for parity, but if you add another drive, that goes down to 25 percent of the space used for parity. Add another, and it goes down to 20 percent.

- How fasts are the needs growing? Remember that your needs are not static. They are changing at all times and probably growing. You can calculate this growth rate manually or you can use capacity-planning tools. If you have different classes of storage, you may want to make this calculation per class rather than overall because the growth rates may be significantly different for different classes.

- Are there major expansions on the table? If you are aware that major additions are occurring, you should reflect that in your growth rate. For example, if you know you adding a datacenter requiring a certain amount of capacity, that capacity should be added to the growth rate.

In many cases you find yourself in a crunch for space at a time when capacity cannot be added. In such cases, you should be aware of techniques for maximizing the space you have. Some of those approaches are as follows:

Using Disk Deduplication Tools   In many cases, data is located on the same drive. Deduplication tools remove this redundancy while still making the data available at any location it was previously located by pointing to the single location. This process can be done after the data is on the drive or it can be implemented inline, which means data being written to the drive is examined first to see if it already exists on the drive. These two processes are shown in Figure 3.2.

FIGURE 3.2   Deduplication techniques

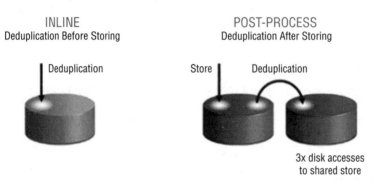

Archiving Older Data   You can also choose to have the older data moved off main storage to backup tapes or media to free up space.

Processes and Services Monitoring

On a more granular basis, you can separate the workload created by specific applications and services on a server. You do this by monitoring performance counters specific to the service or application. Often this exercise is undertaken when a server is experiencing a high workload and you need to determine the source of this workload. If you need to identify the performance counter that applies to an application or service, the best place to go for that information is the application or operating system vendor.

Log Monitoring

When you discover that a service or application is using more resources than normal, you may want to investigate the logs related to that service or application. Most server operating systems create these logs, or you may decide that it is easier to invest in a log monitoring system that can grab these logs off multiple servers and make them available to you in a central interface of some sort. This can be done in Windows by creating what are called *event subscriptions*. This simply means that one server subscribes to access a log on another server and make it available in the console of the first server. This is also called *log forwarding*. This concept is shown in Figure 3.3.

Hardware Maintenance

Like workstations, servers last longer, perform better, and break down less frequently when they get proper care. In this section we'll list regular hardware maintenance activities you should perform and identify specific areas on which you should concentrate.

FIGURE 3.3   Log forwarding

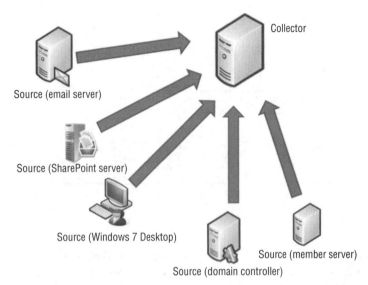

Collector

Source (email server)

Source (SharePoint server)

Source (Windows 7 Desktop)

Source (domain controller)

Source (member server)

Check System Health Indicators

First there are some indicator mechanisms that will be provided by the vendor of the hardware and the software that can give you an early warning that something is amiss or is about to go bad. You should always react to these indicators in the same way you would react to a warning that your car is overheating, because they typically don't come into play until the situation is getting serious.

LEDs

Most network devices, including servers, have LEDs on them that indicate certain things. The LED diagram for a Sun Blade X6250 Server Module is shown in Figure 3.4. The purpose of the LEDS and buttons is as follows:

   #1: LED that helps you identify which system you are working on

   #2: Indicates whether the server module is ready to be removed from the chassis

   #3: Service Action Required

   #4: Power/OK

Error Codes

Many servers come with integrated diagnostics that will generate error codes. These are usually text-based interfaces that you can access even when the server is having significant issues. In other cases, you receive error code messages when you reboot the server (which is often done when issues occur). For example, Dell servers issue these messages and provide tables on their website to help you not only interpret the problem, but in many cases, tell you exactly what to do to resolve the issue.

FIGURE 3.4 LEDs

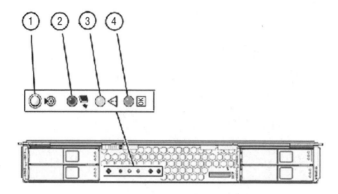

For example, if you receive the following message when rebooting, it indicates that something has changed and it suggests that if this is unexpected (you neither added nor removed memory), you have a piece of bad memory that is not now being included in the memory amount:

```
Amount of memory has changed
```

Beep Codes

Another possible source of information when troubleshooting server issues are the beep codes heard when rebooting the server. Like workstations, servers emit beep codes that indicate the status of the POST during boot. For example, an IBM blade server emits two long beeps followed by a short beep when a microprocessor register test fails. By using the online list of code descriptions (or the documentation), you will find that the document not only lists the meaning of the pattern but tells you exactly what to do (in this instance, reseat the processor). It goes on to tell you that if reseating the processor doesn't work, you should change out the processor, and if that doesn't work, change out the board.

LCD Messages

Many hardware devices like servers also have small LCD screens on the front that may be a source of messages that are helpful during troubleshooting. The Dell PowerEdge has the panel shown in Figure 3.5.

FIGURE 3.5 Dell LCD

Not only is this panel used to make configurations, but it also displays error messages. When it does this, it changes the backlight color from blue to amber so that you notice it quicker. The types of alerts covered are as follows:

- Cable and board presence

- Temperature

- Voltages

- Fans

- Processors

- Memory

- Power supplies

- BIOS

- Hard drives

IBM calls their system *light path diagnostics*. This is a system consisting of an LED panel on the front and a series of LEDs inside the box near various components. One of the LEDs is the Information LED, and when it indicated there is an error, you can open the box and LEDs inside the box might be lit near the problem component, as shown in Figure 3.6.

FIGURE 3.6   IBM Light path diagnostics

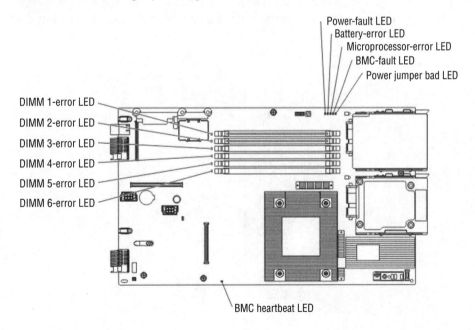

Replace Failed Components

Inevitably, parts will go bad and you will have to replace them. Common components replacements are covered in this section.

Fans

Servers typically have multiple fans. For example, a Dell PowerEdge has a fan on the chassis back panel and a front fan beneath the drive bays. In Exercise 3.2 you'll change out the one in the back panel.

 This exercise applies to the Dell PowerEdge 2400 system. The procedure for your server may vary, so consult the documentation.

EXERCISE 3.2

Replacing the Back Panel Fan in a Dell PowerEdge

1. Turn off the system, including peripherals, and disconnect the AC power cable.

2. Remove the right-side computer cover.

3. Remove the cooling shroud.

4. Disconnect the cooling fan cable from the FAN3 (back fan) connector on the system board.

5. Remove the four fasteners that secure the fan to the back of the chassis by pushing the plunger of each back into the fastener barrel, using a coin or flat-tipped screwdriver.

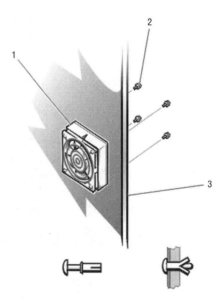

6. On the other side of the back panel, pull the fastener completely out of the back panel.

7. Attach the new fan using the four fasteners you removed.

8. Connect the fan power cord to the system board FAN3 connector.

9. Replace the right-side computer cover and reconnect the power.

10. Turn on the system.

Hard Drives

At one time, hard disk drives had a higher rate of unexpected failures with respect to the mechanical parts and SSDs had a shorter normal lifetime. However, this is changing as SSDs become more and more durable. At any rate, you will at some point have to replace a drive. The exact method depends on the type of drives. In Exercise 3.3 you'll use a Dell 1850 rack server and look at changing out a drive.

This exercise applies to the Dell 1850 system. The procedure for your server may vary, so consult the documentation.

EXERCISE 3.3

Changing a Drive on a Dell 1850

1. Shut down the system.

2. Remove the front bezel.

3. Use the hard drive handle as shown in this graphic.

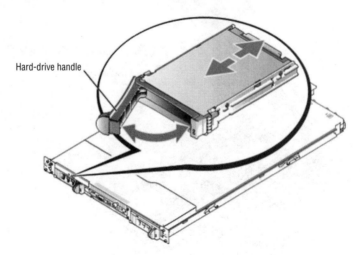

Hard-drive handle

4. Remove the old hard drive from the bay.

5. Insert the hard drive into the empty bay.

6. Lock the drive in place by closing the hard drive handle.

7. If it was removed in step 2, replace the front bezel.

8. In the system diagnostics, run the SCSI Controllers test.

RAM

Replacing RAM in a server is not all that different from doing so in a workstation. The box looks different but otherwise the basic steps are the same. In Exercise 3.4 you'll use an IBM blade server.

 This exercise applies to an IBM blade server. The procedure for your server may vary, so consult the documentation.

EXERCISE 3.4

Changing RAM in an IBM Blade Server

1. If the blade server is installed in a BladeCenter unit, remove it from the BladeCenter unit.

2. Remove the blade server cover.

3. If an optional expansion unit is installed, remove the expansion unit. This may require an extraction device (thumbscrews or levers) and it may not. If one is not provided then, using the blade server cover releases on each side, lift the expansion unit from the blade server as shown in in this graphic.

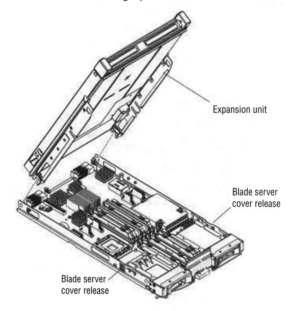

Expansion unit

Blade server cover release

Blade server cover release

4. Locate the DIMM connectors. Determine which DIMM you want to remove from the blade server.

Warning: To avoid breaking the retaining clips or damaging the DIMM connectors, handle the clips gently.

5. Move the retaining clips on the ends of the DIMM connector to the open position by pressing the retaining clips away from the center of the DIMM connector. To access DIMM connectors 7 through 12, use your fingers to lift the DIMM access door as shown in the following graphic.

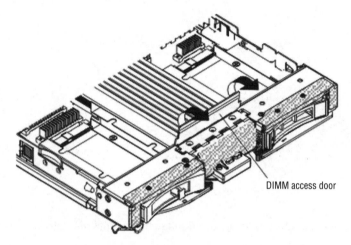

DIMM access door

6. Using your fingers, pull the DIMM out of the connector.

7. Install a DIMM or DIMM filler in each empty DIMM connector.

Note that DIMMs or DIMM fillers must occupy DIMM connectors 1, 2, 13, 14, 15, and 16 for proper cooling on the IBM HS22 blade server.

Backplanes

Servers have backplanes that abut the drives and make a connection with the drive so no cables are required. These can go bad and sometimes need replacing. In Exercise 3.5 you'll do this on a Dell PowerEdge 2650.

 This exercise applies to a Dell 2650 server. The procedure for your server may vary, so consult the documentation.

EXERCISE 3.5

Replacing the SCSI Backplane

1. After powering down the server remove the bezel using the key to unlock it.

2. Loosen the three thumbscrews that secure the cover to the chassis.

3. Slide the back cover backward and grasp the cover at both ends.

4. Carefully lift the cover away from the system.

5. Press the release tab on the control-panel cable cover and lift the cable cover straight up to clear the chassis, as shown in this graphic.

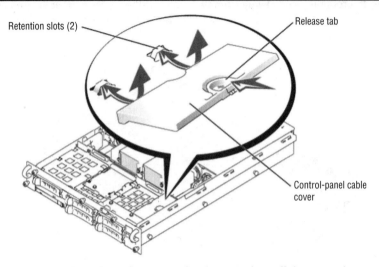

Retention slots (2)

Release tab

Control-panel cable cover

6. Rotate the system board tray levers up simultaneously until the tray releases from the chassis.

7. Pull the system board tray straight back until it stops.

8. Lift the front of the system board tray upward slightly and then pull the tray straight back until it clears the chassis.

9. If the system has a SCSI backplane daughter card, remove it by pulling the retention lever to slide the daughter card away from the SCSI backplane connector.

10. Lift the card up and away from the tabs on the card guide above the drive bay.

11. Grasp the CD/diskette drive tray release handle and pull the tray out of the system, as shown in this graphic.

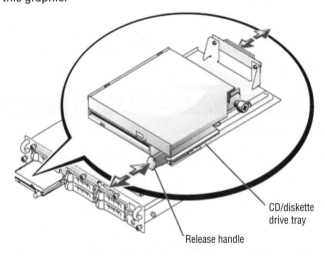

CD/diskette drive tray

Release handle

12. Open the hard drive carrier handle to release the drive(s). Slide them out so they are not connected to the backplane.

13. Loosen the thumbscrew that secures the SCSI backplane board in the system.

14. Slide the backplane board toward the right-side chassis wall about 0.5 inch.

15. Lift the backplane board off its grounding tabs.

16. Lift the backplane board and disconnect the control panel cable from the board.

17. Lift the backplane board out of the system board tray, as shown in the following graphic.

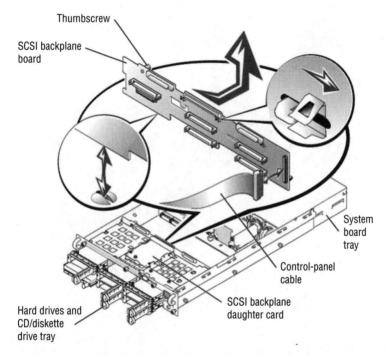

18. Reverse your steps to install the new SCSI backplane and bring the system back up.

Batteries

Yes, servers have system batteries and they can die and need replacing. Always use the type of battery recommended by the vendor. In Exercise 3.6 you'll use an IBM System x3250 M4.

This exercise applies to an IBM server. The procedure for your server may vary, so consult the documentation.

EXERCISE 3.6

Replacing the Battery in an IBM Server

1. After powering down the server remove the cover.

2. If necessary, lift the air baffle out of the way. It is over the fans in the middle of the server, as shown in this graphic.

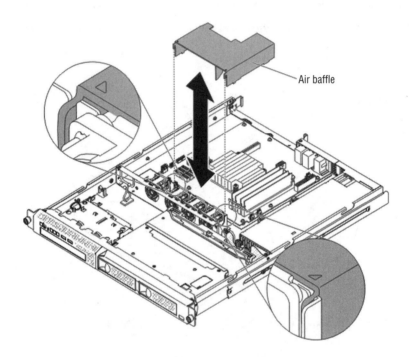

Air baffle

3. Remove the old battery.

4. Insert the new battery:

   a. Position the battery so that the positive (+) symbol is facing toward the power supply.

   b. Tilt the battery so that you can insert it into the socket on the side opposite the battery clip.

   c. Press the battery down into the socket until it snaps into place, as shown in this graphic.

Positive (+) side

Preventive Maintenance

Even when the servers are humming along happily with no issues, there are maintenance tasks that, if performed regularly, will increase the life of your servers and ward off avoidable issues. Two of these will go a long way toward avoiding overheating issues.

Clearing Dust

Dust will accumulate inside the server and, if it is not removed, will act as an insulator to the components and increase the likelihood of overheating. When cleaning the dust, use an antistatic vacuum or use compressed air. If you use compressed air, make sure you are blowing the dust out of the server so it doesn't just go into the air and land back in the same area.

Check Proper Air Flow

Although clearing the dust is important while you are inside the box, you should examine the server while running and ensure that the fans are working together to ensure proper airflow. This will be less of a concern if the server is in the stock condition in which you purchased it because the vendor probably made sure that the fans were positioned properly. But if you have made changes to the server, perhaps adding processors or new cards in the box, the airflow may have been altered in an unfavorable way or may even be significantly blocked.

Generally speaking, you want the air to enter the front of the server and proceed unimpeded toward the back and then to exit the server at the back. Anything added to the server that disrupts this flow needs attention. Also, any fans that may be added should not push hot air toward the front of the server.

Proper Shutdown Procedures

When shutting down the server for maintenance, make sure you follow proper shutdown procedures. There are two types of reboots:

Soft Reboot   Better for the system than a hard reboot, a soft reboot allows the proper shutdown of all running applications and services, yet requires that you be logged in as either administrator or root and that the server be in a responsive state. It is also good to know that since power is not completely removed, memory registers are not cleared.

Hard Reboot   A hard reboot is not good for the system and equivalent to turning off the power and turning it back on. However, in cases where the server is unresponsive, a hard reboot may be the only option.

Always use a soft reboot whenever possible. A hard reboot does not give the server an opportunity to properly shut down all running applications and services.

Fault Tolerance and High Availability Techniques

Since servers are so critical to the operation of the network, in many cases we need to protect ourselves against the negative effects of a server going down. In other cases, we simply need to add more server horsepower to meet a workload. We accomplish these goals through fault tolerance and high availability techniques. This section explores several types of these methods.

Clustering

Clustering is the process of combining multiple physical or virtual servers together in an arrangement called a cluster, in which the servers work together to service the same work-load or application. This may be done to increase performance or to ensure continued access to the service if a server goes down, or its goal could be both. A server cluster is generally recommended for servers running applications that have long-running in-memory state or frequently updated data. Typical uses for server clusters include file servers, print servers, database servers, and messaging servers. Clustering can be implemented in one of two ways: active/active or active/passive.

Active/Active

In an active/active cluster, both or all servers are actively servicing the workload. That doesn't necessarily mean they are running the same applications at all times, but only that they are capable of taking over the workload of an application running on another cluster member if that member goes down. For example, in Figure 3.7 the server on the left is run-ning two applications prior to failing, whereas the server on the right is running only one of the three applications. After the failure, the server on the right takes over the work of all three applications. With this arrangement you must ensure that the remaining server can handle the total workload.

Active/Passive

In an active/passive cluster, at least one of the servers in the cluster is not actively working but simply sitting idle until a failure occurs. This is shown in Figure 3.8. This arrangement comes at the cost of having a server sitting idle until a failure occurs. It has the benefit of providing more assurance that the workload will continue to be serviced with the same level of resources if the servers are alike.

FIGURE 3.7   Active/active cluster

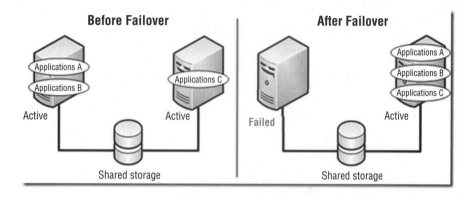

FIGURE 3.8   Active/passive cluster

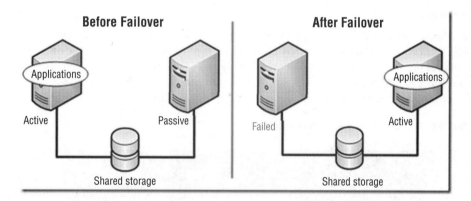

Load Balancing

A second form of fault tolerance that focuses more on providing high availability of a resource is *load balancing*. In load balancing a frontend device or service receives work requests and allocates the requests to a number of backend servers. This type of fault tolerance is recommended for applications that do *not* have long-running in-memory state or frequently updated data. Web servers are good candidates for load balancing. The load balancing device or service can use several methods to allocate the work. Let's look at the most common allocation method, round robin, and also talk about a key function in the load balancing system, the heartbeat.

Round Robin

In a round robin allocation system, the load balancer allocates work requests to each server sequentially, resulting in each getting an equal number of requests. As shown in Figure 3.9, this could mean that a user may make two requests that actually go to two different servers.

FIGURE 3.9   Round robin load balancing

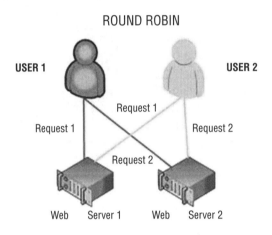

Heartbeat

A heartbeat connection is a connection between servers in a load balancing scenario across which the servers send a signal (called a heartbeat) used to determine when the other server is down. If one server goes down, the other will service the entire workload. The two servers are typically identical (content-wise), and this is used often as a failover technique. It may be a direct physical connection, as shown in Figure 3.10, or it might be done over the network.

FIGURE 3.10   Heartbeat connection

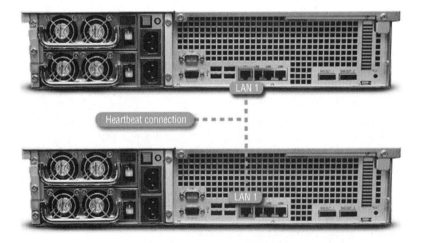

Asset Management and Documentation

You would be amazed at how many network administrators can't tell you exactly how many devices of a certain type they have, and if they can, they can't tell you where they all are. This is the result of a combination of poor record keeping and frequent job turnover. While the job turnover may just be an unfortunate characteristic of the business, it should not cause an issue if proper documentation policies are followed. In this section the proper management of assets through the entire asset life cycle will be covered. We'll also talk about the type of documentation you keep and how it should be handled, especially sensitive information.

Asset Management

Proper asset management is not rocket science. It boils down to knowing exactly what you have, when you got it, where it is, and where the license to use it is. Most server administrators don't set out to intentionally exercise poor asset management; they simply don't assign it the importance it requires to be done correctly. Let's break the process down and talk about its individual parts and why each is important.

Licensing

When you purchase software, you are purchasing the right to use it. At any point in time you may face a software audit from one of the major vendors. When this occurs, you will need to be able to provide written proof that you possess a number of licenses for a particular product that is equal or greater than the number of installations in your network. When that time comes, will you be able to locate these? They should be kept in a safe place where you can put your hand on them at a moment's notice. That does not mean the records can't be digital, but they must be available.

Labeling

Labeling servers, workstations, printers, ports on infrastructure devices (routers and switches), and other items is another form of asset documentation that often doesn't receive enough attention. Not only does this make your day-to-day duties easier, it makes the process of maintaining accurate records simpler and supports a proper asset management plan. When periodic inventories are taken (you are doing that, right?), having these items labeled makes the process so much quicker. This goes for cables in the server room as well.

Warranty

Warranty information should be readily available to you when equipment breaks. You should never spend time or money repairing items that are still under warranty. It should *not* take you hours to locate this information when that time comes. Keep this paperwork or its digital equivalent close at hand in the same way you would the licensing information.

Life-Cycle Management

Managing assets becomes easier if you understand that an asset goes through various stages called its life cycle. Consequently, life-cycle management comprises the activities that we undertake with respect to the asset at various points in the life cycle. Let's examine these stages.

Procurement

This includes all activities that might go into purchasing a product. It includes activities such as product research, requests for bids, product selection, and delivery.

Usage

This stage includes day-to-day maintenance tasks that are involved in using the item. This might encompass things like updating the software or firmware or tasks that would be unique to the device type, such as defragmenting a hard drive.

End of Life

End of life can mean a couple of different things. From the vendor perspective, it probably means that they are no longer providing support for a product. From your perspective, it probably means that the product no longer meets your needs or that you have decided to replace the item with a new version. It could also mean that changes in your business process make the item no longer necessary.

Disposal/Recycling

The final stage in the life of an asset is its disposal. Regardless of your approach—whether it is throwing the item away, donating the item to charity, or turning the item in for recycling—you should ensure that all sensitive data is removed. This requires more than simple deletion, and the extent to which you go with this process depends on how sensitive that data is. Degaussing is a way to remove the data for good. With extremely sensitive data, you may find it advisable to destroy the device.

Proactive Life-Cycle Management

Here's a final word of advice: you may find it beneficial to stagger replacement cycles so that your entire server room doesn't need to be replaced all at once. It's much easier to get smaller upgrades added to the budget.

Inventory

As I mentioned at the start of this section, asset management includes knowing what you have. You can't know something is missing until you take an inventory, so you should take inventory on a regular basis. So what type of information is useful to record? You may choose to record more, but the following items should always be included:

Make   The manufacturer of the device should be recorded as well as the name they give the device.

Model   The exact model number should be recorded in full, leaving nothing out. Sometimes those dangling letters at the end of the model number are there to indicate how this model differs from another, or they could indicate a feature, so record *the entire number*.

Serial Number   The serial number of the device should be recorded. This is a number that will be important to you with respect to the warranty and service support. You should be able to put your hands on this number quickly.

Asset Tag   If your organization places asset tags on devices, it probably means you have your own internal numbering or other identification system in place. Record that number and any other pertinent information that the organization deems important enough to place on the asset tag, such as region and building.

Documentation

Along with a robust asset management plan, you should implement a formal plan for organizing, storing, and maintaining multiple copies in several locations of a wide array of documentation that will support the asset management plan. Just as you should be able to put your hands on the inventory documentation at a moment's notice, you should be able to obtain needed information from any of the following documents at any time.

Service Manuals

All service manuals that arrive with new hardware should be kept. They are invaluable sources of information related to the use and maintenance of your devices. They also contain contact information that may make it easier to locate help at a critical time. Many manuals have troubleshooting flowcharts that may turn a 4-hour solution into a 30-minute one. If a paper copy has not been retained, you can usually obtain these service manuals online at the vendor website.

Network Diagrams

All network diagrams should be kept in both hard copy and digital format. Moreover, these diagrams must be closely integrated with the change management process. The change management policy (covered later in this section) should specifically call for the updating of the diagram at the conclusion of any change made to the network that impacts the diagram and should emphasize that no change procedure is considered complete unless this update has occurred.

Architecture Diagrams

Any diagrams created to depict the architecture of a software program or group of programs should be kept. When the original developers are no longer with the company, they are invaluable to those left behind to understand the workings of the software. There may multiple layers of this documentation. Some may only focus on a single piece of software whereas others may depict how the software fits into the overall business process of the company. An example of such a diagram, called an enterprise architecture diagram, is shown in Figure 3.11.

FIGURE 3.11   Enterprise architecture diagram

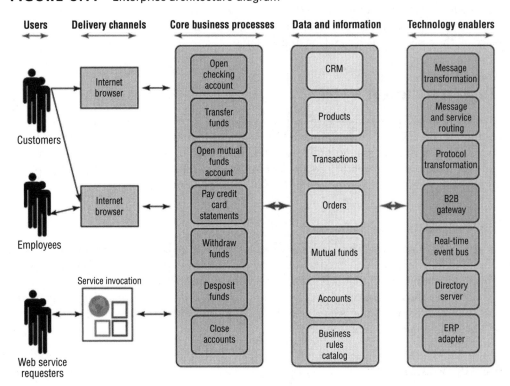

Dataflow Diagrams

While some of your network diagrams will focus on the physical pieces of the network, others will be focused on the flow of data in the network in the process of doing business. So these may depict a workflow and how information involved in a single transaction or business process goes from one logical component in the network to another. An example of a dataflow diagram for an order system is shown in Figure 3.12.

FIGURE 3.12 Data flow for order entry

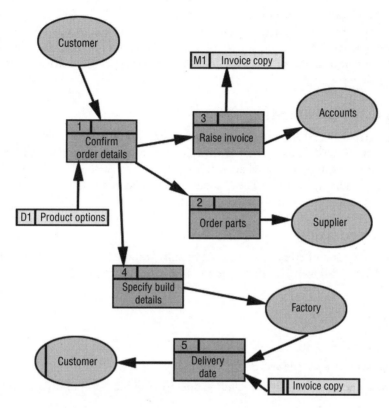

Recovery Documentation

If your organization has a disaster recovery plan, that plan should call for recovery documentation. It should outline, in detail, the order with which devices should be recovered in the event of a disaster that causes either complete or partial destruction of the facility. It should also cover the steps to be taken in lesser events as well, such as a power outage, the theft of a device, or the failure of a device, and data recovery procedures as well.

Baseline Documentation

Earlier you learned the importance of creating performance baselines for major systems. The baselines will be used as a comparison point to readings taken at regular intervals. This means that the baseline data will need to be available at all times. A plan should be in place to consider at regular intervals whether major changes in the network may require new baselines to be taken.

Change Management Policies

As a part of the overall security policy, the change management policy will outline the steps involved in suggesting, considering, planning, executing, and documenting any change in the server configuration. No change should be made without it undergoing this process. The policy should be available at times for consultation when questions arise about making configuration changes.

Service-Level Agreement

Service-level agreements (SLAs) can be made with customers or with departments within the organization. These documents describe the type of service to be provided, in what format, in what time frame, and at what cost. Some SLAs are executed with vendors that provide service to the organization. These documents should be readily available when disagreements arise and clarifications need to be made.

Server Configuration

The exact configuration of every server should be fully recorded and updated any time a change is made. The following is information that should be included:

General

- Server name
- Server location
- Function or purpose of the server
- Software running on the server, including operating system, programs, and services

Hardware

- Hardware components, including the make and model of each part of the system

Configuration Information

- Event logging settings
- Services that are running
- Configuration of any security lockdown tool or setting
- Configuration and settings of software running on the server

Data

- Types of data stored on the server
- Owners of the data stored on the server
- Sensitivity of data stored on the server
- Data that should be backed up, along with its location

- Users or groups with access to data stored on the server
- Administrators, with a list of rights of each
- Authentication process and protocols for users of data on the server
- Authentication process and protocols used for authentication
- Data encryption requirements
- Authentication encryption requirements

Users

- Account settings
- List of users accessing data from remote locations and type of media they access data through, such as the Internet or a private network
- List of administrators administrating the server from remote locations and type of media they access the server through

Security

- Intrusion detection and prevention method used on the server
- Latest patch to operating system and each service running
- Individuals with physical access to the area the server is in and the type of access, such as key or card access
- Emergency recovery disk and date of last update
- Disaster recovery plan and location of backup data

Secure Storage of Sensitive Documentation

No discussion of documentation storage would be complete without covering storage of sensitive documents. There should be a system of data classification that extends to cover sensitive documents such as contracts, leases, design plans, and product details. The data protection method accorded each category should reflect its sensitivity label. Any such documents labeled sensitive should be encrypted and stored separately from other categories of data. Examples of this sort of information are

- Personally identifiable information, which in part or in combination can be used to identify a person
- Human resources information
- Financial documents that are not public
- Trade secrets and propriety methods
- Plans and designs
- Any other documents that the company deems to be sensitive

Summary

In this chapter you learned about server roles and the requirements for those roles. We also covered proper server maintenance techniques such as patch management, performance monitoring, and hardware maintenance. You learned the importance of change management and the steps in replacing components in the server. Finally, we discussed asset management from the perspective of the asset life cycle and the role that proper documentation management plays in proper network management.

Exam Essentials

Compare and contrast server roles and requirements for each.   Understand the possible roles servers can play in the network and describe the hardware requirements of these roles.

Perform proper server maintenance.   Identify the procedures involved in patch management and updating drivers and firmware. Describe how SLAs are used to control the delivery of service to the network. List the major resources that should be monitored during performance monitoring.

Explain the importance of asset management and documentation.   List what should be included when creating an asset inventory. Understand the importance of organizing and maintaining documentation. Describe some of the types of sensitive documents that require special treatment.

Review Questions

You can find the answers in the Appendix.

1. Which server role uses HTTP as its transfer mechanism?
   A. Web
   B. Application
   C. Directory
   D. Database

2. Which resource is stressed the most on an application server?
   A. Disk
   B. NIC
   C. CPU
   D. Memory

3. Which of the following server roles is used to authenticate users to the network?
   A. Web
   B. Application
   C. Directory
   D. Database

4. Which server role automates the process of providing an IP configuration to devices in the network?
   A. DNS
   B. Routing and Remote Access
   C. DHCP
   D. NTP

5. Which server role is critical to the operation of digital certificates?
   A. DNS
   B. Routing and Remote Access
   C. DHCP
   D. NTP

6. Which server role resolves hostnames to IP addresses?
   A. DNS
   B. Routing and Remote Access
   C. DHCP
   D. NTP

7. Which of the following are the software stubs that allow devices to communicate with the operating system?

   A. Drivers

   B. Patches

   C. Shims

   D. Manifests

8. Which of the following describes the average length of time it takes a vendor to repair a device or component?

   A. MTBF

   B. MMTR

   C. MTTR

   D. MTR

9. Which of the following represents aspects of the workload the resource is undergoing?

   A. Counters

   B. Alerts

   C. Metrics

   D. Markers

10. Which of the following is not one of the four major resources?

   A. Memory

   B. CPU

   C. Disk

   D. Pagefile

11. Which of the following is the percentage of time the CPU spends executing a non-idle thread?

   A. Processor\% Processor Time

   B. Processor\% User Time

   C. Processor\% Interrupt Time

   D. System\Processor Queue Length

12. Which of the following is the amount of physical memory, in megabytes, available for running processes?

   A. Memory\% Committed Bytes in Use

   B. Memory\Pool Non-Paged Bytes

   C. Memory\Available Mbytes

   D. Memory\Pool Paged Bytes

13. What is a common disk metric that describes how fast the disk subsystem is able to read and write to the drive?

    A. ILO

    B. IOPS

    C. IOS

    D. TIOS

14. To which component do drives abut and make a connection with the server so no cables are required?

    A. Frontplane

    B. Drive board

    C. Backplane

    D. Disk plane

15. Which of the following allows the proper shutdown of all running applications and services?

    A. Hard reboot

    B. Soft reboot

    C. Slow reboot

    D. Easy boot

16. Which type of fault tolerance is recommended for servers running applications that do not have long-running in-memory state or frequently updated data?

    A. Load balancing

    B. Hot site

    C. Clustering

    D. Cold site

17. Which of the following means that the device is no longer supported by the vendor?

    A. Proprietary

    B. Legacy

    C. End of life

    D. Expiration

18. What drives the amount of memory for a print server?

    A. Number of printers

    B. Number of users assigned to the printer

    C. Size of the network

    D. Fault tolerance required

19. Which of the following protocols is used when mail servers send email?

    A. POP3

    B. SMTP

    C. SNMP

    D. IMAP4

20. Which RAID type increases fault tolerance and performance?

    A. RAID 0

    B. RAID 1

    C. RAID 3

    D. RAID 5

Chapter

4

Storage Technologies

COMPTIA SERVER+ EXAM OBJECTIVES COVERED IN THIS CHAPTER:

✓ **3.1 Given a scenario, install and deploy primary storage devices based on given specifications and interfaces**

- Disk specifications (RPM, dimensions/form factor, capacity, bus width, IOPS, seek time and latency, hotswap vs. non-hotswap components)

- Interfaces (SAS, SATA, SCSI, USB, Fiber Channel)

- Hard drive vs. SSD

✓ **3.3 Summarize hardware and features of various storage technologies**

- DAS

- NAS (iSCSI, FCoE)

- SAN (Fiber Channel, LUN & LUN masking, HBAs and fabric switches)

- JBOD

- Tape (drive, libraries)

- Optical drive

- Flash, compact flash, and USB drive

Servers require storage to hold the operating system and applications and, in some cases, large amounts of data. Although this storage serves the same function as it does for any workstation, the form it takes may be drastically different. In some cases, it is neither directly attached nor does it use standard hard drives. The storage may also reside on a completely different type of network from the rest of the LAN. In this chapter, we'll look at storage technologies you'll probably encounter when dealing with servers.

Hardware and Features of Various Storage Technologies

Servers can use several different technologies to reach their storage devices. Although they can make use of directly attached storage devices in the same way as workstations, the amount of data they sometimes have to store and the performance and fault tolerance requirements of that data make it more likely that other types of storage are preferable. In this section, three major approaches to providing servers with high-performance, fault-tolerant storage will be covered.

Direct Attached Storage (DAS)

Direct attached storage (DAS) is the type of storage used in workstations. In this approach, the drives are attached to the server locally through a SATA, USB, SCSI, or Serial Attached SCSI (SAS) Connection. All these interface types will be covered later in the section "Installing and Deploying Primary Storage Devices;" for now the main concept you need to grasp is that these are local interfaces to the server.

Keep in mind that multiple drives or the presence of fault-tolerant technologies such as RAID can still be considered DAS if the interface to the storage is one of these local technologies. One of the key features of DAS is that there is no network connection standing between the server and the storage, as is the case with the other two technologies we'll be discussing. Although DAS has the advantage of being widely understood and simple to deploy, it has the disadvantage of being more difficult to scale.

Network-Attached Storage (NAS)

Network-attached storage (NAS), as the name implies, consists of storage devices that are attached to the network and not attached locally to the server or servers that may be accessing the NAS. Although the storage may not be attached locally to the server, it is reachable via the TCP/IP network.

In a NAS, almost any machine that can connect to the LAN (or is interconnected to the LAN through a WAN) can use protocols such as NFS, CIFS, or HTTP to connect to a NAS and share files. The advantages and disadvantages of using NAS are listed in Table 4.1.

TABLE 4.1   Advantages and disadvantages of NAS

Advantages	Disadvantages
A NAS is easily accessed over TCP/IP Ethernet-based networks.	A NAS has higher latency and lower reliability than a SAN.
A NAS is inexpensive to implement.	NAS traffic competes with regular data on the network since it is not on its own network.
A NAS typically supports multiple RAID methods.	Packet drops and congestion are inherent in Ethernet.
A NAS offers GUI-based management.	Taking frequent snapshots works better in SAN. (Snapshots are images of operating systems, making a rollback to an earlier state possible.)
A NAS typically contains backup software.	
Ethernet troubleshooting is well understood.	
A NAS supports high throughput.	

Storage Area Networks (SANs)

Classic storage area networks (SANs) consist of high-capacity storage devices that are connected by a high-speed private network (separate from the LAN) using a storage-specific switch. This storage information architecture addresses the collection, management, and use of data. The advantages and disadvantages of a SAN are listed in Table 4.2.

TABLE 4.2   Advantages and disadvantages of SANs

Advantages	Disadvantages
SANs are scalable; it's easy to add additional storage as required.	SANs are expensive.
SANs are available; maintenance can be performed without taking servers offline.	Maintaining SANs requires higher skill levels.
Sharing is made easier by the fact that the SAN is not connected directly to any network or server.	It's not possible to leverage legacy investments.
SANs make it easier to provide physical security. Longer cable runs are made possible because Fibre Channel enables you to access a SAN in a remote location.	There is a relative scarcity of SAN vendors.

Another key difference between the operation of a NAS and that of a SAN is that a SAN provides block-level access to data as opposed to a NAS, which provides file-level access to the data. In file-level access, data is accessed in bulk in the form of a file and the process is controlled by the protocol used by the client. When block-level access is used, data is stored in raw blocks and each block can be controlled like an individual hard drive.

Each of these systems has advantages, as shown in Table 4.3.

TABLE 4.3   File- and block-level access

File level	Block level
Easy to implement and use	Better performance
Stores and presents data as files and folders	Each block can be treated as an independent disk
Less expensive	More reliable
Well suited for bulk file storage	Can support external boot-up of the systems to which it is connected

A comparison of the three storage methods we've discussed so far is shown in Figure 4.1. The FC in the diagram refers to Fibre Channel, which we discuss in the next section.

FIGURE 4.1   Storage technologies

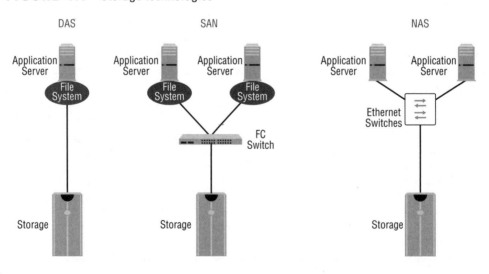

Fibre Channel

In a classic SAN, devices communicate using the Fibre Channel protocol over a fiber network of storage devices typically connected to a Fibre Channel switch. This means that any servers that will be directly connected to this fiber network must have a host bus adapter (HBA) installed that can communicate on the fiber network. Let's take a closer look at these two critical components on a classic SAN.

HBAs and Fabric Switches

The host bus adapters that must be present in the server are usually installed in one of the expansion slots, typically in a PCIe slot. They can come in single or multiple port varieties. In Figure 4.2, a two-port adapter is shown with the fiber network cables that connect to the ports on the HBA. In this instance the fiber connector is an LC connector.

FIGURE 4.2   Fiber HBA

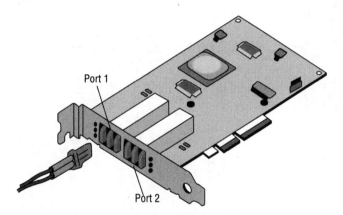

Port 1

Port 2

HBAs have World Wide Names (WWNs) used to identify them. HBAs have two types of WWNs: one that identifies the HBA and is used by all ports on the HBA, and one that identifies each port on the HBA.

HBAs can be allocated to specific devices, connections, and storage zones. (Zones are divisions of the storage created for performance and/or security reasons.) HBA allocation is the process of confining certain ports on the HBA to certain zones for security.

Fabric switches are those that support a Fibre Channel network. If you look back at Figure 4.1, you'll see that the fiber switch connects the storage devices and the servers are accessing the storage devices.

LUN Masking

A logical unit number (LUN) identifies a device addressed by the SCSI protocol or protocols that encapsulate SCSI, such as Fibre Channel or iSCSI. LUN masking or mapping is the process of controlling access to a LUN by effectively "hiding" its existence from those who should not have access. This makes the storage available to some hosts but not to others.

LUN masking can be done at either the HBA level or the storage controller level. Implementing LUN masking at the storage controller level provides greater security because it is possible to defeat it at the HBA level by forging an IP address, MAC address, or WWN. Moreover, if the HBA is moved, it can cause the masking process to become vulnerable. LUN masking is illustrated in Figure 4.3. Each server can only access the LUN to which it is assigned.

FIGURE 4.3 LUN masking

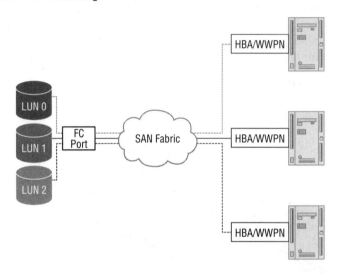

Using iSCSI and FCoE

SANs can also be implemented in such a way that devices that cannot normally communicate by using the Fibre Channel protocol or SCSI commands can access the storage devices. Two technologies that make this possible are covered next.

iSCSI

Internet Small Computer Systems Interface (iSCSI) is an IP-based networking storage standard method of encapsulating SCSI commands (which are used with SANs) within IP packets. This allows you to use the same network for storage that you use for the balance of the network. Whereas iSCSI can also be used in a NAS architecture, we have chosen to include it under SAN as it was first used in a SAN. Figure 4.4 compares a regular SAN and one using iSCSI.

FIGURE 4.4 Classic SAN and SAN with iSCSI

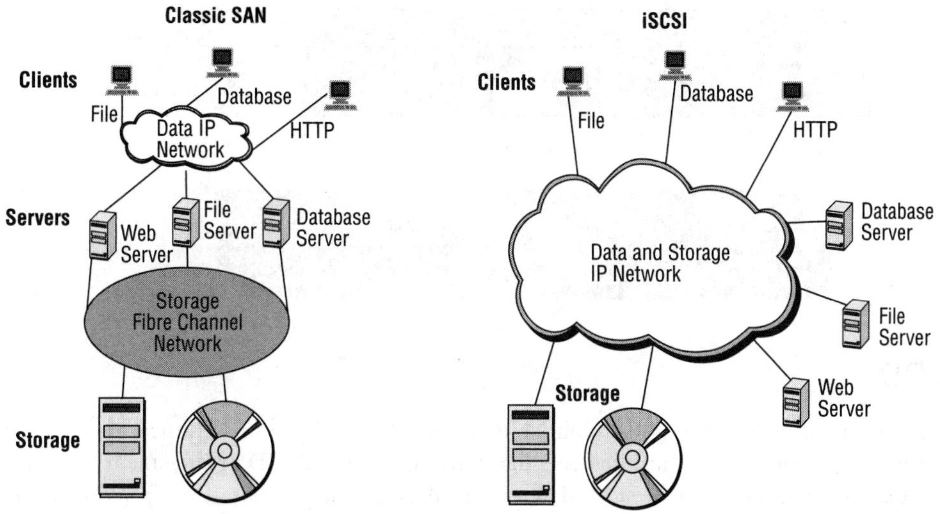

The advantages and disadvantages to using iSCSI are listed in Table 4.4.

TABLE 4.4 Advantages and disadvantages of iSCSI

Advantages	Disadvantages
iSCSI is simple, due to its reliance on Ethernet, which is well known.	Performance issues are possible, due to reliance on software.
iSCSI eliminates distance limitations imposed by SCSI transfers.	iSCSI is susceptible to network congestion.
iSCSI is inexpensive in simple deployments.	In larger deployments, iSCSI can be as expensive as or more expensive than Fibre Channel.

FCoE

Fibre Channel over Ethernet (FCoE) encapsulates Fibre Channel traffic within Ethernet frames much as iSCSI encapsulates SCSI commands in IP packets. However, unlike iSCSI, it does not use IP at all. Figure 4.5 shows the structures of iSCSI and FCoE.

FIGURE 4.5 FCoE and iSCSI

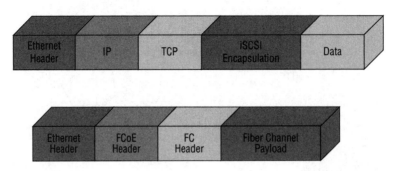

JBOD

The acronym JBOD refers to "just a bunch of disks." The disks in this "bunch of disks" are independent of one another, unlike disks that participate in a RAID arrangement of some sort. Although the data may be striped across the disks, no fault tolerance is provided. It is a cheaper alternative to a RAID system. JBOD uses a process called *concatenation*, which is illustrated in Figure 4.6. In the figure you can see that data is concatenated from the end of disk 0 (block 64) to the beginning of disk 1 (block 65). Notice there is no data redundancy, and regardless of the number of disks in the system, if the data is spanned across the disks, the loss of a single disk means the loss of all data, making backup extremely important.

FIGURE 4.6 JBOD

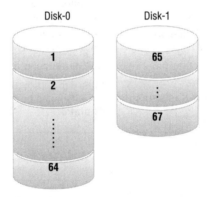

Tape

While there are a number of limitations to backing up data to tape, it is still a widely used method. In this section we'll examine the hardware required and the logical way in which the data can be organized on tapes.

Drive

Tape drives can come in several formats and have ever-increasing capacities. Linear Tape Open (LTO), IBM, and Oracle are some of the major formats available. The LTO drives have been through a number of generations, the latest of which, LTO-6, has a maximum capacity of 2.5 TB and operates at 160 MBps uncompressed. One interesting feature with respect to the various versions of LTO is use of colors to indicate a specific cartridge type. For example, though not a standard, LTO-6 cartridges are typically black whereas LTO-5 cartridges are red (unless they are HP, which has its own color scheme). LTO-7 is expected be out in early 2016. It will support 6 TB native and up to 15 TB compressed and will operate at 700 MBps.

One of the historical shortcomings of tape, its sequential access method, was the driver of the introduction of media partitioning in LTO-5. This has enabled tape to be accessed in a new way, using IBM's Linear Tape File System (LTFS). It allows access to files on a tape in a similar fashion to the way files are accessed on a disk or flash drive. Keep in mind that although it may make the tape drive appear to behave like a hard drive, the data is still sequential.

Libraries

A tape library is a storage device that contains multiple tape drives. It also contains a number of slots to hold tape cartridges and a barcode reader that is used to identify the cartridges. A tape library typically contains a robotic method for loading the tapes. As shown in Figure 4.7, it can be connected to the backup device via SCSI, Fibre Channel, iSCSI.

FIGURE 4.7   Tape library

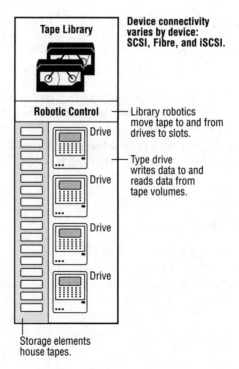

Optical Drive

Servers may also have optical drives connected through SATA connections when the drives are internal or integrated. Alternatively, they may be external and connected with a USB connection. These drives make it easy to install software on the server, transfer data easily, and perform backups.

Flash, Compact Flash, and USB Drive

Increasingly the largest datacenters and organizations are moving toward flash drives or solid state drives (SSDs) rather than using mechanical hard disk drives (HDDs). In the past SSDs have had a shorter life than HDDs. But that is no longer the case, and they are faster than HDDs, which makes them worth the extra expense. SSDs use flash memory and have no moving parts.

These drives can also be implemented through Compact Flash. While originally intended as a form of memory, Compact Flash cards have been connected to adapters that allow the system to use a Compact Flash card as an SSD.

Almost every kind of drive we have discussed in this section can be implemented externally via a USB connection. That includes flash drives, SSD drives, optical drives, and tape drives.

Installing and Deploying Primary Storage Devices

When anticipating the installation or deployment of primary storage devices on servers, you should consider several factors before you even purchase the drives or drives. First, there are a number of disk specifications to understand, as well as a variety of interfaces that you may be dealing with during the installation. Let's consider both of these issues and then we'll end this section by running through the steps in a typical installation.

Disk Specifications

The number of technical specifications you will find listed when shopping for storage solutions can be bewildering at first. But if you understand what each means and how to compare the values attached to these specifications, the process of choosing the right solution can be much easier. In this section, we'll consider the most common characteristics of server storage.

RPM

Revolutions per minute (RPM) is a value that indicates how fast the drive spins. There is an inverse relationship between the RPMs and drive latency. That's means faster spinning drives experience less latency. Disk drives for servers typically have RPM values between 7200 and 15000. Just to be clear, this is a value with meaning only for hard disk drives. SSDs do not spin at all.

Dimensions/Form Factor

It would be pretty embarrassing to buy a drive, get the drive, and then realize it won't fit. Therefore, the size and dimensions (also called the form factor) of the drive must also be considered. The drive must fit into the bay in which it will be installed. The two most common are the 2.5-inch small form factor (SFF) and the 3.5-inch large form factor (LFF). Enterprise-class HDD enclosures typically have a standard length and width. They can vary in height, up to 15 mm for SFF and up to 26.1 mm for LFF. Many SSDs are sized to fit in the same slots used for HDDs. Always consider the bay into which the drive will be installed before purchasing.

Capacity

The capacity of disks can vary widely. The amount of space you need will largely depend on the role the server is playing. If you review the section on server roles in Chapter 3, "Server Maintenance," you will see that some roles, such as file servers, require lots of space whereas other roles do not. The latest standard HDDs can hold up to 8 TB of data. Western Digital has a line of helium-sealed drives that go up to 10 TB, and Samsung has released a solid-state drive that holds almost 16 TB of data.

Bus Width

At one time, the width of the bus to which the disk would attach was a key consideration when selecting a disk, but since most drive technology no longer uses parallel communications, bus width is less important. When SCSI and IDE were in use, the wider the bus, the better. But today's serial attached SCSI (SAS) and serial ATA (SATA) use high-speed serial communication.

   If you are still using SCSI, then ensuring that you buy a disk drive or drives that make full use of the bus width in the server is essential. So if your SCSI bus will support Ultra 640 SCSI, you should purchase drives that also fully support this.

IOPS

Input/Output Operations per Second (IOPS) is a value that describes how fast the drive can read and write to the disk. Keep in mind that one of the advantages of SSDs is their superior IOPS values when compared to HDDs. For more information on common values for both types of drives, see the section "Disk IOPS" in Chapter 3.

Seek Time and Latency

Seek time is the time it takes for the actuator arm to arrive at the proper location where the read or write will occur. Latency is a measure of the time it takes the platter to spin the disk around so that the actuator arm is over the proper section. Latency is largely a function of the RPMs as a faster spinning disk will arrive at the desired location faster than a slower disk.

Given all this, when it comes to SSDs, there are no moving parts, so seek times and latency times will be much lower and cannot be used in comparison with HDDs. For disks in a datacenter you should look for average seek time between 5 ms and 10 ms.

Hot-swap vs. Non-hot-swap Components

Some disks can be changed out with the server running while others cannot. A hot-swap disk is one that can be changed without shutting down the server. In some cases, while the server may be left on, the software in the server may need to be disconnected from the disk being changed and then reconnected after the swap is done. Lower-end SCSI devices may be of this type, which is also called *cold pluggable*.

In other cases, where the device is truly hot pluggable, the system requires no disconnection process because it can detect what is going on when you make the swap. Examples of these types of drives are higher-end SCSI devices, USB, FireWire, and eSATA.

Interfaces

There are five major drive interfaces you may encounter when installing or swapping out disk drives. We've already discussed a number of these, but just for completeness let's run through them all here in one place.

Serial Attached SCSI (SAS)

Serial Attached SCSI (SAS) is a type of SCSI that uses serial operation rather than parallel as the original SCSI did. There are several other ways in which it differs from parallel SCSI. A SCSI bus is a multidrop bus (one on which multiple points of attachment exist) whereas SAS uses point-to-point communication. Also, SAS requires no termination as in parallel SCSI. The latest version of SAS, SAS-3, operates at 12.0 Gbps.

A common SAS setup is shown in Figure 4.8. The cable plugged into the HBA is an external version of the SAS cable using the SFF-8470 connector, while the cable running from the HBA to the drives is an internal variety also called an octopus cable using the SFF-8484 connector to the HBA and SFF-8484 connector to the drives.

FIGURE 4.8 SAS cabling

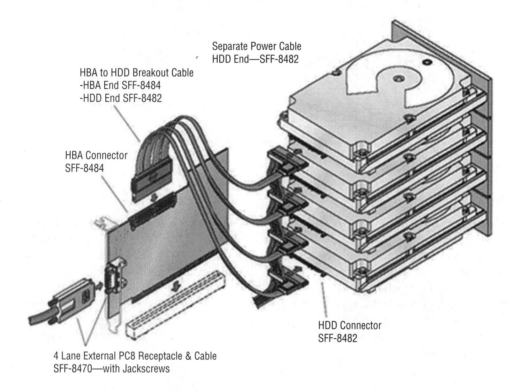

Serial ATA (SATA)

Serial ATA (SATA) is also a serial communication method and began as an enhancement to the original ATA specifications, also known as IDE and, today, PATA. Technology is proving that serial communication is superior to placing multiple bits of data in parallel and trying to synchronize their transmission. Serial transmissions are simpler to adapt to the faster rates than are parallel transmissions. The SAS system receptacle is compatible with both the SAS HDD plug and the SATA HDD plug, as illustrated in Figure 4.9. The opposite is not true: you cannot plug a SAS HDD into a SATA system receptacle.

FIGURE 4.9 SAS system receptacle with the SATA HDD plug

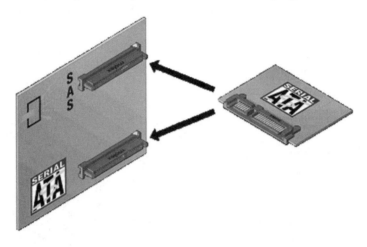

SCSI

The classic SCSI interface differs from SAS in that devices on the SCSI bus are like devices on a LAN and require SCSI IDs. There are many versions of SCSI that differ in the width of the bus and the allowable length of the cables. Internal parallel SCSI cables have two or more 50-, 68-, or 80-pin connectors attached. External cables have 50- or 68-pin connectors at each end, depending on the specific SCSI bus width supported. An 80-pin Single Connector Attachment (SCA) is typically used for hot-pluggable devices. The latest version, Ultra 640 SCSI, can have only 16 devices on the bus and the cable cannot exceed 10 meters in length, but it can achieve 640 MBps. Examples of 50-, 68-, and 80-pin interfaces are shown in Figure 4.10.

FIGURE 4.10 SCSI interfaces

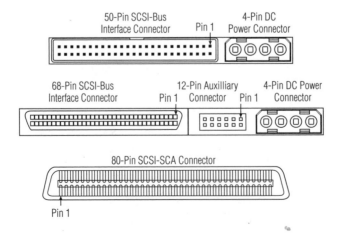

SCSI has also been implemented to work on fiber interfaces as well using Fibre Channel Protocol (FCP) for SCSI and on USB interfaces using USB-Attached SCSI (UAS).

USB

As you already know, USB can provide an interface to practically any type of device, including storage devices. This includes the ability to use special adapter cables to connect a SCSI drive to a USB 3.0 port using the UAS. One of the cables you would use in such a situation is shown in Figure 4.11.

FIGURE 4.11 USB to SCSI

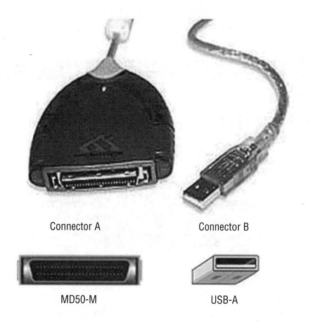

Connector A	Connector B
MD50-M	USB-A

Fibre Channel

A very common interface for storage in servers is a Fibre Channel interface. These are used to connect devices in a high-speed fiber storage network. These networks typically use a fiber switch with devices connected to the switch using Fibre Channel interfaces. Servers will require some implementation of a fiber HBA. Each HBA has a unique World Wide Name (WWN), which like a MAC address uses an Organizationally Unique Identifier (OUI) assigned by the IEEE. A two-port version of a fiber HBA was shown in the section "HBAs and Fabric Switches" earlier in this chapter. An example of a fiber switch to which the cables from the HBAs on the servers would attach is shown in Figure 4.12.

FIGURE 4.12 Fiber switch

Hard Drive vs. SSD

In Chapter 3 you learned that while traditional HDDs are less expensive than SSDs, SSDs are faster and suffer fewer failures not due to old age. Also remember that SSDs exhibit much higher IOPS values than traditional HDDs. For example, a 10,000 rpm SATA drive with 3 Gbps is listed to deliver ~125–150 IOPS, whereas a SSD with a SATA 3 Gbps interface is listed at ~8,600 IOPS (and that is one of the slower SSD drives). Finally, one characteristic that you did not learn about in Chapter 3 is that SSDs, unlike HHDs, are unaffected by magnetism, so they cannot be erased using magnetism as you can do with an HDD. In Exercise 4.1, you will change out a hard drive in an HP ProLiant DL380p Gen8 Server. In the HP ProLiant, both HDDs and SDDs can be changed out without shutting down the server. You server may be different. Consult your vendor documentation.

EXERCISE 4.1

Installing a SATA Drive

1. Remove a drive blank. This is simply a cover over one of the drive bays, as shown here.

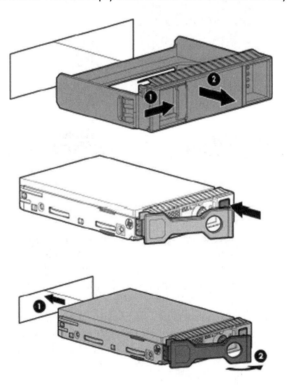

2. Prepare the drive and install the drive back into the slot, as shown in the previous graphic in steps labeled 1 and 2.

3. Observe the status of the LEDs on the front of the drive, as shown here.

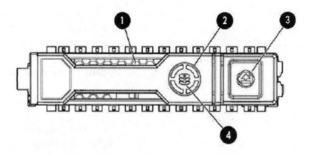

4. Use the following chart to assess the status of the newly installed drive.

LED number	LED name	Status	Definition
1	Locate	Solid blue	Drive is being identified by host application.
		Flashing blue	Firmware is being updated or requires an update.
2	Activity ring	Rotating green	Drive activity.
		Off	No drive activity.
3	Do not remove	Solid white	Do not remove the drive. Removing the drive causes one or more of the logical drives to fail.
		Off	Removing the drive does not cause a logical drive to fail.
4	Drive status	Solid green	The drive is a member of one or more logical drives.
		Flashing green	The drive is rebuilding or performing a RAID migration, stripe size migration, capacity expansion, or logical drive extension, or is erasing.
		Flashing amber/green	The drive is a member of one or more logical drives and predicts the drive will fail.

LED number	LED name	Status	Definition
		Flashing amber	The drive is not configured and predicts the drive will fail.
		Solid amber	The drive has failed.
		Off	The drive is not configured by a RAID controller.

Summary

In this chapter you learned about a number of storage technologies, including DAS, NAS, and SAN. We looked at the advantages and disadvantages of each of these techniques. We also discussed various implementations of multiple storage devices such as JBOD. We explored the use of tape drives and tape libraries.

In the second half of the chapter, we talked about the specifications, such as RPMs, form factor, capacity, and bus width, you should consider when purchasing drives. Finally, we covered the most common interfaces you may encounter, such as SAS, SCSI, SATA, USB, and Fibre Channel.

Exam Essentials

Compare and contrast storage technologies.   Understand the difference between DAS, NAS, and SAN. Describe the advantages and disadvantages of each.

Describe some of the physical implementations of tape systems.   Explain tape drives and tape libraries and the role they play in backing up and restoring data.

Explain the limitations of JBOD.   Describe what JBOD means and what the fault tolerance limitations are when using such a setup of drives. Describe the advantages and disadvantages.

Understand the various specifications used to compare drives.   These include RPMs, IOPS, form factor, bus width, seek time, and latency.

Identity various drive interfaces.   Be able to differentiate SAS, SATA, SCSI, USB, and Fibre Channel interfaces and ports.

Review Questions

You can find the answers in the Appendix.

1. In which storage technology are all storages devices attached locally?
   - **A.** NAS
   - **B.** SAN
   - **C.** DAS
   - **D.** PAS

2. Which of the following is not an advantage of NAS?
   - **A.** A NAS has lower latency and higher reliability than a SAN.
   - **B.** A NAS typically supports multiple RAID methods.
   - **C.** A NAS supports high throughput.
   - **D.** Implementing a NAS is inexpensive.

3. In which of the following is the storage natively reachable through a TCP/IP network?
   - **A.** NAS
   - **B.** SAN
   - **C.** DAS
   - **D.** PAS

4. Which of the following is an advantage of a SAN?
   - **A.** Ethernet troubleshooting is well understood.
   - **B.** Implementing a SAN is inexpensive.
   - **C.** It's possible to leverage legacy investments.
   - **D.** Sharing is made easier by the fact that the SAN is not connected directly to any network or server.

5. Which of the following uses the Fibre Channel protocol?
   - **A.** NAS
   - **B.** SAN
   - **C.** DAS
   - **D.** PAS

6. Which of the following is used as identifiers for host bus adapters?
   - **A.** MAC addresses
   - **B.** World Wide Names

   C. IP addresses

   D. LUNs

7. Which of the following are divisions of storage created for performance and/or security reasons?

   A. Zones

   B. Domains

   C. Organizers

   D. Quadrants

8. Which of the following identifies a device addressed by the SCSI protocol or protocols that encapsulate SCSI?

   A. LUN

   B. Zone

   C. WWW

   D. Mask

9. Which of the following is an IP-based networking storage standard method of encapsulating SCSI commands?

   A. HBA

   B. iSCSI

   C. FCoE

   D. Fibre Channel

10. Which of the following is not an advantage of iSCSI?

   A. Inexpensive in simple deployments

   B. Eliminates distance limitations imposed by SCSI transfers

   C. Simple, due to its reliance on Ethernet, which is well known

   D. Impervious to network congestion

11. Which of the following describes FCoE?

   A. Encapsulates Fibre Channel traffic within Ethernet frames

   B. Encapsulates Fibre Channel traffic within IP frames

   C. Encapsulates SCSI traffic within Ethernet frames

   D. Encapsulates SCSI traffic within IP frames

12. Which of the following is defined as the use of multiple disks, which operate independently of one another?

   A. RAID 1

   B. RAID 5

    C. JBOD

    D. vRAID

13. What is the latest version of an LTO drive?

    A. 4

    B. 5

    C. 6

    D. 7

14. What is a storage device that contains multiple tape drives?

    A. JBOD

    B. Tape library

    C. Disk box

    D. Tape box

15. Which of the following is not a specification of an SSD?

    A. IOPS

    B. RPMs

    C. Seek time

    D. Form factor

16. Which of the following describes how fast the drive can read and write to the disk?

    A. IOPS

    B. RPMs

    C. Seek time

    D. Form factor

17. Which of the following is the time it takes for the actuator arm to arrive at the proper location where the read or write will occur?

    A. IOPS

    B. RPMs

    C. Seek time

    D. Form factor

18. Which of the following is the time it takes for the platter to spin the disk around so the actuator arm is over the proper section?

    A. IOPS

    B. RPMs

    C. Seek time

    D. Latency

19. Which of the following describes a drive that needs to be disconnected from the software in the server before begin changed out and then reconnected after the swap is done?

    A. Hot pluggable

    B. Warm pluggable

    C. Cold pluggable

    D. Hot swappable

20. Which of the following is a type of SCSI that uses serial operation rather than parallel as the original SCSI did?

    A. SATA

    B. SAS

    C. FCP

    D. UAS

Chapter
5

Identifying Capacity and Fault Tolerance Requirements

COMPTIA SERVER+ EXAM OBJECTIVES COVERED IN THIS CHAPTER:

✓ **3.4 Given a scenario, calculate appropriate storage capacity and plan for future growth**

- Base10 vs. Base2 disk size calculation (1000 vs. 1024)

- Disk quotas

- Compression

- Capacity planning considerations (operating system growth [patches, service packs, Log files], temporary directories, databases, application servers, file servers, archival)

✓ **3.2 Given a scenario, configure RAID using best practices**

- RAID levels and performance considerations (0, 1, 5, 6, 10)

- Software vs. hardware RAID (performance considerations)

- Configuration specifications (capacity, bus types, drive RPM)

- Hotswap support and ramifications

- Hot spare vs. cold spare

- Array controller (memory, battery-backed cache, redundant controller)

When designing and deploying a server solution, you need to know some basic information to guide the implementation of the storage system. Naturally one of the drivers will be the amount of storage you need or the capacity of the storage solution. As you will learn in this chapter, this includes what you need now and what additional needs you anticipate in the future.

Perhaps even more important than capacity, however, is the ability to restore data that has been intentionally or unintentionally deleted or lost through hardware failures. Frequent backups are a part of the fault tolerance solution, but in some cases the time it takes to locate the proper tape and perform the restore operation is more than can be tolerated. In that scenario you may want to implement a solution that allows the system to maintain access to the data even with the loss of a drive. In this chapter, we'll look at both capacity considerations and fault tolerance technologies.

Calculating Appropriate Storage Capacity and Planning for Future Growth

Planning for the capacity requirements of a server can be challenging. You must take into account the current needs and those that may occur in the future. Predicting the future is not easy, even when you have data from the past to use as a benchmark. Often you have to factor in somewhat vague assessments of future needs from department managers who may or not be able to do this accurately. At any rate, an attempt must be made to plan for now and the future. In this section, we'll look at terms used to discuss capacity, some factors that impact the amount of space you need, and scenarios that may require more space.

Base 10 vs. Base 2 Disk Size Calculation

The question is one that has been asked many times: "Why does the advertised capacity of my drive not equal what I see in Windows?" The answer lies in the way the capacity is calculated. When there is a mismatch of this type, you typically have the vendor using one method and Windows using another.

There are two ways to calculate the space. Vendors typically count using the Base 10 number system, whereas Windows does so using the Base 2 number system. Let's look at how using these two systems can arrive at different answers.

1000 vs. 1024

One gigabyte as defined by a manufacturer is 1,000,000,000,000 bytes. In metric base 10, we define *kilo-* as 1000, *mega-* as 1,000,000, and *giga-* as 1,000,000,000,000.

Windows, however, calculates the disk size in a Base 2 system. In Base 2

2^{10} is 1024 bytes, which is 1 kilobyte

2^{20} is 1048576 bytes, or 1 megabyte

2^{30} is 1073741824 bytes, or 1 gigabyte

When the hard disk manufacturer advertises a 120-gigabyte hard drive, they are selling you 120,000,000,000 bytes. Windows divides this number by what it considers a GB (1073741824) and reports the hard disk size as

120000000000 (bytes) / 1073741824 (bytes per GB) = 111.8 GB

So just be aware of this and ensure that when comparing drive capacities you are comparing apples to apples.

Disk Quotas

One of the ways you make capacity planning easier when dealing with a server where users will be storing their data is to implement disk quotas. These are limits assigned to each user. These limits can be implemented with a warning to users when they are filling their allotted space, so they can delete some data or take some action that keeps them within their limits. This is implemented in Windows Server 2012 R2 at the disk properties, as shown in Figure 5.1. In the figure all users are being given 1 GB of space and will be warned when they get to 50 MB.

FIGURE 5.1   Disk quotas

Users that may require a different setting would need to be configured using the Quota entries button.

The reason this helps with capacity planning is that if you know how much space each user is given, it becomes simple math to determine what you need based on the number of current and prospective users. You should keep in mind that quotas ignore compression and calculate use based on the *uncompressed* space taken.

Compression

Another tactic you can use to better utilize the space you have is to compress files that are used infrequently. This can be done in Windows at both the file and the folder level. In the advanced attributes of the file or folder properties, "Compress contents to save disk space," as shown in Figure 5.2.

FIGURE 5.2   Disk compression

Be aware that when you do this to files and folders that are frequently accessed, you will placing a load on the CPU of the server because it decompresses the file to make it available and then compresses it again when saved. For that reason, use this tool with caution.

Capacity Planning Considerations

As you have already learned, capacity planning needs to consider current needs and future needs. A number of things go into making that educated guess about the future. In this section, we'll look at issues that impact the amount of space a healthy server requires.

Operating System Growth

Although the number and size of the basic operating system files don't change, the fact is that as you install different sorts of updates, the operating system does in fact take up more space. It also gobbles up space over time monitoring and reporting on the operation of the system. These logs are useful but they take up space. Let's look at three ways in which the operating system can grow over time.

Patches

Patches are the security- or performance-related additions to the operating system code that are issued between service packs. When you add patches, the system may also make a backup or snapshot of the system for rollback purposes. If it doesn't delete these, that's a double whammy on your space.

Service Packs

In the past, all service packs used to be cumulative—meaning you needed to load only the last one. Starting with XP SP3, however, all Windows service packs released, including those for servers, have been incremental, meaning that you must install the previous ones before you can install the new one. Of course, this will never be a consideration if you maintain all of your updates. However, if you are bringing a new server up to date on service packs and patches, you need to know this.

One of the things that you can do in Windows to mitigate the amount of space used by constant updates is to manage a folder called the *component store*. This folder, called windows\winsxs, contains all the files that are required for a Windows installation. Any updates to those files are also held within the component store as the updates are installed. This means that over time this directory can get huge.

To reduce the size of the component store directory on a Windows installation, you can elect to install a service pack permanently and reclaim used space from the service pack files. You can also use Disk Cleanup on the directory. Doing either of these actions will make the service pack installation permanent, and not removable.

For complete information on several ways to clean up the component store and/or control the growth of its size, see

https://technet.microsoft.com/en-us/library/dn251565.aspx.

Log Files

Servers also create useful logs that you may or may not be using. Even if you are using the logs (and you should!), you shouldn't allow them to slowly eat up all the space. You can control the behavior of log files in Windows in several ways:

- You can limit the amount of space used for each log.
- You can determine the behavior when the log is full.
- You can choose to save a log for later viewing.

To set the maximum size for a log file, access the properties of the log in Event Viewer. In the Maximum Log Size option, use the spinner control to set the value you want and click OK, as shown in Figure 5.3.

FIGURE 5.3   Event Log properties

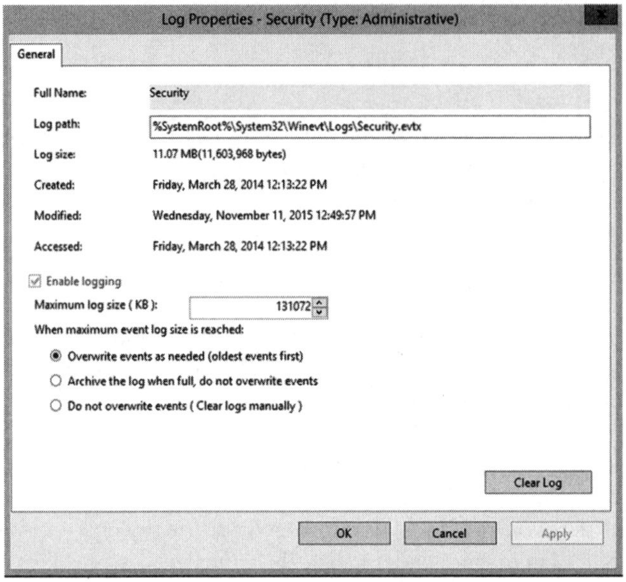

You can also use the command line using the following command, inserting the name of log file and the maximum size in bytes:

```
wevtutil sl <LogName> /ms:<MaxSizeInBytes>
```

To determine what happens when the log is full, access the same dialog box shown in Figure 5.3 and select one of the three options:

- Overwrite Events As Needed (Oldest Events First)
- Archive The Log When Full, Do Not Overwrite Events
- Do Not Overwrite Events (Clear Logs Manually)

This can also be done at the command line using the following command:

```
wevtutil sl <LogName> /r:{true | false} /ab:{true | false}
```

The r parameter specifies whether you want to retain the log, and the ab parameter specifies whether to automatically back up the log.

Use the following combinations to achieve the desired result:

- Overwrite Events As Needed (Oldest Events First): r = false, ab = false
- Archive The Log When Full, Do Not Overwrite Events: r = true, ab = true
- Do Not Overwrite Events (Clear Logs Manually): r = true, ab = false

Temporary Directories

Temporary directories are created in many instances by the services and applications on the server. These files can cause program issues in some cases, so cleaning these directories up is not just a space issue. It is always safe to delete these directories—any that are required will be built again.

Manually performing a disk cleanup will allow you to get rid of these files (and many other useless files as well), but if you would like to create a batch file, you can automate the process. The following batch file will do the trick.

```
rd /s /q %temp%
md %temp%
rd /s /q %systemroot%\temp
md %systemroot%\temp
```

Keep in mind that if this process encounters any files in use, the entire operation will be aborted. Therefore, schedule this batch file to run when no applications are running (perhaps as a logon script). Also keep in mind that you should not use this approach if you are installing applications that require a reboot. Many software installers use Windows temporary directories to hold the installer's files while the process completes. If those files are deleted, the installer won't be able to complete or may crash outright.

Databases

When servers contain databases, you must also manage the database and its size. Although database management is beyond the scope of this book, you should understand the importance of attempting to predict the growth of the database over time to plan for adding storage as needed. One of a database administrator's worst nightmare is an out-of-space error. You must account for not just the data but also the log files that are created as a natural process of the database operating. For help in estimating required space for data and logs, consult the vendor.

Application Servers

As you learned in Chapter 3, "Server Maintenance," in the section on server roles, application servers place more of a workload on the NIC and processor than the disk. However, each type of application interacts in a different way with the hard drive. Some use space temporarily (and may not delete that temporary file), whereas others do not. For that reason, we can't make a definitive statement about that here, but you will find guidance from the vendor of the application when it comes to allowing enough space for proper functioning and good performance. Thus planning should precede the installation of the application and would be best done in the initial planning of the server.

File Servers

File servers exist to provide storage space for users. The amount of space you need will be determined by answering the following questions:

- How many users will store data on the server?
- What is the average amount of space each will use?
- What is the growth rate for the number of users and the amount of space used?
- Where is your organization in the hardware upgrade life cycle—will you have additional space coming online?

Here is an area where the use of disk quotas, as discussed in the section "Disk Quotas" earlier in this chapter, can be a help in planning. See that section for more details.

Archives

An archive is a collection of files from a server packaged together and saved to another location to free up space on the server. There will be some information that resides on the server that you do not want to throw away. But you don't use it frequently enough to justify its use of space—yet you want to have it for reference later or you are legally obligated to keep it. This information (event logs and so on) can be saved, as described in the earlier section "Log Files."

Many organizations have taken a more proactive approach to managing data throughout its life cycle by implementing hierarchical storage systems. These are automated systems that move data from one type of storage to another as it ages. This places the most recent and most important data on the most expensive and fastest form of storage while moving data to cheaper storage as it ages. This concept is illustrated in Figure 5.4.

FIGURE 5.4   Hierarchical storage systems

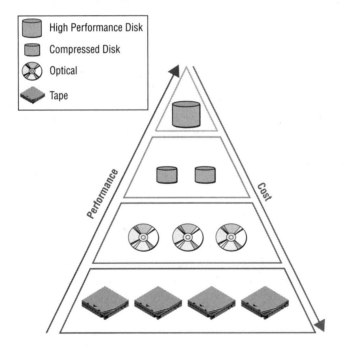

Configuring RAID

In some cases you may want to maintain access to data even when there is a single drive failure (although this is not a replacement for making frequent backups). You can do so by deploying a version of RAID. As you learned in Chapter 2, "Installing and Configuring

Servers," RAID stands for Redundant Array of Independent Disks. It's a way of combining the storage power of more than one hard disk for a special purpose such as increased performance or fault tolerance. RAID is more commonly done with SAS drives, but it can be done with IDE or SATA drives.

RAID Levels and Performance Considerations

Not all versions of RAID provide fault tolerance, and they have varying impacts on performance. Let's look at each type.

RAID 0

RAID 0 is also known as *disk striping*. For details on RAID 0, see Chapter 2. RAID 0 is illustrated in Figure 5.5.

FIGURE 5.5 RAID 0

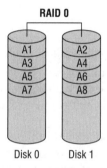

RAID 1

RAID 1 is also known as *disk mirroring*. For details on RAID 1, see Chapter 2. RAID 1 is illustrated in Figure 5.6.

FIGURE 5.6 RAID 1

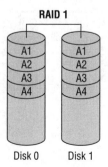

RAID 5

RAID 5 combines the benefits of both RAID 0 and RAID 1 and is also known as *striping with parity*. For details on RAID 5, see Chapter 2. RAID 5 is illustrated in Figure 5.7.

FIGURE 5.7 RAID 5

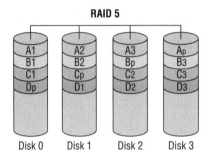

RAID 6

RAID 6 writes parity information across the drives as is done in RAID 5, but it writes two stripes, which allows the system to recover from two drive failures whereas RAID 5 cannot. As each set of parities must be calculated separately, performance is slowed during writing to the drive. The cost is higher due to the two drives dedicated to parity information.

RAID 6 uses $2/n$ (n = the number of drives in the array) for parity information (for example, two thirds of the space in a three-drive array), and only $1 - (2/n)$ is available for data. So if three 250-GB drives are used in the array (for a total of 750 GB), 250 GB will be the available drive space. In Figure 5.8 you can see the parity blocks are indicated with a small letter next to each and that they are in pairs. RAID 6 is illustrated in Figure 5.8.

FIGURE 5.8 RAID 6

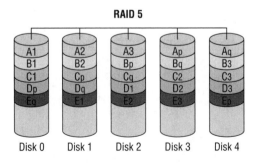

RAID 10

RAID 10 is also known as RAID 1+0. Striped sets are mirrored (a minimum of four drives, and the number of drives must be even). It provides fault tolerance and improved performance but increases complexity. Since this is effectively a mirrored stripe set and a stripe set gets 100 percent use of the drive without mirroring, this array will provide half of the total drive space in the array as available drive space. For example, if there are four 250 GB drives in a RAID 10 array (for a total of 1,000 GB), the available drive space will be 500 GB. RAID 10 is illustrated in Figure 5.9.

FIGURE 5.9   RAID 10

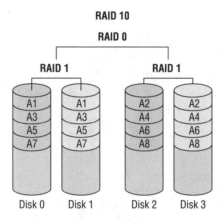

Software vs. Hardware RAID

RAID can be implemented using disk software that comes with an operating system such as Microsoft Windows Server 2012 R2, but it can also be implemented using hardware, in which case it will be managed, not in the operating system but using a RAID utility built into the drive controller. When using hardware RAID, the disk array is presented to the operating system as a single disk. This has an impact both on performance and on the types of RAID that are available to you in certain situations. Let's look at these issues.

Performance Considerations

The advantages of using software RAID are

- Lower cost
- The ability to implement disk duplexing

Disk Duplexing

Disk duplexing is the use of separate controller cards for each disk when implementing disk mirroring (RAID 1), thus providing fault tolerance at both the disk level and at the disk controller level, protecting against both a single disk failure and a single controller card failure. This concept is illustrated in the following graphic, where a mirrored disk without duplexing is compared to one with duplexing.

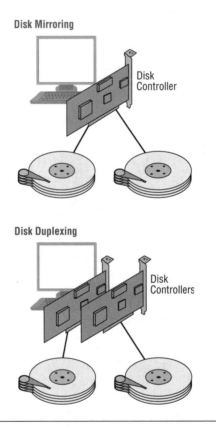

The advantages of using hardware RAID are

- Faster, more reliable performance than software RAID
- Support for online spares
- Support for RAID 10
- Decreased processor load

- User-friendly configuration utilities
- No operating system interface required when starting a rebuild

If you look at the comparison of the operation of software and hardware RAID shown in Figure 5.10, you can see how much less the operating system is involved in reading and writing both data and parity information with hardware RAID.

FIGURE 5.10   Hardware and software RAID

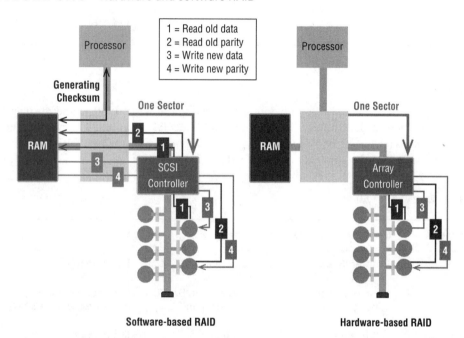

Configuration Specifications

When configuring RAID, you will need to consider a number of issues surrounding the drives you select for the array. Most of these issues we have touched on already, but just to be complete and cover all these issues in one place, let's examine them again.

Capacity

Always keep in mind the cost in capacity of implementing each type of RAID. While there are plenty of RAID capacity calculators available on the Internet (you can access one at www.raid-calculator.com), Table 5.1 indicates the capacity yielded by each method when using various numbers of 500-GB disks. RAID 0 is not listed as it provides no fault tolerance and thus costs nothing in capacity.

TABLE 5.1   RAID capacities

Type	# of 500-GB Disks	Usable space
RAID 1	4	1000 GB
RAID 5	4	750 GB
RAID 6	4	1000 GB
RAID 10	4	1000 GB

Bus Types

The bus type of the array will have a big impact on the speed of the solution and the length of the cables involved. The three main choices are SATA, SCSI, and fiber. The types cannot be mixed in the same array. As you would expect, the options with the best performance cost the most. Table 5.2 compares the three methods in several ways.

TABLE 5.2   Bus types

Bus type	Maximum cable length	Speed	Cost
SATA	1 meter (3 feet)	Slowest	Least costly
SCSI	12 or 25 meters, depending on version	Faster than SATA, slower than FC	Less costly than FC, more costly than SATA
Fiber channel	10K in single mode	Fastest	Most costly

Drive RPM

Although it is possible to mix drives with different RPMs in the same pool, it is not recommended. As a matter of fact, mixing any of the following drive specifications in the same array will result in the entire array using the least capable specification (also called "dumbing down" the array):

- Slowest speed (performance)
- Smallest size; for example, 750 GB + 1 TB (250 GB of the 1 TB is lost)
- Smallest buffer

Hot-Swap Support and Ramifications

Another consideration when choosing a RAID type is hot-swap support. If you need to be able to swap out a bad drive without shutting down the server, then you require a solution that supports hot swapping. Keep in mind, however, that while you need not shut down the server, in some instances you still may need to logically disconnect the server from the bad disk and then reattach it logically when it has been replaced.

You should also know that if you are using SATA disks, hot swapping is inherently supported due to the pin layout. In any case, hot swapping must be supported by the controller and any drive enclosures or backplanes that are in use. It also must be a hardware RAID implementation and the operating system must support it (although most server operating systems do).

Hot Spare vs. Cold Spare

While hot swapping is convenient, even more convenient are hot spares. These are disks attached to the array that are not in use but are available to take the place of a bad disk automatically. A cold spare, on the other hand, is one that is attached to the system and available but cannot replace the bad disk without administrator intervention and in some cases a reboot.

Array Controller

The heart of a hardware array is the array controller. When choosing the controller you should be concerned with three issues. Let's talk about these three issues.

Memory

RAID cards will come with memory right on the card. This memory is used to cache information, and the more you buy, the faster the performance of the array. For example, a card with 512 MB onboard would be a better choice than one with 256 MB onboard. This memory can be configured into two caches: a read cache and a write cache. A common ratio used for the two is 75:25 write:read.

Battery-Backed Cache

Another interesting aspect of the cache that comes on a RAID controller is that it is typically supported by a battery, so that if there is a loss of power, there is not a loss of the information that may be residing in the cache. This can also include changes to data that have not yet been written to the disk as well. A RAID card is shown in Figure 5.11. The battery pack is shown connected to the back of the card.

FIGURE 5.11   Battery-backed cache

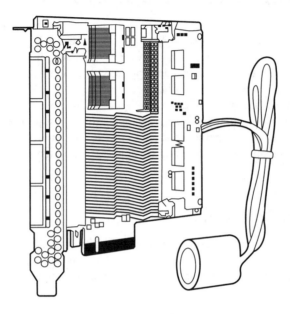

Redundant Controller

To take the redundancy provided by RAID a step further, you can implement multiple RAID controllers so that you have fault tolerance not only at the disk level but at the controller level as well. An example of a single piece RAID controller that provides redundancy is shown in Figure 5.12.

FIGURE 5.12   Redundant RIAD controller

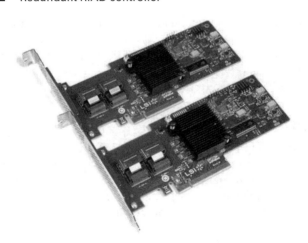

Summary

In this chapter you learned about topics related to planning for storage, implementing storage, and providing fault tolerance for the data residing within. This included a discussion of disk size calculation methods and options available to minimize the use of disk space such as disk quotas and compression.

You also learned about using RAID for fault tolerance and performance. This included looking at RAID 0, 1, 5, 6, and 10 and talking about the difference between software and hardware RAID. We also discussed types of hot-swappable components and some of the specifications you should be mindful of when purchasing drives. Finally, we differentiated between hot and cold spares and discussed the characteristics of array controllers.

Exam Essentials

Discuss disk size calculation techniques.   Understand the difference between using Base 10 and Base 2 numbering when calculating disk size.

Describe methods used to minimize disk usage.   Explain methods such as disk quotas, which allow you to control disk usage, a compression, which can save space on the drive as well.

Explain operating system growth issues.   Describe the types of operating system growth that need to be taken into consideration when planning for capacity. This includes the addition of patches and service packs, and the growth of log files and temporary directories.

Understand every type of RAID.   Detail the performance and fault tolerance characteristics of RAID 0, 1, 5, 6, and 10 and describe when each is indicated.

Review Questions

You can find the answers in the Appendix.

1. If a hard drive has 120 GB as calculated using the Base 10 number system, what will be the capacity reported by Windows?

   A. 120 GB

   B. 110 GB

   C. 111.8 GB

   D. 122.5 GB

2. Which of the following is the best candidate for compression in the server?

   A. A folder accessed on average once a month

   B. A folder accessed on average once a day

   C. A folder accessed on average three times a day

   D. A folder accessed on average once a year

3. Which of the following folders is the component store directory?

   A. `C:\windows`

   B. `C:\windows/winsxs`

   C. `C:\winsxs`

   D. `C:\winnt/winsxs`

4. Which command-line utility can be used to manage the size of log files?

   A. `winsxs`

   B. `wevtutil`

   C. `nlookup`

   D. `logutil`

5. Which of the following actions can empty temporary directories?

   A. Running `wevutil`

   B. Running Disk Cleanup

   C. Running `defrag`

   D. Running Disk Check

6. Which of the following provides *no* fault tolerance?

   A. RAID 0

   B. RAID 1

   C. RAID 5

   D. RAID 6

7. Which of the following is also called disk mirroring?

   A. RAID 0

   B. RAID 1

   C. RAID 5

   D. RAID 6

8. If three 250 MB disks are present in a RAID 5 array, how much space is actually usable for data?

   A. 125 MB

   B. 200 MB

   C. 250 MB

   D. 500 MB

9. What is the minimum number of disk required for RAID 5?

   A. 2

   B. 3

   C. 4

   D. 5

10. RAID 6 writes parity information across the drives as is done in RAID 5, but it writes two stripes. What is the effect of writing two stripes?

   A. Speeds performance

   B. Allows the cable to be longer

   C. Hurts performance

   D. Allows you to use only two drives

11. Which of the following is an advantage of software RAID over hardware RAID?

   A. Better performance

   B. Lower cost

   C. Better security

   D. Faster recovery

12. Which of the following is *not* an advantage of hardware RAID over software RAID?

   A. Decreased processor load

   B. Ability to do disk duplexing

    C. Support for online spares

    D. Faster performance

13. You have four 500 GB disks in a RAID 10 array. How much space is available for data?

    A. 500 GB

    B. 750 GB

    C. 1000 GB

    D. 2500 GB

14. When separate controller cards are used for each disk, what is it called?

    A. Disk jukebox

    B. JBOD

    C. Disk duplexing

    D. Disk triplexing

15. Which of the following allows a cable to be a maximum of 1 meter in length?

    A. SATA

    B. SCSI

    C. Fibre Channel

    D. iSCSI

16. Which of the following is the most costly to implement?

    A. SATA

    B. SCSI

    C. Fibre Channel

    D. iSCSI

17. Which of the following RPMs will provide the fastest access speed when discussing hard disk drives?

    A. 4800

    B. 5400

    C. 7200

    D. 10000

18. You have three drives that have capacities of 500 MB, 750 MB, and 1000 MB. Setting the cost of parity information aside, what is the total capacity of the array?

    A. 1500 MB

    B. 2250 MB

    C. 3000 MB

    D. 3500 MB

19. Which of the following technologies supports hot swapping inherently?

    A. SAS

    B. SATA

    C. SCSI

    D. Fibre Channel

20. Which of the following is attached to the system but cannot replace a bad disk without manual intervention?

    A. Hot swap

    B. Hot spare

    C. Cold spare

    D. Standby

Chapter

6

Securing the Server

COMPTIA SERVER+ EXAM OBJECTIVES COVERED IN THIS CHAPTER:

✓ **4.1 Compare and contrast physical security methods and concepts**

- Multifactor authentication (something you have, something you know, something you are)

- Security concepts (mantrap, RFID chip, ID card, biometric, keypad, access list, security guard, security camera, keys and locks [cabinet, rack mount, server], safe)

✓ **4.2 Given a scenario, apply server hardening techniques**

- OS hardening (stopping unneeded services/closing unneeded ports, install only required software, install latest operating system patches)

- Application hardening (install latest patches, disabling unneeded services/roles/features)

- Endpoint security (HIDS, anti-malware)

- Remediate security issues based on a vulnerability scan

- Hardware hardening (disabling unneeded hardware and physical ports/devices, BIOS password, disable WOL [Wake on LAN], set up boot order, chassis locks/intrusion detection)

✓ **4.6 Given a scenario, implement proper environmental controls and techniques**

- Power concepts and best practices (UPS [runtime vs. capacity, automated graceful shutdown of attached devices, periodic testing of batteries, maximum load, bypass procedures, remote management], PDU [connect redundant rack PDUs to separate circuits], capacity planning [PDU ratings, UPS ratings, total potential power draw], multiple circuits [connect redundant power supplies to separate PDUs])

- Safety (ESD procedures, fire suppression, proper lifting techniques, rack stability, floor load limitations, sharp edges and pinch points)

- HVAC (room and rack temperature and humidity [monitoring and alert notifications], air flow [rack filler/baffle/blanking panels], hot aisle and cold aisle)

Once you've deployed your server and verified that it is functioning, you also maintain the server and ensure that the server is secured from attacks from insiders as well as outsiders. Securing the server means that it is capable of providing the three tenets of security: confidentiality, integrity, and availability (CIA). Confidentiality means that the data is accessible only to those who have that right, integrity means that its data has not been altered or corrupted, and availability means that the server is always there as a resource. To provide those three tenets the server must not only be secured but maintained so that it is not overloaded or down for service.

Physical Security Methods and Concepts

Although there are many logical security methods that can be used to protect the data on a server, if users can attain physical access to the server, the options available to them to compromise the server increase dramatically. For this reason, servers and other infrastructure equipment should be locked away. In this section, we'll look at not only the physical methods used to achieve this but also authentication concepts that relate to gaining physical access.

Multifactor Authentication

As attaining access to a server room should be a right held only by a few, the method used to authenticate those attempting to enter the server room should be robust. Names and passwords are simple to create, manage, and use, but you can increase the security of the authentication solution by implementing *multifactor* authentication.

There are three factors of authentication. When more than one of these factors is required to authenticate, it is called multifactor authentication. It is *not* multifactor if it uses two forms of the same factor of authentication. Let's look at three forms and examples of each.

Something You Have

When the system requires something you have, it means that something in your possession, like a smart card, must be inserted into a reader that will verify that the security credentials on the card are correct and that they correspond to the other factor that you presented.

Something You Know

When the system requires something you know, it means that something that resides in your memory is required such as a password, a username, or a PIN.

Something You Are

When the system requires something you are, it will examine some unique physical feature such as a fingerprint or retina scan. This is called *biometrics*. Although the use of biometrics offers a high level of security, you should know that they are expensive to implement and can be prone to false positives (letting a user in that should not be in) and false negatives (denying a legitimate user).

Remember, when more than one of these factors is required to authenticate it is called multifactor authentication. It is *not* multifactor if it uses two forms of the same factor of authentication such as a username and password (both something you know).

Security Concepts

There are many ways to provide physical security. Let's explore the terms used to discuss physical security and the mechanisms available to achieve it.

Mantrap

A *mantrap* is a series of two doors with a small room between them. The user is authenticated at the first door and then allowed into the room. At that point additional verification will occur (such as a guard visually identifying the person) and then the user is allowed through the second door. These doors are typically used only in very high security situations. Mantraps also typically require that the first door is closed, prior to enabling the second door to open. A mantrap design is shown in Figure 6.1.

FIGURE 6.1   Mantrap

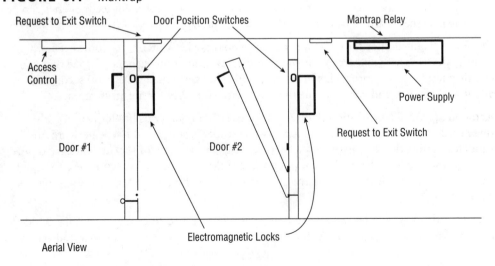

RFID Chip

An increasingly popular method of tracking physical assets is to tag them with radio frequency identification (RFID) chips. This allows for tracking the location of the asset at any time. This technology uses either bar codes or magnetic strips to embed information that can read wirelessly from some distance. The main components of this are

RFID Reader   This device has an antenna and an interface to a computer.

Transponder   This is the tag on the device that transmits its presence wirelessly.

The reader receives instructions from the human using the software on the computer that is attached to the reader. This causes the reader to transmit signals that wake up or energize the transponder on the device. The device then responds wirelessly, thus allowing the reader to determine the location of the device and display that location to the user on the computer.

The tags can be one of two types: passive and active. Active tags have batteries whereas passive tags receive their energy from the reader when the reader interrogates the device. As you would expect, the passive tags are cheaper but have a range of only a few meters whereas the active tags are more expensive but can transmit up to 100 meters.

The drawbacks of this technology are that the tag signal can be read by any reader in range, multiple readers in an area can interfere with one another, and multiple devices can interfere with one another when responding.

Finally, given the distance limitations, once the stolen item is a certain distance away, you lose the ability to track it, so this technology should only be a part of a larger program that includes strong physical security. As you will see in the next section, asset tracking is not the only use of RFID tags.

ID Card

All users should possess and wear identification cards, but it becomes even more important when those users have access to the server room. A number of different technologies can be used to make these cards part of the authentication process:

Key Fobs   Named after the chains that used to hold pocket watches to clothes. They are security devices that you carry with you that display a randomly generated code that you can then use for authentication. This code usually changes quickly (every 60 seconds is about the average), and you combine this code with your PIN for authentication.

Radio Frequency Identification (RFID)   A wireless, no-contact technology used with these cards and their accompanying reader. The reader is connected to the network and validates against the security system. This increases the security of the authentication process because you must be in physical possession of the smart card to use the resources. Of course, if the card is lost or stolen, the person who finds the card can access the resources it allows.

Smart Card   A type of badge or card that gives you access to resources, including buildings, parking lots, and computers. It contains information about your identity and access privileges. Each area or computer has a card scanner or a reader in which you insert your card. Smart cards are difficult to counterfeit, but they're easy to steal. Once a thief has a smart card, that person has all the access the card allows. To prevent this, many organizations don't put any identifying marks on their smart cards, making it harder for someone to utilize them. Many modern smart cards require a password or PIN to activate the card, and they employ encryption to protect the card's contents.

Physical Tokens   Anything, including key fobs, that users must have on them to access network resources. They are often associated with devices that enable users to generate a one-time password authenticating their identity. SecurID, from RSA, is one of the best-known examples of a physical token; learn more at `www.rsa.com/node.aspx?id=1156`.

Biometric

For high-security scenarios that warrant the additional cost and administrative effort involved, biometrics is a viable option. Biometric devices use physical characteristics to identify the user. Such devices are becoming more common in the business environment. Biometric systems include hand scanners, retinal scanners, and soon, possibly, DNA scanners. To gain access to resources, you must pass a physical screening process. In the case of a hand scanner, this may include identifying fingerprints, scars, and markings on your hand. Retinal scanners compare your eye's retinal pattern, which are as unique as fingerprints, to a stored retinal pattern to verify your identity. DNA scanners will examine a unique portion of your DNA structure to verify that you are who you say you are.

With the passing of time, the definition of *biometric* is expanding from simply identifying physical attributes about a person to being able to describe patterns in their behavior. Recent advances have been made in the ability to authenticate someone based on the key pattern they use when entering their password (how long they pause between each key, the amount of time each key is held down, and so forth). A company adopting biometric technologies needs to consider the controversy they may face (some authentication methods are considered more intrusive than others). It also needs to consider the error rate and that errors can include both false positives and false negatives.

Keypad

An older technology that is still enjoying widespread use are door keypads, where the user enters a code into the keypad that identifies her, authenticates her, and if allowed, opens the door for her. In many cases these device can also be configured with an emergency code that can be used when a personal code doesn't work and an alarm code that opens the door but alerts police or other authorities that a hostage scenario is underway.

Access List

An *access list* can be either a digital list of allowed users that resides on an authentication system or a physical entry roster monitored by a security guard at an entry point.

At any physical location where users are arriving and departing the facility or the server room, users should be authenticated through one of the mechanisms discussed in this section. There should be a recording of each user arriving and departing. This can be either a record of all successful and unsuccessful authentications on a log or, in the case of visitors who have no network account, a physical identification process of some sort. In any case, there should be an entry control roster in the form of a physical document that shows when each person entered and left the facility. This will serve as a backup in case the log is lost.

Security Guard

Security guards offer the most flexibility in reacting to whatever occurs. Guards can use discriminating judgment based on the situation, which automated systems cannot do. This makes them an excellent addition to the layers of security you should be trying to create. One of the keys to success is adequate training of the guards so they are prepared for any eventuality. There should be a prepared response for any possible occurrence.

Security Camera

If you use security guards, you can make them more effective by implementing closed-circuit television (CCTV) systems. These are cameras that can be monitored in real time, allowing guards to monitor larger areas at once from a central location. Even in the absence of guards, these systems can record days of activity that can be viewed as needed at a later time.

Keys and Locks

One of the easiest ways to prevent people intent on creating problems from physically entering your environment is to lock your doors and keep them out. A key aspect of access control involves physical barriers. The objective of a physical barrier is to prevent access to computers and network systems. The most effective physical barrier implementations require that more than one physical barrier be crossed to gain access. This type of approach is called a multiple-barrier system. This means a lock to protect the facility, another to protect the server room, and another to open the rack. Let's look at some of these points where locks should be present.

Cabinet

Any cabinets that are used to hold spare equipment or tools should be locked and all keys should be accounted for. Any cabinets that enclose racks of servers should be locked as well. This includes all types of equipment enclosures. Some of these locks can be integrated into your access control system, and some also alert you when a cabinet door is opened. An example of one of these locks is shown in Figure 6.2.

FIGURE 6.2   Cabinet lock with alarm

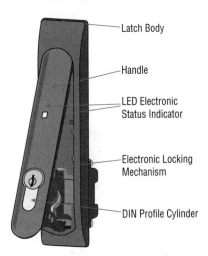

- Latch Body
- Handle
- LED Electronic Status Indicator
- Electronic Locking Mechanism
- DIN Profile Cylinder

Rack Mount

Rack-mounted servers may come with locks that prevent removing the server from the rack without opening the lock. Whereas many of these locks are on cabinets that enclose the servers as discussed in the previous section, others are a part of the server case itself such as the one shown in Figure 6.3.

FIGURE 6.3   Rack mount lock

Server

There may also be servers you need to physically secure from tampering that are not located in racks or lockable server cabinets. Perhaps you still have some tower servers you are using. These servers can be secured using a lockable rack such as the one you see in

Figure 6.4. This connects to a cable that you secure to an immovable object as you would secure a laptop.

FIGURE 6.4   Tower server lock

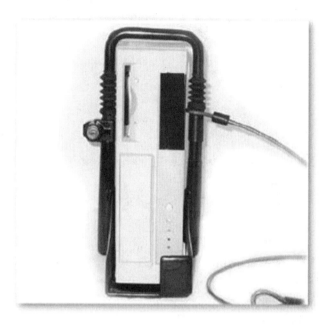

You also can secure a tower in a lockable cabinet made for just such a situation as shown in Figure 6.5. Usually these come with a ventilation system to keep the server cool.

FIGURE 6.5   Tower cabinet

Safe

You also have items that need to be secured that are not servers. Installation CDs and DVDs, network diagrams, disaster recovery plans, and backup tapes are all examples of these items. When considering a safe, you should focus on two items, the ease with which the safe can be compromised, and the ability of the safe to withstand a fire.

In the United States, United Laboratories (UL) assigns ratings to safes that you can use to assess the suitability of the safe. These ratings typically assign a recommended maximum dollar figure for which any item that you wish to protect with the safe should not exceed. Use these values to guide your choice.

With respect to fire, first understand that no safe is fireproof. Many are fire resistant and will protect a document from being destroyed, which occurs at a much higher temperature than many of the other items (such as backup tapes and CDs) can tolerate without damage. For this reason, items such as backup tapes should be stored offsite.

Server Hardening Techniques

Hardening the server involves reducing the available options a hacker or attacker might have to compromise the system. It involves hardening the system logically—that is, hardening the operating system and applications—and hardening the server physically by ensuring the device cannot be tampered with by someone who can touch the server. Both concepts are covered in this section.

OS Hardening

Hardening the server should start with hardening the operating system. This involves a series of steps that should result in a server that offers a minimum of attack points to a hacker. Let's look at six steps that can lead to this result.

Stopping Unneeded Services/Closing Unneeded Ports

Any services that are not required on the server should be disabled. Only those required for the server to perform its role in the network should be left on. The easiest way to do this is to install a host firewall on the system and adopt a "disable by default" policy with respect to services. Then manually enable any you need.

If you need to disable services, see the exercises "Disabling a Service in Windows Server 2012 R2" and "Disabling a Service in Linux" in Chapter 2, "Installing and Configuring Servers."

Installing Only Required Software

It also hardens the system to remove any software the server does not require. Often server operating systems come with certain applications already installed, although this habit has been somewhat discredited in the industry and many vendors are moving away from the practice. You should examine all installed applications and retain only those you need. Not only does unnecessary software eat resources, it can create security loopholes in some cases.

Installing Latest Operating System Patches

It almost feels silly at this point in the discussion to have to say this, but I'll say it anyway: Always keep the server updated with all operating system patches and service packs. Arrive at some process or procedure that automates the process such as using a Windows Server Update Services server or at the very least, set the server to check for and download updates. It's not a great idea to install them automatically because you want to test them first and make sure they don't break something on the server.

Implementing Application Hardening

Application hardening follows the same conceptual process as operating system hardening. Applications can have many features and embedded programs that you may not make use of. Determine which of these you require and, in cases where it is possible, disable all other features. If you have any applications your enterprise has developed, ensure the applications have been developed with security in mind and follow secure coding principles when creating these applications.

Installing Latest Patches

Don't forget about the applications that may be running on the server. Applications can also be attacked by hackers. That's why software vendors are also periodically issuing security updates. As security issues are reported, they respond by fixing the software. For Windows applications, these updates can accompany the operating system updates if you choose to enable them.

Other applications may be more of a challenge, but it's hard to find vendors today that don't either automatically send and install the updates or, at the very least, notify you that one is available.

Disabling Unneeded Services/Roles/Features

Server operating systems come with a lot of features, utilities, tools, and roles. In all probability you won't need many of these, even when the server is performing more than one role in the network. In the old days, Windows servers came with many of these roles running. Today, thankfully, that is no longer the case and you can simply refrain from enabling or installing the role or feature rather than uninstalling it.

In Linux and Unix, most versions don't install anything to the kernel. You are required to enable or install these features or services. This makes it easier to restrict the running features to those you desire and trust.

Endpoint Security

When discussing network security, an endpoint is any point of entry into the network. A typical example of an endpoint is a laptop connected to the network with a remote access connection. Therefore, the process of providing endpoint security is the process of ensuring that every endpoint (including servers) has been secured in the same way in which you would secure the network gateway. It is based on the assumption that any device that is connected to the network—either permanently, as a server typically is, or temporarily, as when a remote access connection is made—is a potential entryway if the device is compromised. There are two main issues to consider when providing endpoint security: identifying intrusions when they occur and preventing the spread of malware. Let's look at both of these issues.

HIDS

An IDS (intrusion detection system) is a system responsible for detecting unauthorized access or attacks. The most common way to classify an IDS is based on its information source: network based and host based. A host-based intrusion detection system (HIDS) is installed on the device (for the purpose of our discussion, a server) and the system focuses solely on identifying attacks on that device only. This is in contrast to a network-based system, which monitors all traffic that goes through it looking for signs of attack on any machine in the network.

These systems can use several methods of detecting intrusions. The two main methods are

Signature Based   Analyzes traffic and compares patterns, called *signatures*, that reside within the IDS database. This means it requires constant updating of the signature database.

Anomaly Based   Analyzes traffic and compares it to normal traffic to determine if the traffic is a threat. This means any traffic out of the ordinary will set off an alert.

An HIDS can be configured to also focus on attacks that may be relevant to the role that the server is performing (for example, looking for DNS pollution attacks on DNS servers). But there are drawbacks to these systems; among them are

- A high number of false positives can cause a lax attitude on the part of the security team.
- Constant updating of signatures is needed.
- A lag time exists between the release of the attack and the release of the signature.
- An HIDS cannot address authentication issues.
- Encrypted packets cannot be analyzed.
- In some cases, IDS software is susceptible itself to attacks.

Despite these shortcomings, an HIDS can play an important role in a multilayer defense system.

Anti-Malware

Although the installation of an HIDS may not be indicated if a network IDS is in place and you want to avoid the issues mentioned in the last section that come along with an HIDS, antimalware software will need to be installed on all endpoints, including servers. Many texts discuss antivirus and antimalware software separately, but for the purposes of our discussion, we are talking about software that addresses all types of malicious software, including, viruses, worms, Trojan horses, adware, and spyware.

The primary method of preventing the propagation of malicious code involves the use of antivirus software. Antivirus software is an application that is installed on a system to protect it and to scan for viruses as well as worms and Trojan horses. Most viruses have characteristics that are common to families of virus. Antivirus software looks for these characteristics, or fingerprints, to identify and neutralize viruses before they impact you.

Millions of known viruses, worms, bombs, and other malware have been defined. New ones are added all the time. Your antivirus software manufacturer will usually work very hard to keep the definition database files current. The definition database file contains all known viruses and countermeasures for a particular antivirus software product. You probably won't receive a virus that hasn't been seen by one of these companies. If you keep the virus definition database files in your software up to date, you won't be overly vulnerable to attacks.

Remediating Security Issues Based on a Vulnerability Scan

It is impossible to accurately access the security posture of a server without approaching the server in the same manner in which an attacker would. One of the ways to accomplish this is to perform a vulnerability scan of the server. This can be done with software products developed for just such a purpose. While using these products is important, it is also important that the person performing the assessment is trained in the process. This training not only covers the use of the tools, but also explains a structured approach that takes into consideration the mind-set of a hacker.

For your Windows servers, an excellent tool is the Microsoft Baseline Security Analyzer (MBSA). This tool can identify missing security patches, weak passwords, and other security issues that are specific to installed products. MBSA version 2.3, the latest, does not support client systems beyond Windows 8.1, but it supports all Windows servers up to Windows Server 2012 R2.

In Figure 6.6, an example of the results of a scan of a new installation of Windows Server 2012 R2 is shown. In the output the issues found on a host are rated with the worst issues at the top. For the computer scanned in this output, we see that there is one High severity issue (that it could not check for security updates, which occurred because the system was not connected to the Internet) and one cautionary issue (that some of the user accounts have nonexpiring passwords).

FIGURE 6.6   MBSA results

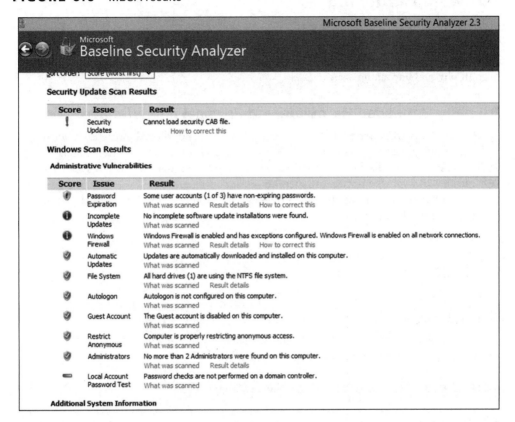

For non-Windows systems there are other tools as well. Nessus is a proprietary vulnerability scanner developed by Tenable Network Security that scans any type of system. It is free of charge for personal use in a non-enterprise environment. It can be deployed from the cloud or from your premises. An example of a Nessus scan is shown in Figure 6.7. It organizes the issues by severity, with the most critical issues at the top of the list.

FIGURE 6.7   Nessus output

Plugin ID	Count	Severity	Name	Family
32315	1	High	Firebird Default Credentials	Databases
51192	2	Medium	SSL Certificate Cannot Be Trusted	General
18405	1	Medium	Microsoft Windows Remote Desktop Protocol Server Man-in-the-Middle Weaknes	Windows
24244	1	Medium	Microsoft .NET Custom Errors Not Set	Web Servers
57608	1	Medium	SMB Signing Disabled	Misc.
57690	1	Medium	Terminal Services Encryption Level is Medium or Low	Misc.
30218	1	Low	Terminal Services Encryption Level is not FIPS-140 Compliant	Misc.
14272	15	Info	netstat portscanner (SSH)	Port scanners
10736	7	Info	DCE Services Enumeration	Windows

Hardware Hardening

While securing the servers from an attack from across a network is certainly important, you must also harden the servers against any physical attacks that may take place. Some of these issues we have already touched upon in earlier sections, but for completeness, let's cover all physical hardening issues.

Disabling Unneeded Hardware and Physical Ports/Devices

The closing of any software ports that are not in use is part of digital hardening, but the disabling of any physical ports or connections on the server is a part of physical hardening. This encompasses disabling unused devices on the server as well, such as CD drives or DVD burners that may be present. Remember, though, the aim is to do so without preventing the server from performing its role in the network. Some of the items that should be considered for disabling are

- USB ports

- NICs

- Serial ports

- Firmware ports

- Thunderbolt ports

Most of this work can be done in Device Manager if you are working with Windows. For example, in Figure 6.8 you can see how to disable the USB ports.

FIGURE 6.8 Disabling USB ports in Device Manager

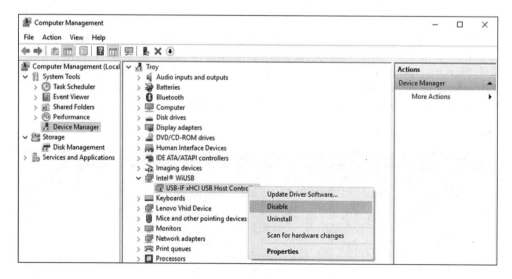

This can also be done in the BIOS or UEFI settings. Figure 6.9 shows disabling the USB ports in the BIOS.

FIGURE 6.9   Disabling USB ports in the BIOS

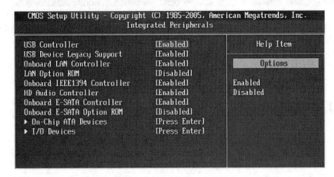

In Exercise 6.1 you will disable the network adaptor in Windows Server 2012 R2.

EXERCISE 6.1

Disabling the Network Adaptor in Windows Server 2012 R2

1. Open the Server Manager tool if it is not already open.

2. From the Tools menu select Computer Management.

3. In the Computer Management console select Device Manager.

4. Locate and expand the Network Adaptors device category as shown in Figure 6.10.

FIGURE 6.10   Expanding the Network adaptors category

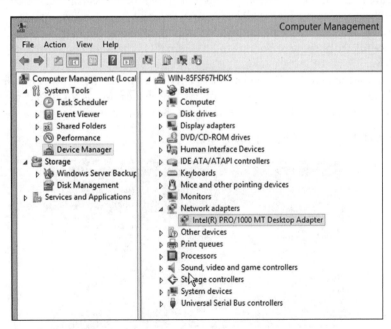

EXERCISE 6.1 *(continued)*

5. Right click the network adaptor you wish to disable (this server has only one, but your server may have more than one) and select Disable from the menu.

6. You can verify your work by looking for the black down arrow next to the adaptor as shown in Figure 6.11.

FIGURE 6.11　Disable adaptor

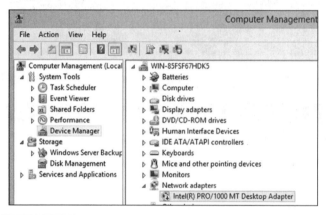

BIOS Password

While you are in the BIOS, set a password for it. This will be a password that anyone attempting to boot the device to the BIOS will be required to know. This can prevent someone with physical access to the server from booting to the BIOS, changing the boot order, and enabling a boot device for the purpose of booting to an external OS that they can use to take data off the hard drive.

As you can see in Figure 6.12, you can set one for users and another for the administrator (called the Supervisor password in the BIOS). The critical one is for the administrator because that is the password that allows access to the setup utility.

FIGURE 6.12　Setting a BIOS password

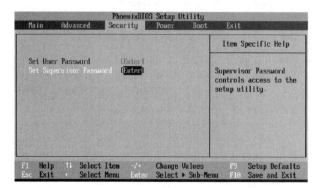

Disable WOL (Wake on LAN)

Many NICs are capable of a function called Wake on LAN (WOL). This allows the device to be started up from the network by sending a special packet to the NIC (which is not ever actually off). Although this feature can be helpful, it can also be abused by attackers. The magic packets are Layer 2 frames, which can be sent by any device on the same LAN as the target. While this only allows the startup of the server and does not remove any other authentication required to access the server, it may be a function you want to disable, especially if you don't use it.

This is another configuration that can be done in the BIOS settings in a similar fashion to the way we disabled the USB ports. Figure 6.13 shows where this is done in the BIOS settings. In this case WOL is disabled.

FIGURE 6.13   Disabling WOL

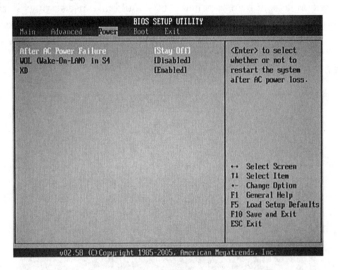

Setup Boot Order

You learned earlier that the boot order can be set in the BIOS or UEFI settings. You should set this boot order so that booting to a device other than the hard drive is difficult, if not impossible. If you lock access to the BIOS settings, this order cannot be changed. Accessing the boot settings on a Dell PowerEdge server is shown in Figure 6.14.

FIGURE 6.14   Accessing boot settings

Once you have accessed boot settings, use the Boot sequence settings to arrive at the desired order, as shown in Figure 6.15.

FIGURE 6.15 Changing the boot order

Chassis Locks/Intrusion Detection

Although securing the BIOS can keep the server from being accessed by booting to another operating system, it cannot prevent theft of memory or hard drives. You should put locks on the case to prevent it from being opened. You should also use settings in the BIOS to alert you when the case has been opened. These settings are shown in Figure 6.16. In this case the open case warning has *not* been enabled yet.

FIGURE 6.16 Open case warning in the BIOS

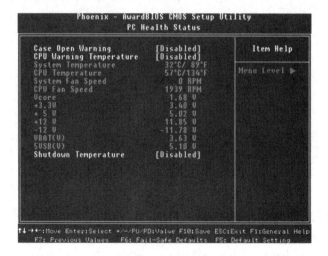

Proper Environmental Controls and Techniques

You might think it a bit off topic to discuss environmental controls in a security chapter. However, it makes perfect sense to do so if you consider what the A in the security triad CIA stands for. CIA is an acronym for the three goals of security: to provide confidentiality (data can be read only by those for which it is intended), integrity (the data has not been altered in any way), and availability (the data is available to those who need it when they need it).

It is the goal of availability that maintaining proper environmental control serves. When proper environmental practices are not in place, servers lock up, shut down, and suffer any number of ailments that make them unable to perform their role or make their resources available. With that said, let's close this chapter with a section covering best practices.

Power Concepts and Best Practices

Power is the lifeline of the datacenter. One of your goals is to ensure that all systems have a constant, clean source of power. In this section, we'll look at the proper use of uninterruptable power supplies (UPSs) and discuss what power distribution units are (PDU). We'll also talk about how to plan to ensure you have sufficient capacity to serve your devices. Finally, we'll explore the use of redundant power supplies and the use of multiple circuits to enhance availability.

UPS

All systems of any importance to the continued functioning of the enterprise should be connected to a UPS. These devices have a battery attached that can provide power to the systems in the case of a power outage. You may also be aware that these systems are designed to provide only short-term power to the systems; that is a length of time sufficient to allow someone to gracefully shut down the devices. In this section, we'll dig a bit deeper and identify some of the features of these devices. We'll also go over best practices with regard to ensuring your UPS solution provides the protection you intended.

Runtime vs. Capacity

Two important metrics that are related but *not* the same when assessing a UPS are its run-time and its capacity. The *runtime* is the amount of time that the UPS can provide power at a given power level. This means you can't evaluate this metric without knowing the amount of load you will be placing on the UPS. Documentation that comes with the UPS should reveal to you the number of minutes expected at various power levels. So if you doubled the number of like devices attached to the UPS, you should expect the time to be cut in half (actually, it will be cut more than in half in reality because the batteries discharge quicker at higher loads).

Capacity is the maximum amount of power the UPS can supply at any moment in time. So if it has a capacity of 650 volt amperes (VA) and you attempt to pull 800 VA from the UPS, it will shut itself down. So both of the values must be considered. You need to know the total amount of power the devices may require (capacity) and, based on that figure, select a UPS that can provide that for the amount of time you will need to shut down all the devices.

One good thing to know is that some UPS vendors can supply expansion packs for existing units that increase their capacity and runtime. That would be a favorable feature to insist on to allow your system to grow.

Automated Graceful Shutdown of Attached Devices

Today's enterprise-level UPS system tends to offer the ability to shut down a server to which it is attached when the power is lost. If all devices were thus equipped, it could reduce the amount of runtime required and eliminate the race to shut servers down.

There are several approaches that vendors have taken to this. In some cases if you purchase a special network card for the UPS, a single UPS can provide the automatic shutdown to multiple servers. The agent on each server communicates with the network card in the UPS.

Another option is to use a dedicated UPS for each server and attach the server to the UPS using a serial or USB cable. The disadvantage of this approach is that it requires a UPS for each device and you will be faced with the cable length limitations of serial and USB cables.

In either case, using the software that comes with the UPS, you can also have scripts run prior to the shutdown, and you can configure the amount of time to wait for the shutdown so the script has time to execute, as shown in Figure 6.17. You can set a notification of this event.

FIGURE 6.17   Automatic shutdown

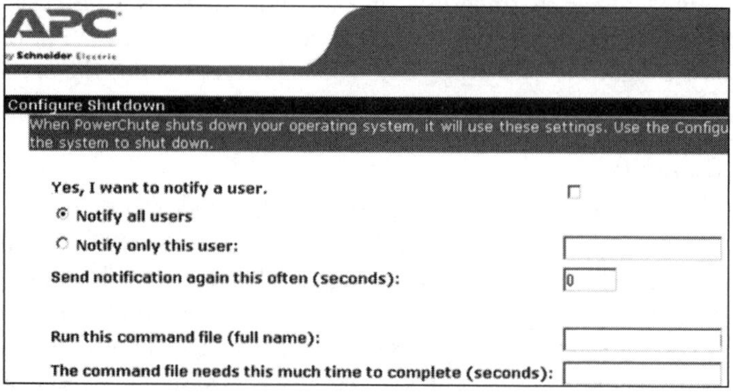

Periodic Testing of Batteries

Just as you would never wait until there is a loss of data to find out if the backup system is working, you should never wait until the power goes out to see whether the UPS does its job. Periodically you should test the batteries to ensure they stand ready to provide the expected runtime.

While the simplest test would be to remove power and see what happens, if you have production servers connected when you do this it could cause a resume generating event (RGE). In most cases, the software that came with the UPS will have the ability to report the current expected runtime based on the current state of the battery, as shown in Figure 6.18.

FIGURE 6.18 Checking battery level

Even with this information, it is probably advisable to test the units from time to time with devices connected that you don't care about just to make sure the process of switching over to the battery succeeds and the correct runtime is provided.

Maximum Load

Although the capacity of a UPS is rated in volts ampere (VA), that is not the same as maximum load. The capacity value assumes that all of the attached devices are pulling the maximum amount of power, which they rarely do. As a rule of thumb, if you multiply the VA times 0.8, you will get a rough estimate of the maximum load your UPC may undergo at any particular time. So a UPS that is rated for 650 VA cannot provide more than 520 watts. If either of these values is exceeded during operation, the UPS will fail to provide the power you need.

Bypass Procedures

Putting a UPS in bypass mode removes the UPS from between the device and the wall output conceptually, without disconnecting it. A *static bypass* is one in which the UPS, either by the administrator invoking the bypass manually or by an inverter failure in the UPS, switches the power path back to the main line and removes itself from the line.

A *maintenance bypass* is possible when the UPS is augmented with an external appliance called the bypass cabinet. This allows for enabling the bypass and then working with the UPS without concerns about the power being on (although it can be enabled while leaving the power to the UPS on). This concept is shown in Figure 6.19. Notice the two switches on the bypass cabinet that can be opened and shut to accomplish this power segregation.

FIGURE 6.19 Maintenance bypass

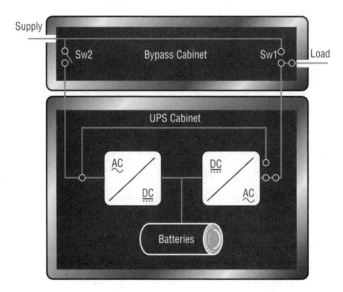

Remote Management

Most enterprise-level UPS systems also allow for remote management of the system. In most cases, this will be through the use of a special network card such as the one described in the earlier section, "Automated Graceful Shutdown of Attached Devices." These cards are installed in slots on the UPS, as shown in Figure 6.20. A slot cover is removed and replaced with the card. Once installed, the card is given an IP address, subnet mask, and gateway. Once the card is on the network, you will be able to use several protocols, such as SMTP, HTTP, SMTP, Telnet, and SSH, to access it.

FIGURE 6.20 Installing the remote management card

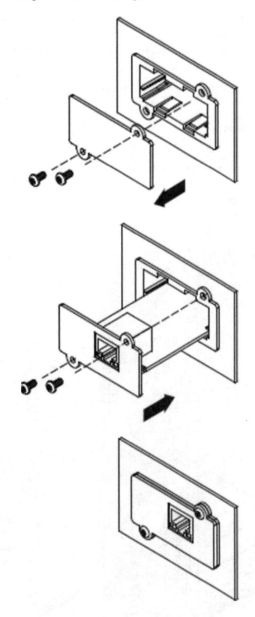

Keep in mind that these cards come with varying levels of functionality. Some give you total control of the device, whereas others may only allow you to monitor the device environment.

PDU

A power distribution unit (PDU) is a device that looks much like a simple power strip with multiple outlets, but depending on the model it can be much more than that. Some are large, freestanding devices. Some of the features these devices can provide besides multiple outlets are

- Power conditioning (evening out sags and surges)
- Surge protection
- Environmental monitoring
- Case alarms

Figure 6.21 shows an example of a rack mount PDU that is installed in a rack cabinet.

FIGURE 6.21   Rack PDU

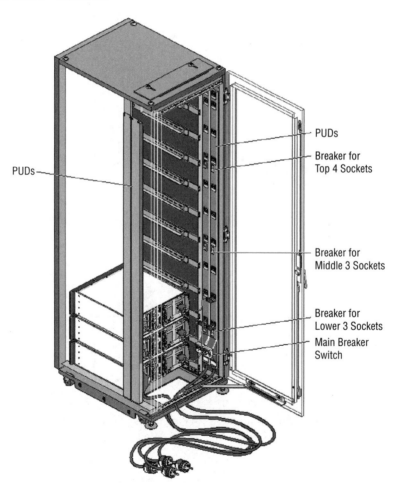

Connecting Redundant Rack PDUs to Separate Circuits

In cases where every possible effort must be made to keep the servers running, you may decide to deploy multiple rack PDUs in a rack or cabinet, as shown in Figure 6.22, where there are two PDUs.

FIGURE 6.22   Redundant PDUs

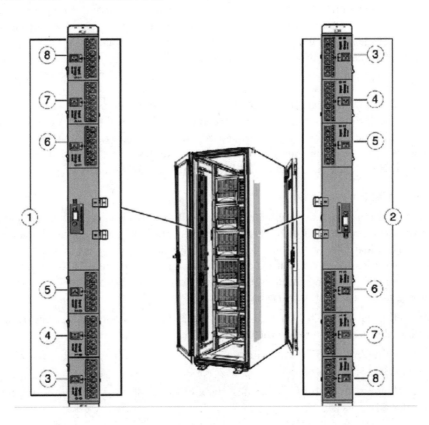

If you do this it for redundancy, you may want to connect each to different circuits so that if one entire circuit goes dead, the rack can still be powered by the second power source.

Capacity Planning

When planning your power system, you want to ensure that you have sufficient capacity to handle all the devices both during normal operation and during any power outages that may occur, when you might be operating on battery or generator. To do so, you need to understand several terms related to capacity planning and some of the metrics that are used when describing products.

PDU Ratings

PDUs are rated according to the power load they can handle. You should ensure that no single PDU is connected to more devices than it can handle. So a PDU that is rated at 24 amps cannot provide more power at a time to the servers to which it is connected than that. It is also useful to know that PDUs will have two ratings in that regard. The National Electric Code, which is published by the National Fire Protection Association, requires that the continuous current drawn from a branch circuit not exceed 80 percent of the circuit's maximum rating. Therefore, PDUs have a maximum input value and a de-rated value. The de-rated value will be 80 percent of the maximum input value. So a PDU with a maximum value of 30 amps will have a de-rated value of 24 amps.

UPS Ratings

You also must ensure that you have enough UPS devices and that they can support the power required during an outage. As you learned earlier, you need to consider both the total capacity of the UPS and its runtime. Moreover, with respect to capacity, don't forget to consider both the VA value and the maximum load values. For more information on this, review the section, " Power Concepts and Best Practices," earlier in this chapter.

Total Potential Power Draw

The power consumption of any individual server will vary. It's unlikely but there may be a point in time when all of your devices require what's called *critical power* at the same time. You need to calculate that value and ensure that if this occurs, you have sufficient power. If the circuit is overloaded, it can cause a complete outage. This means every link in the chain, including the PDU, UPS, and the circuit to these devices, must be capable of the load. When determining that load, use the following guidelines:

- Add up the wattages listed on each device. If the wattage is not listed on the device, multiply the current (amps) by the voltage of the device to get the VA.

- Multiply the VA by 0.67 to estimate the actual power, in watts, that the critical load will represent.

- Divide the number by 1000 to establish the kilowatt (kW) load level of the anticipated critical load.

Don't forget that your needs will not be static, so build in some additional capacity to allow for growth.

Multiple Circuits

If you have a single power circuit and it fails, you will only be up as long as your batteries last or as long as the generator can run. Many datacenters commission multiple power circuits to prevent this. A comparison of a center with a single circuit to one with two circuits is shown in Figure 6.23. In this case the engineers have gone beyond circuit redundancy and implemented a main power panel, auto transfer switch, power panel, maintenance bypass (MBP), and UPS redundancy as well. An MBP is used to bypass the UPS when either changing the UPS or performing maintenance on it.

FIGURE 6.23 Multiple circuits

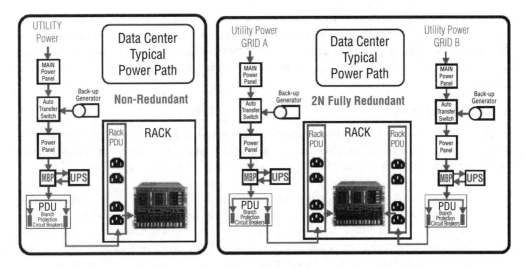

Connect Redundant Power Supplies to Separate PDUs

If you deploy multiple PDUs for redundancy, you may want to connect each to different circuits so that if one entire circuit goes dead, the rack can still be powered by the second power source. Another approach is to attach two UPSs to the PDU, with one going to the main power and the other to secondary power or to a generator, as shown in Figure 6.24.

FIGURE 6.24 Redundant UPS with single PDU

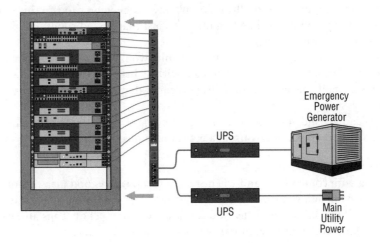

Safety

All of the technology an organization possesses is important to its mission, but the most important resource of the organization is its people. For this reason, safety is critical in a datacenter. The same goes for the devices. If they are handled improperly, they can be damaged. In this final section of the chapter, we'll discuss what keeping devices and people safe entails.

ESD Procedures

Electrostatic discharge (ESD) is one of the most dangerous risks associated with working with computers. Not only does ESD have the potential to damage components of the computer, but it can also injure you. Not understanding the proper way to avoid it could cause you great harm.

Electrostatic discharge is the technical term for what happens whenever two objects of dissimilar charge come in contact—think of rubbing your feet on a carpet and then touching a light switch. The two objects exchange electrons in order to equalize the electrostatic charge between them. If the device receiving the charge happens to be an electronic component, there is a good chance it can be damaged.

The likelihood that a component will be damaged increases with the use of complementary metal-oxide semiconductor (CMOS) chips because these chips contain a thin metal oxide layer that is hypersensitive to ESD. The previous generation's transistor–transistor logic (TTL) chips are more robust than the CMOS chips because they don't contain this metal-oxide layer. Most of today's integrated circuits (ICs) are CMOS chips, so ESD is more of a concern lately.

The lowest static voltage transfer that you can feel is around 3,000 volts (it doesn't electrocute you because there is extremely little current). A static transfer that you can *see* is at least 10,000 volts! Just by sitting in a chair, you can generate around 100 volts of static electricity. Walking around wearing synthetic materials can generate around 1,000 volts. You can easily generate around 20,000 volts simply by dragging your smooth-soled shoes across a carpet in the winter. (Actually, it doesn't have to be winter to run this danger; it can occur in any room with very low humidity. It's just that heated rooms in wintertime generally have very low humidity.)

It would make sense that these thousands of volts would damage computer components. However, a component can be damaged with as little as 300 volts. That means if your body has a small charge built up in it, you could damage a component without even realizing it.

Just as you can ground yourself by using a grounding strap, you can ground equipment. This is most often accomplished by using a mat or a connection directly to a ground.

Antistatic Bags

When working with components and when storing them, it is a good idea to store them in antistatic bags. Although you can buy these bags, replacement parts usually come in antistatic bags, and if you keep these bags, you can use them later. These bags also can serve as a safe place to lay a component temporarily when working on a device.

ESD Straps

There are measures you can implement to help contain the effects of ESD. The easiest one to implement is the *antistatic wrist strap*, also referred to as an *ESD strap*.

 The ESD that we are speaking about here does not have the capability to kill you since it doesn't have the amperage. What does represent a threat, though, is using a wrist strap of your own design that does not have the resistor protection built into it and then accidentally touching something with high voltage while wearing the wrist strap. Without the resistor in place, the high voltage would be grounded through you!

You attach one end of the ESD strap to an earth ground (typically the ground pin on an extension cord) and wrap the other end around your wrist. This strap grounds your body and keeps it at a zero charge. Figure 6.25 shows the proper way to attach an antistatic strap.

FIGURE 6.25   Proper ESD strap connection

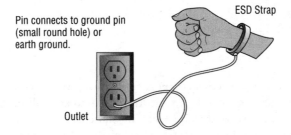

Pin connects to ground pin (small round hole) or earth ground.

ESD Strap

Outlet

If you do not have a grounded outlet available, you can achieve partial benefit simply by attaching the strap to the metal frame of the PC case. Doing so keeps the charge equalized between your body and the case so that there is no electrostatic discharge when you touch components inside the case.

 An ESD strap is a specially designed device to bleed electrical charges away safely. It uses a 1 megaohm resistor to bleed the charge away slowly. A simple wire wrapped around your wrist will not work correctly and could electrocute you!

 Do not wear the antistatic wrist strap when there is the potential to encounter a high-voltage capacitor, such as when working on the inside of a monitor or power supply. The strap could channel that voltage through your body.

ESD Mats

It is possible to damage a device simply by laying it on a bench top. For this reason, you should have an *ESD mat* (also known as an *antistatic mat*) in addition to an ESD strap. This mat drains excess charge away from any item coming in contact with it (see Figure 6.26). ESD mats are also sold as mouse/keyboard pads to prevent ESD charges from interfering with the operation of the computer.

You can also purchase ESD floor mats for technicians to stand on while performing computer maintenance. These include a grounding cord, usually 6 to 10 feet in length.

FIGURE 6.26   Proper use of an ESD mat

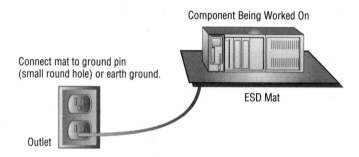

Vendors have methods of protecting components in transit from manufacture to installation. They press the pins of ICs into antistatic foam to keep all the pins at the same potential, and circuit boards are shipped in antistatic bags, discussed earlier. However, keep in mind that unlike antistatic mats, antistatic bags do not drain the charges away—they should never be used in place of antistatic mats.

Self-Grounding

Grounding is the electrical term for providing a path for an electrical charge to follow to return to earth. This term was mentioned earlier as it relates to ESD straps and mats. Grounding saves you from harm in the event of an electrical discharge as the charge passes to ground. The easiest way to ground yourself is to use a grounding strap.

Fire Suppression

You also must protect yourself and the equipment from fire. While having the proper fire extinguishers handy is important, what happens if no one is there? Fire suppression systems are designed to detect the fire and address the situation. There are several types of systems you can use.

Wet Pipe   Wet pipe systems use water contained in pipes to extinguish the fire. In some areas, the water may freeze and burst the pipes, causing damage. These systems are not recommended for rooms where equipment will be damaged by the water.

Dry Pipe   In this system the water is not held in the pipes but in a holding tank. The pipes hold pressurized air, which is reduced when fire is detected, allowing the water to enter the pipe and the sprinklers. This minimizes the chance of an accidental discharge. A comparison of a wet pipe and dry pipe system is shown in Figure 6.27.

FIGURE 6.27   Wet and dry systems

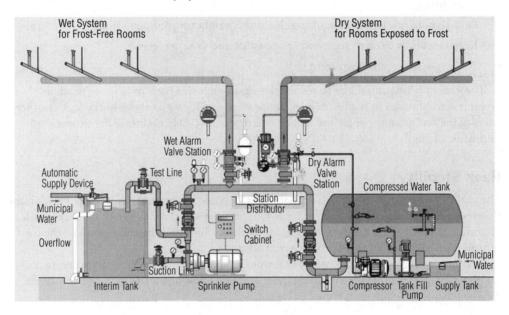

Preaction   This system operates like a dry pipe system except that the sprinkler head holds a thermal-fusible link that must be melted before the water is released. This is currently the recommended system for a computer room.

Deluge   This system allows large amounts of water to be released into the room, which obviously makes this a poor choice for where computing equipment will be located.

At one time, fire suppression systems used Halon gas, which works well by suppressing combustion through a chemical reaction. However, these systems are no longer used because they have been found to damage the ozone layer.

EPA-approved replacements for Halon include

- Water
- Argon
- NAF-S-III

Another fire suppression system that can be used in computer rooms that will not damage computers and is safe for humans is FM-200. NAS-S-III shows physical characteristics similar to those of Halon 1301 without the ozone-depleting characteristics. FM-200 is an alternative to Halon from DuPont.

Proper Lifting Techniques

An easy way to get hurt is by moving equipment in an unsafe or improper way. Here are some safe lifting techniques to always keep in mind:

- Lift with your legs, not your back. When you have to pick something up, bend at the knees, not at the waist. You want to maintain the natural curve of the back and spine when lifting.

- Be careful to not twist when lifting. Keep the weight on your centerline.

- Keep objects as close to your body as possible and at waist level.

- Where possible, push instead of pull.

The goal in lifting should be to reduce the strain on lower back muscles as much as possible since muscles in the lower back aren't nearly as strong as those in the legs or other parts of the body. Some people use a back belt or brace to help maintain the proper position while lifting.

Rack Stability

The racks in your server room will probably hold significant amounts of weight. The devices that reside there can be fragile, so for both your and the equipment's safety the racks must be stable. Racks that are solidly connected to both the floor and the ceiling will be the least of your worries if they are properly secure at all posts.

Considering that some racks may be on wheels, you may want to consider using rack stabilizers to prevent them from falling over. Then go underneath the rack and secure the rack to the floor, as shown in Figure 6.28.

FIGURE 6.28   Rack stabilizer

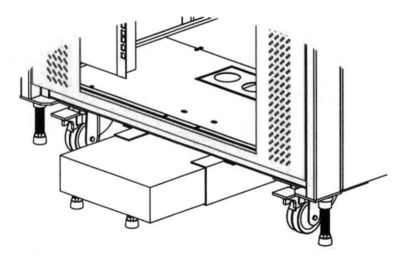

Floor Load Limitations

Whether your server room or datacenter has a raised floor (which is highly advisable) or not, you must ensure that the floor has the ability to support the weight of the equipment. You should determine the total weight of all the equipment and the racks in the room. This includes everything that will be in the room. Then when the raised floor is constructed, you must ensure it has the load capacity. If you are in an area where earthquakes are possible, then you need go beyond that and consult load experts who can tell you how much additional load capacity may be required for the intensity of any of these events that occur.

Most server room or datacenter floors have tile panels that can be removed to access things such as cabling that might be under the floor. Your floor load calculations should be done with the tiles installed because they will increase the load capacity when they are all in place.

Sharp Edges and Pinch Points

In the process of working with the servers and the racks in which they may be installed, there will be several inescapable hazards you may encounter, but a dose of patience and awareness can help you avoid them. Although manufacturers try to minimize this fact, you may encounter sharp edges that can cut you if you aren't careful. These include metal corners of cases, edges of cards, and subassemblies. If you go slow and exercise care, you can avoid cutting yourself.

There also will be occasions when certain procedures may expose you to a "pinch point," which is simply an opportunity to pinch your fingers between two objects when performing the procedure. In some cases the documentation describing the procedure will call out this hazard, another good reason to "read the directions." For example, Figure 6.29 shows a callout that precedes instructions on removing the power distribution board on a Sun Netra 440 server. Always heed these warnings.

FIGURE 6.29   Pinch point warning

 Caution - There are several pinch points on the power supplies, so use caution when removing or installing a power supply in the system. Refer to the caution label on the power supplies for more information.

HVAC

As stated in the beginning of this chapter, ensuring availability of resources stored on the servers is also a part of the security function. This cannot be done unless the environment in which the servers operate meets certain standards. In this section, we'll focus on the heating, ventilation, and air conditioning (HVAC) systems and best practices for ensuring the server room is providing an optimal operational environment to the devices.

Room and Rack Temperature and Humidity

A critical issue that must be considered is maintaining the proper temperate and humidity level for the devices. Maintaining an ambient temperature range of 68° to 75°F (20° to 24°C) is optimal for system reliability. When temperatures rise, bad things start to occur such as server rebooting. Computers can tolerate (and enjoy) slightly colder temperatures without troubles, as long as there aren't huge fluctuations.

A humidity level between 45 percent and 55 percent is recommended for optimal performance and reliability. When the level is too high, it causes condensation, which is bad news for any electronics. When the level is too low, the dry air is conducive to ESD.

MONITORING AND ALERT NOTIFICATIONS

When either the humidity or the temperature is outside of the recommended range, you need to know it. Even if you are in the room when this occurs, you may not notice it. For this reason, you need to have an environmental monitoring system in place and that system should have the ability to alert someone.

Hardware devices are made (usually rack mountable) that can do this monitoring. Most can also tell you when water is present and when cases or cabinets have been opened. Figure 6.30 shows an example of a monitor in a rack. On the back are connections to various types of sensors. Sensor data can be retrieved from the system using HTTP requests. It also can be monitored from a web interface as well. If an event occurs, it can alert you via email, SNMP, or SMS.

FIGURE 6.30 Rack monitor

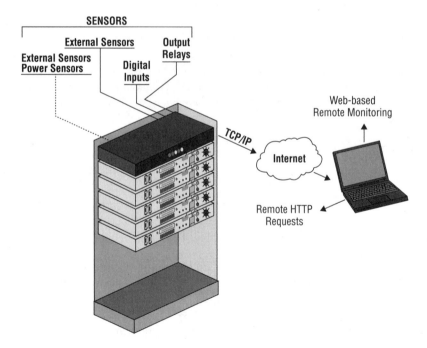

Airflow

Another important issue is to maintain airflow in the facility so that hot air is sent out of the room and replaced with cold air. This needs to be approached in a holistic manner, ensuring that no pockets of hot air are created in this process. You may remember that we talked about airflow within a server case and how the location of the fans must be considered in tandem with the presence of cards and other objects in the box that may impede airflow. With respect to the overall airflow in the room, the vent system must take these things into consideration.

As each server must be able to successfully vent hot air out of the box, any server cabinets must be able to vent air out of the cabinet or rack and all the room systems must be able to pick up that hot air and move it out of the room. It's a symphony of operations that work together. Sometimes this means you have to alter the airflow in the room using rack fillers, baffles, and blanking panels. Let's talk about those.

RACK FILLERS, BAFFLES, AND BLANKING PANELS

Rack fillers, also called filler panels, are used to cover the space between two racks or the space between racks and the wall. They can be used to eliminate spaces to help to create the airflow that is needed. An example is shown in Figure 6.31.

FIGURE 6.31   Rack fillers or filler panels

Baffles attach to the top of racks and cabinets and may or may not be angled. They are typically used when the air on one side of the row of racks needs to be channeled a certain way. In a hot aisle/cold aisle arrangement (covered in the next section more fully), baffles usually are used on the hot aisle to prevent the hot air from recirculating back into the hot aisle. Figure 6.32 shows an example.

FIGURE 6.32 Baffles

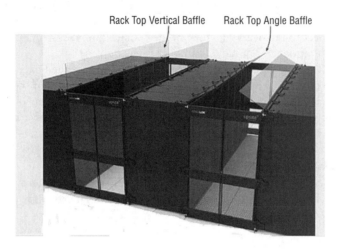

Blanking panels are used to cover spaces in a rack where no devices are located and are used to close those openings, like a slot cover closes the hole on the back of a computer. They come in both solid and vented versions. In Figure 6.33 a rack is shown before and after the installation.

FIGURE 6.33 Blanking panels

Hot Aisle and Cold Aisle

A common way to ensure that hot air is removed and cool air is introduced properly is to establish the racks in a hot aisle/cold aisle arrangement. A version of this arrangement is shown in Figure 6.34. Hot air is vented upward and then out of the room on the hot aisles, and cold air is introduced from the floor and vented into the backs of the same racks that just vented hot air upward. When done correctly, this creates a room flow that accomplishes your goal.

FIGURE 6.34 Hot aisle and cold aisle

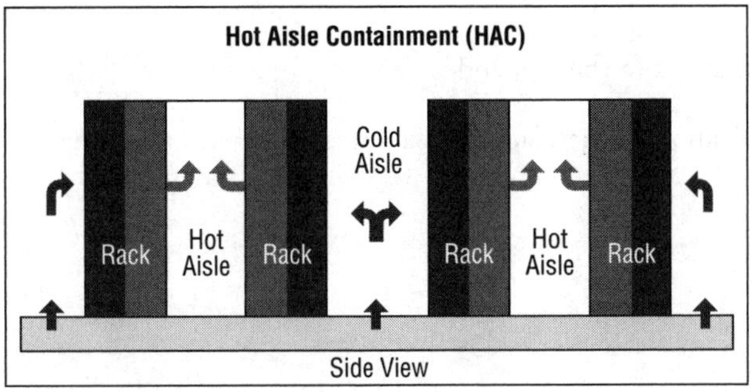

Summary

In this chapter, you learned concepts related to securing the server. These included physical security methods such as locking cabinets and server rooms and deploying strong authentication methods for accessing those rooms. We also covered server techniques such as stopping unneeded services, installing only needed software, and keeping up to date on security patches. Finally, we explored concepts related to ensuring that you can satisfy the availability requirement of the CIA security triad by maintaining the proper environment in which the servers operate.

Exam Essentials

Compare and contrast physical security methods and concepts. Among these methods are multifactor authentication, mantraps, RFID chips, and access lists. You should also be familiar with all types of locks, including server, rack, and cabinet locks.

Describe what hardening the server entails. Explain the value of stopping unneeded services, closing unneeded ports, installing only required software, and installing the latest operating system patches. You should also know about physical hardening, including disabling unneeded hardware and physical ports, implementing a BIOS password, disabling WOL (Wake on LAN), and using chassis locks.

List proper environment controls and techniques. Identify the steps required to ensure availability of the resources on the servers. These include implementing UPS systems, using redundant rack PDUs, and provisioning multiple circuits. It also entails monitoring the temperature and humidity to ensure they are at the recommended levels. Finally, the layout of the server room should be such that it promotes airflow that removes heat.

Review Questions

You can find the answers in the Appendix.

1. Which authentication mechanism is an example of something you have?
   A. Password
   B. Username
   C. Smart card
   D. Retina scan

2. Which of the following is a series of two doors with a small room between them?
   A. Mantrap
   B. Bi-gate
   C. Holding cell
   D. Visual check door

3. Which of the following is *not* a drawback of using active RFID chips?
   A. The tag signal can be read by any reader in range.
   B. The tag signal can only go a few feet.
   C. Multiple readers in an area can interfere with one another.
   D. Multiple devices can interfere with one another when responding.

4. Which of the following authentication methods is *not* an example of biometrics?
   A. Password
   B. Hand scanners
   C. Fingerprint scan
   D. Retina scan

5. Which of the following offers the most flexibility in reacting to security events?
   A. Cameras
   B. Security guards
   C. Motion sensors
   D. Intrusion prevention systems

6. Which of the following statements is false with respect to safes?
   A. All safes are fireproof.
   B. United Laboratories (UL) assigns ratings to safes that you can use to assess the suitability of the safe.
   C. Those that are fire resistant will protect a document from being destroyed.
   D. When considering a safe, you should focus on two items: the ease with which the safe can be compromised and the ability of the safe to withstand a fire.

7. Which of the following is a physical hardening technique?

    A. Stopping unneeded services

    B. Closing unneeded ports

    C. Installing only required software

    D. Assigning a BIOS password

8. When discussing security, which of the following is defined as any point of entry into the network?

    A. Access point

    B. Endpoint

    C. Drop point

    D. Access link

9. Which of the following is not true of an HIDS?

    A. A high number of false positives can cause a lax attitude on the part of the security team.

    B. An HIDS cannot address authentication issues.

    C. Encrypted packets cannot be analyzed.

    D. An HIDS monitors all traffic that goes through it looking for signs of attack on any machine in the network.

10. Which of the following is a vulnerability scanner for Windows only?

    A. MBSA

    B. Nessus

    C. NIDS

    D. Tripwire

11. Which of the following is *not* an example of physical hardening of the server?

    A. Disabling USB ports

    B. Implementing strong authentication to log into the server

    C. Installing locks on server racks

    D. Installing locks on the server room door

12. Which of the following allows a device to be started up from the network by sending a special packet to the NIC?

    A. RAID

    B. WOL

    C. JBOD

    D. LANwake

13. Which of the following describes the amount of time a UPS can provide a given level of power?

   A. Capacity

   B. Volts ampere

   C. Runtime

   D. Charge time

14. What is the maximum amount of power a UPS can supply at any moment in time?

   A. Capacity

   B. Volt limit

   C. Ceiling

   D. Maximum volts

15. Which of the following modes removes a UPS from between the device and the wall output conceptually, without disconnecting it?

   A. Override

   B. Link switch

   C. Bypass

   D. Closed circuit

16. Which of the following is a device that looks much like a simple power strip with multiple outlets but can provide case alarms and environmental monitoring as well?

   A. HIDS

   B. PDU

   C. Surge protector

   D. UPS

17. Which of the following is the de-rated value of a PDU with a maximum input value of 30 amps?

   A. 35 amps

   B. 30 amps

   C. 24 amps

   D. 20 amps

18. When determining the critical load of all devices, by what value should you multiply the total wattage listed on each device?

   A. 1.5

   B. 0.9

   C. 0.75

   D. 0.67

19. What is the lowest static voltage one can feel?

A. 1500 volts

B. 2000 volts

C. 2500 volts

D. 3000 volts

20. Which of the following is no longer legal to use in a fire suppression system?

A. Halon

B. Water

C. Argon

D. NAS-S-III

Chapter

7

Securing Server Data and Network Access

COMPTIA SERVER+ EXAM OBJECTIVES COVERED IN THIS CHAPTER:

✓ **4.3 Explain basic network security systems and protocols**

- Firewall (network-based, host-based)
- Port security/802.1x/NAC
- Router access list
- NIDS
- Authentication protocols (LDAP, RADIUS, TACACS, TACACS+)
- PKI (private key, public key, certificate authority, SSL/TLS)
- VPN
- IPsec
- VLAN
- Security zones (DMZ, public and private, intranet and extranet)

✓ **4.4 Implement logical access control methods based on company policy**

- Access control lists (users, groups [roles], resources [file system, network ACLs, peripheral devices, administrative rights, distribution lists])
- Permissions (read, write/modify, execute, delete, full control/ superuser, file vs. share)

✓ **4.5 Implement data security methods and secure storage disposal techniques**

- Storage encryption (file level encryption, disk encryption, tape encryption
- Storage media (soft wipe [file deletion], hard wipe [zero out all sectors], physical destruction, remote wipe)

While securing the server from physical access is of immense importance, securing the data that resides on the server is also critical and requires a different approach. Logical or technical controls are used to protect this data. We have to be concerned about the security of the data when it is en route to the user across the network and when it is at rest on the storage media. In addition, we have to ensure that, when storage media is disposed of, the data that resided on the media is removed completely.

Basic Network Security Systems and Protocols

A number of security mechanisms can be used to protect data on media and on the network. These mechanisms include hardware devices, procedures, authentication processes, encryption algorithms, and secure network design principles. All of these components must work together to achieve the goal of securing the network and its resources. In this section we'll break down these building blocks and examine each one.

Firewall

Firewalls are used to filter out unwanted traffic while allowing desired traffic. They perform this function in a number of different ways. In this section, we'll look at two types of firewalls: network-based and host-based firewalls.

Network-Based

Network-based firewalls are one of the first lines of defense in a network. There are different types of firewalls, and they can either be standalone systems or they can be included in other devices such as routers or servers. You can find firewall solutions that are marketed as hardware only and others that are software only. Many firewalls, however, consist of add-in software that is available for servers or workstations.

 Although solutions are sold as "hardware only," the hardware still runs some sort of software. It may be hardened and in ROM to prevent tampering, and it may be customized—but software is present nonetheless.

The basic purpose of a firewall is to isolate one network from another. Firewalls are becoming available as appliances, meaning they're installed as the primary device separating two networks. *Appliances* are freestanding devices that operate in a largely self-contained manner, requiring less maintenance and support than a server-based product.

Firewalls function as one or more of the following:

- Packet filter
- Proxy firewall
- Stateful inspection firewall

To understand the concept of a firewall, it helps to know where the term comes from. In days of old, dwellings used to be built so close together that if a fire broke out in one, it could easily destroy a block or more before it could be contained. To decrease the risk of this happening, firewalls were built between buildings. The firewalls were huge brick walls that separated the buildings and kept a fire confined to one side. The same concept of restricting and confining is true in network firewalls. Traffic from the outside world hits the firewall and isn't allowed to enter the network unless otherwise invited.

The firewall shown in Figure 7.1 effectively limits access from outside networks, while allowing inside network users to access outside resources. The firewall in this illustration is also performing proxy functions.

FIGURE 7.1 A proxy firewall blocking network access from external networks

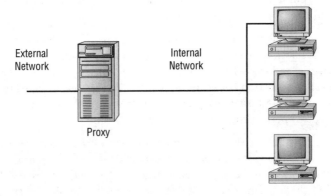

The following list discusses three of the most common functions that firewalls perform:

Although firewalls are often associated with outside traffic, you can place a firewall anywhere. For example, if you want to isolate one portion of your internal network from others, you can place a firewall between them.

Packet Filter Firewalls   A firewall operating as a *packet filter* passes or blocks traffic to specific addresses based on the type of application. The packet filter doesn't analyze the data of a packet; it decides whether to pass it based on the packet's addressing information. For instance, a packet filter may allow web traffic on port 80 and block Telnet traffic on port 23. This type of filtering is included in many routers. If a received packet request asks for a port that isn't authorized, the filter may reject the request or simply ignore it. Many packet filters can also specify which IP addresses can request which ports and allow or deny them based on the security settings of the firewall.

Packet filters are growing in sophistication and capability. A packet filter firewall can allow any traffic that you specify as acceptable. For example, if you want web users to access your site, then you configure the packet filter firewall to allow data on port 80 to enter. If every network were exactly the same, firewalls would come with default port settings hard-coded, but networks vary, so the firewalls don't include such settings.

Proxy Firewalls   A *proxy firewall* can be thought of as an intermediary between your network and any other network. Proxy firewalls are used to process requests from an outside network and those outbound from inside the network. The proxy firewall examines the data and makes rule-based decisions about whether the request should be forwarded or refused. The proxy intercepts all the packages and reprocesses them for use internally. This process includes hiding IP addresses.

The proxy firewall provides better security than packet filtering because of the increased intelligence that a proxy firewall offers. Requests from internal network users are routed through the proxy. The proxy, in turn, repackages the request and sends it along, thereby isolating the user from the external network. The proxy can also offer caching, should the same request be made again, and can increase the efficiency of data delivery.

A proxy firewall typically uses two network interface cards (NICs). Any type of firewall that has two NICs is referred to as a *dual-homed* firewall. One of the cards is connected to the outside network, and the other is connected to the internal network. The proxy software manages the connection between the two NICs. This setup segregates the two networks from each other and offers increased security. Figure 7.2 illustrates a dual-homed firewall segregating two networks from each other.

The proxy function can occur at either the application level or the session level of the OSI model. *Application-level proxy* functions read the individual commands of the protocols that are being served. This type of server is advanced and must know the rules and capabilities of the protocol used. An implementation of this type of proxy must know the difference between GET and PUT operations (these are HTTP commands used to read and write to a web page), for example, and have rules specifying how to execute them. A *circuit-level proxy* creates a circuit between the client and the server and doesn't deal with the contents of the packets that are being processed.

A unique application-level proxy server must exist for each protocol supported. Many proxy servers also provide full *auditing, accounting*, and other usage information that wouldn't normally be kept by a circuit-level proxy server.

FIGURE 7.2   A dual-homed firewall segregating two networks from each other

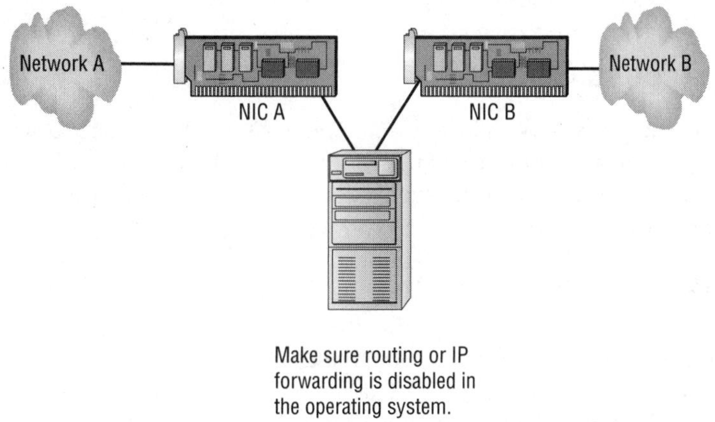

Make sure routing or IP
forwarding is disabled in
the operating system.

Stateful Inspection Firewalls   This last section on firewalls focuses on the concept of stateful inspection. *Stateful inspection* is also referred to as *stateful packet filtering*. Most of the devices used in networks don't keep track of how information is routed or used. After a packet is passed, the packet and path are forgotten. In stateful inspection (or stateful packet filtering), records are kept using a state table that tracks every communications channel. Stateful inspections occur at all levels of the network and provide additional security, especially in connectionless protocols such as *User Datagram Protocol (UDP)* and *Internet Control Message Protocol (ICMP)*. This adds complexity to the process. Denial-of-service (DoS) attacks present a challenge because flooding techniques are used to overload the state table and effectively cause the firewall to shut down or reboot.

Host-Based

Host-based firewalls are software installed on a single device that protects only that device from attacks. Many operating systems today come with personal firewalls or host-based firewalls. Many commercial host-based firewalls are designed to focus attention on a particular type of traffic or to protect a certain application.

On Linux-based systems, a common host-based firewall is iptables, replacing a previous package called ipchains. It has the ability to accept or drop packets. Firewall rules are created, much like creating an access list on a router. An example of a rule set follows:

```
iptables -A INPUT -i eth1 -s 192.168.0.0/24 -j DROP
iptables -A INPUT -i eth1 -s 10.0.0.0/8 -j DROP
iptables -A INPUT -i eth1 -s 172. -j DROP
```

This rule set blocks all incoming traffic sourced from either the 192.168.0.0/24 network or from the 10.0.0.0/8 network. Both of these are private IP address ranges. It is quite common to block incoming traffic from the Internet that has a private IP address as its source because this usually indicates IP spoofing is occurring.

Network Access Control

Access of users to the network both locally and remotely should be strictly controlled. This can be done at a number of levels of the OSI model, and it can be accomplished in a decentralized or centralized manner. In this section, we'll cover three forms of network access control and how they work.

Port Security

Port security applies to ports on a switch, and since it relies on monitoring the MAC addresses of the devices attached to the switch ports, we call it Layer 2 security. While disabling any ports not in use is always a good idea, port security goes a step further and allows you to keep the port enabled for legitimate devices while preventing its use by illegitimate devices.

There are several things you can accomplish with port security. It can be used to

- Set the maximum number of MAC addresses that can be seen on a port.
- Define exactly which MAC addresses are allowed on the port.
- Take a specific action when a port violation occurs.

The following scenarios can be prevented through the use of port security:

- A malicious individual enters the facility, unplugs a legitimate computer, and plugs in his computer.
- Users in a department violate policy by attaching a hub to one of the switch ports so they can connect more devices.
- A student in a computer lab disconnects one of the lab computers and connects her laptop to the network.

802.1x

The IEEE 802.1x security standard describes a method of centralizing the authentication, authorization, and accounting of users that connect either locally or remotely to the network. It is sometimes called port-based access control because in an 802.1x architecture, the user's port to the network is not opened until the process is complete. The 802.1x architecture can be applied to both wireless and wired networks and uses three components:

Supplicant   The user or device requesting access to the network

Authenticator   The device through which the supplicant is attempting to access the network

Authentication Server   The centralized device that performs authentication

The role of the authenticator can be performed by a wide variety of network access devices, including remote access servers (both dial-up and VPN), switches, and wireless access points. The role of the authentication server can be performed by a Remote Authentication Dial-in User Service (RADIUS) or a Terminal Access Controller Access

Control System+ (TACACS+) server. Each of these server types centralizes the authentication process on behalf of the multiple authenticators.

The authenticator requests credentials from the supplicant and, upon receipt of those credentials, relays them to the authentication server where they are validated. Upon successful verification, the authenticator is notified to open the port for the supplicant to allow network access. This process is illustrated in Figure 7.3.

FIGURE 7.3   802.1x process

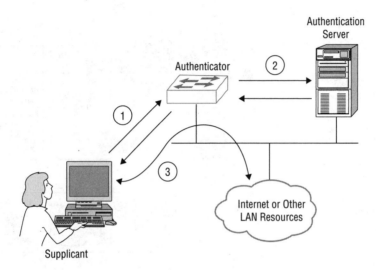

While RADIUS and TACACS+ perform the same roles, they do have different characteristics. Take these differences into consideration when you are choosing the method. Also keep in mind that although RADUIS is a standard, TACACS+ is Cisco proprietary. Enabling 802.1x authentication on all devices is considered by many to be the best protection you can provide a network. RADIUS and TACACS+ are covered more completely later in this chapter.

NAC

Network Access Control (NAC) is a service that goes beyond authentication of the user. NAC includes an examination of the state of the computer the user is introducing to the network when making a remote access or VPN connection to the network.

These services are called Network Admission Control in the Cisco world and Network Access Protection (NAP) in the Microsoft world. The goals of the features are the same: to examine all devices requesting network access for malware, missing security updates, and any other security issues the device could potentially introduce to the network.

The steps that occur in Microsoft NAP are shown in Figure 7.4. The health state of the device requesting access is collected and sent to the Network Policy Server (NPS), where the state is compared to requirements. If requirements are met, access is granted and if requirements are not met, access is usually limited or denied.

FIGURE 7.4 Microsoft Network Access Protection

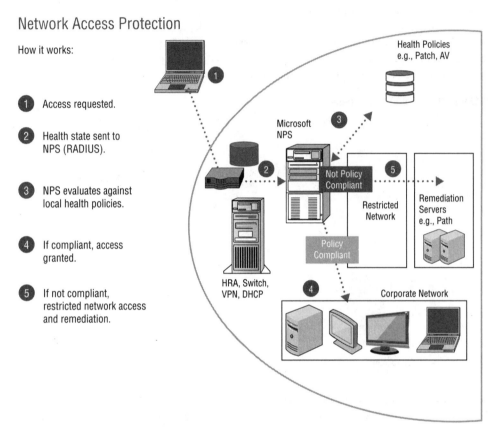

Network Access Protection

How it works:

1. Access requested.

2. Health state sent to NPS (RADIUS).

3. NPS evaluates against local health policies.

4. If compliant, access granted.

5. If not compliant, restricted network access and remediation.

Health Policies
e.g., Patch, AV

Microsoft NPS

Not Policy Compliant

Restricted Network

Remediation Servers
e.g., Path

Policy Compliant

HRA, Switch, VPN, DHCP

Corporate Network

Router Access List

Although firewalls can be used to keep unwanted and perhaps malicious traffic types out of the network, and port security and NAC can help keep intruders out of the network, within the network there will be occasions when you don't want to allow communication between certain devices. Perhaps you want to prevent users in the Sales subnet from accessing data in the Finance subnet. In these scenarios, you can use access control lists (ACLs) on the router.

The inherent limitation of ACLs is their inability to detect whether IP spoofing is occurring. IP address spoofing is one of the techniques used by hackers to hide their trail or to masquerade as another computer. The hacker alters the IP address as it appears in the packet. This can sometimes allow the packet to get through an ACL that is based on IP addresses. It also can be used to make a connection to a system that only trusts certain IP addresses or ranges of IP addresses.

Access control lists are ordered sets of rules that control the traffic that is permitted or denied the use of a path through the router. These rules can operate at Layer 3, making these decisions on the basis of IP addresses, or at Layer 4, when only certain types of traffic are allowed based on a TCP or UDP port number. When this is done, the ACL will typically reference a port number of the service or application that is allowed or denied.

When creating ACL rule sets, keep the following design considerations in mind:

- The order of the rules is important. If traffic matches the first rule, the action specified by the rule will be applied, and no other rules will be read. Place more specific rules at the top of the list and more general ones at the bottom.

- On many devices (such as Cisco routers), an implied deny all rule is located at the end of all ACLs. If you are unsure, it is always best to configure an explicit deny all rule at the end of the ACL list. An implied deny all is a rule that doesn't actually appear in the list but is assumed in all lists. An explicit deny is implemented by specifying "deny all" as the last rule in the list.

- It is also possible to log all traffic that meets any of the rules.

NIDS

An IDS (intrusion detection system) is a system that detects unauthorized access or attacks. A network-based IDS (NIDS) monitors network traffic on a local network segment. This is in contrast to a host-based IDS (HIDS) that monitors a single machine.

One of the disadvantages of an NIDS (which is an advantage of an HIDS) is that it cannot monitor any internal activity that occurs within a system, such as an attack against a system that is carried out by logging on to the system's local terminal.

Most IDSs are programmed to react certain ways in specific situations. Event notification and alerts are crucial to IDSs. These notifications and alerts inform administrators and security professionals when and where attacks are detected.

To monitor traffic on the network segment, the network interface card (NIC) must be operating in promiscuous mode. Moreover, an NIDS is affected by a switched network because generally an NIDS only monitors a single network segment and each switch port is a separate collision domain.

Authentication Protocols

We can't discuss authentication frameworks such as 802.1x without talking about the authentication protocols we might use in this process. The protocols covered in this section are not all authentication protocols—there are many others for use in operations such as remote access—but these are the ones that relate most closely to the 802.1x process and are used commonly in that process.

LDAP

Lightweight Directory Access Protocol (LDAP) is a protocol that provides a mechanism to access and query directory services systems. These directory services systems are most likely to be Microsoft's Active Directory but could also be Novell Directory Services (NDS). Although LDAP supports command-line queries executed directly against the directory database, most LDAP interactions are via utilities such as an authentication program (network logon) or involve locating a resource in the directory through a search utility.

An LDAP-based server can participate in 802.1x systems as the authentication server. It could be that the RADIUS server is integrated with the LDAP server as well.

RADIUS

Remote Authentication Dial-In User Service (RADIUS) is a networking protocol that provides centralized authentication and authorization. It can be run at a central location, and all of the access devices (AP, remote access, VPN, and so forth) can be made clients of the server. Whenever authentication occurs, the RADIUS server performs the authentication and authorization. This provides one location to manage the remote access policies and passwords for the network. Another advantage of using these systems is that the audit and access information (logs) are not kept on the access server.

RADIUS is a standard defined in RFC 2865. It is designed to provide a framework that includes three components. The *supplicant* is the device seeking authentication. The *authenticator* is the device to which they are attempting to connect (AP, switch, remote access server), and the *RADIUS server* is the authentication server. With regard to RADIUS, the device seeking entry is *not* the RADIUS client. The authenticating server is the RADIUS server, and the authenticator (AP, switch, remote access server) is the RADIUS client.

TACACS

Terminal Access Controller Access Control System (TACACS) is a Cisco proprietary service that operates in Cisco devices, whereas RADIUS is a standard defined in RFC 2138. A TACACS server can also perform the role of authenticator in the 802.1x architecture.

TACACS+

Cisco has implemented several versions of TACACS over time. It went from TACACS to Extended TACACS (XTACACS) and then to the latest version, TACACS+. The latest version provides authentication, accounting, and authorization, which is why it is sometimes referred to as an AAA service. TACACS+ employs tokens for two-factor, dynamic password authentication. It also allows users to change their passwords.

PKI

A public key infrastructure (PKI) includes systems, software, and communication protocols that distribute, manage, and control public key cryptography. In public key cryptography, two keys are used: a public key and a private key. These two keys are not the same, but they are mathematically related in such a way that if you encrypt data with one of them you can decrypt it with the other. Users and devices are issued public/private key pairs that are bound to a digital document called a digital certificate. This certificate (more specifically, the keys to which it is bound) can be used for a variety of things, including

- Encrypting data
- Authenticating users and devices

- Encrypting email
- Digitally signing software

Let's take a closer look at the components that make up a PKI.

Private Key

The private key that is generated as part of the key pair is only made available to the user or device to which it was issued. This key may be stored on software in the user's computer, or it might be stored on a smart card if it is to be used for authentication. At any rate, the key concept here is that it is *only* available to the user or device to which it was issued.

Public Key

The public key that is generated as part of the key pair is made available to anyone to whom the certificate is presented because it is part of the information contained in this digital document. In some cases, public keys may be kept in a repository so they can be requested by an entity if required. Regardless of the method used to obtain the public key, the thing to remember is that it is available to anyone.

Putting It Together

These keys work together to perform both encryption and digital signatures. To provide encryption, the data is encrypted with the receiver's public key, which results in cipher text that only the receiver's private key can decrypt. To digitally sign a document, the sender creates what is called a *hash value* of the data being sent, encrypts that value with the sender's private key, and sends this value along with the message. The receiver decrypts the hash using the sender's public key. The receiver then, using the same hashing algorithm, hashes the message. The sender then compares the decrypted hash value to the one just generated. If they are the same, the signature (and the integrity of the data) has been verified.

Certification Authority

The certification authority (CA) is the entity that creates and signs digital certificates, generates the key pairs, maintains the certificates, and revokes them when necessary. To participate in the PKI, an entity must contact the CA and request a digital certificate. It is the ultimate authority for the authenticity for every participant in the PKI and signs each digital certificate. The certificate binds the identity of the participant to the public key.

SSL/TLS

Secure Sockets Layer (SSL) is a Transport layer protocol that provides encryption, server and client authentication, and message integrity. SSL was developed by Netscape to transmit private documents over the Internet. Transport Layer Security (TLS) is an open-community standard that provides many of the same services as SSL. TLS 1.0 is based on SSL 3.0 but is more extensible. The main goal of TLS is privacy and data integrity between two communicating applications.

SSL is related to a PKI in that a certificate is required on the server end and optionally can be used on the client end of an SSL communication. If the user verifies the server certificate and the server verifies the user certificate, the process is called mutual authentication. In the operation of SSL, the public and private keys of the server are used to encrypt the data and protect its integrity.

VPN

Virtual private network (VPN) connections are remote access connections that allow users to securely connect to the enterprise network and work as if they were in the office. These connections use special tunneling protocols that encrypt the information being transferred between the user and the corporate network. In any case where users, business partners, or vendors are allowed remote access to the network, VPN connections should be used. Examples of tunneling protocol that can be used are

- Point-to-Point Tunneling Protocol (PPTP)
- Layer 2 Tunneling Protocol (L2TP)

In VPN operations, tunneling protocols wrap around or encapsulate the original packet when this process occurs. PPTP will encrypt the result using Microsoft Point-to-Point Encryption (MPPE). L2TP has no encryption mechanism but is usually combined with IPsec (covered in the next section) to provide the encryption.

IPsec

Internet Protocol Security (IPsec) is a suite of protocols that establishes a secure channel between two devices. IPsec is commonly implemented over VPNs but that is not its only use.
Components of IPsec include

Authentication Header (AH)   Provides authentication and integrity

Encapsulating Security Payload (ESP)   Provides authentication, integrity, and encryption (confidentiality)

Security Associations (SAs)   A record of a device's configuration needs to participate in IPsec communication.

Security Parameter Index (SPI)   A type of table that tracks the different SAs used and ensures that a device uses the appropriate SA to communicate with another device. Each device has its own SPI.

IPsec runs in one of two modes: transport mode or tunnel mode. Transport mode only protects the message payload, whereas tunnel mode protects the payload, routing, and header information. Both of these modes can be used for gateway-to-gateway or host-to-gateway IPsec communication. IPsec does not specify which hashing or encryption algorithm is used. That choice is up to the designer of the connection, but the parameters must match on both ends.

One of the challenges with IPsec is how to generate an encryption key for the session (each session key is unique). Internet Key Exchange (IKE) is the key exchange method that is most commonly used by IPsec. IKE with IPsec provides authentication and key exchange.

The authentication methods that can be used by IKE with IPsec include preshared keys, certificates, and public key authentication. The most secure implementations of preshared keys require a PKI. But a PKI is not necessary if a preshared key is based on simple passwords.

VLAN

Virtual local area networks (VLANs) are logical subdivisions of a switch that segregate ports from one another as if they were in different LANs. VLANs offer another way to add a layer of separation between sensitive devices and the rest of the network. For example, if only one device should be able to connect to the Finance server, the device and the Finance server could be placed in a VLAN separate from the other VLANs. As traffic between VLANs can only occur through a router, access control lists (ACLs) can be used to control the traffic allowed between VLANs.

These VLANs can also span multiple switches, meaning that devices connected to switches in different parts of a network can be placed in the same VLAN regardless of physical location.

VLANs have many advantages and only one disadvantage. These are listed in Table 7.1.

TABLE 7.1   Advantages of VLANs

Advantages	Disadvantages
Cost: Switched networks with VLANs are less costly than routed networks because routers cost more than switches.	Managerial overhead securing VLANs
Performance: By creating smaller broadcast domains (each VLAN is a broadcast domain), performance improves.	
Flexibility: Removes the requirement that devices in the same LAN (or in this case, VLAN) be in the same location.	
Security: Provides one more layer of separation at Layers 2 and 3.	

A VLAN security issue you should be aware of is called *VLAN hopping*. By default, a switch port is an access port, which means it can only be a member of a single VLAN. Ports that are configured to carry the traffic of multiple VLANs, called trunk ports, are used to carry traffic between switches and to routers. A VLAN hopping attack's aim is to receive traffic from a VLAN of which the hacker's port is not a member. It can be done two ways:

Switch Spoofing   Switch ports can be set to use a protocol called Dynamic Trunking Protocol (DTP) to negotiate the formation of a trunk link. If an access port is left configured to use DTP, it is possible for hackers to set their interface to spoof a switch and use DTP to create a trunk link. If this occurs, they can capture traffic from all VLANs. To prevent this, disable DTP on all switch ports.

Double Tagging   Trunk ports use an encapsulation protocol called 802.1q to place a VLAN tag around each frame to identify the VLAN to which the frame belongs. When a switch at the end of a trunk link receives an 802.1q frame, it strips this off and forwards the traffic to the destination device. In a double tagging attack, the hacker creates a special frame that has two tags. The inner tag is the VLAN to which the hacker wants to send a frame (perhaps with malicious content), and the outer tag is the real VLAN of which the hacker is a member. If the frame goes through two switches (which is possible since VLANs can span switches), the first tag gets taken off by the first switch, leaving the second, which allows the frame to be forwarded to the target VLAN by the second switch.

Double tagging is only an issue on switches that use "native" VLANs. A native VLAN is used for any traffic that is still a member of the default VLAN, or VLAN 1. To mitigate double tagging, either move all ports out of VLAN 1 or change the number of the native VLAN from 1 to something else. If that is not possible, you can also enable the tagging of all traffic on the native VLAN. None of these settings are the defaults, so it will require configuration on your part.

Security Zones

One of the most basic design principles for a secure network calls for creating *security zones*. These are logical divisions of the network with access controls applied to control traffic between the zones. By organizing resources in these zones and applying the proper access controls, we can reduce the possibility that unauthorized access to data is allowed. In this section, we'll explore three common security zones.

DMZ

A *demilitarized zone (DMZ)* is an area where you can place a public server for access by people you might not trust otherwise. By isolating a server in a DMZ, you can hide or remove access to other areas of your network. You can still access the server using your network, but others aren't able to access further network resources. This can be accomplished using firewalls to isolate your network.

When establishing a DMZ, you assume that the person accessing the resource isn't necessarily someone you would trust with other information. By keeping the rest of the network from being visible to external users, this lowers the threat of intrusion in the internal network.

Any time you want to separate public information from private information, a DMZ is an acceptable option.

The easiest way to create a DMZ is to use a firewall that can transmit in three directions:

- To the internal network
- To the external world (Internet)
- To the public information you're sharing (the DMZ)

From there, you can decide what traffic goes where; for example, HTTP traffic would be sent to the DMZ, and email would go to the internal network.

Intranet and Extranet

While DMZs are often used to make assets publicly available, extranets are used to make data available to a smaller set of the public—for example, a partner organization. *Intranet* is a term to describe the interior LAN; an extranet is a network logically separate from the intranet, Internet, and the DMZ (if both exist in the design), where resources that will be accessed from the outside world are made available. Access may be granted to customers, business partners, and the public in general. All traffic between this network and the intranet should be closely monitored and securely controlled. Nothing of a sensitive nature should be placed in the extranet.

Public and Private

The purpose of creating security zones such as DMZs is to separate sensitive assets from those that require less protection. Because the goals of security and of performance/ease of use are typically mutually exclusive, not all networks should have the same levels of security.

Information that is of a public nature, or that you otherwise deem not to be of a sensitive nature, can be located in any of the zones you create. However, you should ensure that private corporate data and especially personally identifiable information (PII)—information that can be used to identify an employee or customer and perhaps steal their identity—is located only in secure zones and never in the DMZ or the extranet.

Logical Access Control Methods

Controlling access to resources has a physical component that includes locking the server room door and training users to lock their machines when they step away. But for the most part, we use logical or technical methods to control users' access to resources. This is done by applying ACLs to the resources that define who has access and specifically what access they have. In this section, we'll see how ACLs and permissions are used to accomplish logical access control.

Access Control Lists

While ACLs on routers are used to control the types of traffic that are allowed, ACLs on resources control which users have access to the resources and operations that access allows. You can think of these ACLs as comprising a table that lists each user and the access to which they have been assigned. Each time a user attempts to access a resource, the list is checked. This establishes the security relationship between users or groups of users and the resources that exist in the network. Let's talk about these three concepts.

Users

Every user is issued an account when hired that is his or hers alone. However, there are some default accounts in many operating systems that you should be aware of as well. The most common types of default accounts in an operating system are as follows.

Administrator Account (Root in Linux and Unix)

The Administrator account is the most powerful of all; it has the power to do everything from the smallest task all the way up to removing the operating system. Because of the great power it holds, and the fact that it is always created, many who try to do harm will target this account as the one they try to break into. To increase security, during the installation of a Windows operating system, you are prompted for the name of a user who will be designated as the Administrator. The power then comes not from being truly called "Administrator" (it might now be tmcmillan, mcmillant, or something similar) but from being a member of the Administrators group (notice we use plural for the group and singular for the user).

Guest Account

This account is created by default (and should be disabled) and is a member of the group called Guests. For the most part, members of Guests have the same rights as users except they can't get to log files. The best reason to make users members of the Guests group is if they are accessing the system only for a limited time.

 As part of operating system security, we usually recommend that you rename the default Administrator and Guest accounts that are created at installation.

Standard User Account

This is the default that standard users belong to. Members of this group have read/write permission to their own profile. They cannot modify system-wide Registry settings or do much harm outside of their own account. Under the principle of least privilege, users should be made a member of the Users group only unless qualifying circumstances force them to have higher privileges.

Groups

One of the easier ways to assign permissions to a large number of users with the same needs is to put them all in a group and assign the permissions or rights to the group. There are default groups in Windows operating systems that have standard collections of privileges that you can use if desired, but generally it is better to create your own. One of the best examples is the Administrators group.

Since members of the Administrators group have such power, they can inadvertently do harm (such as by accidentally deleting a file that a regular user could not). To protect against this, the practice of logging in with an Administrator account or as a member of the Administrators group for daily interaction is strongly discouraged. Instead, we suggest that system administrators log in with a user account (lesser privileges) and change to the Administrators group account (elevated privileges) only when necessary.

When creating groups to use for assigning access, you should group users together that need the *same* access. This might be easier if you define roles and create the groups according to these roles. Let's look at roles.

Roles

When you create a role-based group, you should define what actions this role will be capable of. The choice of permissions or rights you assign to the group that represents this role (for example, customer service rep) should be driven by the tasks required and the resources required to do that job. This is an area where you should exercise a security principle called *least privilege*. This principle states that no user should be given access to any resource that is not required to do the job.

Resources

As a part of creating the access control policy, you need to identify all resources to ensure that all are secured. There are a number of different types of resources to consider besides just files and folder. Creating an access control policy also goes beyond controlling access to resources and encompasses defining what other actions the users can take on the network. In this section, we'll look at all of these issues.

Filesystem

Access to information stored in the filesystems of the various servers located on your network will be controlled by the ACLs that are attached to these files and folders. These resources can be arranged in a hierarchy that allows you to leverage the inheritance of access permissions that operates by default in these filesystems.

Although you can alter this inheritance property, by carefully classifying the data by its sensitivity and by arranging it according to the groups that need to access it, you can allow this inheritance to make your job easier.

The NTFS filesystem used in Windows allows you to assign permissions at the folder and the file levels. A file will inherit the permissions assigned to the folder in which it resides, but you can modify that by assigning a different permission to the file directly. By default, any change made to the permissions assigned at the folder level will be reflected in the permissions inherited at the file level. You can also disable the inheritance completely if desired.

The FAT filesystem does not allow assigning permissions at the file level, and therefore you must be much more careful in placing files in folders because they will take on the permissions assigned to that folder. In Linux and Unix systems, a new file created or placed in a folder will inherit the permissions from the folder; however, changes made to the permissions at the folder level will not affect the permissions on the file.

Network ACLs

Access control lists that are used to control network traffic are typically applied to the interfaces of routers and firewalls. These are quite different from the ACLs that are applied to resources in the filesystem. They do not reference users but rather traffic types as identified by information such as

- Source and destination IP address
- Source and destination port number
- Direction (inbound or outbound)

These lists are what make packet filtering firewalls work. Using these lists, an administrator can, at a very granular level, define who can send specific types of traffic to specific locations. For example, we could prevent Jack from using Telnet to connect to the Sales server without preventing him from using Telnet to any other devices and without any of his other activities or those of any other users.

We could prevent Jack's access to the Sales server from using Telnet by creating an ACL that includes a rule that references Jack's IP address (192.168.5.5/24) as the source IP address, the port number for Telnet as the traffic type (23), and the IP address of the Sales server (192.168.6.20/24) as the destination IP address:

```
deny host 192.168.5.5 0.0.0.255 host 192.168.6.20 0.0.0.255 eq 23
```

Access control lists operate on a deny-by-default principle, meaning that any traffic *not* specifically allowed in the list is denied. So we would include a rule following this rule that would allow all other traffic types such as the following:

```
permit ip any any
```

Once the access control list has been created on the router or firewall, it must be applied to an interface, and that interface must be in the path between Jack and the Sales server. If there is more than one path from Jack to the Sales server, the ACL may need to be applied in two places. Typically, though, we could avoid that by assigning the ACL to the router interface that is the default gateway of the Sales server and by applying it outbound on that interface.

Peripheral Devices

One constant security threat is the attachment of peripheral devices by users to company computers. Personal peripherals such as USB drives and flash drives can introduce malware, and they constitute a pathway for sensitive corporate data to leave the network. For this reason, many organizations choose to control the ability to use personal peripherals, if permitting their use at all.

The use of peripherals is considered a right in the Windows world, where rights are used to control actions and permissions are used to control the access to resources such as file folders and printers. The right to connect peripherals to the USB ports can be controlled on a wide scale by using Group Policies. A number of different policies exist that are created to control the use of USB ports.

In Figure 7.5, the domain security policy that prevents the use of USB ports is shown from a Windows Server 2012 R2 domain controller. If you enable this policy from a domain level, all users in the domain will be prevented from using USB devices. This system allows you to identify certain users who can be exempted from the policy if their job requires them to attach these devices to their computers.

FIGURE 7.5   USB policies

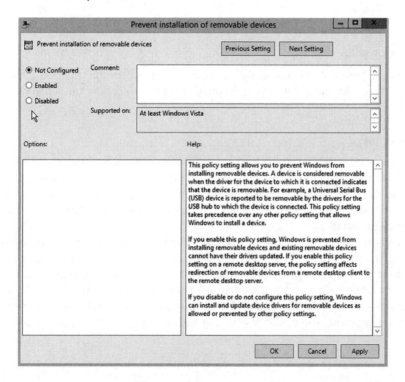

Administrative Rights

Administrative rights should be the most closely controlled rights that exist. There is very little that cannot be done with administrative rights. These rights can be granted as a whole by assigning a user to the Administrators group or by copying the rights assigned to an administrator to the rights assigned to the user. It is also possible to assign only a subnet of the rights assigned to the administrator.

When an administrator needs to delegate some of the rights to a user, it can be done two ways. The administrator can directly assign the right to perform certain functions to the user; when done this way, rights are assigned on the object to which those rights apply. For example, to allow a user to manage a printer, the Manage Printer right could be assigned to the user on the printer object in question.

In some cases, however, it may be desirable to assign that right on *all* printer objects. In that case, it will be easier to use the second way to delegate this right: using one of the built-in groups in Windows that exist for such a situation. Placing the user in the Domain Print Operators group ensures that the user will be granted the right to manage all printers in the domain. A number of such built-in groups exist for such a purpose. Here are some additional examples:

- Network Configuration operators
- Server operators
- Performance Log users
- Event Log readers

Each of these groups possesses all rights required to perform the function for which the group was created and allows the right on all relevant objects in the scope of the group.

Distribution Lists

All of the groups we have discussed thus far are *security* groups. Security groups are used to assign rights and permissions. A second type of group is a *distribution* group, also called a distribution list. These are groups used in email. When a distribution group is created, its main function is to serve as a group to which an email can be sent and every member of the group receives the email.

There is an interesting relationship between security groups and distribution groups. While a security group can also be used as a distribution group, a distribution group cannot be used as a security group. To illustrate, if a Sales security group exists, it can also be as a distribution group for the purpose of sending an email to all members of the security group. On the other hand, if a distribution group was created for the members of the Finance department, you cannot assign any rights or permission to that distribution group.

Permissions

Although some of the names for permissions may be slightly different from one filesystem to another, most filesystems have the same basic permissions that can be applied to resources. In this section, we'll look at those basic permissions and also discuss the difference between the operations of file and share permissions. While certainly not the only filesystems you will encounter, Table 7.2 shows the NTFS folder permissions and what these permissions allow, and Table 7.3 shows the NTFS file permissions and what these permissions allow. These tables offer a close approximation of what these permissions allow in any filesystem.

TABLE 7.2 NTFS Folder permissions

NTFS permission	Meaning
Full Control	Gives the user all the other choices and the ability to change permission. The user also can take ownership of the directory or any of its contents.
Modify	Combines the Read & Execute permission with the Write permission and further allows the user to delete everything, including the folder.
Read & Execute	Combines the permissions of Read with those of List Folder Contents and adds the ability to run executables.
List Folder Contents	The List Folder Contents permission (known simply as List in previous versions) allows the user to view the contents of a directory and to navigate to its subdirectories. It does not grant the user access to the files in these directories unless that is specified in file permissions.
Read	Allows the user to navigate the entire directory structure, view the contents of the directory, view the contents of any files in the directory, and see ownership and attributes.
Write	Allows the user to create new entities within the folder, as well as to change attributes.

TABLE 7.3 NTFS file permissions

NTFS permission	Meaning
Full Control	Gives the user all the other permissions as well as permission to take ownership and change permission
Modify	Combines the Read & Execute permission with the Write permission and further allows the user to delete the file
Read	Allows the user to view the contents of the file and to see ownership and attributes
Read & Execute	Combines the Read permission with the ability to execute
Write	Allows the user to overwrite the file, as well as to change attributes and see ownership and permissions

Superuser

The term *superuser* applies to any user account that has total control and access to a system. This user will possess the Full Control permission to every resource and object on the device for which the user possesses this account type. Various operating systems attach different names to this account. Windows systems call this the Administrator account; other systems call it root, admin, or supervisor. Whatever this account is called, security best practices call for the account to be used only when required. Users who are members of any group accounts (like the Administrators group) that possess these rights or who are superuser account holders should use standard user accounts for all day-to-day activities and only log on using the superuser account when required.

File vs. Share

The Windows New Technology File System (NTFS) was introduced with Windows NT to address security problems. Before Windows NT was released, it had become apparent to Microsoft that a new filesystem was needed to handle growing disk sizes, security concerns, and the need for more stability. NTFS was created to address those issues.

Although FAT was relatively stable if the systems that were controlling it kept running, it didn't do well when the power went out or the system crashed unexpectedly. One of the benefits of NTFS was a transaction tracking system, which made it possible for Windows NT to back out of any disk operations that were in progress when Windows NT crashed or lost power.

With NTFS, files, directories, and volumes can each have their own security. NTFS's security is flexible and built in. Not only does NTFS track security in ACLs, which can hold permissions for local users and groups, but each entry in the ACL can specify what type of access is given—such as Read, Write, Modify, or Full Control. This allows a great deal of flexibility in setting up a network. In addition, special file-encryption programs encrypt data while it was stored on the hard disk.

Microsoft strongly recommends that all network shares be established using NTFS. Several current OSs from Microsoft support both FAT32 and NTFS. It's possible to convert from FAT32 to NTFS without losing data, but you can't do the operation in reverse (you would need to reformat the drive and install the data again from a backup tape).

> If you're using FAT32 and want to change to NTFS, the convert utility will allow you to do so. For example, to change the E drive to NTFS, the command is convert e: /FS:NTFS.

Share permissions apply only when a user is accessing a file or folder through the network. Local permissions and attributes are used to protect the file when the user is local. With FAT and FAT32, you do not have the ability to assign "extended" or "extensible" permissions, and the user sitting at the console is effectively the owner of all resources on the system. As such, they can add, change, and delete any data or file that they want.

With NTFS as the filesystem, however, you are allowed to assign more comprehensive security to your computer system. NTFS permissions are able to protect you at the file level. Share permissions can be applied to the directory level only. NTFS permissions can affect users logged on locally or across the network to the system where the NTFS permissions are applied. Share permissions are in effect only when the user connects to the resource via the network.

How Do NTFS and Share Permissions Work Together?
Share and NTFS permissions are not cumulative; permission must be granted at both levels to allow access. Moreover, the effective permission that the user has will be the most restrictive of the combined NTFS permissions as compared to the combined share permissions.

Allow vs. Deny

Within NTFS, permissions for objects fall into one of three categories: allow, not allow, and deny. When viewing the permissions for a file or folder, you can check the box for Allow, which effectively allows that group to perform that action. You can also deselect the Allow check box so that group cannot perform that action. Alternatively, you can select the Deny check box, which prevents that group from using that action. There is a difference between not allowing (a cleared check box) and Deny (which specifically prohibits), and you tend not to see Deny used often. Deny, when used, trumps other permissions. This can be a problem for users with permissions derived from multiple groups.

Permissions set at a folder are inherited down through subfolders, unless otherwise changed. Permissions are also cumulative; if a user is a member of a group that has read permission and a member of a group that has write permission, the user effectively has both read and write permissions.

Data Security Methods and Secure Storage Disposal Techniques

While controlling access to files and folders is important, it does nothing for you if a device is stolen because it's possible to access the data using an operating system on an external drive. To prevent that, encrypting the data is the solution. In this final section, we'll look at various levels of encryption and how they differ. We'll also talk about securely removing data from a storage device when that device is decommissioned.

Storage Encryption

When using encryption to protect data that resides on storage devices (called *data at rest*), we can apply the encryption at different levels with different results. Let's look at three types of encryption.

File-Level Encryption

Encryption at the file level is performed on each file or on a folder that contains files. In Windows this is done using the Encrypting File System (EFS). EFS is an encryption tool built into all Enterprise versions of Windows. It allows a user to encrypt files that can only be decrypted by the user who encrypted the files. It can only be used on NTFS volumes but is simple to use.

Linux and Unix do not have a system like EFS, but you can encrypt a file use the gpg command. It is an encryption and signing tool for Linux- and Unix-like operating systems such as FreeBSD/Solaris and others. To encrypt a file named Sales.txt, you would execute this command:

```
$ gpg -c Sales.txt
```

This will generate the following output, to which you must respond with a password:

```
Enter passphrase:<YOUR-PASSWORD>
Repeat passphrase:<YOUR-PASSWORD>
```

Disk-Level Encryption

Disk-level encryption encrypts an entire volume or entire disk and may use the same key for the entire disk or, in some cases, a different key for each partition or volume. This can help prevent data loss by the theft of the computer or the hard drive.

Disk-level encryption may also use a Trusted Platform Module (TPM) chip. This chip is located on the motherboard of the system and provides password protection, digital rights management (DRM), and full disk encryption. It protects the keys used to encrypt the computer's hard disks and provide integrity authentication for a trusted boot pathway. Since the key in the TPM chip is required to access the hard drive, if it is removed, decryption of the data on the drive becomes impossible.

In Windows, full disk encryption is done using BitLocker. In Linux and Unix, open source tools such as TrueCrypt have been used in the past. While development of that tool has been halted, other open source tools such as dm-crypt exist to accomplish full disk encryption.

Tape Encryption

It is also possible to encrypt data that resides on backup tapes. Starting with version 4 of the Linear Tape Open tape standard (LTO-4), encryption is a supported feature. You should keep in mind the following issues:

- Choose a product that will perform compression prior to performing encryption. Otherwise, the tape will not compress because encryption effectively scrambles the data, removing the redundancy that compression algorithms rely on.

- All of your tape drives must support the encryption used with LTO-4 drives.

- Ensure that you have a robust key management system; the loss of a key will mean the loss of the data that was encrypted with the key.

Storage Media

At some point in time, storage media must be decommissioned. When that occurs, all sensitive data must be removed. There are a number of ways this can be done, with the results varying widely. We'll discuss data removal methods in this section.

Soft Wipe

A soft wipe describes any method that deletes data in such a way that the data can be recovered later using special data forensics software. The best example of this is the simple file deletion process.

File Deletion

When you simply right-click on a file and select Delete, the data is not immediately deleted—the area of the hard drive where that data is located is marked for deletion. That simply means that the filesystem is now given permission to write data over the old data in that location. Until that overwrite occurs, the data is still there on the hard drive. Moreover, even after the data is overwritten, unless the overwriting has occurred many times, the data can be recovered using data recovery software.

Hard Wipe

A *hard wipe* is a term used to describe any deletion process that cannot be reversed using data recovery or forensics software. Most disk management software will provide this type of deletion and may refer to it in various terms, such as "scrubbing" the drive. Let's look at how this process works.

Zero Out All Sectors

When a hard wipe is performed, the area where the file is located is zeroed out, meaning all 0s are written to the sectors where the data is located. This is followed by writing all 1s to the same location, followed by another round of all 0s. This process may continue many times. The more times it's done, the more effective the data wipe.

Physical Destruction

Ultimately the most effective method of protecting sensitive data located on a hard drive is to destroy the hard drive. While the focus is on hard drives, you can also physically destroy other forms of media, such as flash drives and CD/DVDs.

Shredder

When it comes to DVDs and CDs, many commercial paper shredders include the ability to destroy them. Paper shredders, however, are not able to handle hard drives, and you need a shredder created for just such a purpose. Jackhammer makes a low-volume model that will destroy eight drives a minute and carries a suggested list price of just under $30,000.

Drill/Hammer

If you don't have the budget for a hard drive shredder, you can accomplish similar results in a much more time-consuming way with a power drill. The goal is to physically destroy the platters in the drive. Start the process by removing the cover from the drive—this is normally done with a Torx driver (while #8 does not work with all, it is a good one to try first). You can remove the arm with a slotted screwdriver and then the cover over the platters using a Torx driver. Don't worry about damaging or scratching anything because nothing is intended to be saved. Everything but the platters can be tossed away.

As an optional step, you can completely remove the tracks using a belt sander, grinder, or palm sander. The goal is to turn the shiny surface into fine powder. This adds one more layer of assurance that nothing usable remains. Always be careful to wear eye protection and not breathe in any fine particles that you generate during the grinding/destruction process.

Following this, use the power drill to create as small a set of particles as possible. A drill press works much better for this task than trying to hold the drive and drill it with a handheld model.

   Even with practice, you will find that manually destroying a hard drive is time-consuming. There are companies that specialize in this and can do it efficiently. One such company is Shred-it, which will pick it up from you and provide a chain-of-custody assurance and a certificate of destruction upon completion. You can find out more about what it offers here:

www.shredit.com/shredding-service/What-to-shred/Hard-drive-destruction.aspx

Electromagnetic/Degaussing

Degaussing involves applying a strong magnetic field to initialize the media. This process helps ensure that information doesn't fall into the wrong hands.

Since degaussing uses a specifically designed electromagnet to eliminate all data on the drive, that destruction also includes the factory prerecorded servo tracks (These are tracks put on at the factory.). You can find wand model degaussers priced at just over $500 or desktop units that sell for up to $30,000.

Incineration

A final option that exists for some forms of storage is to burn the media. Regardless of whether the media is a hard drive, CD, DVD, solid-state drive, or floppy disk, the media must be reduced to ash, or in the case of hard drive platters, the internal platters must be physically deformed from heating.

Certificate of Destruction

Certificates of destruction are documents that attest to either the physical destruction of the media on which sensitive data was located or of a scientifically approved method of removing the data from a drive.

These documents are typically issued to the organization by a storage vendor or cloud provider to prove either that the data has been removed or that the media has been destroyed.

Remote Wipe

While a remote wipe is most often used to erase the data in a mobile device, there may be instances when you need to remotely wipe a server. Using SSH, the command to wipe a Linux or Unix server would be

```
shred [option(s)] file(s)_or_devices(s)
```

By default, this command will overwrite the specified drive or file 25 times. There are options you can use to increase that number if desired.

In Windows, the remote wipe feature is available only for mobile devices and not for servers.

Summary

In this chapter you learned about basic network security systems and protocols. This included a discussion of physical security devices such as firewalls, NIDs, and routers. We also talked about authentication protocols such as LDAP, TACACS, TACACS+, and RADIUS and the components that make up a PKI. You also learned about controlling access to data on servers using logical control methods. Finally, we covered secure methods of data storage and disposal, including various levels of encryption that are available and techniques for removing sensitive data from media such as soft wipes, hard wipes, and degaussing.

Exam Essentials

Identify common methods of controlling network traffic.   Among these methods are the deployment of both host-based and network-based firewalls, the implementation of port-based security and 802.1x, and the implementation of VLANs.

Describe logical access control methods.   Explain the proper use of access control lists (ACLs) to protect resources. Use groups to apply role-based access control. List common permissions and identify the tasks they enable when working with resources.

Implement secure storage methods and secure data disposal techniques.   Describe various levels at which encryption can be applied and the implications of each. List the techniques for removing sensitive data from storage devices. Understand the advantages and disadvantages of each method.

Review Questions

You can find the answers in the Appendix.

1. Which of the following devices can also provide web caching services?

   A. Proxy firewall

   B. Packet filtering firewall

   C. Stateful firewall

   D. Host-based firewall

2. Which of the following can read the individual commands of the protocols that are being served?

   A. Stateful firewall

   B. Packet filtering firewall

   C. Application-level proxy

   D. Host-based firewall

3. In which of the following devices are records kept using a table that tracks every communications channel?

   A. Stateful firewall

   B. Packet filtering firewall

   C. Application-level proxy

   D. Host-based firewall

4. In which operating system is `iptables` used?

   A. Windows

   B. Sun Solaris

   C. Linux

   D. Novell

5. Which of the following packets will be allowed according to the `iptables` rule that follows?

   `iptables -A INPUT -i eth1 -s 192.168.0.0/24 -j DROP`

   A. A packet from 192.168.1.6/24

   B. A packet from 192.168.0.6/24

   C. A packet from 192.168.0.1/24

   D. A packet from 192.168.0.240/24

6. Which of the following cannot be accomplished using port security?

   A. Set the minimum number of MAC addresses that can be seen on a port.

   B. Take a specific action when a port violation occurs.

   C. Define exactly which MAC addresses are allowed on the port.

   D. Set the maximum number of MAC addresses that can be seen on a port.

7. Which standard describes centralized port-based access control?

   A. 802.11i

   B. 802.1x

   C. 802.12

   D. 802.10

8. When discussing 802.1x, which of the following roles is played by the RADIUS server?

   A. Supplicant

   B. Authenticator

   C. Authentication server

   D. Imperative

9. Which of the following is *not* an example of an authenticator in an 802.1x architecture?

   A. 802.1x capable switch

   B. Access point

   C. RADIUS server

   D. VPN server

10. Which statement is false with respect to router ACLs?

    A. The order of the rules is important.

    B. An implied deny all rule is located at the end of all ACLs.

    C. It is possible to log all traffic that meets any of the rules.

    D. All rules in the list are considered before the traffic is allowed.

11. Which of the following provides a mechanism to access and query directory services systems?

    A. TACACS

    B. LDAP

    C. TACACS+

    D. RADIUS

12. Which of the following would Joe use to encrypt a message that only Sally could decrypt?

   A. Joe's private key

   B. Sally's private key

   C. Joe's public key

   D. Sally's public key

13. Which of the following is true of the requirements to use SSL on a website?

   A. The web server must have a certificate.

   B. The client must have a certificate.

   C. The web server and the client must have a certificate.

   D. Neither the web server nor the client must have a certificate.

14. What type of encryption does PPTP use?

   A. AES

   B. IPsec

   C. MPPE

   D. Triple DES

15. Which of the following IPsec components provides authentication and integrity *only*?

   A. SPI

   B. SA

   C. ESP

   D. AH

16. Which of the following is a type of table that tracks IPsec security associations?

   A. SPI

   B. SA

   C. ESP

   D. AH

17. Which of the following is used to generate each session key in IPsec?

   A. IKE

   B. SA

   C. ESP

   D. AH

18. You have two devices that are connected to the same switch with IP addresses in the same network. After placing the two devices in separate VLANs, they can no longer ping one another. At what layer of the OSI model are the VLANs providing separation?

    A. Network

    B. Data link

    C. Session

    D. Transport

19. Using which of the following protocols can expose your switches to a switch spoofing attack?

    A. SSL

    B. VTP

    C. DTP

    D. STP

20. Which is the only security zone in which PII should be located?

    A. DMZ

    B. Extranet

    C. Intranet

    D. Public cloud

Chapter 8

Networking

COMPTIA SERVER+ EXAM OBJECTIVES COVERED IN THIS CHAPTER:

✓ **5.1   Given a scenario, configure servers to use IP addressing and network infrastructure services**

- IPv4 vs. IPv6
- Default gateway
- CIDR notation and subnetting
- Public and private IP addressing
- Static IP assignment vs. DHCP
- DNS (FQDN, default domain suffix/search domain)
- WINS
- NetBIOS
- NAT/PAT
- MAC addresses
- Network interface card configuration (NIC teaming, Duplexing [full, half, auto], speeds [10/100/1000 Mbps, 10 Gbps])

✓ **5.2   Compare and contrast various ports and protocols**

- TCP vs. UDP
- SNMP 161
- SMTP 25
- FTP 20/21
- SFTP 22
- SSH 22
- SCP 22
- NTP 123
- HTTP 80
- HTTPS 443

- TELNET 23

- IMAP 143

- POP3 110

- RDP 3389

- FTPS 989/990

- LDAP 389/3268

- DNS 53

- DHCP 68

✓ **5.3 Given a scenario, install cables and implement proper cable management procedures**

- Copper (patch cables [crossover, straight through, rollover], CAT5, CAT5e, CAT6)

- Fiber (singlemode, multimode)

- Connectors (ST, LC, SC, SFP, RJ-45, RJ-11)

- Cable placement and routing (cable channels, cable management trays [vertical, horizontal])

- Labeling

- Bend radius

- Cable ties

If you really wanted to secure your servers from network attacks, you could remove them from the network. Unfortunately servers that are not connected to a network are not of much use to us. Therefore you need to know how to connect servers to a network and manage any issues that may arise. Moreover, as networking servers involves working with cabling, you need to know how to manage all that spaghetti that may reside in the server room or data center. This chapter is about all things networking.

Configuring Servers to Use IP Addressing and Network Infrastructure Services

Servers, like any other network host, require an IP address and a subnet mask to operate on the network. In almost all cases, they require a default gateway and the IP address of a DNS server as well. Moreover, there are a host of networking services that servers typically rely on. To successfully configure a server to operate on the network, you must understand all of these functions and services. First, let's spend time learning and/or reviewing infrastructure services and the configurations required to allow a server to make use of these services.

IPv4 vs. IPv6

IPv4 uses a 32-bit addressing scheme that provides for over 4 billion unique addresses. Unfortunately, a lot of IP-enabled devices are added to the Internet each and every day—not to mention the fact that not all of the addresses that can be created are used by public networks (many are reserved, in classes D and above, and are unavailable for public use). This reduces the number of addresses that can be allocated as public Internet addresses.

IPv6 offers a number of improvements, the most notable of which is its ability to handle growth in public networks. IPv6 uses a 128-bit addressing scheme, allowing a huge number of possible addresses: 340,282,366,920,938,463,463,374,607,431,768,211,456. Table 8.1 compares IPv4 to IPv6.

In IPv6 addresses, leading zeroes in a hextet can be left out and consecutive hextets consisting of all zeroes can represented with a double colon, so colons next to each other in the address indicate one or more sets of zeroes for that section. The double colon may only be used once in this fashion, however.

TABLE 8.1   IPv4 vs. IPv6

Feature	IPv4	IPv6
Loopback address	127.0.0.1	0:0:0:0:0:0:0:1 (::1)
Private ranges	10.0.0.0 172.16.0.0 –172.31.0.0 192.168.0.0	FEC0:: (proposed)
Autoconfigured addresses	169.254.0.0	FE80::

Default Gateway

In TCP/IP, a gateway is the address of the machine to send data to that is not intended for a host on this network (in other words, a default gateway). It is the router that allows traffic to be sent beyond the internal network. Hosts are configured with the address of a gateway (called the default gateway), and if they need to correspond with a host outside the internal network, the data is sent to the gateway to facilitate this. When you configure TCP/IP on a host, one of the fields you should provide is a gateway field, which specifies where data not intended for this network is sent in order to be able to communicate with the rest of the world.

CIDR Notation and Subnetting

Subnetting your network is the process of taking a single network and dividing it into smaller networks. When you configure TCP/IP on a host, you typically need to give only three values: a unique IP address, a default gateway (router) address, and a subnet mask. It is the subnet mask that determines the network on which the host resides. The default subnet mask for each class of network is shown in Table 8.2.

Purists may argue that you don't need a default gateway. Technically this is true if your network is small and you don't communicate beyond it. For all practical purposes, though, most networks need a default gateway.

TABLE 8.2   Default subnet values

Class	Default subnet mask
A	255.0.0.0
B	255.255.0.0
C	255.255.255.0

When you use the default subnet mask, you're requiring that all hosts be at one site and not be subdividing your network. This is called *classful* subnetting. Any deviation from the default signifies that you're dividing the network into multiple subnetworks, a process known as *classless* subnetting.

The problem with classful subnetting is that it only allows for three sizes of networks: Class A (16,777,216 hosts), Class B (65,536 hosts), and Class C (254 hosts). Two of these are too large to operate efficiently in the real world, and when enterprises were issued public network IDs that were larger than they needed, many public IP addresses were wasted. For this reason, and simply to allow for the creation of smaller networks that operate better, the concept of classless routing, or Classless Interdomain Routing (CIDR), was born.

Using CIDR, administrators can create smaller networks called subnets by manipulating the subnet mask of a larger classless or major network ID. This allows you to create a subnet that is much closer in size to what you need, thus wasting fewer IP addresses and increasing performance in each subnet. The increased performance is a function of the reduced broadcast traffic generated in each subnet.

Public and Private IP Addressing

Within each of the three major classes of IP v4 addresses, a range is set aside for *private addresses*. These addresses cannot communicate directly with the Internet without using a proxy server or network address translation to do so. Table 8.3 lists the private address ranges for Class A, B, and C addresses.

TABLE 8.3   Private address ranges

Class	Range
A	10.0.0.0/8 to 10.255.255.255 /8
B	172.16.0.0/16 to 172.31.255.255 /16
C	192.168.0.0/16 to 192.168.255.255 /16

Automatic Private IP Addressing (APIPA) is a TCP/IP feature Microsoft added to their operating systems. If a DHCP server cannot be found and the clients are configured to obtain IP addresses automatically, the clients automatically assign themselves an IP address, somewhat randomly, in the 169.254.*x.x* range with a subnet mask of 255.255.0.0. This allows them to communicate with other hosts that have similarly configured themselves but are unable to connect to the Internet. If a computer is using an APIPA address, it will have trouble communicating with other clients if those clients do not use APIPA addresses.

In IPv6, there is a type of address called a *link local address* that is like an APIPA address in many ways in that the device will generate one of these addresses for each interface with no intervention from a human—as is done with APIPA. The scope of the address is also the same in that it is not routable and is only good on the segment on which the device is located.

As is the case with APIPA addresses, if two devices connected to the same segment generate these addresses, they will be in the same network and the two devices will be able to communicate. This is because the devices always generate the address using the same IPv6 prefix (the equivalent of a network ID in IPv4), which is FE80::/64. The remainder of the address is created by spreading the 48-bit MAC address across the last 64 bits, yielding an IPv6 address that looks like this:

```
FE80::2237:06FF:FECF:67E4/64
```

Static IP Assignment vs. DHCP

The two methods of entering address information for a host are *static* and *dynamic*. Static means that you manually enter the information for the host and it does not change. Dynamic means that Dynamic Host Configuration Protocol (DHCP) is used for the host to lease information from a DHCP server.

DHCP issues IP configuration data. Rather than administrators having to configure a unique IP address for every host added on a network (and *default gateway* and *subnet mask*), they can use a DHCP server to issue these values. That server is given a number of addresses in a range that it can supply to clients.

For example, the server may be given the IP range (or *scope*) 192.168.12.1 to 192.168.12.200. When a client boots, it sends out a request for the server to issue it an address (and any other configuration data) from that scope. The server takes one of the numbers it has available and leases it to the client for a length of time. If the client is still using the configuration data when 50 percent of the lease has expired, it requests a renewal of the lease from the server; under normal operating conditions, the request is granted. When the client is no longer using the address, the address goes back in the scope and can be issued to another client.

DHCP is built on the older Bootstrap Protocol (BOOTP) that was used to allow diskless workstations to boot and connect to a server that provided them with an operating system and applications. The client uses broadcasts to request the data and thus—normally—can't communicate with DHCP servers beyond their own subnet (broadcasts don't route). A DHCP relay agent, however, can be employed to allow DHCP broadcasts to go from one network to another. The relay agent can be one of the hosts on the local network or a router that the hosts in the local network use as their gateway. The positioning of the relay agent is shown in Figure 8.1.

FIGURE 8.1 DHCP relay agent

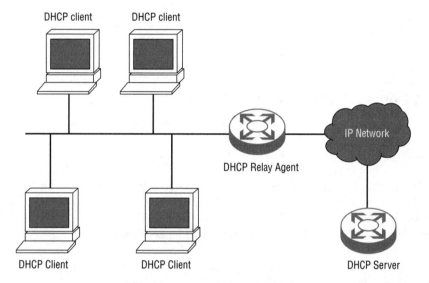

While the primary purpose of DHCP is to lease IP addresses to hosts, when it gives the IP address, it also often includes the additional configuration information as well: DNS server, router information, and so on.

DNS

Every computer, interface, or device on a TCP/IP network needs an *IP address*. Because of the Internet, TCP/IP is the most commonly used networking protocol today. You can easily see that it's difficult for most users to memorize these numbers, so hostnames are used in their place. *Hostnames* are alphanumeric values assigned to a host; any host may have more than one hostname.

For example, the host 192.168.12.123 may be known to all users as Gemini, or it may be known to the sales department as Gemini and to the marketing department as Apollo9. All that is needed is a means by which the alphanumeric name can be translated into its IP address. There are a number of methods for doing so, but for this exam, you need to know only one: DNS. On a large network, you can add a server to be referenced by all hosts for the name resolution. Multiple DNS servers can serve an area and provide fault tolerance for one another. In all cases, the DNS servers divide their area into zones; every zone has a primary server and any number of secondary servers. DNS works with any operating system and any version.

FQDN

Fully qualified domain names (FQDNs) identify the host and the location of the hostname in the DNS namespace of the organization. FQDNs consists of at least two parts and perhaps more. All FQDNs will have a host name and a domain name. If the DNS namespace of the organization is subdivided into subdomains, it could have a subdomain section as well. For example, in the FQDN tmcmillan.acme.com, *tmcmillan* is the hostname and acme.com is the domain name. In the example tmcmillan.atlanta.acme .com, *tmcmillan* is the hostname, *atlanta* identifies the subdomain, and *acme.com* is the domain name.

Default Domain Suffix/Search Domain

While tmcmillan.acme.com describes a FQDN, if we just consider the hostname portion, *tmcmillan* without the domain name, we would call the name *unqualified* because it is lacking information that fully qualifies or describes its location in the DNS namespace.

In many instances, users make references to unqualified hostnames when accessing resources. When this occurs, DNS needs to know how to handle these unqualified domain names. The treatment of these names by default will be for DNS to append or add domain names (called suffixes) to the unqualified hostname until a match is found in the DNS namespace. If the device has been assigned a domain name, then it uses that as a suffix to unqualified hostnames.

It is also possible to configure a list of domain names for the DNS to append to unqualified hostnames and the order in which they should be tried. In Microsoft this can be done in several ways. It can be done through the use of a Group Policy that is pushed down to the clients, or it can be done manually on the interface of the device. Exercise 8.1 will demonstrate the manual method, and Exercise 8.2 will demonstrate use of a Group Policy. This task can also be done with a Registry edit, but Microsoft recommends these two methods as the safest.

EXERCISE 8.1

Configuring a Suffix Search List

1. Access the TCP/IP properties of the network interface. You should be seeing the dialog box shown in Figure 8.2.

2. At the bottom of the screen click the Advanced button. Then select the DNS tab and you will be presented with the dialog box shown in Figure 8.3, open to the DNS tab.

3. In the middle of this page are two radio buttons, one of which is selected by default and tells DNS to append the parent DNS suffix to any unqualified hostnames. The second button, Append These DNS Suffixes (In Order) is the one you select to create a list of domain names to attempt when an unqualified hostname is encountered. Select that radio button.

FIGURE 8.2 TCP/IP properties

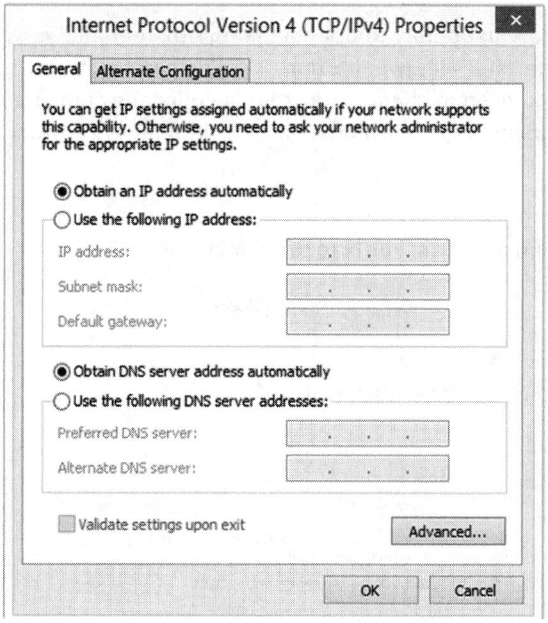

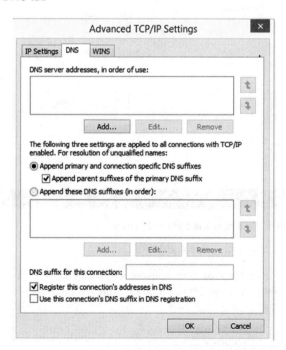

FIGURE 8.3 DNS tab

EXERCISE 8.1 *(continued)*

4. Click the Add button just below to open a dialog box that allows you to enter a domain suffix to the list, as shown in Figure 8.4. You can do this repeatedly until the list is finished. If you need to change the order in which they are attempted, use the up and down arrows next to the list box. Then click OK at the bottom of the page to finalize the list.

FIGURE 8.4   Adding a domain suffix to the search list

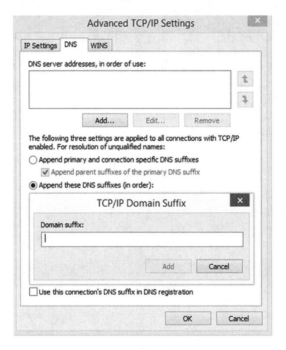

EXERCISE 8.2

Configuring a Suffix Search List as a Policy

Note: This exercise uses Windows Server 2012 R2.

1. Access the Group Policy Management console, choosing it from the Tools menu in Server Manager. Right-click the default domain policy in the tree and click Edit, as shown in Figure 8.5.

2. In the Group Policy window, navigate to Computer Configuration ➢ Administrative Templates ➢ Network ➢ DNS Client, as shown in Figure 8.6.

FIGURE 8.5   Group Policy

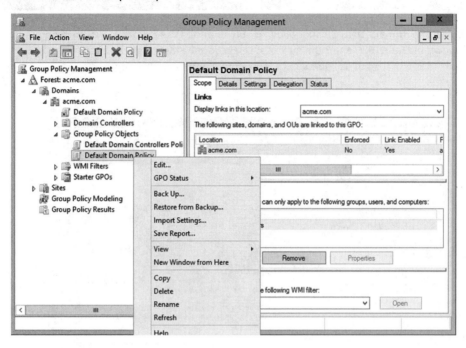

FIGURE 8.6   DNS client settings

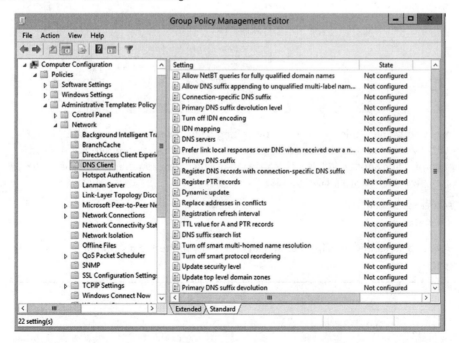

3. Select the Primary DNS Suffix policy, enable it, and in the Primary DNS suffix box (shown in Figure 8.7) enter the suffixes. Use a comma-delimited string to enter multiple addresses, such as "acme.com, ajax.com," and then click Apply.

FIGURE 8.7 Primary DNS suffix

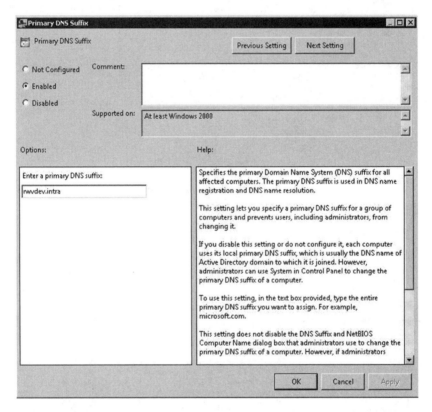

In a Linux environment this can be done by editing a file called the resolv.conf, which is located at /etc/resolv.conf. Open the file using either the vi command or the sudi vi command. Then simply add search entries to the file. For example, to add the suffix acme.com, use the following commands:

```
# vi /etc/resolv.conf
search acme.com
```

Then save and close the file. The search list is currently limited to six domains with a total of 256 characters.

NetBIOS

NetBIOS (Network Basic Input/Output System) allows applications on different computers to communicate within a local area network and was first developed by IBM and later adopted by Microsoft. In today's networks, NetBIOS normally runs over TCP/IP via the NetBIOS over TCP/IP (NBT) protocol.

Devices have multiple NetBIOS names, unlike DNS in which each device typically has a single hostname (although they can be configured with other names or aliases). Each of these names represents a service on the device. A NetBIOS name consists of 16 ASCII characters; however, Microsoft limits the hostname to 15 characters and reserves the 16th character as a NetBIOS suffix. The NetBIOS suffix is written in hex and identifies the service; it is what is unique to each of these names on a device.

WINS

Windows Internet Name Service (WINS) is an alternate method of locating devices that is based on the use of NetBIOS names. While mostly used in Windows environments, it might be used in any environment where NetBIOS-based applications requiring the resolution of NetBIOS names are in use.

WINS servers perform NETBIOS name resolution on behalf of WINS clients. In the absence of a WINS server, clients requiring NetBIOS name resolution will resort to other methods that create much more network traffic, such as a broadcast. Although the use of WINS servers has declined with the decline of NetBIOS-based applications, you still may need to know how to configure a server to use a WINS server. In Exercise 8.3, this task is demonstrated.

EXERCISE 8.3

Configuring a Server to Use a WINS Server

Note: This exercise uses Windows 2012 R2.

1. Access the TCP/IP properties of the network interface. You should see the dialog box from Figure 8.2 earlier.

2. Click the Advanced button and select the WINS tab, as shown in Figure 8.8.

3. Click the Add button, and in the box provided, enter the address of the WINS server, as shown in Figure 8.9. Then click OK to finalize the configuration.

FIGURE 8.8   WINS tab

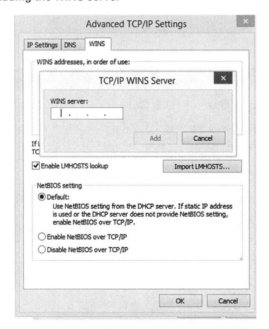

FIGURE 8.9   Adding the WINS server

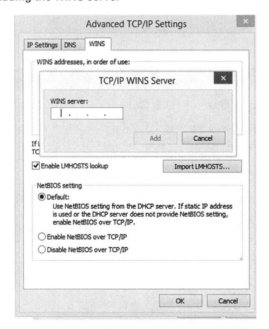

NAT/PAT

While not created as a security mechanism, *Network Address Translation* (NAT) provides a unique opportunity to assist in the security of a network.

Originally, NAT extended the number of usable Internet addresses. It translates private IP addresses to public addresses. Now it allows an organization to present a single address to the Internet for all computer connections. The NAT server provides IP addresses to the hosts or systems in the network and tracks inbound and outbound traffic.

A company that uses NAT presents a single connection to the network. This connection may be through a router or a NAT server. The only information that an intruder will be able to get is that the connection has a single address.

NAT effectively hides your network from the world, making it much harder to determine what systems exist on the other side of the router. Most new routers support NAT.

It's important to understand that NAT acts as a proxy between the local area network (which can be using private IP addresses) and the Internet.

Most NAT implementations assign internal hosts private IP address numbers and use public addresses only for the NAT to translate to and communicate with the outside world. The private address ranges, all of which are nonroutable, are discussed earlier in the section "Public and Private IP Addressing."

In addition to NAT, Port Address Translation (PAT) is possible. Whereas NAT can use multiple public IP addresses, PAT uses a single one for every packet that leaves the network and keeps track of the original sender by recording the dynamic port number that the device used as the source port when the transmission was initiated.

MAC Addresses

Each network interface card (NIC) has a unique hardware address, called a Media Access Control (MAC) address. If two NICs or interfaces on the same network have the same hardware address, neither one will be able to communicate. For this reason, the IEEE has established a standard for hardware addresses and assigns blocks of these addresses to NIC manufacturers, who then hard-wire the addresses into the cards.

MAC addresses, also called *physical addresses*, which reside on the Network Access layer of the TCP/IP model, are applied to network interface adapters of various types. These permanent addresses, sometimes called *burned-in addresses (BIAs)*, are assigned to the adapters by the manufacturer.

MAC addresses use the hexadecimal numbering system and follow standard formats that identify both the manufacturer and the individual device. Two formats are set forth by the IEEE; the more common is the MAC-48 format. A newer format, the EUI-64 format, is used with IPv6. As the use of IPv6 increases in North America (still lagging behind the rest of the

world), the use of the EUI-64 format will increase. Even when EUI-64 is used, it doesn't actually change the format of the physical 48-bit MAC address. It is a method of spreading the
48-bit MAC across 64 bits so that it can be used as the last 64 bits of the 128-bit IPv6 address.
It does so by ensuring 16 bits in the middle of the MAC address are always set to FF:FE in hex.

Some examples of items that have MAC addresses using the MAC-48 identifier are as
follows:

- Wired Ethernet adapters
- Wireless network adapters
- Router interfaces
- Bluetooth devices
- Token Ring network adapters
- FDDI network adapters

The standard format for these addresses is six groups of two hex digits separated by a hyphen
or a colon. It is also sometimes displayed in the three groups of four hex digits separated by a
period. It's important to note that although we view and discuss these MAC addresses in their
hexadecimal format, they are transmitted over the medium (cabling or wireless) in binary.
Figure 8.10 shows an example of a MAC address as displayed by executing the `ipconfig/all`
command on a computer at the command prompt. This command will display information
about the network interfaces of the computer, including the MAC address.

FIGURE 8.10   MAC address output

```
::\Users\tmcmillan>ipconfig/all

Ethernet adapter Local Area Connection:

    Connection-specific DNS Suffix  . : alpha.kaplaninc.com
    Description . . . . . . . . . . . : Broadcom NetXtreme 57xx Gigabit Controlle
    Physical Address. . . . . . . . . : 00-1A-A0-E1-95-AB
    DHCP Enabled. . . . . . . . . . . : Yes
    Autoconfiguration Enabled . . . . : Yes
    Link-local IPv6 Address . . . . . : fe80::ada3:8b73:a66e:6bc0%11(Preferred)
    IPv4 Address. . . . . . . . . . . : 10.88.2.177(Preferred)
    Subnet Mask . . . . . . . . . . . : 255.255.254.0
    Lease Obtained. . . . . . . . . . : Friday, April 08, 2011 7:05:01 PM
    Lease Expires . . . . . . . . . . : Friday, May 06, 2011 7:08:43 AM
    Default Gateway . . . . . . . . . : 10.88.2.6
    DHCP Server . . . . . . . . . . . : 10.88.10.55
```

Each part of this address communicates information. The address is divided into two sec-
tions, as shown in Figure 8.11. The left half of the address is called the *Organizationally
Unique Identifier (OUI)*. The right half is called the Universally Administered Address (UAA).
Together they make a globally unique MAC address.

FIGURE 8.11   OUI and UAA

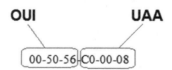

Depending on the manufacturer of the device, and the tool in which you are viewing the MAC address, this MAC address may be represented in the following formats:

```
00-50-56-C0-00-08
00:50:56:C0:00:08
0050.56C0.0008
```

Network Interface Card Configuration

The most basic configuration you can apply to a NIC is assigning an IP address and a subnet mask, but most devices also require a default gateway and a DNS server. But you may have to make other changes to the NIC that go beyond this, and you need to understand and appreciate the importance of setting the NIC to the proper speed and duplex. Finally, there may be cases where you need to combine the bandwidth of multiple NICs into what we call a NIC team. In this section, we'll discuss all of those issues.

NIC Teaming

NIC teaming is the process of combining multiple physical network connections into a single logical interface. This process goes by other names as well, including link aggregation and link bonding. Combining these physical links can be done using proprietary methods, and there is also an IEEE standard for the process called 802.3ad, later replaced by 802.1ax-2008. When the standard method is used, a protocol called Link Aggregation Control Protocol (LACP) controls the establishment of the aggregated link based on the proper combination of settings of the ends of the multiple links and upon the agreement of certain settings on all physical links in the "bundle" (speed and duplex among them).

The advantages to using a NIC team are increased bandwidth and fault tolerance. You have two physical links, so if one is lost the other is still functional. For links that run between switches, it is better than using two links that are *not* aggregated, because in switch networks that include redundant links (which they should, according to best practices) a switching loop prevention protocol called Spanning Tree Protocol (STP) will disable one of the links. When the links are aggregated, STP considers them to be a single link and does not shut any of the ports in the aggregation.

In Exercise 8.4, you will set up a NIC team on a Windows Server 2012 R2 server.

EXERCISE 8.4

Configuring a NIC Team

Note: This exercise uses Windows Server 2012 R2.

1. Open Server Manager and determine if NIC teaming has been enabled, as shown in Figure 8.12. If not, double-click on the Disabled link.

2. If NIC teaming is disabled, double-click on the Disabled link and the NIC Teaming window will open, as shown in Figure 8.13.

FIGURE 8.12   Server Manager

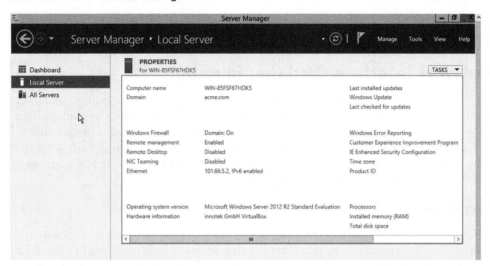

FIGURE 8.13   NIC Teaming

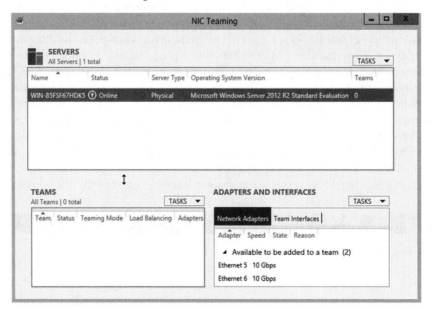

3. Select New Team from the Tasks drop-down box above the Teams panel on the lower-left side, as shown in Figure 8.14.

4. A new dialog box will appear. Select the network adapters that will be members of the team you are creating. As shown in Figure 8.15, we are selecting Ethernet 5 and Ethernet 6.

FIGURE 8.14   New Team

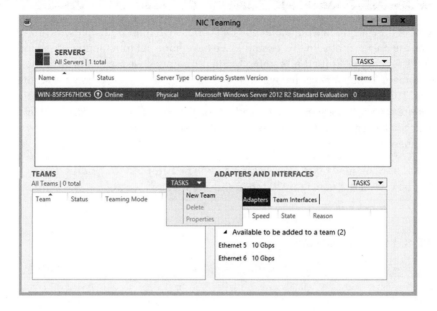

FIGURE 8.15   NIC team settings

Also note that it is on this page that you can choose whether both adapters are active or if one is only standby. In this example, we have none set for standby, meaning both are functional. From the Teaming Mode drop-down, we have chosen Switch Independent, which means that we intend to connect each adapter to a different switch. The Load Balancing drop-down allows you to select the method used to distribute the traffic between the two adapters. We set it to Address Hash, which means it will keep all traffic that is part of the same conversation or session on the same adapter.

5. Click OK and the new team is created. You will be returned to the previous dialog box, with the new team listed in the Teams pane, as shown in Figure 8.16.

FIGURE 8.16   New NIC team

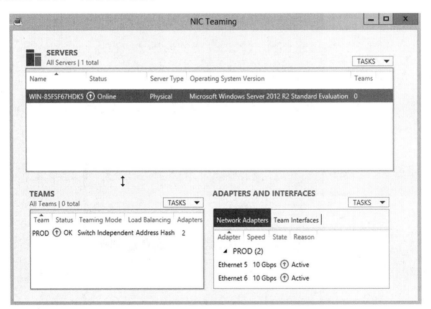

This can also be done in Linux. In Exercise 8.5, you will create a NIC team from two adapters, Ethernet 1 and Ethernet 2, and they will be teamed into an object called Bond0. You will implement round robin, in which both adapters are used.

EXERCISE 8.5

Configuring a NIC Team

Note: This exercise uses Linux.

1. Configure Ethernet 1 to be used as a slave by bond0 by opening the `ifcfg-eth1` file and editing it as follows:

```
# vi /etc/sysconfig/network-scripts/ifcfg-eth1
DEVICE="eth1"
TYPE=Ethernet
ONBOOT="yes"
BOOTPROTO="none"
USERCTL=no
MASTER=bond0
SLAVE=yes
```

2. Repeat the same procedure on Ethernet 2 as shown here:

```
# vi /etc/sysconfig/network-scripts/ifcfg-eth2
DEVICE="eth2"
TYPE=Ethernet
ONBOOT="yes"
BOOTPROTO="none"
USERCTL=no
MASTER=bond0
SLAVE=yes
```

3. Create the bond0 interface in the `/etc/sysconfig/network-scripts/` directory called `ifcfg-bond0` and configure channel bonding.

```
# vi /etc/sysconfig/network-scripts/ifcfg-bond0
DEVICE=bond0
ONBOOT=yes
IPADDR=192.168.246.130
NETMASK=255.255.255.0
BONDING_OPTS="mode=0 miimon=100"
```

Bonding mode=0	means round robin.
miimon=100	is the polling interval.

4. Restart the network to make the team functional as shown here:

```
# service network restart
```

Duplexing

Duplexing is the means by which communication takes place. There are three settings:

- With *full duplexing*, adapters can send and receive at the same time. The main advantage of full-duplex over half-duplex communication is performance. NICs can operate twice as fast in full-duplex mode as they do normally in half-duplex mode.

- With *half duplexing*, communications travel in both directions, but in only one direction at any given time. Think of a road where construction is being done on one lane—traffic can go in both directions but in only one direction at a time at that location.

- With *auto duplexing*, the mode is set to the lowest common denominator. If a card senses another card is manually configured to half duplex, then it also sets itself at half-duplex.

You set duplexing by using the Configuration button in the Properties window of the network card in Device Manager, as shown in Figure 8.17.

FIGURE 8.17   Setting Speed & Duplex

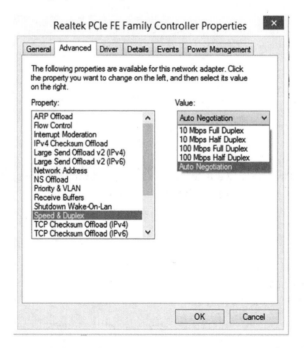

Speeds

The speed allows you to configure (or not) whether the card should run at its highest possible setting. You often need to be compatible with the network on which the host resides. If, for example, you are connecting a workstation with a 10/100BaseT card to a legacy network, you will need to operate at 10 MBps to match the rest of the network. This is done along with duplex, as shown in Figure 8.17.

10/100/1000 Mbps

While the example shown in Figure 8.15 uses a NIC capable of only 10/100 speeds, you are more likely to encounter network adapters on servers that have greater capability. When you are setting speed and duplex, you are presented with the 10/100/1000 Mbps option, which means the card is a Gigabit Ethernet card capable of 1 Gbps of speed. Therefore, you should set it to this highest setting if the switch and the cabling that the server is connected to is also capable of that speed (which it likely will be).

10 Gbps

In some cases, the NIC in the server will be even more capable than a Gigabit Ethernet card. If the card is capable of 10 Gbps, by all means make use of that speed and remember to ensure it is plugged into a port in the switch and the cabling that is also capable of this speed.

If the switch port to which the server is connected and the NIC on the server are set to either a speed mismatch or a duplex mismatch, you will suffer degraded performance and potentially no connection. Make sure the ends are set to match!

Ports and Protocols

Communication across a TCP/IP-based network takes place using various protocols, such as FTP to transfer files, HTTP to view web pages, and POP3 or IMAP to work with email. Each of these protocols has a default port associated with it, and CompTIA expects you to be familiar with them for this exam.

Both TCP and UDP use port numbers to listen for and respond to requests for communication using various protocols. There are a number of protocols and their port numbers that you must know for this exam, as well as the differences between TCP and UDP.

TCP vs. UDP

There are two transport layer protocols in the TCP/IP stack. TCP provides guaranteed, connection-oriented delivery whereas UDP provides nonguaranteed, connectionless delivery. Each protocol or service uses one of the two transport protocols (and in some cases both). There will be additional information later in this chapter on TCP and UDP.

TCP and UDP both use port numbers to listen for and respond to requests for communications. RFC 1060 defines common ports for a number of services routinely found in use, and these all have low numbers—up to 1,024. You can, however, reconfigure your service to use another port number (preferably much higher) if you're concerned about security and you don't want your site to be available to anonymous traffic.

SNMP 161

Simple Network Management Protocol (SNMP) is a protocol that facilitates network management functionality. It is not, in itself, a network management system (NMS) but is simply the protocol that makes a NMS possible. It operates over port 161.

SMTP 25

Simple Mail Transfer Protocol (SMTP) is a protocol for sending email between SMTP servers. Clients typically use either IMAP or POP to access their email server and use SMTP to send email. SMTP uses port 25 by default.

FTP 20/21

The File Transfer Protocol (FTP) is both a TCP/IP protocol and software that permits the transferring of files between computer systems. Because FTP has been implemented on numerous types of computer systems, files can be transferred between disparate systems (for example, a personal computer and a minicomputer). It uses ports 20 and 21 by default. FTP can be configured to allow or deny access to specific IP addresses and can be configured to work with exceptions. Although the protocol can be run within most browsers, a number of FTP applications are available; FileZilla (http://filezilla-project.org) is one of the most popular.

SFTP 22

Secure File Transfer Protocol over SSH, or SFTP, is a version of FTP that is encrypted by SSH. Since it operates over an SSH session and SSH uses port 22, SFTP uses port 22.

SSH 22

Secure Shell is a remote administration tool that can serve as a secure alternative to using Telnet to remotely access and configure a device like a router or switch. Although it requires a bit more setup than Telnet, it provides an encrypted command-line session for managing devices remotely. As you learned in the section on SFTP, it is used to provide security to a number of other protocols as well. It uses port 22.

SCP 22

Secure Copy (SCP) is a secure method of transferring files from one device to another. It is another example of a protocol that runs over SSH, which actually provides the encryption; as such, SCP also uses port 22.

NTP 123

Network Time Protocol (NTP) is used to keep all of the devices in the network synced to the same time source. This helps keep the timestamps of all network events that may be sent to a central server synchronized so that the events can be placed in the order in which they occurred. Time synchronization of all devices is also critical for proper function of digital certificates and services such as Active Directory. It operates on port 123.

HTTP 80

Hypertext Transfer Protocol (HTTP) is the protocol used for communication between a web server and a web browser. It uses port 80 by default.

HTTPS 443

Hypertext Transfer Protocol over Secure Sockets Layer (HTTPS), or HTTP Secure, is a protocol used to make a secure web connection. It uses port 443 by default.

Telnet 23

Telnet is a protocol that functions at the Application layer of the OSI model, providing terminal-emulation capabilities. Telnet runs on port 23, but it has lost favor to SSH due to the fact that Telnet sends data—including passwords—in plain-text format.

IMAP 143

Internet Message Access Protocol (IMAP) is a protocol with a store-and-forward capability. It can also allow messages to be stored on an email server instead of downloaded to the client. The current version of the protocol is 4 (IMAP4), and the counterpart to it is Post Office Protocol (POP). IMAP runs on port 143.

POP3 110

The Post Office Protocol (POP) is a protocol for receiving email from a mail server. The alternative to POP (which runs on port 110) is IMAP.

RDP 3389

The Remote Desktop Protocol (RDP) is used in a Windows environment to make remote desktop communications possible. It uses port 3389.

FTPS 989/990

File Transfer Protocol over TLS/SSL (FTPS) secures the FTP file transfer process as SFTP does but does so in a different way. Whereas SFTP is version of FTP that is encrypted by SSH, FTPS uses SSL for the encryption. Therefore, unlike all of the protocols secured by SSH that use port 22, FTPS uses ports 989 and 990.

LDAP 389/3268

Lightweight Directory Access Protocol (LDAP) is a protocol that provides a mechanism to access and query directory services systems. These directory services systems are most likely to be Microsoft's Active Directory but could also be Novell Directory Services (NDS). Although LDAP supports command-line queries executed directly against the directory database, most LDAP interactions are done via utilities such as an authentication program (network logon) or by locating a resource in the directory through a search utility. LDAP uses ports 389 and 3268.

DNS 53

As mentioned earlier, DNS is the Domain Name Service, and it is used to translate hostnames into IP addresses. DNS is an example of a protocol that uses both UDP and TCP ports.

DHCP 68

DHCP has been discussed a few times already in this chapter. It serves the useful purpose of issuing IP addresses and other network-related configuration values to clients to allow them to operate on the network. DHCP uses port 68 as well as port 67.

Cable Management Procedures

To manage server connectivity, you must be familiar with all of the various types of cable to which a server may be connected and the capabilities and shortcomings of these media types. You also need to understand cable management techniques to use in the datacenter or server room to not only prevent the room from looking messy but to also avoid causing devices to overheat from masses of unruly cabling. In this section, those will be our areas of focus.

Copper

Copper cabling uses electrical signals to represent the ones and zeroes in a transmission. The most common type of copper cabling in use is twisted pair cabling. There are two primary types of twisted pair cabling: shielded twisted pair (STP) and unshielded twisted pair (UTP). In both cases, the cabling consists of pairs of wires twisted around each other, as shown in Figure 8.18.

FIGURE 8.18   Twisted pair cable

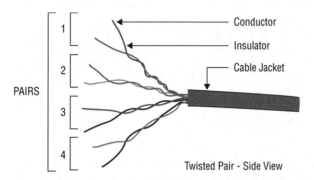

UTP offers no shielding (hence the name) and is the network cabling type most prone to outside interference. The interference can be from fluorescent light ballast, an electrical motor, or other such source (known as electromagnetic interference [EMI]) or from wires being too close together and signals jumping across them (known as crosstalk). STP adds a foil shield around the twisted wires to protect against EMI.

Patch Cables

While any twisted pair cable can be called a patch cable, there are actually three types of patch cables (different in the way in which they are wired and in the situation in which they are required), and these cables come in specifications called categories used to describe their capabilities. Let's first look at the three ways in which these cables can be wired.

Crossover and Straight Through

Two wiring standards are commonly used with twisted-pair cabling: T568A and T568B (sometimes referred to simply as 568A and 568B). These are telecommunications standards from TIA and EIA that specify the pin arrangements for the RJ-45 connectors on UTP or STP cables. The number 568 refers to the order in which the wires within the Category 5 cable are terminated and attached to the connector. The signal is identical for both.

T568A was the first standard, released in 1991. Ten years later, in 2001, T568B was released. Figure 8.19 shows the pin number assignments for the 568A and 568B standards. Pin numbers are read left to right, with the connector tab facing down. Notice that the pin-outs stay the same, and the only difference is in the color coding of the wiring.

FIGURE 8.19   Pin assignments for T568A and T568B

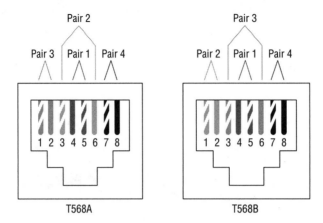

The bottom line here is that if the same standard is used on each end, the cable will be a straight-through cable, and if a different standard is used on either end, it will be a cross-over cable.

Crossover cables are used to connect like devices, while straight-through cables are used to connect dissimilar devices. For example, to connect a router to another router or a switch to another switch, use a crossover cable. To connect a router to a switch or a computer to a switch, use a straight-through cable. There is one exception: to connect a host to a router, use crossover. Having said all that, most NICs today have the ability to sense the required pin-out pattern for the connection and use that. This function is called Auto-MDI-X.

Rollover

A rollover cable is a cable using a completely reversed wiring pattern. It is used to connect to a router, switch, or access point console port to manage the device using a HyperTerminal application. The pin-out is shown in Figure 8.20.

FIGURE 8.20   Rollover pin-out

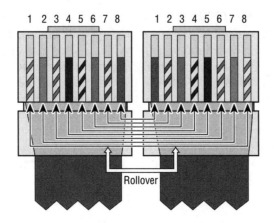

CAT5

Category 5 cabling transmits data at speeds up to 100 Mbps and is used with Fast Ethernet (operating at 100 Mbps) with a transmission range of 100 meters. It contains four twisted pairs of copper wire to give the most protection. Although it had its share of popularity (it's used primarily for 10/100 Ethernet networking), it is now an outdated standard. Newer implementations use the 5e standard.

CAT5e

CAT5e cabling transmits data at speeds up to 1 Gbps (1000 Mbps). Category 5e cabling can be used up to 100 meters, depending on the implementation and standard used, and it provides a minimum of 100 MHz of bandwidth. It also contains four twisted pairs of copper wire, but they're physically separated and contain more twists per foot than Category 5 to provide maximum interference protection.

CAT6

CAT6 cabling transmits data at speed up to 10 Gbps, has a minimum of 250 MHz of bandwidth, and specifies cable lengths up to 100 meters (using CAT6a). It contains four twisted pairs of copper wire and is used in 10GBaseT networks. Category 6 cable typically consists of four twisted pairs of copper wire, but its capabilities far exceed those of other cable types. Category 6 twisted pair uses a longitudinal separator, which separates each of the four pairs of wires from each other and reduces the amount of crosstalk possible.

Fiber

Because fiber-based media use light transmissions instead of electronic pulses, such problems as EMI and crosstalk become nonissues. Fiber gets around the limitations on almost everything else except cost and is well suited for transferring data, video, and voice transmissions. Since anyone trying to access data signals on a fiber-optic cable must physically tap into the medium, it is the most secure of all cable media. It does have distance limitations based on the mode in use and the cable type.

Types (Single-Mode vs. Multimode)

Two types of fiber-optic cable are available: single-mode and multimode. As the name implies, single-mode uses a single direct beam of light, thus allowing for greater distances and increased transfer speeds. With multimode, a lot of light beams travel through the cable, bouncing off the cable walls; this weakens the signal, reducing the length that the data signal can travel.

The most common types of fiber-optic cable include the following:

- 8.3 micron core/125 micron cladding single mode
- 50 micron core/125 micron cladding multimode
- 62.5 micron core/125 micron cladding multimode

Speed and Transmission Limitations

Table 8.4 lists the speed and transmission limitations for the most common fiber-optic implementations.

TABLE 8.4   Fiber speeds and limitations

Characteristic	100BaseFX	1000BaseSX	1000BaseLX	10GBaseER
Speed	100 Mbps	1000 Mbps	1000 Mbps	10,000 Mbps
Distance (multimode)	412 meters	220 to 550 meters	550 meters	(not used)
Distance (single mode)	10,000 meters	(not used)	5 km	40 km

Connectors

You're expected to know the basic concepts of networking as well as the different types of cabling that can be used. For the latter, you should be able to identify connectors and cables from figures even if those figures are crude line art (think shadows) appearing in pop-up boxes.

There are two specific types of network cables, and the connectors associated with each, that you must know for this exam: fiber and twisted pair. Fiber is the more expensive of the two and can run the longest distance. A number of types of connectors can work with fiber, but four you must know are SC, ST, LC, and SFP.

Twisted pair is commonly used in office settings to connect workstations to hubs or switches. It comes in two varieties: unshielded (UTP) and shielded (STP). The two types of connectors commonly used are RJ-11 (four wires and popular with telephones), and RJ-45 (eight wires and used with *x*BaseT networks—100BaseT, 1000BaseT, and so forth).

Let's take a closer look at all of these connectors.

ST

The straight tip (ST) fiber-optic connector, developed by AT&T, is probably the most widely used fiber-optic connector. It uses a BNC attachment mechanism that makes connections and disconnections fairly easy. The ease of use of the ST is one of the attributes that makes this connector so popular. Figure 8.21 shows an ST connector along with an SC and LC connector.

FIGURE 8.21   Fiber connectors ST, SC, and LC

SC

The subscriber connector (SC), also sometimes known as a square connector, is also shown in Figure 8.19. SCs are latched connectors, making it virtually impossible for you to pull out the connector without releasing its latch, usually by pressing a button or release. SCs work with either single-mode or multimode optical fibers. They aren't as popular as ST connectors for LAN connections.

LC

The local connector (LC), which was developed by Lucent Technologies, is a mini form factor (MFF) connector, especially popular for use with Fibre Channel adapters, fast storage area networks, and Gigabit Ethernet adapters (see Figure 8.21).

SFP

The small form-factor pluggable (SFP) is a compact, hot-pluggable transceiver that, though not standardized by any governing body like the IEEE, was created through a multisource agreement (MSA) between competing manufacturers. For this reason, you may find that there is not full compatibility among these from various sources.

These devices allow for adding functionality to a device. For example, you plug in a fiber SFP into an open SFP slot in a device and add a fiber connection where there was none. SFP sockets are found in Ethernet switches, routers, firewalls, and network interface cards. You will find them in storage devices as well. An example of a fiber SFP is shown in Figure 8.22. The example shows a fiber cable plugged into the SFP module, which is then plugged into the SFP slot. The SFP slot is shown removed from a generic slot on a Cisco device.

FIGURE 8.22   Fiber SFP

SFP cards can be added to servers if you need to add a connection type currently not present. These cards can be added to a PCI-Express slot. An example of one of these cards is shown in Figure 8.23. This particular model accepts two SFP+ connectors, requiring either Direct Attach Cable (DAC) for copper environments, or fiber transceivers supporting short haul (SR) optics plus fiber cables for fiber-optic environments.

FIGURE 8.23   HP 2-port server adapter

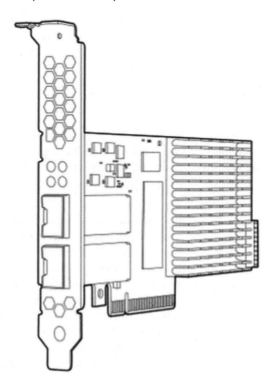

RJ-45 and RJ-11

Twisted pair cabling uses a connector type called an RJ (registered jack) connector. You are probably familiar with RJ connectors. Most landline phones connect with an RJ-11 connector. The connector used with UTP cable is called RJ-45. The RJ-11 has room for two pairs (four wires), and the RJ-45 has room for four pairs (eight wires). In almost every case, UTP uses RJ connectors; a crimper is used to attach an RJ connector to a cable. Figure 8.24 shows an RJ-11 and an RJ-45 connector.

FIGURE 8.24   RJ-45 and an RJ-11 connector

Cable Placement and Routing

It can be time-consuming to tie cables up, run them in channels, and snake them through walls, but it is time well spent when it keeps one person from harm. It is all too easy to get tangled in a cable or trip over one that is run across the floor. Take the extra time to manage cables, and it will increase your safety as well as that of others who work in that environment. These final sections will discuss cable management in the server room or datacenter.

Cable Channels

Cable channels are used to route cables across floors and other surfaces. They enclose the cables and protect them from damage while also preventing someone from tripping over them. In some cases, these trays may be integrated into the floor of the datacenter as well. An example of a cable channel is shown in Figure 8.25.

FIGURE 8.25   Cable channel

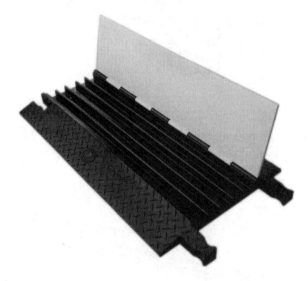

Cable Management Trays

While cable channels are good for floors, in some cases cable must be run up and over racks of equipment. In such instances you can use cable trays, which come in two types: vertical and horizontal.

Vertical

Vertical trays are used to route a group of cables up or down. For example, you may need to get cable from the back of a rack to the ceiling, where it may intersect with horizontal trays that lead the cabling out of the room or to another rack in the room. With vertical installation, cables on cable trays must be fixed by clips or suitable binding materials. An example of a vertical tray is shown in Figure 8.26.

FIGURE 8.26 Attaching cable to vertical trays

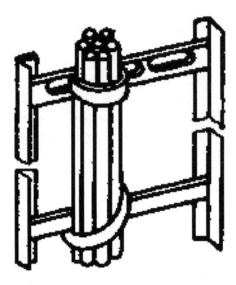

Horizontal

Horizontal trays are used to route cable across the room on the floor, the ceiling, or anywhere in between. A horizontal tray is shown in Figure 8.27.

FIGURE 8.27 Horizontal cable tray

Labeling

In a datacenter, server room, or wiring closet, correct and updated labeling of ports, systems, circuits, and patch panels can prevent a lot of confusion and mistakes when configuration changes are made. Working with incorrect or incomplete (in some cases nonexistent) labeling is somewhat like trying to locate a place with an incorrect or incomplete map. In this section, we'll touch on some of the items that should be correctly labeled.

Port Labeling

Ports on switches, patch panels, and other systems should be properly labeled, and the wall outlets to which they lead should match. You should agree on a naming convention to use so that all technicians are operating from the same point of reference. In any case, the labels should be updated where changes are made that dictate an update.

System Labeling

Other systems that are installed in racks, such as servers, firewall appliances, and redundant power supplies, should also be labeled with IP addresses and DNS names that the devices possess.

Circuit Labeling

Circuits entering the facility should also be labeled. Label electrical receptacles, circuit breaker panels, and power distribution units. Include circuit information, voltage and amperage, the type of electrical receptacle, and where in the datacenter the conduit terminates.

Naming Conventions

A naming system or convention guides and organizes labeling and ensures consistency. No matter what name or numbering system you use, be consistent.

Patch Panel Labeling

The key issue when labeling patch panels is to ensure that they're correct. Also, you need to make sure that the wall outlet they're connected to is the same. The American National Standards Institute/Telecommunications Industry Association (ANSI/TIA) 606-B Administration Standard for Telecommunications Infrastructure for identification and labeling approved in April 2012 provides clear specifications for labeling and administration best practices across all electrical and network systems premise classes, including large datacenters.

Bend Radius

When working with cables, especially fiber cables, you must recognize that every cable has a maximum bend radius, which you cannot exceed without damaging the cable. The smaller the allowable bend radius, the greater the material flexibility. If you exceed the recommended bend radius, you will damage the cable. For twisted pair cabling, this is much less of an issue, but the bend radius should not exceed four times the cable diameter for horizontal UTP cables and 10 times the cable diameter for multipair backbone UTP cables.

For fiber-optic cables, if no specific recommendations are available from the cable manufacturer, the cable should not be pulled over a bend radius smaller than 20 times the cable diameter.

Cable Ties

Throughout the datacenter or server room, you will need to organize bundles of cable and in some cases attach these bundles to trays and channels. For this operation, you will use cable ties, which come in various sizes and strengths. You should have plenty of these ties in all sizes at all times. In Figure 8.28 a variety of cable ties are shown along with a bundle of cable neatly organized using the cable ties.

FIGURE 8.28 Cable ties

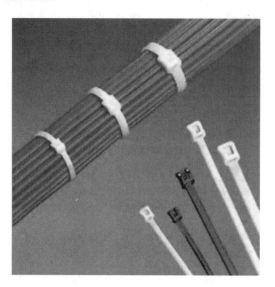

Summary

In this chapter, you learned about networking servers. That included configuring the server with an IP address, default gateway, subnet mask, and DNS server—the essential settings in most cases. You also learned how to enable a server for NetBIOS communication using a WINS server. We covered the use of Network Address Translation and Private IP addressing to enable Internet access while saving public IP addresses. We examined various NIC settings, including setting the speed and duplex, and enabling NIC teaming.

Common protocols, their function, and the port number used by these protocols were also explored in this chapter. Among the more common ones we discussed were HTTP, SNMP, FTP, and SSH. Finally, we explored cables and the connectors they use. That topic included fiber and copper variants. You also learned the value of proper management of cabling in the server room or datacenter.

Exam Essentials

Identify the most common and important network settings.   A server usually requires an IP address, a subnet mask, a default gateway, and the address of a DNS server to function on a network. In some cases, it may also require the address of a WINS server. Also understand the purpose of NAT and its use with private IP addressing. Finally, know how to configure a NIC properly for speed and duplex and, when required, for teaming.

Compare and contrast protocols and ports numbers.   List the port numbers used by well-known network protocols and services including but not restricted to FTP, SNMP, DNS, SHCP, HTTP, and SSH. Describe the functionality provided by each as well.

Implement proper cable management procedures.   Describe the various types of fiber and copper cabling. Understand the proper use of crossover, straight-thorough, and rollover cables. Know how to use cable channels and trays in conjunction with cable ties to organize router cabling in the server room or datacenter.

Review Questions

You can find the answers in the Appendix.

1. Which of the following is the loopback address in IPV6?
   A. 127.0.0.1
   B. FE80::
   C. ::1
   D. FEC0:

2. Which of the following is the IPv6 prefix of an autoconfigured address?
   A. 127.0.0.1
   B. FE80::
   C. ::1
   D. FEC0:

3. When implementing CIDR, what configuration setting is manipulated to size the subnet as desired?
   A. IP address
   B. Subnet mask
   C. Default gateway
   D. Duplex

4. Which of the following is *not* a private IP address?
   A. 10.0.0.5
   B. 172.16.5.9
   C. 192.168.5.9
   D. 172.32.63

5. Which of the following is an APIPA address?
   A. 168.254.3.3
   B. 172.16.5.9
   C. 192.168.5.9
   D. 169.254.5.6

6. Which of the following is an example of a link local IPv6 address?
   A. FE80::2237:06FF:FECF:67E4/64
   B. FE80::1/64
   C. ::1
   D. FEC0: 2237:06FF:FECF:67E4/64

7. Which of the following is *not* a FQDN?

    A. tmcmillan

    B. tmcmillan.acme.com

    C. ws5.ajax.com

    D. smitht.smithcorp.com

8. When does a device use a DNS suffix search list?

    A. At all times

    B. When an unqualified hostname is encountered

    C. When an FQDN is encountered

    D. When the users select to use the list

9. Which of the following do you edit to affect a DNS suffix search list in Linux?

    A. resolv.conf

    B. suffix.lst

    C. search.lst

    D. resolv.sfx

10. Which statement is false with regard to WINS?

    A. It is an alternate method of locating devices that is based on the use of NetBIOS names.

    B. It performs hostname name resolution on behalf of WINS clients.

    C. It is mostly used in Windows environments.

    D. In the absence of a WINS server, clients requiring NetBIOS name resolution will resort to other methods that create much more network traffic.

11. Which of the following is a method of spreading the 48-bit MAC across 64 bits so that it can be used as the last 64 bits of the 128-bit IPv6 address?

    A. TACACS

    B. EIU-64 format

    C. TACACS+

    D. MAC-48 format

12. Which of the following parts of a MAC address identify the manufacturer of the interface?

    A. UAA

    B. BAA

    C. OUI

    D. EUI-64

13. Which of the following is a standard method of implementing NIC teaming?

    A. 802.1ax-2008

    B. 802.3

    C. 802.1x

    D. 802.3g

14. What file do you edit in Linux to configure the Ethernet 6 interface to be used in a NIC team?

    A. `ifcfg-eth1`

    B. `ifcfg-bond0`

    C. `ifcfg-eth6`

    D. `ifcfg-bond6`

15. Which of the following tools is used to set the speed and duplex of an interface in Windows?

    A. Network and Sharing

    B. Device Manager

    C. Server Manager

    D. Devices and Printers

16. Which of the following is the port number for SMTP?

    A. 21

    B. 161

    C. 25

    D. 20

17. Which of the following services uses port number 22?

    A. SFTP

    B. NTP

    C. HTTP

    D. HTTPS

18. Which of the following has lost favor to SSH because it sends data—including passwords—in plain-text format?

    A. POP3

    B. Telnet

    C. RDP

    D. IMAP

19. Using which pair of configurations will result in a crossover cable?

    A. T568A and T568A

    B. T568B and T658B

    C. T568A and T568B

    D. T568A and a completely reversed wiring pattern

20. Which is the category of cable required for 10 Gbps transmissions?

    A. CAT 3

    B. CAT 5

    C. CAT 5e

    D. CAT 6

Chapter

9

Disaster Recovery

COMPTIA SERVER+ EXAM OBJECTIVES COVERED IN THIS CHAPTER:

✓ **6.1 Explain the importance of disaster recovery principles**

- Site types (hot site, cold site, warm site)
- Replication methods (disk to disk, server to server, site to site)
- Continuity of operations (disaster recovery plan, business continuity plan, business impact analysis [who is affected, what is affected, severity of impact])

✓ **6.2 Given a scenario, implement appropriate backup techniques**

- Methodology (full/normal [copy], incremental, differential, snapshot, selective, bare metal, open file, data vs. OS restore)
- Backup media (linear access [tape], random access [disk, removable media, optical media])
- Media and restore best practices (labeling, integrity verification, test restorability, tape rotation and retention)
- Media storage location (offsite, onsite, security considerations, environmental considerations)

Despite all of our planning and efforts to prevent them, disasters still occur. Although their level of devastation may vary, their occurrence is inevitable. What is not inevitable is that these events, ranging in seriousness from a single file deletion to the complete loss of an office or location, cripple the organization or prevent it from continuing to do business. What separates organizations that survive the same disaster from those that do not is preparation. In large measure, the success of that preparation is determined by the selection and implementation of appropriate backup techniques.

Disaster Recovery Principles

Disaster recovery principles are based on accepting the inevitability of these events and taking steps to ensure that when they do occur the organization can, in a timely manner, recover both its data and the underlying infrastructure on which it depends. This may entail the establishment of a second site from which the enterprise might operate in severe events that destroy an office. In any case there should be several plans created *before* an event occurs that are used to guide the organization through every type of event. In this first section of the chapter, we'll explore types of backup sites, methods of replicating data to backup sites, and the type of plans and documents that should be created to ensure both disaster recovery and business continuity.

Site Types

Although a secondary site that is identical in every way to the main site with data kept synchronized up to the minute would be ideal, the cost cannot be justified for most organizations. Cost–benefit analysis must be applied to every business issue, even disaster recovery. Thankfully, not all secondary sites are created equally. They can vary in functionality and cost. We're going to explore three types of sites in this section.

Hot Site

A *hot site* is a leased facility that contains all the resources needed for full operation. This environment includes computers, raised flooring, full utilities, electrical and communications wiring, networking equipment, and uninterruptible power supplies (UPSs). The only resource that must be restored at a hot site is the organization's data, usually only partially. It should only take a few minutes to bring a hot site to full operation.

Although a hot site provides the quickest recovery, it is the most expensive to maintain. In addition, it can be administratively hard to manage if the organization requires proprietary hardware or software. A hot site requires the same security controls as the primary facility and full redundancy, including hardware, software, and communication wiring.

Cold Site

A *cold site* is a leased facility that contains only electrical and communications wiring, air conditioning, plumbing, and raised flooring. No communications equipment, networking hardware, or computers are installed at a cold site until it is necessary to bring the site to full operation. For this reason, a cold site takes much longer to restore than a hot or warm site.

A cold site provides the slowest recovery, but it is the least expensive to maintain. It is also the most difficult to test.

Warm Site

A *warm site* is somewhere between the restoration time and cost of a hot site and a cold site. It is the most widely implemented alternate leased location. Although it is easier to test a warm site than a cold site, a warm site requires much more effort for testing than a hot site.

A warm site is a leased facility that contains electrical and communications wiring, full utilities, and networking equipment. In most cases, the only thing that needs to be restored is the software and the data. A warm site takes longer to restore than a hot site but less time than a cold site.

Replication Methods

When multiple sites are implemented for fault tolerance, the current state of the data in the main site must be replicated to the secondary site. This is especially critical when using hot sites or what are called mirrored sites, where the two sites are kept up to date with one another constantly.

There are several methods you can use to implement this replication. In this section, we'll look at three common replication methods.

Disk to Disk

When implementing *disk-to-disk replication* (also sometimes called storage- or array-based replication) the data is copied from the local disk on the server to either another disk on the same server or to another disk in the remote office. An example of its operation in the simplest form is when RAID 1 is implemented, which creates a mirror of one disk on another local disk. But it can also be implemented to replicate to a disk in another office, as shown in Figure 9.1, where Server B and its disk are located in another office.

FIGURE 9.1   Disk to disk

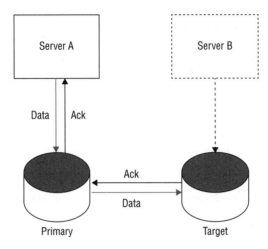

In disk-to-disk or array replication, the replication process is offloaded from the servers and therefore will not impact their performance. Because the replication software is part of the storage array, it requires that the destination array be from the same vendor.

Server to Server

In server-to-server replication, also called host-based replication, software on the servers handle the replication process. Server-to-server replication is typically less costly than disk- (array-)based, but it will impact the performance of the servers on which it is running. The replication software may also require updating from time to time as patches and service packs are installed. This process is shown in Figure 9.2.

FIGURE 9.2   Server to server

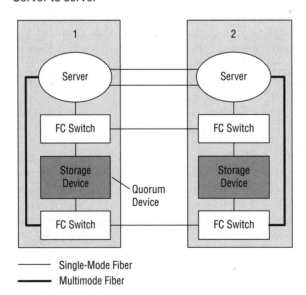

In Figure 9.2, the server and the storage device are connected to a Fibre Channel (FC) switch. The connections are therefore fiber cables. The cables from the servers to the local switches use multimode (which means they can carry more data but a shorter distance) and the cables between the offices are single mode (which means they carry less data but can go long distances).

Site to Site

Site-to-site replication (sometimes called network-based replication) uses FC switches to replicate from one site to another. The switch copies writes performed on the local site to the alternate site. This removes the process from the servers and eliminates any requirement that the local and remote systems be alike. It is also likely the most expensive solution. This process is shown in Figure 9.3.

FIGURE 9.3   Site to site

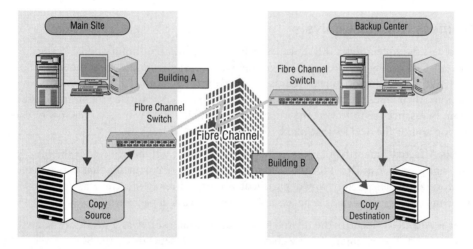

Continuity of Operations

When a disaster occurs, the amount of damage to the organization is a function of the extent to which the enterprise can continue to operate while recovery is under way. Even a reduced level of operations is preferable to a complete shutdown of operations. This continuity cannot occur without planning. There are a number of interrelated documents that should be developed to guide the company through the difficult recovery process while still maintaining some degree of operations. Let's take a look at these documents.

Disaster Recovery Plan

A *disaster recovery plan* (DRP) minimizes the effect of a disaster and includes the steps necessary to resume normal operation. Disaster recovery must take into consideration all organizational resources, functions, and personnel. Efficient disaster recovery will sustain an organization during and after a disruption due to a disaster.

Each organizational function or system will have its own DRP. The DRP for each function or system is created as a direct result of that function or system being identified as part of the business continuity plan (covered in the next section). The DRP is implemented when the emergency occurs and includes the steps to restore functions and systems. The goal of DRP is to minimize or prevent property damage and prevent loss of life.

Business Continuity Plan

The *business continuity plan* (BCP) considers all aspects that are affected by a disaster, including functions, systems, personnel, and facilities. It lists and prioritizes the services that are needed, particularly the telecommunications and IT functions. As such it serves to identify the process, functions, and hardware devices that should be addressed in the DRP.

Continuity planning deals with identifying the impact of any disaster and ensuring that a viable recovery plan for each function and system is implemented. Its primary focus is how to carry out the organizational functions when a disruption occurs.

Business Impact Analysis

A *business impact analysis* (BIA) occurs as part of business continuity and disaster recovery. Performing a thorough BIA will help business units understand the impact of a disaster. The resulting document that is produced lists the critical and necessary business functions, their resource dependencies, and their level of criticality to the overall organization. In essence the following information is assembled with respect to the loss of each function and/or the devices that make that function possible:

Who Is Affected   Identify all users and departments that will be affected if the function or process is lost. Don't forget to consider any other departments that may depend on information generated by any department you have already identified as vulnerable. Unfortunately, in many cases it begets a tidal wave across departments.

What Is Affected   Identify the related processes that may suffer as a result of the loss of each function. For example, if the web commerce server depends on the SQL server and the SQL server is unavailable, the commerce server will also be unable to function.

Severity of Impact   Finally, the impact of the loss of each function must be assigned a severity level. The importance of this is that this information will be used to prioritize the recovery of functions such that the most critical are recovered first.

Backup

While somewhat related, backup has a different purpose than replication. The goal of replication is to provide quick if not seamless access to data in a second site, whereas the goal of regular backups is to provide the organization with the ability to restore the data in the event of a replication issue or in cases where there is no second site. In this section, we'll explore the various types of backup, the media options available for storing the backup, and best practices for managing the backup process. Finally, we'll look at options for storing the backup media and the implications of each option.

Methodology

There are many types of backup that you can choose from, and the difference between the methods lies in how each method handles a property of each file called the *archive bit*. This is a bit that is used to communicate to the backup system whether a particular file has changed since the last backup. When the archive bit is cleared (0), it communicates that the file has been backed up already and has not changed since. When the bit is on (1), it communicates that the file has had changes since the last backup and should be backed up again. Its value lies in its ability to prevent an unchanged file from being backed up again needlessly. In this section, we'll compare various methodologies with respect to the handling of the archive bit and the implications for your backup schedule.

Full/Normal

With a full or normal backup, all data is backed up. During the full backup, the current status of the archive bit is ignored, everything is backed up, and the archive bit for each file is cleared. A full backup takes the longest time and the most space to complete. However, if an organization only uses full backups, then only the latest full backup needs to be restored, meaning it is the quickest restore. A full backup is the most appropriate for offsite archiving.

Copy

Copy backups are similar to normal backups but do not reset the file's archive bit. Another backup type that treats the archive bit this way is the daily backup, which uses a file's time stamp to determine if it needs archiving. Daily backups are popular in mission-critical environments where multiple daily backups are required because files are updated constantly.

Incremental

In an incremental backup, all files that have been changed since the last full or incremental backup will be backed up. During the incremental backup process, the archive bit for each file is cleared. An incremental backup usually takes the least amount of time and space to complete. In an organization that uses a full/incremental scheme, the full backup and each subsequent incremental backup must be restored. The incremental backups must be restored in order. For example, if your organization completes a full backup on Sunday and an incremental backup daily Monday through Saturday, you will need the last full and every incremental backup created since.

Differential

In a differential backup, all files that have been changed since the last full backup will be backed up. During the differential backup process, the archive bit for each file is not cleared. Each differential backup will back up all the files in the previous differential backup if a full backup has not occurred since that time. In an organization that uses a full/differential scheme, the full and only the most recent differential backup must be restored, meaning only two backups are needed to perform a restoration.

Snapshot

Using special backup utilities, you can also perform what are called *snapshot backups*. These are lists of pointers or references to the data and are somewhat like a detailed table of contents about the data at a specific point in time. They can speed the data recovery process when it is needed. There are two types of snapshots: copy-on-write and split mirror.

Keep in mind that snapshots are *not* a replacement for regular backups. In many cases the snapshot is stored on the same volume as the data so if the drive goes bad you will also lose the snapshot.

Copy-on-Write

This type of snapshot is taken every time a user enters data or changes data, and it only incudes the changed data. It allows for rapid recovery from a loss of data, but it requires you to have access to all previous snapshots during recovery. As changes are made, multiple copies of snapshots will be created. Some will contain changes not present in others. There will also be some data that remains unchanged in all of them.

Split Mirror

This type of snapshot also is created every time a change is made, but it is a snapshot of everything rather than just the changes. However, as you can imagine it takes significant storage space and the restore process will be slower.

Selective

A selective backup is one in which the user or the technician selects specific files to be backed up and *only* those files are backed up. Many backup tools allow you to decide whether or not to clear the archive bit when creating this backup type.

Bare Metal

A bare-metal backup is one in which the entire system, including operating system, applications, configuration data, and files, are saved. It rapidly speeds the recovery process because there is no need to reinstall the operating system and the applications and configure the server again before restoring the data. It is called bare metal because this type of backup can be restored to a system with no operating system.

Open File

Typically, when a file is open during a backup, the backup system will skip that file. Normally, open files are locked by the application or operating system. However, backup programs that use the Windows Volume Shadow Copy Service (VSS) can back up open files. But you should know that when you back up open files in this manner, changes that may have been made to the file while it was open and the backup job was proceeding will *not* be present in the backup of the open file and will not be recorded until the next backup.

Data vs. OS Restore

Backup can be done on the data present on a system, the operating system, or both. When the operating system is backed up, the configuration of the operating system, sometimes called the system state, is what is saved. When the data and the OS are backed up, it is sometimes called a complete PC backup. It is important to know that a system state backup alone does not back up any data, only system files. Conversely a data-only backup will not preserve the OS. Finally, neither of these backup types will back up your applications. To preserve those as well, you must do a complete PC backup or an image-based backup.

In Exercise 9.1, you will perform a bare-metal backup on a Windows Server 2012 R2 server. You will send the backup to an external hard drive.

EXERCISE 9.1

Creating a Bare-Metal Backup

1. If the Windows Server Backup feature has not been installed (it is not by default), navigate to the Server Manager page and select Add Roles And Features in the Configure This Server panel at the top of the page.

2. On the Before You Begin page, click Next. On the Select Installation Type page, select Role-Based Or Feature-Based Installation as shown here and then click Next.

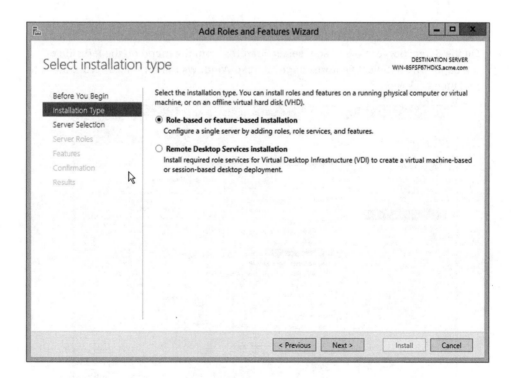

3. On the Select Destination Server page, leave the Select A Server From The Server Pool radio button selected and, from the list of servers in the pool, highlight the name of the local server (it may be the only one). Then click Next.

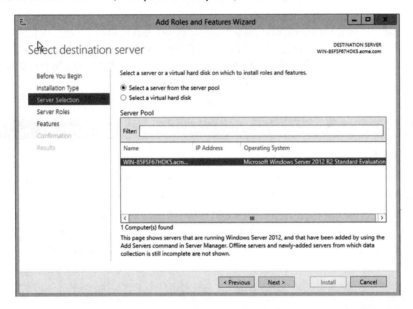

4. On the Select Server Roles page, select Features from the menu on the left side of the page. On the Select Features page, choose Windows Server Backup from the list, and then click Next.

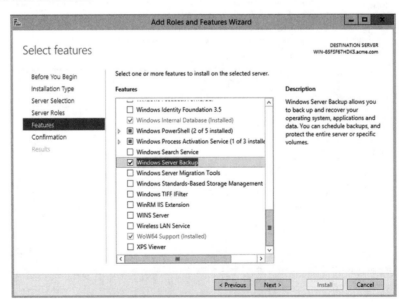

5. On the Confirmation page, check the Restart The Server If Required check box and select Install.

6. When the installation is complete, click Close. After the server restarts, return to the Server Manager page and select Windows Server Backup from the Tools menu.

7. On the Local Backup page, right-click Local Backup in the menu on the left and select Backup Once. On the Backup Options page, leave the Different Options radio button selected and click Next.

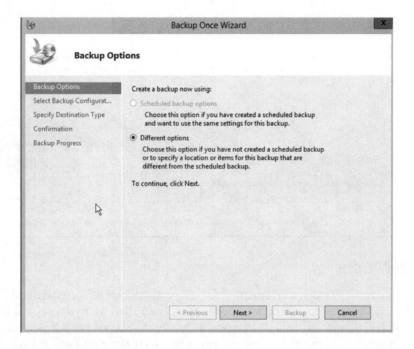

8. On the Select Backup Configuration page, select Custom and click Next. On the Select Items For Backup page, select the items by checking their boxes and then click OK.

9. Click Next and on the Specify Destination page leave Local Drives selected and click Next.

10. On the Select Backup Destination page, select the external drive you have connected. These can be internal, external, tape, or flash drives.

11. On the Confirmation page, click Backup. Monitor the process until it is complete.

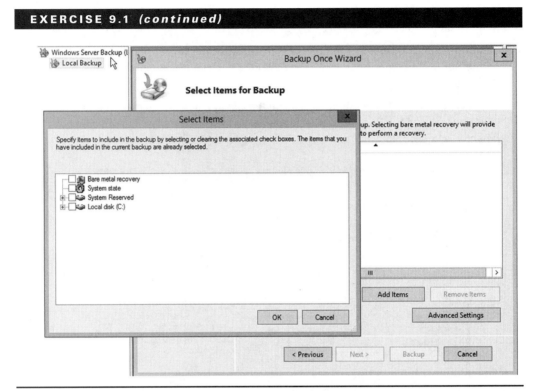

Backup Media

When choosing backup media, it is important to understand the advantages and disadvantages of various technologies. In general backup media, you should allow for two types of access to the data stored on the media: linear and random access. In this section, we'll look at the difference between these access methods as well as types of media that use the two methods.

Linear Access

Technologies that provide linear access to the data require you to position the data reader on the part of the media where the specific data is located before that data can be accessed. An example of a technology that provides linear access only is tape.

Tape

Tapes have been the default backup media for many years and only recently have been replaced by other media types like CDs, DVDs, and external drives. Although younger technicians may be unfamiliar with the task of rewinding or fast-forwarding a music tape or cassette to access a particular song, it illustrates the way linear access works. A song cannot be played until the tape head (reader) is positioned over the location where that song resides.

Tapes cannot provide instant access (also called random access) to any location on the tape (as can be done with CDs, DVDs, and external drives), but they are the most economical media. They are also still the most widely used media, although that is changing. The lack of random access has been a shortcoming that technicians were willing to accept until recently when technologies that provide random access have become more widespread.

Tapes are also less durable than CDs and DVDs. They are more susceptible to damage from temperature extremes and provide a limited number of times you can record data to them. While the maximum capacity of a standard tape drive has been 10 TB, Sony released a new cassette tape in 2014 that will hold 185 TB of data by storing the data very densely on the tape.

In 2010, IBM introduced the Linear Tape File System (LTFS), which allows you to access files on tape in the same way as on a disk filesystem, meaning random access is available using tapes.

Random

Any backup media that allows you to instantly access a single file regardless of its location is providing random access. You are probably quite familiar with this type of access as it is provided on hard drives, CDs, and DVDs. In this section, we'll go over the most common of these.

Disk

Hard disk drives are the most common example of a storage device that provides random access. By using either the command line or operating system file utilities such as Windows Explorer, you can access a single file regardless of its location on the hard drive. This is true whether the drive is solid state, magnetic disk drive, or hybrid drive.

Removable Media

Removable media such as external drives, flash drives, and USB drives also are examples of storage media that provide random access. Using the filesystem of the drive, you can browse to any location and access it instantly.

Optical Media

Despite the fact that optical drives use a completely different technology than hard disk and removable drives, they still provide the same type of random access. They may use a different filesystem to locate the data, but you will still browse to it using that filesystem and can instantly access that file regardless of its sequence on the drive.

Media and Restore Best Practices

Unless the backup process is managed properly, you may find that data is unavailable when you need to restore it. All backup procedures must be clear to all and based on best practices developed over years. The best practices covered in this section can help prevent issues and ensure that restoration processes go smoothly.

Labeling

All backup media should be clearly marked or labeled to prevent any confusion about which tape or DVD to use for the night's backup. The labeling logic will largely depend on the media rotation scheme that you choose. Media rotation schemes are covered later in this section. The most important takeaway is that all media should be labeled following the selected rotation scheme.

Integrity Verification

Verifying the integrity of a backup is an optional but important procedure. It verifies that the backup completed successfully. If you create the backup using checksums (which is an option with many utilities), it will allow you to check that the data has not changed since it was made or that it has been corrupted or damaged. It is important to perform a verification after you back up and again before you restore, so you don't restore any damaged data.

Test Restorability

Although many backup utilities offer a "verification process," nothing beats actually attempting to restore the data. Test restorations may not be appropriate after every backup, but they should be done often to ensure that you have not been creating corrupt backups for days on end.

Tape Rotation and Retention

The amount of time you should retain tapes or other backup media will be driven by several issues:

- Any regulations that may apply to the industry in which the company operates
- The criticality of the data
- Any company policies that may exist

Cost and storage considerations often dictate that backup media be reused after a period of time. You should adopt a system of rotating the media you are using, especially when that media is tape, which can only be used a certain number of times reliably. If this reuse is not planned in advance, media can become unreliable due to overuse. Two of the most popular backup rotation schemes are grandfather/father/son and first in, first out:

Grandfather/Father/Son (GFS)   In this scheme, three sets of backups are defined. Most often these three definitions are daily, weekly, and monthly. The daily backups are the sons, the weekly backups are the fathers, and the monthly backups are the grandfathers. Each week, one son advances to the father set. Each month, one father advances to the grandfather set.

First In, First Out (FIFO)   In this scheme, the newest backup is saved to the oldest media. Although this is the simplest rotation scheme, it does not protect against data errors. If an error in data occurs, this system over time may result in all copies containing the error.

Figure 9.4 displays a typical five-day GFS rotation using 21 tapes. The daily tapes are usually differential or incremental backups. The weekly and monthly tapes must be full backups.

FIGURE 9.4   Grandfather/father/son

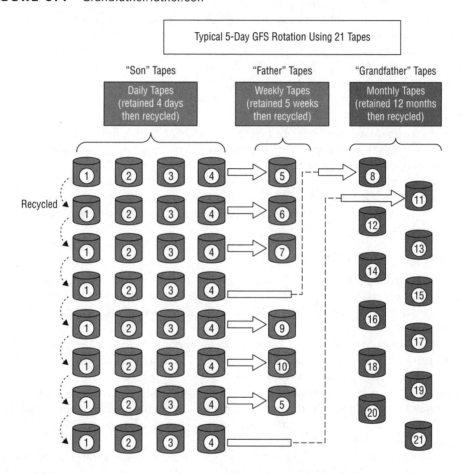

Media Storage Location

Safe storage of the media is a critical consideration when designing the backup system. While certainly quick access to media that contains data requiring restoration is a key consideration, other considerations are just as, if not more, important. In the final analysis, you may find it desirable to use both methods. Let's look at some of the issues to consider when deciding where and how to store the backup media.

Offsite

Storing backup media offsite helps to ensure that if the worst-case scenario occurs (the entire building is destroyed), backup media exists to re-create all the data lost. If you are storing it offsite for this reason, make sure it is far enough away from the office that it escapes the fate that befalls the office.

The only disadvantage to storing media offsite is that there will be some delay transporting the media onsite when a restoration is required. It is also worth noting that offsite storage in today's world may mean the data is backed up over a WAN link to a vendor with retrieval over a WAN link when required. In this case, a disadvantage is the time it may take to retrieve the data over the WAN link. In many cases, this method also results in a higher cost per GB for the protection provided.

Onsite

Storing backup media onsite has the advantage of ensuring the media is readily available if needed and results in a quicker restoration process when compared to storing media offsite. It also is cheaper per GB of data than offsite storage.

On the other hand, it introduces a high amount of risk to the backup process. If a disaster destroys the office where both the live data and the backup media are stored, there will be no option for replacing the data. Storing the media onsite also introduces the risk of vandalism or theft of the backup media.

Security Considerations

Offsite and onsite storage present you with different security issues and concerns. With onsite storage the media must be accounted for at every step in the process, in the same way a chain of custody is created for evidence. A log must be maintained that describes who made it, who handled it, and where it is stored. Keep in mind that organizations have the most to fear from their own employees because they have unique access to the facility and the network. It also may be advisable to encrypt the data in the backup media. This provides another hurdle to anyone who steals or copies the media.

Chain of custody becomes even more important when media is physically transported to an offsite location. When third parties are involved in the transport, these third parties should be vetted to ensure they can be trusted to secure the media and strictly follow any procedures for creating a paper trail.

When backup data is transmitted across a WAN link to a backup location, steps must be taken to ensure that the transmission is properly encrypted to prevent its disclosure in the event of its capture with sniffing utilities.

Environmental Considerations

Backup media, both tape and optical, can become damaged and useless if not provided with the proper environment. They should be locked away in an area where humidity and temperature are controlled. With regard to magnetic tape, it should be

- Kept away from contaminants like dirt, dust, cigarette smoke, and ashes
- Kept out of strong sunlight

- Stored on end and not lying flat
- Stored in an environment of not more than 110 degrees F (43 degrees C) or less than 32 degrees F (0 degrees C).
- Stored in a location with 40% humidity. More humid conditions promote fungal growth, which can damage the tape.

Optical media should be stored at a temperature between 41 and 68 degrees F (5 to 20 degrees C). The humidity should be 30 to 50 percent. This media should be kept out of direct sunlight, although the effect on some variants of optical media (disks that are read/write) is minimal. Optical disks should also be kept dry.

Summary

In this chapter you learned the importance of implementing proper disaster recovery principles. This included a discussion of various types of alternate sites and the replication methods used to synchronize data between the main and backup site. You also learned how ensuring continuity of operations during a disaster requires the creation of a business continuity plan based on the results of a properly executed business impact analysis.

You also learned about various backup methodologies, among them, full, incremental, and differential backups. We also covered the types of media that can be used to store data that has been backed up, both those that supply linear access (tape) and those that supply random access (optical). Managing the media was also discussed, including topics on media storage, labeling, and retention. Finally, the advantages and disadvantages of onsite and offsite storage of backup media ended the chapter.

Exam Essentials

Identify key principles of disaster recovery.   Describe the pros and cons of various alternate site types, such as hot, warm, and cold sites. Differentiate replication methodologies, including disk to disk, server to server, and site to site. Understand the way in which the creation of various documents such as a disaster recovery plan, business continuity plan, and business impact analysis serves as the foundation of ensuring continued operation during a disaster.

Implement appropriate backup techniques.   Differentiate backup methodologies, including but not restricted to full, incremental, and differential backups. Describe the access techniques of various backup media such as tape and optical media. Identify and implement best practices for media storage and labeling. Discuss the security and environmental considerations of storing media offsite and onsite.

Review Questions

You can find the answers in the Appendix.

1. Which of the following site types contains only electrical and communications wiring, air conditioning, plumbing, and raised flooring?

   A. Mirrored

   B. Warm

   C. Cold

   D. Hot

2. Which of the following replication methods is also called array-based replication?

   A. Differential

   B. Disk to disk

   C. Site to site

   D. Server to server

3. Which method has the biggest impact on the performance of the host being replicated?

   A. Bare metal

   B. Disk to disk

   C. Site to site

   D. Server to server

4. Which of the following replication methods is the most expensive?

   A. Bare metal

   B. Full

   C. Site to site

   D. Server to server

5. Which document provides the information necessary to create the DRP?

   A. BCP

   B. DCP

   C. BIA

   D. DIA

6. Which of the following describes who and what are affected by the loss of each business process or function?

   A. BCP

   B. DCP

   C. BIA

   D. DIA

7. What file attribute is used to communicate to the backup system whether a particular file has changed since the last backup?

   A. Read only

   B. Archive

   C. System

   D. Hidden

8. Which backup method does *not* clear the archive bit? (Choose two.)

   A. Full

   B. Differential

   C. Incremental

   D. Copy

9. Which of the following always requires exactly two tapes to restore?

   A. Full

   B. Differential

   C. Incremental

   D. Copy

10. You do a full backup every Saturday at 1 a.m. and an incremental backup every other day of the week at 1 a.m. A drive failure occurs on Thursday afternoon at 5:30. How many backup tapes do you need to restore?

    A. 1

    B. 3

    C. 4

    D. 6

11. Which snapshot type is taken every time a user enters data or changes data and it only includes the changed data?

    A. Site to site

    B. Copy-on-write

    C. Array-based

    D. Split mirror

12. Which of the following is required to be supported to perform an open file backup?

    A. VSS

    B. BAA

    C. OUI

    D. EUI-64

13. Which of the following is another name for the system configuration data?

   A. Bare metal

   B. System state

   C. Head files

   D. BCD

14. Which backup media type provides linear access to the data?

   A. CD

   B. Tape

   C. DVD

   D. External hard drive

15. What is the purpose of creating a backup using checksums?

   A. For integrity verification

   B. To encrypt the data

   C. To speed restoration

   D. To deduplicate the data

16. Which of the following is *not* an issue that affects retention time?

   A. The amount of data

   B. Regulations that may apply to the industry

   C. Criticality of the data

   D. Company policies

17. Which of the following uses three sets of backup tapes?

   A. GFS

   B. Tower of Hanoi

   C. FIFO

   D. LIFO

18. Which of the following rotation schemes does not protect against data errors?

   A. GFS

   B. Tower of Hanoi

   C. FIFO

   D. LIFO

19. Which of the following is false with regard to using offsite storage for backup media?

   A. It results in a higher cost per GB for the protection provided.

   B. There will be some delay transporting the media onsite when a restoration is required.

   C. It increases the risk of vandalism or theft of the backup media.

   D. It protects against worst-case scenarios (such as the destruction of the entire building).

20. What is a safe temperature range for tape media?

   A. 32–74 degrees

   B. 50–90 degrees

   C. 32–100 degrees

   D. 60–80 degrees

Chapter

10

Troubleshooting Hardware and Software Issues

COMPTIA SERVER + EXAM OBJECTIVES COVERED IN THIS CHAPTER:

✓ **7.1 Explain troubleshooting theory and methodologies**

- Identify the problem and determine the scope (question users/stakeholders and identify changes to the server/ environment, collect additional documentation/logs; if possible, replicate the problem as appropriate; if possible, perform backups before making changes)

- Establish a theory of probable cause (question the obvious, determine whether there is a common element of symptom causing multiple problems)

- Test the theory to determine cause (once theory is confirmed, determine next steps to resolve problem; if theory is not confirmed, establish new theory or escalate)

- Establish a plan of action to resolve the problem and notify impacted users

- Implement the solution or escalate as appropriate (make one change at a time and test/confirm the change has resolved the problem, if the problem is not resolved, reverse the change if appropriate and implement new change)

- Verify full system functionality and if applicable implement preventative measures

- Perform a root cause analysis

- Document findings, actions, and outcomes throughout the process

✓ **7.2 Given a scenario, effectively troubleshoot hardware problems, selecting the appropriate tools and methods**

- Common problems (failed POST, overheating, memory failure, onboard component failure, processor failure, incorrect boot sequence, expansion card failure, operating system not found, drive failure, power supply failure, I/O failure)

- Causes of common problems (third-party components or incompatible components, incompatible or incorrect BIOS, cooling failure, mismatched components, backplane failure)

- Environmental issues (dust, humidity, temperature, power surge/failure)

- Hardware tools (power supply tester [multimeter], hardware diagnostics, compressed air, ESD equipment)

✓ **7.3 Given a scenario, effectively troubleshoot software problems, selecting the appropriate tools and methods**

- Common problems (user unable to log on, user cannot access resources, memory leak, BSOD/stop, OS boot failure, driver issues, runaway process, cannot mount drive, cannot write to system log, slow OS performance, patch update failure, service failure, hangs on shut down, users cannot print)

- Cause of common problems (user account control [UAC/SUDO], corrupted files, lack of hard drive space, lack of system resources, virtual memory [misconfigured, corrupt], fragmentation, print server drivers/services, print spooler)

- Software tools (system logs, monitoring tools [resource monitor, performance monitor], defragmentation tools, disk property tools [usage, free space, volume or drive mapping])

Just as surely as it is a given that devices and device components will fail from time to time, it is also a given that hardware and software will malfunction or at least appear to be malfunctioning from time to time as well. In some cases, it is a true failure and in others it is simply the result of misconfiguration, human error, a misunderstanding of how the hardware or software operates, or an unrealistic expectation of what the hardware or software can deliver. In this chapter we are going are to discuss a general troubleshooting approach that has proven effective and specific troubleshooting approaches to specific issues.

Troubleshooting Theory and Methodologies

If you type the term **troubleshooting methodology** in a search engine, you will find that they are many approaches. Most of them follow the same basic steps with some variation because years of experience have taught us what works and what doesn't work. CompTIA has a specific methodology that you should know for the exam. In this first section of the chapter well cover the steps involved.

Identifying the Problem and Determining the Scope

Although it may sound obvious, you can't troubleshoot a problem without knowing what the problem is. In some cases, the problem will be obvious. But in others, especially when relying on the description of the problem by the user, it will appear to be one thing on the surface when in actuality the issue the user is experiencing is a symptom of a different, possibly larger problem.

One of the first things you should attempt to do when a user reports an issue is to determine the scope the problem. By that I mean "how widespread is the issue?" Is this the only user experiencing the issue or is it everyone in his subnet or department or VLAN? Is it everyone in an office? Is it the entire network? When the issue is affecting other users it becomes less likely the issue is the reporting user's machine and more likely that the source is an infrastructure device or service that many are depending on.

If you do determine that the issue is widespread, have a clear understanding of the potential impact of any changes you make, and always ensure that a rollback plan has been established in advance. Whenever you determine that a change has the potential to cause widespread issues, try to make the change in a test environment or on a small, low-impact section of the network.

In this section, processes that can help bring clarity to the situation are discussed.

Question Users/Stakeholders and Identify Changes to the Server/Environment

Identify the problem by questioning the user and identifying user changes to the computer. Before you do anything else, ask the user the following:

- What the problem is
- When the last time was that the problem didn't exist
- What has changed since

When performing this step, be wary of accepting the user's diagnosis of the problem at face value. For example, a user may start the conversation with the statement, "The email server is down." At this point, ask the question, "Is there anything else you cannot do besides open your email?" Ask them to try accessing a shared folder or the Internet. If either of those tasks fails, the problem is probably not the email server but basic network connectivity of their computer.

If in fact you do find that the issue lies in the server environment, then you may ask yourself or the system owner of the suspected server the same questions you asked the reporting user—that is, what is the problem, when was the last time the problem didn't exist, and what has changed since then?

Collect Additional Documentation/Logs

One of your best sources of information when answering some of these questions are the logs that the servers produce and any support documentation that may have been developed over time in the process of solving earlier issues. This is one of the reasons that best practices call for keeping a log in some format for every server that lists issues that have occurred and what was done to resolve them.

Creating and maintaining this documentation not only can help to speed the resolution of issues that have already been solved but it can identity trends that may indicate that earlier solutions only treated symptoms and not the root problem when an issue reoccurs over and over.

When you combine this with information gleaned from the server logs it can help map the appearance of the issue to events that occurred in the logs and changes that may have been made. If you make these connections, it can suggest theories of probable cause and possible solutions.

If Possible, Replicate the Problem as Appropriate

Once you have examined the logs and the documentation you may attempt to replicate the issue. In many cases, attempting to replicate the issue may be desirable from a troubleshooting standpoint but impossible or inadvisable because of the mayhem that may ensue. For example, you shouldn't re-create a DNS failure, which typically will bring the entire network down, no matter how valuable the resulting information may be.

However, when appropriate, if you can re-create the issue, it means that you have a very good handle on what's happening and what to do to fix the problem. Unfortunately, in many cases you can't do that (or at least not at first) and the problem may appear to be intermittent, a type of issue that can prove to be the moist difficult to solve.

If Possible, Perform Backups Before Making Changes

You may find yourself attempting significant changes on a server in an attempt to locate and/or solve the issue. Be sure that you do a backup before you make any changes so that all your actions can be undone, if necessary. If you have virtual servers or if you have the ability to make a disk image of a physical server, you may want to do the troubleshooting on an restored image of the live server (or a snapshot in the case of a virtual server) to prevent making the issue worse in the production network.

Establish a Theory of Probable Cause (Question the Obvious)

As you get answers to your initial questions, theories will begin to evolve as to the root of the problem.

Once you have developed a list of possible causes, develop a list of tests you can perform to test each to narrow the list by eliminating each theory one by one. Don't forget to consider the obvious and make no assumptions. Just because the cable has worked every day for the last five years doesn't mean the person cleaning the office may not have caught the vacuum cleaner on the cable and damaged its connector last night.

Determine Whether There Is a Common Element of Symptom Causing Multiple Problems

In some cases, it may appear that several issues are occurring at once. While it is always possible that multiple unrelated issues are occurring at the same time, always treat that possibility with distrust. Often there is a single element that is causing what may appear to be unrelated issues. The more you know and understand about the details of the inner workings of a device or piece of software the easier it will be for you to look at a set of issues and have that "ah ha" moment where you realize what could cause all the issues to occur.

For this reason, never hesitate to seek the counsel of others who may be subject matter experts. That might mean others in your organization or it might mean colleagues in other organizations. Finally, you may want to consult blogs and discussion groups that may address the issue. The bottom line is it's not cheating or a sign of weakness to ask for help!

Test the Theory to Determine Cause

Test related components, including connections and hardware and software configurations; use Device Manager; and consult vendor documentation. Whatever the problem may be, the odds are good that someone else has experienced it before. Use the tools at your disposal—including manuals and websites—to try to zero in on the problem as expeditiously as possible.

Once Theory Is Confirmed, Determine Next Steps to Resolve Problem

If your theory is confirmed, then determine the next steps you need to take to resolve the problem. In cases where you have determined the device where the problem lies but you have no expertise in that area, escalate the problem to someone as needed. For example, if you have narrowed down the problem to the router and you don't understand or manage the router, escalate the problem to the router administrator.

If Theory Is Not Confirmed, Establish New Theory or Escalate

If your theory is not confirmed, then come up with a new theory, or bring in someone with more expertise (escalate the problem). If you make changes to test one theory, make sure you reverse those changes before you test another theory. Making multiple changes can cause new problems and make the process even more difficult.

Establish a Plan of Action to Resolve the Problem and Notify Impacted Users

Evaluate the results, and develop an action plan of steps to fully resolve the problem. Keep in mind that it's possible that more than one thing is causing the problem. If that is the case, you may need to solve one problem and then turn your attention to the next.

Once you have planned your work, work your plan. Methodically make the required changes while always having a back-out plan if your changes cause a larger problem.

Implement the Solution or Escalate as Appropriate

Remember that if a solution evades you because of lack of experience with an issue, escalate the problem to someone who has the skills to address the issues. Don't forget that if no such person is available in the organization, you need to make full use of documentation, online resources and any other sources of expertise. If all else fails, consider involving any vendors or third-party experts that are available.

Make One Change at a Time and Test/Confirm the Change Has Resolved the Problem

Throughout the troubleshooting process, make a single configuration change at a time and at every step, stop to test and analyze the results. When you make multiple changes at a time, those changes might interact with one another and make the picture even muddier. If any change resolves the problem, proceed to verifying that the change didn't introduce new issues and there is full functionality (see this step later in this section).

If the Problem Is Not Resolved, Reverse the Change If Appropriate and Implement New Change

If a change does not solve the issue, roll that change back before making any additional changes. Only operating in this manner can you truly judge the effects of each individual configuration change. Remember, making multiple changes at a time not only makes it impossible to correctly assess the effect of each change, it may result in making the issue worse!

Verify Full System Functionality and If Applicable Implement Preventative Measures

When the problem is believed to be resolved, verify that the system is fully functional. If there are preventive measures that can be put in place to keep this situation from recurring, take those measures on this machine and on all others where the problem may exist. Also keep in mind that times like this are great learning moments to teach users what role they may have played and what actions they may be able to take on their own in the future to prevent the problem, if that is appropriate.

Perform a Root Cause Analysis

While solving the immediate issue is certainly satisfying and it is tempting to assume the issue is resolved, keep in mind that in many cases you may have treated the symptom and not the root cause. If you have any lingering doubts that the issue is solved continue to work at finding the root cause. This is one of the benefits of keeping track of all issues and all changes made in attempts to resolve issues for every server. When you see an issue continues to rear its head time and again, it's a pretty good indication that your changes are treating a symptom and not a root cause.

Document Findings, Actions, and Outcomes Throughout the Process

Document your activities and outcomes. Experience is a wonderful teacher, but only if you can remember what you've done. Documenting your actions and outcomes will help you (or a fellow administrator) troubleshoot a similar problem when it crops up in the future.

In some cases, you may think you have solved a problem only to find it occurs again later because you only treated the symptom of a larger problem. When this type of thing occurs, documentation of what has occurred in the past can be helpful in seeing patterns that otherwise would remain hidden.

Troubleshooting Hardware Problems

While problems can occur with the operating system with little or no physical warning, that is rarely the case when it comes to hardware problems. Your senses will often alert you that something is wrong based on what you hear, smell, or see. This section discusses common issues with the main players.

Common Problems

Once you have performed troubleshooting for some time, you will notice a pattern. With some exceptions, the same issues occur over and over and usually give you the same warnings each time. This section covers common symptoms or warning signs. When you learn what these symptoms are trying to tell you, it makes your job easier.

Failed POST

During the bootup of the system, a power-on self-test (POST) occurs, and each system critical device is checked for functionality. If the system boots to the point where the video driver is loaded and the display is operational, any problems will be reported with a numeric error code.

If the system cannot boot to that point, problems will be reported with a beep code. Although each manufacturer's set of beep codes and their interpretation can be found in the documentation for the system or on the website of the manufacturer, one short beep almost always means everything is OK. Some examples of items tested during this process include the following:

- RAM
- Video card
- Motherboard

To interpret the beep codes in the case where you cannot read the error codes on the screen, use the chart provided at www.computerhope.com/ beep.htm.

During startup, problems with devices that fail to be recognized properly, services that fail to start, and so on, are written to the system log and can also be viewed with Event Viewer. If no POST error code prevents a successful boot, this utility provides information about what's been going on system-wise to help you troubleshoot problems. Event Viewer shows warnings, error messages, and records of things happening successfully. You can access it through Computer Management, or you can access it directly from the Administrative Tools in Control Panel.

Overheating

Under normal conditions, the server cools itself by pulling in air. That air is used to dissipate the heat created by the processor (and absorbed by the heat sink). When airflow is restricted by clogged ports, a bad fan, and so forth, heat can build up inside the unit and cause problems. Chip creep—the unseating of components—is one of the more common byproducts of a cycle of overheating and cooling inside of the system.

Since the air is being pulled into the machine, excessive heat can originate from outside the server as well because of a hot working environment. The heat can be pulled in and cause the same problems. Take care to keep the ambient air within normal ranges (approximately 60–90 degrees Fahrenheit) and at a constant temperature.

Replacing slot covers is vital. Servers are designed to circulate air with slot covers in place or cards plugged into the ports. Leaving slots on the back of the computer open alters the air circulation and causes more dust to be pulled into the system.

Memory Failure

Memory problems include a bad or failing memory chip, using memory whose speed is incompatible with the motherboard, or using applications that require more memory than is present in the server. These issues typically manifest themselves with system freezes or lockups. If the issue is serious enough the server may fail the POST. Replace and upgrade the memory as required.

Here are some error messages that may indicate a memory issue:

Data_Bus_Error   This error is usually a hardware issue. This could include the installation of faulty hardware, or the failure of existing hardware. In many cases it is related to defective memory of some sort (RAM, L2 cache, or video RAM). If you just added something, remove it and test the results.

Unexpected_Kernel_Mode_Trap   Several items can cause this error. One of them is overclocking the CPU. Try executing the hardware diagnostics provided with the system, especially the memory system. Again, if you just added hardware, remove it and test the result.

Page_Fault_in_nonpaged_area   Thius is another message that can be the result of adding faulty hardware or of hardware (usually memory of some type) going bad. Use the hardware diagnostics provided with the system to gain more information about the error. And as always, if you just added something, remove it and test the results.

Onboard Component Failure

Onboard components (also called integrated components) are those that are built into the motherboard. Unfortunately, when these components fail, a replacement of the motherboard is usually required. Although it is possible to make some component replacements, it requires soldering and in many cases cause more issues than it solves. Even if you have the skills, always weigh the value of the time taken to attempt the repair (you may waste the time in vain) against the cost of a new mother board. Having said all this, if the board is a newer board, you may be able to disable the defective on board component and set the system to use a replacement component installed in one of the expansion slots.

Processor Failure

When processors fail, it is typically a catastrophic event for the server. This is why many server vendors are implementing multiple CPUs for both redundancy and improved performance. CPU failures can be caused by a number of issues, the most common of which is a failure of a transistor or of the interconnections within the CPU. Overheating is usually the culprit when these failures occur. If you have replaced a CPU at some point, and if you used too much thermal paste between the heat sink and the CPU, it can also cause a processor failure. The amount you use should be about the size of a grain of rice. It will spread sufficiently when you clamp the CPU down. Degradation of transistors doesn't always cause a complete failure. In some cases, it causes a degradation in the performance of the CPU. If you find the performance is declining, consider this possibility.

Incorrect Boot Sequence

When multiple volumes or partitions exist on the computer or there are multiple hard drives and maybe CD/DVD and floppy drives as well, there are multiple potential sources for the boot files. If the system delivers an "operating system not found" message, it could be that the system is looking in the wrong location for the boot files.

The boot order is set in the BIOS. Check the boot order and ensure that it is set to boot to the partition, volume, and hard drive where the boot files are located. If the device still has a floppy drive, check first whether there is a floppy in the floppy drive. When the system is running down the list of potential sources of boot files, in all other cases if it looks in a location and finds no boot files, it will move on to the next location in the list. However, if a floppy is in the floppy drive and it checks the floppy drive and no boot files are present, it does not proceed but stops and issues the nonsystem disk message.

Expansion Card Failure

When an expansion card fails in a server, the solution is to replace the card with a new card. However, you should always make sure the card is the culprit first. Many servers come with onboard hardware diagnostics that can help you determine if it is the card or the slot in which it resides. While each server's documentation might provide different steps to determine this, the steps in Exercise 10.1 might serve as a guide at using the diagnostic tools.

The following exercise applies a Dell PowerEdge T110. Your server may differ. Consult the documentation.

EXERCISE 10.1

Troubleshooting Expansion Cards in a Dell PowerEdge T110

1. Run an online diagnostic test. As the system boots, press F10.

2. Click Hardware Diagnostics in the left pane and click Run Hardware Diagnostics in the right pane.

3. When the screen changes select Run Diags as shown in Figure 10.1.

FIGURE 10.1 Selecting Run Diags

4. Select Test One Device as shown in Figure 10.2.

FIGURE 10.2 Test one device

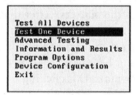

5. When the test has completed, view the results for both the slot and the card in question.

Operating System Not Found

If the system delivers an "operating system not found" message, it could be that the system is looking in the wrong location for the boot files or that the file has been corrupted. See the earlier section "Incorrect Boot Sequence."

Boot problems can also occur with corruption of the boot files or missing components. Luckily, during the installation of the OS, log files are created in the %SystemRoot% or %SystemRoot%\Debug folder (C:\WINNT and C:\WINNT\DEBUG or C:\Windows and C:\Windows\Debug, depending on the operating system). If you have a puzzling problem, look at these logs to see whether you can find error entries there. These are primarily helpful during installation. For routine troubleshooting, you can activate boot logging by selecting Enable Boot Logging from the Windows Advanced Options menu (Access the menu by turning on your computer and pressing the F8 key before Windows starts.) to create an ntbtlog.txt log file in the %systemroot% folder.

Drive Failure

Hard drives typically exhibit symptoms before they fail. Learning to read these clues is critical to troubleshooting. This section discusses the most common of these clues and symptoms.

Read/Write Failure

Read/write failures occur when areas of the hard drive require repeated attempts before successful reads or writes occur. This is because these areas are at least partially damaged, although perhaps not enough for these areas to be marked as bad sectors.

Slow Performance

Another symptom of hard drive issues is slow access to the drive. Oddly, one of the potential causes of this is insufficient memory. When this is the case, it causes excessive paging. Another cause can be a drive that needs to be defragmented. A fragmented drive results in it taking much longer for all the parts of a file to be located before the file will open. Other issues that cause slow performance are controller cards that need updating, improper data cables, and slower devices sharing the same cable with the hard drive.

Loud Clicking Noise

A loud clicking noise, sometimes referred to as the *click of death*, is caused by the read/write heads making contact with the platters. After that happens, both the heads and the platters become damaged, and the system becomes unable to establish a successful starting point to read the drive. (Keep in mind that a bad fan can also make a clicking noise). This is serious damage and cannot be repaired. Be aware that solid state drives have no moving parts and thus will never make this clicking noise. Back up all the data if that's still possible. If the drive is beyond readable, the only option to recover the data is with the help of a professional data recovery service. At that point, you must balance the cost of the recovery with the value of the data. This is a case where performing regular backups saves the day!

Failure to Boot

A failure of the system to boot can be caused by a number of issues.

- Failure of the system to locate the boot files. See the section "Incorrect Boot Sequence."

- If you are presented with an "IDE drive not ready" at startup, the drive may not be spinning fast enough to be read during startup. Enable or increase the hard disk predelay time.

- If you receive the message "Immediately back up all your data and replace your hard drive. A fault may be imminent," take it seriously. This means the drive is using Self-Monitoring, Analysis, and Reporting Technology (SMART) to predict a failure.

- The hard drive data or power cable may have become unseated. Sometimes even if the cable appears to be seated fine, reseating it can have a positive effect. Also ensure that the data cable has not been reversed.

Drive Not Recognized

If the system does not recognize the drive, the problem could be one of the following:

- The hard drive data or power cable may have become unseated. Sometimes even if the cable appears to be seated fine, reseating it can have a positive effect. Also ensure that the data cable has not been reversed.

- If you just added a drive, ensure that both drives have not been set to master or slave and that the boot drive is set as master on the first channel.

- If the system uses serial ATA and you just added a drive, ensure that all the onboard SATA ports are enabled.

- If you just added a drive, ensure that there is no conflict between the new drive and another device.
- If you receive the "No boot device available, strike F1 to retry boot, F2 for setup utility" message, it could be incorrect drive geometry (probably not the case if this drive has been functioning properly), a bad CMOS battery, or an inability to locate the active partition or master boot record. You should check the BIOS and ensure that the system is detecting the drive correctly.

Power Supply Failure

While power supply failures do occur, power problems usually involve the following issues and scenarios:

- Check the power cord, and if it's plugged into a power strip or UPS, ensure the strip is plugged in (and if it has a breaker, check to see whether it was tripped by a surge or whether the switch that turns off the entire strip has been inadvertently turned to the off position). In the case of a UPS, check whether the UPS battery is dead and if the outlet is still receiving power.
- Try replacing the power supply with a known good unit to see whether the power supply failed.
- Power supply problems can cause reboots as well. The power supply continually sends a Power_Good signal to the motherboard, and if this signal is not present momentarily, the system will reset.
- Power supplies can also provide too much power, that will fry components in the path. For example, you replace fried memory and the new memory is fried immediately. It could be the power supply is providing too much power.

I/O Failure

I/O errors are typically related to the system reading or writing to its storage. An I/O error can occur with different types of hardware devices or media:

- External hard drives
- SD cards
- USB flash drives or pen drives
- CD-Rom or DVD drives
- CD or DVD discs

   One of the most common error messages related to this says

   `The request could not be performed because of an I/O device error`

   When this message or other messages referencing I/O issues are generated, some possible causes are

1. The hardware drivers are damaged or incompatible.
2. The optical disk that you are trying to access is dirty or damaged.

3. The operating system is trying to use a transfer mode that the hardware device cannot use.

4. The device that you are trying to access is damaged or defective.

5. There is a connection problem, such as a bad cable.

A general approach to these issues is as follows:

1. Restart the server, and then try to access the drive or disk again.

2. Use a cleaner disc to clean the disk.

3. Move the disk or drive to another server and attempt to access the data to confirm that the drive or disk is not damaged.

4. If no alternate and compatible server is available, try a different disk or drive on the original server to make sure that the problem is with the computer and not with the original disk.

If this doesn't solve the issue, check all cable connections and perform a clean boot of the server.

Clean Boot

When you start the server in a clean boot, it starts by using a preselected minimal set of drivers and startup programs, and because the computer starts with a minimal set of drivers, some programs may not work as you expected.

Causes of Common Problems

While incompatible programs and drivers are a possible cause of issues such as I/O problems, they are not the only causes of some of the issues raised in this section. We'll look at some other issues that can plague any computer and some that are specific to servers in the data center.

Third-Party Components or Incompatible Components

While vendors of both server hardware and software attempt to cram as much functionality as they can into their products, inevitably customers want systems to do things for which they were not designed or to exhibit functionality not currently present in the product. To meet this demand third parties often enter the picture and create components that when added to the system deliver said functionality or something close to it.

While these components will certainly find a market, the vendors of these products cannot always ensure that these add-ons will play nice with every operating system or with all of your hardware. In their defense, while it is to their benefit to test the component with as many potential interfacing systems (hardware and software) as possible, there is no way they can anticipate every combination of these variables.

For this reason, always consult the vendor websites of your server hardware manufacturer and the operating system and those of any applications that may be installed on the server for guidance regarding supported third-party components. Having done this, you should still test these components for compatibility as there could be some unusual quirks in your specific configuration that render the component incompatible.

Incompatible or Incorrect BIOS

At startup, the BIOS will attempt to detect the devices and components at its disposal. The information that it gathers, along with the current state of the components, will be available for review in the BIOS settings. It is required that the BIOS support the devices that it discovers during this process. Otherwise the system will either fail the POST, fail to start, or the component will fail to function after the server starts.

In some cases, you can solve this problem by performing a BIOS upgrade, also called flashing the BIOS. Server BIOSs don't go bad; they just become out of date or contain bugs. In the case of a bug, an upgrade will correct the problem. An upgrade may also be indicated when the BIOS doesn't support some component that you would like to install—a larger hard drive or a different type of processor, for instance.

Most of today's BIOSs are written to an Electrically Erasable Programmable Read-Only Memory (EEPROM) chip and can be updated through the use of software. Each manufacturer has its own method for accomplishing this. Check out the documentation for complete details. It means the old instructions are erased from the EEPROM chip and the new instructions are written to the chip.

UEFI (Unified Extensible Firmware Interface) is a standard firmware interface for PCs designed to replace the BIOS. Some advantages of UEFI firmware include

- Better security—protects the pre-boot process
- Faster startup times and resuming from hibernation
- Support for drives larger than 2.2 terabytes (TB)
- Support for 64-bit firmware device drivers
- Capability to use BIOS with UEFI hardware

UEFI can also be updated by using an update utility from the motherboard vendor. In many cases the steps are as follows:

1. Download the update file to a flash drive.
2. Insert the flash drive and reboot the machine.
3. Use the specified key sequence to enter the BIOS settings.
4. If necessary disable secure boot.
5. Save the changes and reboot again.
6. Re-enter the BIOS settings again.
7. Chose boot options and boot from the flash drive.
8. Follow the specific directions with the update to locate the upgrade file on the flash drive.

9. Execute the file (usually by typing flash).

10. While the update is completing ensure you maintain power to the device.

Cooling Failure

CPUs produce heat, and the more powerful the CPU the more heat it produces. Heat is an enemy to the server in general as it causes problems such as random reboots. Methods of cooling the CPU and in turn the overall interior of the case have evolved with the increasing need to remove this heat.

When cooling fails, it is usually a fan or air flow issue. If the scope of the issue is such that many servers are involved, the issue may be the cooling in the data center itself. Always have the contact information of an HVAC expert close at hand for those situations.

When you have determined that a single server is involved, consider the following possible causes:

▪ Dead fan

▪ Blockage from dust or debris of front or back panel vents

▪ Improperly installed components or cables that can block the flow of air through the server

▪ Dividers, baffles, component filler panels, and server top covers that may be missing or installed improperly

Mismatched Components

When adding such components you must ensure that the components match and are compatible with any existing instances of that hardware or software and with the system at large. Memory is a good example of components that must be matched to both the existing memory and to the CPU.

Another example is power supply units (PSU). Most server systems can utilize redundant power supplies and many come with them already installed. If multiple power supplies were installed at the factory there should be no issue as they will be the same model. On the other hand, if you add new power supplies you must ensure that these PSUs are compatible. PSU mismatches occur when two or more PSUs do not share the same feature sets.

CPUs are another scenario where a mismatch of feature sets can cause issues. All of these issues can be avoided by simply making use of the documentation that came with the server. If you lose this or if you have reason to believe the documentation may have been updated, access the latest version from the vendor website and do your homework before you purchase a replacement or additional component.

Backplane Failure

Backplanes are advantageous in that they provide data and control signal connectors for the hard drives. They also provide the interconnect for the front I/O board, power and locator buttons, and system/component status LEDs.

Unfortunately, this creates a serious single point of failure because if the backplane fails, we lose communication with the servers to which it is connected. While this generally is considered a highly unlikely event, that won't make you feel better when it happens to you! If the servers using the backplane are mission critical, you may want to invest in both a spare backplane and the spare cables required to connect the backplane. Before you connect the backplane, make sure you have considered a cable failure as well.

Environmental Issues

Three items closely related to an environmentally friendly computing environment are temperature, humidity, and ventilation. We will cover the most important elements with all three and end this section with a discussion of power issues.

Dust

One of the most harmful atmospheric hazards to a computer is dust. Dust, dirt, hair, and other airborne contaminants can get pulled into computers and build up inside. Because computer fans work by pulling air through the computer (usually sucking it in through the case and then pushing it out the power supply), it's easy for these items to enter and then become stuck. Every item in the computer builds up heat, and these particles are no exception. As they build up, they hinder the fan's ability to perform its function, and the components get hotter than they would otherwise. The dust also serves as insulation to all it covers causing more heat; and since it can conduct electricity, it can lead to fried parts. Figure 10.3 shows the inside of a system in use for only six months in an area with carpeting and other dusty surroundings.

FIGURE 10.3 Dust builds up inside the system.

You can remove dust and debris from inside servers with *compressed air* blown in short bursts. The short bursts are useful in preventing the dust from flying too far out and entering another machine, as well as in preventing the can from releasing the air in liquid form. Compressed air cans should be held 2–3 inches from the system and always used upright so the content is released as a gas. If the can becomes cold to the touch, discontinue using it until it heats back up to room temperature.

WARNING   It's possible to use an air compressor instead of compressed-air cans when you need a lot of air. If you take this approach, make sure you keep the pounds per square inch (PSI) at or below 40, and include measures on the air compressor to remove moisture.

Humidity

Another preventive measure you can take is to maintain the relative humidity at around 50 percent. Be careful not to increase the humidity too much to the point where moisture starts to condense on the equipment! It is a balancing act keeping humidity at the right level since low humidity causes electrostatic discharge (ESD) and high humidity causes moisture condensation. Both extremes are bad but have completely different effects.

Also, use antistatic spray, which is available commercially, to reduce static buildup on clothing and carpets. In a pinch, a solution of diluted fabric softener sprayed on these items will do the same thing.

At the very least, you can be mindful of the dangers of ESD and take steps to reduce its effects. Beyond that, you should educate yourself about those effects so you know when ESD is becoming a major problem.

Temperature

Heat and computers don't mix well. Many computer systems require both temperature and humidity control for reliable service. The larger servers, communications equipment, and drive arrays generate considerable amounts of heat; this is especially true of mainframe and older minicomputers. An environmental system for this type of equipment is a significant expense beyond the actual computer system costs. Fortunately, newer systems operate in a wider temperature range. Most new systems are designed to operate in an office environment.

If the servers you're responsible for require special environmental considerations, you'll need to establish cooling and humidity control. Ideally, systems are located in the middle of the building, and they're ducted separately from the rest of the heating, ventilation, and air conditioning (HVAC) system. It's a common practice for modern buildings to use a zone-based air conditioning environment, which allows the environmental plant to be turned off when the building isn't occupied. A computer room will typically require full-time environmental control.

Power Surge/Failure

A number of power-related threats can harm servers. Among them are the following:

Blackout   This is a complete failure of the power supplied.

Brownout   This is a drop in voltage lasting more than a few minutes.

Sag   This is a short-term voltage drop.

Spike   The opposite of a sag, this is a short (typically under 1 second) increase in voltage that can do irreparable damage to equipment.

Surge   This is a long spike (sometimes lasting many seconds). Though a surge is typically a less intense increase in power, it can also damage equipment.

The three solutions for issues are battery backups, surge suppressors, and line conditioners. While surge protectors will only prevent damaging surges and a UPS will prevent total loss of power, a line conditioner take the power out of the wall and delivers it smoothly to the device with no sags or surges.

Hardware Tools

There are troubleshooting tools that you should be familiar with that can aid you. This section discusses some of the most important tools.

Power Supply Tester (Multimeter)

A multimeter combines a number of tools into one. There can be slight variations, but a multimeter always includes a voltmeter, an ohmmeter, and an ammeter (and is sometimes called VOM as an acronym). With one basic multimeter, you can measure voltage, current, and resistance (some will even measure temperature).

Inexpensive devices called power supply testers can go a bit beyond simply checking the voltage of the power cables. One of the things these devices can check is the proper operation of the Power_Good signal. If this signal is not working correctly, the computer will not boot from the power button but will do so when you press Ctrl+Alt+Del.

Hardware Diagnostics

Diagnostic utilities are available for troubleshooting hardware issues. First well talk about the most basic tools available in the BIOS or UEFI and then we'll look at tools that may come with the server operating system.

Although you may not realize it, every time you start the computer, built-in diagnostics are at work. Every computer, including servers, has a diagnostic program built into its BIOS called the *power-on self-test* (POST). When you turn on the server, it executes this set of diagnostics. Many steps are involved in the POST, but they happen very quickly, they're invisible to the user, and they vary among BIOS versions. The steps include checking the CPU, checking the RAM, checking for the presence of a video card, and so on. The main reason to be aware of the POST's existence is that if it encounters a problem, the boot process stops. Being able to determine at what point the problem occurred can help you troubleshoot.

One way to determine the source of a problem is to listen for a *beep code*. This is a series of beeps from the computer's speaker. The number, duration, and pattern of the beeps can sometimes tell you what component is causing the problem. However, the beeps differ depending on the BIOS manufacturer and version, so you must look up the beep code in a chart for your particular BIOS. Different BIOS manufacturers use the beeping differently. AMI BIOS, for example, relies on a raw number of beeps, and uses patterns of short and long beeps.

Another way to determine a problem during the POST routine is to use a *POST card*. This is a circuit board that fits into an Industry Standard Architecture (ISA) or Peripheral Component Interconnect (PCI) expansion slot in the motherboard and reports numeric codes as the boot process progresses. Each of those codes corresponds to a particular component being checked. If the POST card stops at a certain number, you can look up that number in the manual that came with the card to determine the problem.

BIOS Central is a website containing charts detailing the beep codes and POST error codes for many different BIOS manufacturers.

Most server vendors also include a hardware diagnostic utility in what Dell calls the pre-operation system. As this utility has a physical (as opposed to logical) view of the attached hardware, it can identify hardware problems that the operating system and other online tools cannot identify. You can use the hardware diagnostics utility to validate the memory, I/O devices, CPU, physical disk drives, and other peripherals.

For an example of the use of hardware diagnostics, review Exercise 10.1 earlier in this chapter in the section "Expansion Card Failure."

Compressed Air

You can remove dust and debris from inside servers with *compressed air* blown in short bursts. Review the "Dust" section earlier in this chapter.

ESD Equipment

Preventing ESD was covered in Chapter 6 in the section "Safety."

Troubleshooting Software Problems

Because it's software and there are so many places where things can go wrong, the operating system can be one of the most confusing components to troubleshoot. Sometimes it seems a miracle that they even work at all considering the hundreds of files that work together to make the system function. In this section, common operating system issues and their solutions are covered.

Common Problems

What follows in this section can seem like a daunting list of symptoms the operating system can exhibit. With a proper plan of action and good backup (always have a backup!), you can approach any of these problems with confidence. In many cases today, technicians have ceased to spend significant amounts of time chasing operating system issues since most important data is kept on servers and computers can be reimaged so quickly troubleshooting doesn't warrant the effort. Nevertheless, you should know these basic symptoms and the approach to take when they present themselves.

User Unable to Log On

When users have difficulty logging on to a server, it can be one of several things:

- User error typing the password
- Incorrect password
- Account disabled
- Account expired
- Inability to contact the domain controller
- DNS server failure
- Incorrect DNS server IP address on the server
- Unauthorized user

If you have verified that the user is using the correct password and typing it correctly, you need to check to see if the user's account has been either disabled or has expired. If the server is performing local authentication, you will look in the user account settings on the server. If the server is using domain authentication (more likely) you will check this in Active Directory (AD). It is also possible that in the case where the server is using Active Directory the server may not be able to locate and connect to the AD server. If the DNS settings on the server are incorrect it could cause this or if there is an issue with Active Directory or if the AD server is down.

Finally, it is possible that the user simply does not have permission to access that server. You can verify this by contacting his department head or superior.

User Cannot Access Resources

Your approach to solving resource access issues is not that much different than the approach you take with system logon issues. The possible causes are

- Unauthorized user
- Error in permission settings
- Inability to connect to the resource server caused by the following issues:
  - Incorrect DNS server address on client
  - DNS server failures
  - Active Directory failure

If the user simple can't connect to the resource server check her (see above) DNS server settings. If they are correct proceed to verify if the DNS server is functional. If it is *not*, neither will Active Directory be functional. If DNS is working, check the domain controller to ensure it is functioning.

If the user can connect but is denied access to the resource, check the permissions applied to the resource. If the user has no permission or the permissions listed do not match what the user tells you, tell the user you must check with his boss and verify permissions. If you need to make changes to the permissions, make sure you tell the user to log out and log back in so those changes will be reflected.

Finally, in Windows, make sure you have checked both the NTFS permissions and the share permissions. The effective permission will be the most restrictive of the combined NTFS permissions (as a user or member of any group) as compared to the combined share permissions (as a user or member of any group).

Memory Leak, BSOD/Stop

Memory leaks occur when an application is issued some memory to use and does not return the memory and any temporary file to the operating system after the program no longer needs it. Over time the available memory for that application or that part of the operating system becomes exhausted and the program can no longer function. This is caused by poor coding practices. While the application that is causing this should be investigated and perhaps updated, a quick solution is to reboot the server. Make sure when you do this it is a cold boot. Many of the latest operating systems don't actually reboot when you restart, they just sleep.

A more serious issue is a STOP message or Blue Screen of Death (BSOD) message. Once a regular occurrence when working with Windows, blue screens have become less common. Occasionally, systems will lock up; you can usually examine the log files to discover what was happening when this occurred and take steps to correct it. Remember, when dealing with a blue screen, always ask yourself "What did I just install or change?" In many cases, the change is involved in the BSOD. Also keep in mind that (as the instructions on the blue screen will tell you) a simple reboot will often fix the problem. Retaining the contents of the BSOD can help troubleshoot the issue. In most instances, the BSOD error will be in Microsoft's knowledgebase to help with troubleshooting.

OS Boot Failure in Windows

Common error messages include an invalid boot disk and inaccessible boot drive. On Windows servers, additional messages could be missing NTLDR and missing BOOTMGR. In Windows Server 2012 R2, there are four main issues that cause this:

- Corrupted system file
- Corrupted boot configuration data (BCD)
- Corrupted boot sector
- Corrupted master boot record (MBR)

Each if these issues can be addressed by booting the system to the installation disk and, during the process, selecting to repair the system. In Exercise 10.2 you will execute the four commands that address these issues.

EXERCISE 10.2

Repairing Boot Files in Windows Server 2012 R2

1. Put the Windows Server 2012 R2 installation disc into the disc drive, and then restart the server.

2. When the message "Press any key to boot from CD or DVD ..." appears, press a key.

3. Select a language, a time, a currency, and a keyboard or another input method, and then click Next.

4. Click Repair Your Computer.

5. Click the operating system that you want to repair, and then click Next.

6. In the System Recovery Options dialog box, click Command Prompt.

7. To ensure the system files are all intact, execute the following command at the command prompt:

    `sfc /scannow`

8. To rebuild the boot configuration data (BCD), execute the following command:

    `Bootrec /RebuildBcd`

9. To repair the boot sector, execute the following command:

    `BOOTREC /FIXBOOT`

10. To repair the Master Boot record, execute the following command:

    `BOOTREC /FIXMBR`

11. Finally, to apply the master boot code that is compatible with BOOTMGR, execute the following command, where `Drive` is the drive where the installation media resides:

    `Drive:\boot\Bootsect.exe /NT60`

Missing GRUB/LILO

The GRUB is the bootloader package in Linux and UNIX systems. If it is not present the system may not boot. In some cases when you install Windows it will overwrite the GRUB. If this occurs, or in any case where you need to reinstall or recover the GRUB, follow these steps, which are based on Ubuntu:

1. Mount the partition your Ubuntu Installation is on.

2. Bind the directories to which GRUB needs access to detect other operating systems.

3. Using chroot install, check, and update GRUB.

4. Exit the chrooted system and unmount everything.

5. Shut down and turn your computer back on, and you will be met with the default GRUB screen.

For More Information

For more detailed assistance with this process go to http://howtoubuntu
.org/how-to-repair-restore-reinstall-grub-2-with-a-ubuntu-live-cd.

While most distributions of UNIX and Linux now use GRUB, some older systems use
a bootloader called LILO. For some of the same reasons as with GRUB, it may become
corrupted or, after a Windows installation, it may be missing. This can also be recovered
by reinstalling it. To do so:

1. Boot into Linux some other way, either using Loadlin or a Linux boot floppy.

2. At the Linux command prompt just type **/sbin/lilo**.

3. Reboot, and LILO will be back.

Driver Issues

Usually when devices fail to start or are not detected by the system, and you have eliminated
a hardware issue, the problem involves drivers. Drivers are associated with devices, and you
can access them by looking at the properties for the device. The following, for example, are
the three most common tabs (In Windows Server 2012 R2 there are five tabs) of an adaptor's Properties dialog box in Device Manager (tabs that appear are always dependent on
the type of device and its capabilities):

General   This tab displays the device type, manufacturer, and location. It also includes
information regarding whether the device is currently working properly.

Driver   This tab displays information on the current driver and digital signer. Five command
buttons allow you to see driver details and uninstall or update the driver. It also offers the
option to roll back the driver to the previous driver when a new driver causes an issue.

Resources   This tab shows the system resources in use (I/O, IRQ, and so on) and whether
there are conflicts.

The most common driver-related device issue is device failure when a new driver is
installed. If this occurs, you can use the Roll Back Driver option in Device Manager or
boot into the Last Known Good Configuration.

Runaway Process

A runaway process is one that has taken control of the server and may lock the system up or
at the least lock up a service or application. Keep in mind that some forms of malware can
cause this issue, but we are going to focus on legitimate processes that become runaway.

In Windows you can use Task Manager to stop runaway processes. To do so access the
Processes tab and click the CPU and Memory columns to sort the list of running process
according to CPU and memory usage. This will allow you to identity the process using all
the CPU or memory. Highlight the process and select End Now.

In Linux you can use the kill command to stop the process. To do so, you must identity the guilty process using the ps command. To list and sort the processes by CPU usage, use this command (the head-5 option limits it to the top five processes):

```
$ ps aux --sort=-pcpu | head -5
USER PID %CPU %MEM    VSZ    RSS TTY        STAT START    TIME COMMAND
root    1  2.6  0.7  51396  7644 ?          Ss   02:02   0:03 /usr/lib/systemd/
systemd --switched-root --system --deserialize 23
root 1249  2.6  3.0 355800 30896 tty1       Rsl+ 02:02   0:02 /usr/bin/X
-background none :0 vt01 -nolisten tcp
root  508  2.4  1.6 248488 16776 ?          Ss   02:02   0:03 /usr/bin/python /
usr/sbin/firewalld --nofork
silver 1525  2.1  2.3 448568 24392 ?         S    02:03   0:01 /usr/bin/python /
usr/share/s
```

Once you have identified the process, locate the PID and use the kill command to stop it as follows (we are killing process 1249):

```
kill -SIGKILL 1249
```

Cannot Mount Drive

Before a device or drive can be used it must be mounted. This occurs automatically for currently mounted drives and devices, but it can be done manually. This is done in Linux with the mount command that follows where -t is the device type and destination is the mount point in the file system.

```
mount -t type device destination_dir
```

Usually issues occur when mounting an external drive such as a CD or DVD drive. Make sure the drive is attached and that there are no cabling issues. You may also need to install the driver for the storage device as well.

Cannot Write to System Log

When the system cannot write to the System log, it is usually because the log is full. In Windows, by default, the System log will overwrite the oldest events with new events but it is possible to set the log to *not* do so, which means when it gets full it stops collecting events. To avoid this issue, you have two choices. First you can set the log to overwrite older events, which means you may lose some older events. Frequent archives of the log can mitigate this loss. The other option is to leave it set as is and increase the size of the log file. Regardless of the solution you choose, you should still archive the log on a regular basis.

Probably the most important log in Linux is the file /var/log/messages, which records a variety of events, including system error messages, system startups, and system shutdowns. To use the logrotate command to manage log file in Linux see the link http://www.linuxcommand .org/man_pages/logrotate8.html.

Slow OS Performance

Slow system performance can come from many issues. For the purposes of this discussion, we are going to focus on performance that deteriorates after being acceptable as opposed to system performance that is poor from the outset (which could be a matter of insufficient resources such as RAM). Here is a list of possibilities:

- Defragment the hard drive. The more fragmented it is, the slower the disk access will be.

- Check the space on the hard drive. When the partition or volume where the operating system is located becomes full, performance will suffer. This is why it is a good idea to store data and applications on a different partition from the one holding the system files.

- Ensure the latest updates are installed. In many cases, updates help to solve performance problems, so make sure they are current.

- Use Task Manager to determine if a process is using too much memory or CPU or is simply locked up (not responding) and, if necessary, end the process.

- Finally, check for the presence of a virus or other malware. If the system seems to have an overabundance of disk activity, scan it for viruses using a virus program that resides externally on a CD/DVD or memory stick.

Patch Update Failure

When security and system patches are applied, in some cases they fail. While there have been cases of patches being issued that were problematic in and of themselves, in most cases that is not the issue. If the updates are being installed automatically from either the patch source or from a centralized patch server like Window Server Update Services, the issue could be an interruption of the transfer of the patch to the device. In this case you can either wait until the next scheduled update or you can try the update manually and it will succeed if a network issue was the problem. It could also be that there is insufficient drive space to hold the update. It could also be that the patch arrived at the device corrupted. Finally ensure that the firewall is allowing updates.

Service Failure

Sometimes when the system is started you receive a message that tells you a service failed to start. When that occurs, use the event log to determine the service that failed. Then to interact with service, access the Administrative Tools section of Control Panel and choose Services. This starts up the Services console. You can right-click any service and choose to start, stop, pause, resume, or restart it. You can also double-click the service to access its properties and configure such things as the startup type, dependencies, and other variables.

If the service refuses to start, it could be that a service on which it depends will not start. To determine what services must be running for the problem service to start, select the Dependencies tab of the service's Properties dialog box, as shown in Figure 10.4.

FIGURE 10.4   Service dependencies

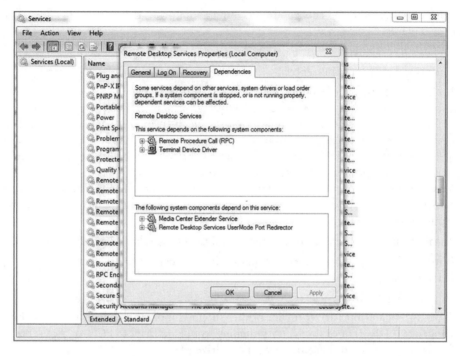

In the figure you can see that the Remote Desktop Services depend on both the RPC and the Terminal Device Driver to function. Try starting these components first. In some cases, you may need to trace the dependencies up several levels to get things going.

Hangs on Shut Down

In some cases, the system hangs during the shutdown of the system. If the system will not shut down without using the power button, use the button to shut it down and reboot in safe mode. Then attempt to shut down. If this works you should explore driver issues.

Some other things you can try are:

- Check for a BIOS update
- Toggle (reverse) the setting of the following registry entry (make a backup first!!)

```
HKEY_LOCAL_MACHINE\SOFTWARE\Microsoft\Windows NT\CurrentVersion\Winlogon
```

  - The key to change is called "PowerdownAfterShutdown".
  - If it's set to 1 change it to 0.
  - If it's set to 0 change it to 1.

You will need to restart after this change, but the next time you shut down it should stay offline. If not, reverse the change, restart and it should work from there.

Users Cannot Print

If you have eliminated a bad cable and users still cannot print, the issue could be located in one of two places:

- The user's computer
- The print device (or print server)

Check to see if others are having an issue and if so, the problem is probably the print device or print server. Sometimes the printer will not print and all attempts to delete print jobs or clear the print queue fail. It's almost as if the printer is just frozen. When this occurs, the best thing to do is restart the print spooler service on the computer that is acting as the print server. Unfortunately, all users will have to resend their print jobs after this, but at least the printer will be functional again.

Moreover, a printer can have several types of memory errors as well. The most common is insufficient memory to print the page. Sometimes you can circumvent this problem by doing any of the following:

- Turn off the printer to flush out its RAM and then turn it back on and try again.
- Print at a lower resolution. (Adjust this setting in the printer's properties in Windows.)
- Change the page being printed so it's less complex.
- Try a different printer driver if your printer supports more than one Printer Description Language (PDL). (For example, try switching from PostScript to PCL, or vice versa.) Doing so involves installing another printer driver.
- Upgrade the memory, if the printer allows.

If only the user is having an issue, check the user's connectivity to the print server. To determine whether it is a connectivity problem to a remote printer, ping the IP address of the printer. If you cannot ping the printer by IP address, that problem must be solved or all other troubleshooting of settings and drivers will be wasted effort.

Finally, printers are considered resources just like files and folders and as such can have permissions attached to them. When a user receives an access denied message, the user lacks the print permission. Typically a printer that has been shared will automatically give all users the print permission, but when permissions have been employed to control which users can print to a particular printer, that default has been altered.

When checking permissions, keep in mind that in Windows, users may have permissions derived from their personal account and from groups of which they are a member. You must ensure that users have not been explicitly denied print permission through their accounts or through any groups of which they are members. A single Deny will prevent them from printing, regardless of what other permissions they may have to the printer.

Also, print availability or print priority can affect access to the printer. Print availability is used to permit certain users to print only during certain times. With print priority, print jobs from certain users or groups are assigned a higher priority than other users or groups. These settings, usually set by an administrator, can prevent or delay successful printing.

Cause of Common Problems

While troubleshooting software issues may seem like looking for a needle in a haystack sometimes, there are a number of common causes that you may find yourself coming back to over and over. This is why some experienced technicians say that they sometimes just have a hunch what the issue is. What they really mean is that they have seen so many common issues that they begin to make quicker connections between issues and cause. Although we have covered some of these causes in prior sections, here are some the most common source of problems.

User Account Control (UAC/SUDO)

Administrator and root accounts are the most highly privileged accounts in an operating system. When a server is left logged on with a privileged account it creates a huge security issue. Most of the server operating systems you will encounter today incorporate the ability of an administrator or a root account holder to use a non-privileged account as standard operating procedure and elevate his privileges as needed without logging off and logging back in as root.

The User Account Control feature in Windows and the use of the sudo command in Linux make this possible. Using either system an administrator can elevate his privileges for a specific task and that security context ends when he is finished with that task.

In Windows this can be done in the GUI by right clicking the icon representing the task and selecting Run As Administrator as shown in Figure 10.5.

FIGURE 10.5   Run as Administrator

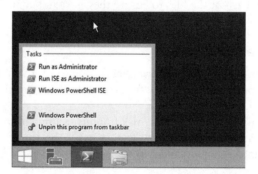

At the command line in Windows the same can be accomplished by prefacing the command with the run as command, as shown below, opening the command prompt as administrator.

```
runas /user:troym@mcmillan.com\administrator cmd
```

In Linux the same can be done using the sudo command. The sudo command can be added at the front of a command to execute the command using root privileges. For example, to remove a package with root privileges, the command is as follows:

```
sudo apt-get remove {package-name}
```

The su command is used to change from one user account to another. When the command is executed, you will be prompted for the password of the account to which you are switching, as shown here:

```
$ su mact
password:
mact@sandy:~$
```

Corrupted Files

File can get corrupted, especially when they are being transferred across a network or when the storage where it resides is damaged. In almost all cases a transmitted file that is corrupted will be detected at the destination using a frame check sequence (FCS). However a file gets corrupted, in many cases the file is of no use at that point.

While this is a sad state of affairs for any file, hopefully you have backup of the file if it is of importance. In the case of corrupted system files, the issue becomes more serious because now something may not work in the operating system. Many times this is caused by malware that alters or changes system files.

Whatever the source of system file corruption, in Windows you can use the System File Checker (SFC) to validate the system files and replace them if required. If you have any doubts about the integrity of important system files, execute the command sfc / scannow. The SFC will check the file structure. If the SFC discovers that a protected file has been overwritten, it retrieves the correct version of the file from the systemroot\system32\dllcache folder, and then replaces the incorrect file.

Another tool you can use in either Linux or Windows is the Tripwire utility. While this requires you to take a hash of all of the system files (and update it each time you update the system) it checks the hash of the files to ensure they have not changed since you took the hash.

Lack of Hard Drive Space

Regardless of how much storage space a server has, at some point you may fill that space! While lack of space in and of itself can slow the system down, issues that accompany the filling hard drive make the situation worse.

For one, this is typically accompanied by disk fragmentation (covered later in this section). Also as more data is added to the system, its takes the anti-malware program longer and longer to scan the system, and while it is doing this, in the background the performance dips.

There is one area that can be affected by lack of space if the situation gets critical. If the system has insufficient memory and frequently makes use of page or swap files on the hard drive, the lack of space will impact performance. The simplest solution to this issue is to add more space or archive some data and remove it from the drive.

Lack of System Resources

Sometimes a system will suddenly find it has insufficient system resources to handle the current workload. If the situation is temporary or transitory, it could be that a service or application is monopolizing all resources due to a malfunction or simply to shoddy coding. In that case you can use the techniques discussed earlier in the section "Runaway Process" to solve the issue.

It is possible that you need to add more physical resources. Use Task Manager and/or the Performance tool (discussed later in the "Software Tools" section) to determine if it is the memory or the CPU that is the issue and add more.

Virtual Memory (Misconfigured, Corrupt)

Virtual memory is a portion of the hard drive to which data is temporarily moved when the current available memory is insufficient for the task at hand. Earlier you learned that when the hard drive fills it limits the amount of space that can be used for this reducing performance.

The system should properly set the size of the file automatically based on the amount of memory present, but you can increase the size of the file and change its location using the System tools in Control Panel. Keep in mind that if this is a continual situation you need to add more RAM.

This utility allows you to view and configure various system elements. The System applet in Windows Server 2012 R2 is shown in Figure 10.6.

FIGURE 10.6   System

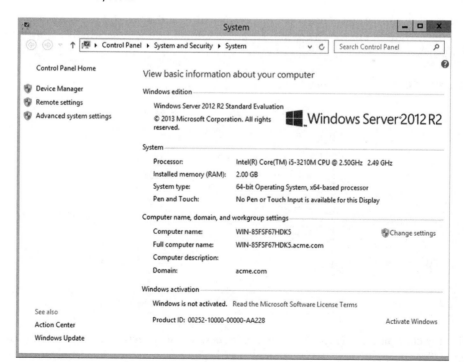

Selecting the Advanced System Settings option in the menu on the left opens the box in Figure 10.7.

FIGURE 10.7   System Properties Advanced tab

Next select the Settings button next to Performance and when the next box open, select the Advanced tab (yes, a second Advanced tab) and the box shown in Figure 10.8 will open.

FIGURE 10.8   Performance Options

Finally click on the Change button in the Virtual Memory section. In the box shown in Figure 10.9 you can change the location of the file and adjust its size. Earlier you learned that moving the file to a drive other than the operating system drive may help performance. To make either of these changes you have to clear the Automatically Manage Paging File Size For All Drives option.

FIGURE 10.9   Virtual memory settings

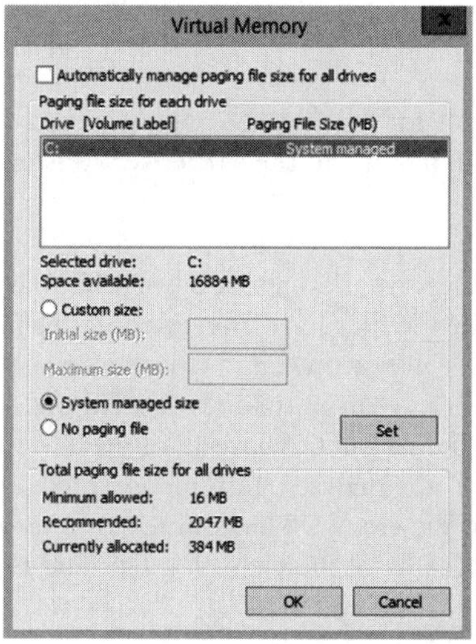

Fragmentation

Over time as data is written and erased from a drive, the data becomes fragmented, which mean that pieces of the same file are scattered in various locations on the drive. This makes it more difficult for the system to find all the pieces when reading the drive so performance slows. This can be addressed by using a defragmentation tool (discussed later in the "Defragmentation Tools" section).

Print Server Drivers/Services

In many cases today enterprise printers have a built-in print server, but you still may have a server that is acting as the print server for less-capable print devices. When that scenario is in effect, you must make sure that the server has all of the drivers required to communicate with the various printers it manages and for all of the operating systems that use it as the print server. While many of the drivers will be already in the operating system, some may not be and you may have to provide them to the server. The best place to obtain these drivers is the vendor website or Windows Update.

The most important and also the most problematic print service to monitor and manage is covered in the next section.

Print Spooler

In some cases, the printer will not print and jobs just seem to be stuck in the queue. The print spooler service controls the print queue. This service can be stopped and started to solve many software-related problems. Locate this service in the Services console and right-click it; you can first start and then stop the service. This can also be done at the command line using the `net stop spooler` and `net start spooler` commands.

Software Tools

A number of tools are available for troubleshooting operating system problems, some of which have been mentioned in passing in the earlier sections on common symptoms.

System Logs

All operating systems collect information about events that have occurred that are stored in log files. There are typically log files for different components, such as a security log, an application log, or a system log. These file can be used to troubleshoot operating system issues, and events related to this are usually in the System log.

If the enterprise is large, you may want to have all of the devices send their logs to a central server where they can be stored and analyzed. In Windows these logs can be viewed, filtered, and saved using a tool called Event Viewer. We'll look more closely at that tool later in this section.

In Linux the following are some of the major log files and their locations:

- `/var/log/messages`: General and system related
- `/var/log/auth.log`: Authentication logs
- `/var/log/kern.log`: Kernel logs
- `/var/log/cron.log`: Cron logs (cron job)
- `/var/log/maillog`: Mail server logs
- `/var/log/qmail/`: Qmail log directory (more files inside this directory) (qmail is a mail transfer agent (MTA) that runs on Unix)
- `/var/log/httpd/`: Apache access and error logs directory (Apache is a web server.)
- `/var/log/lighttpd/`: Lighttpd access and error logs directory (lighttpd is an open-source web server)
- `/var/log/boot.log`: System boot log
- `/var/log/mysqld.log`: MySQL database server log file
- `/var/log/secure` or `/var/log/auth.log`: Authentication log
- `/var/log/utmp` or `/var/log/wtmp`: Login records file
- `/var/log/yum.log`: Yum command log file (Yellowdog Updater, Modified (yum) is an open-source command-line package-management utility for Linux operating systems using the RPM Package Manager.)

Windows employs comprehensive error and informational logging routines. Every program and process theoretically could have its own logging utility, but Microsoft has come up with a rather slick utility, Event Viewer, which, through log files, tracks all events on a particular Windows computer. Normally, though, you must be an administrator or a member of the Administrators group to have access to Event Viewer.

With Windows Server 2012 R2, you can access Event Viewer from the Tools menu in Server Manager as shown in Figure 10.10.

FIGURE 10.10   Tools menu

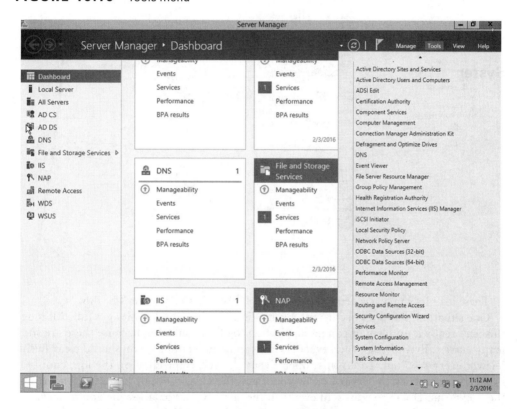

Once Event Viewer is selected, the opening page is shown in Figure 10.11.

- The System log file displays alerts that pertain to the general operation of Windows.

- The Application log file logs application errors.

- The Security log file logs security events such as login successes and failures.

- The Setup log will appear on domain controllers and will contain events specific to them.

- The Forwarded Events log contains events that have been forwarded to this log by other computers.

FIGURE 10.11 The opening interface of Event Viewer

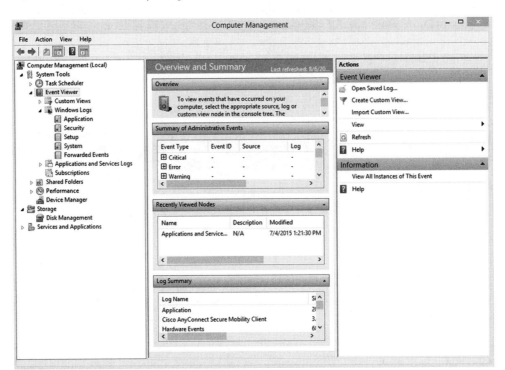

These log files can give a general indication of a Windows computer's health.

One situation that does occur with Event Viewer is that the log files get full. Although this isn't really a problem, it can make viewing log files confusing because there are so many entries. Even though each event is time- and date-stamped, you should clear Event Viewer every so often. To do this, open Event Viewer, right-click on the log, choose Properties, and click the Clear Log button; in earlier OSs, choose Clear All Events from the Log menu. Doing so erases all events in the current log file, allowing you to see new events more easily when they occur. You can set maximum log size by right-clicking on the log and choosing Properties. By default, when a log fills to its maximum size, old entries are deleted in first in, first out (FIFO) order. Clearing the log, setting maximum log size, and setting how the log is handled when full are done on the Log Properties dialog as shown in Figure 10.12.

You can save the log files before erasing them. The saved files can be burned to a CD or DVD for future reference. Often, you are required to save the files to CD or DVD if you are working in a company that adheres to strict regulatory standards.

FIGURE 10.12 Event log Properties

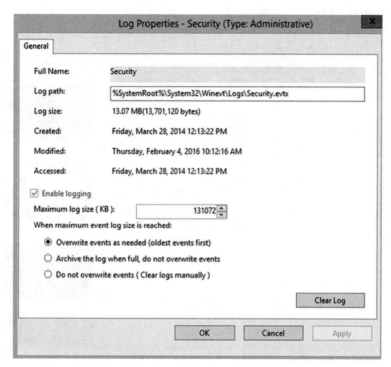

In addition to just erasing logs, you can configure three different settings for what you want to occur when the file does reach its maximum size. The first option is "Overwrite events as needed (oldest events first)," and this replaces the older events with the new entries. The second option is "Archive the log when full, do not overwrite events," and this will create another log file as soon as the current one runs out of space. The third option, "Do not overwrite events (Clear logs manually)," will not record any additional events once the file is full.

Monitoring Tools (Resource Monitor, Performance Monitor)

There are a number of tools available in Windows Server 2012 R2 to monitor the use of resources. The two tools we'll discuss are Resource Monitor and Performance monitor.

Resource Monitor

Resource Monitor, available from the same Tools menu in Server Manager where we accessed Event Viewer, can track the use of the CPU, memory, disk system, and network card in real time. It has a tab for each and an Overview tab as shown in Figure 10.13.

FIGURE 10.13 Resource Monitor

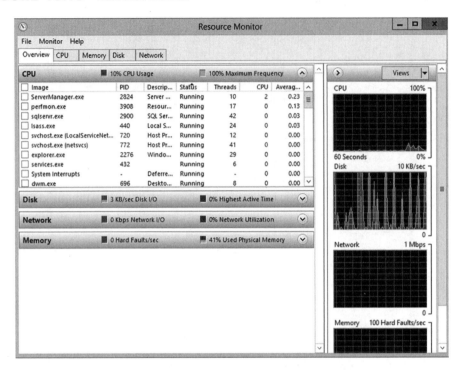

On each tab there are real-time details on the use of each resource. For example, in Figure 10.14 the Memory tab shows a graph of the memory usage (scrolling across in real time) and at the bottom, a bar chart shows how much memory is used, available, and so on.

Performance Monitor

Performance Monitor displays performance counters that represent various aspects of the system use of an object (objects are resources). It will collect the counter information and then send it to a console (such as the one in front of the admin so they can be aware of the problem) or event log.

Where it differs from Resource Monitor is that it allows you to choose a counter for an object with granularity. For example, perhaps you know that the CPU is working harder than usual; rather than just view the overall performance, you can choose to add the % Privileged time counter. Privileged, or kernel, mode is the processing mode that allows code to have direct access to all hardware and memory in the system. A counter that has been added is shown in Figure 10.15. Any of the resources can be broken down this way.

FIGURE 10.14 Memory tab

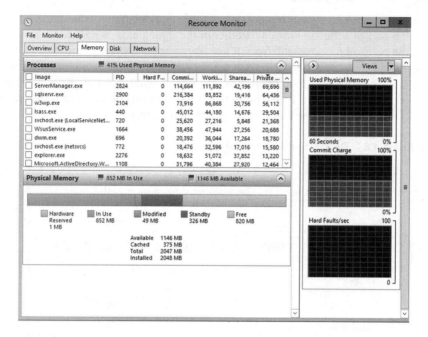

FIGURE 10.15 Adding a counter

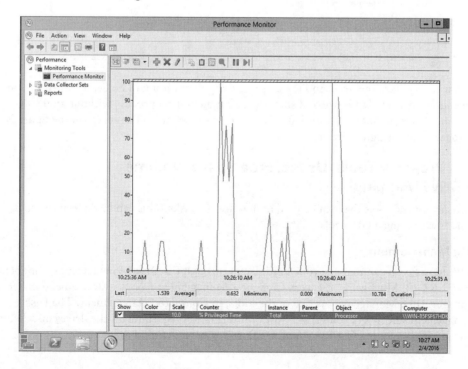

Defragmentation Tools

Defragmentation tools are used to reorganize the physical location of the data on the hard drive so all pieces of a file are located together in the same place. When this is done, it improves the performance of the drive. All server operating systems come with built-in defragmentation tools, and their operation can be scheduled for a time convenient to the user. This also frees the user (and the technician) from having to think about running the tool on a regular basis. Figure 10.16 shows the Drive Optimization tool in Windows Server 2012 R2. This tool is available from the Tools menu in Server Manager.

FIGURE 10.16   Drive Optimization tool

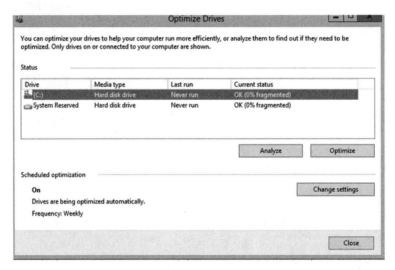

You can analyze the drive and the degree of fragmentation will be determined, or you can choose to select Optimize and start the defragmentation process without analyzing. You can also make schedules so that this occurs automatically. The server in the figure is set for weekly defragmentation.

Disk Property Tools (Usage, Free Space, Volume or Drive Mapping)

There are several tools that can be used to monitor the disks. This can be done at the command line or using a GUI tools.

Disk Management

In Windows, you can manage your hard drives through the Disk Management component. To access Disk Management, access Computer Management from the Tools menu in Server Manager. Disk Management is one of the tools, in Computer Management. The Disk Management screen lets you view a host of information regarding all the drives installed in your system, including CD-ROM and DVD drives, as shown in Figure 10.17.

FIGURE 10.17   Disk Management

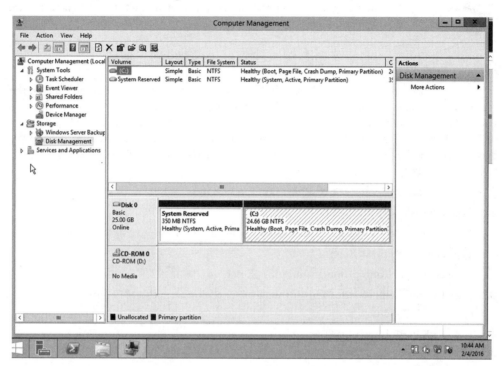

The list of devices in the top portion of the screen shows you additional information for each partition on each drive, such as the filesystem used, status, free space, and so on. If you right-click a partition in either area, you can perform a variety of functions, such as formatting the partition and changing the name and drive letter assignment. For additional options and information, you can also access the properties of a partition by right-clicking it and selecting Properties.

DRIVE STATUS

The status of a drive can have a number of variables associated with it (System, Boot, and so on) but what really matters is whether it falls into the category of *healthy* or *unhealthy*. As the title implies, if it is healthy, it is properly working and if it is unhealthy, you need to attend to it and correct problems. In Figure 10.18, in the Status column of Disk Management, we can see that all drives are Healthy.

MOUNTING

Drives must be mounted before they can be used. Within Windows, most removable media (flash drives, CDs, and so forth) are recognized when attached and mounted. Volumes on basic disks, however, are not automatically mounted and assigned drive letters by default. To mount them, you must manually assign them drive letters or create mount points in Disk Management.

You can also mount from the command line using either the Diskpart or the Mountvol utilities.

INITIALIZING

Initializing a disk makes it available to the disk management system, and in most cases, the drive will not show up until you do this. Once the drive has been connected or installed, you should do this. Initializing the drive can be done at the command line using diskpart or in the Disk Management tool. You need to know that initialization will wipe out the drives contents! To use diskpart to perform the initialization on 2TB drives and smaller follow these steps:

1. Open the Start Menu, type **diskpart**, and press Enter.

2. Type **list disk**, and press Enter.

3. Type **select disk X** (where X is the number your drive shows up as), and press Enter.

4. Type **clean**, and press Enter.

5. Type **create partition primary**, and press Enter.

6. Type **format quick fs=ntfs** (This formats the partition with the NTFS file system.), and press Enter.

7. Type **assign**, and press Enter.

8. Type **exit**, and press Enter.

To use diskpart to perform the initialization on drives that are 2.5 TB and larger follow these steps:

1. Open the Start Menu, type **diskpart**, and press Enter.

2. Type **list disk**, and press Enter.

3. Type **select disk X** (where X is the number your drive shows up as), and press Enter.

4. Type **clean**, and press Enter.

5. Type **convert gpt**, and press Enter.

6. Type **create partition primary**, and press Enter.

7. Type **format quick fs=ntfs**, and press Enter.

8. Type **assign**, and press Enter.

9. Type **exit**, and press Enter.

To use Disk Management, follow this procedure:

1. Install the drive and reboot the device.

2. In the search line, type **Disk Management** and press Enter. With the drive connected you will get the pop-up box shown in Figure 10.18.

3. Choose either MBR or GPT (GPT brings with it many advantages, but MBR is still the most compatible and is required for older operating systems.) and click OK.

FIGURE 10.18   Initialize disk pop-up

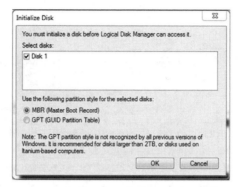

4. Assuming you get this pop-up, right click and select to initialize the newly added drive under where the disk number is listed as shown in the Disk # as shown in Figure 10.19.

FIGURE 10.19   Initialize disk

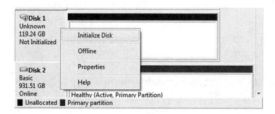

EXTENDING PARTITIONS

It is possible to add more space to partitions (and logical drives) by extending them into unallocated space. This is done in Disk Management by right-clicking and choosing Extend or by using the Diskpart utility.

SPLITTING PARTITIONS

Just as you can extend a partition, you can also reduce the size of it. While generically known as splitting the partition, the menu option in Disk Management is Shrink. By shrinking an existing partition, you are creating another with unallocated space that can then be used for other purposes. You can only shrink basic volumes that use the NTFS filesystem (and space exists) or that do not have a filesystem.

SHRINKING PARTITIONS

It is also possible to shrink a volume from its size at creation. To do so in Disk Management, access the volume in question, right click the volume, and select Shrink Volume as shown in Figure 10.20.

FIGURE 10.20 Shrink Volume

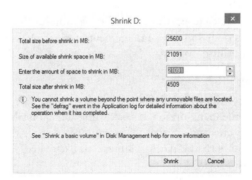

This will open another box that will allows you to control how much you want to shrink the volume as shown in Figure 10.21.

FIGURE 10.21 Set volume size

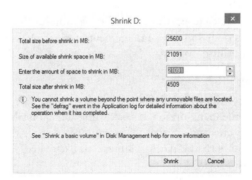

ASSIGNING/CHANGING DRIVE LETTERS

Mounting drives and assigning drive letters are two tasks that go hand in hand. When you mount a drive, you typically assign it a drive letter in order to be able to access it.

Right-clicking on a volume in Disk Management gives the option choice Change Drive Letter And Paths as shown in Figure 10.22.

FIGURE 10.22   Change Drive Letter

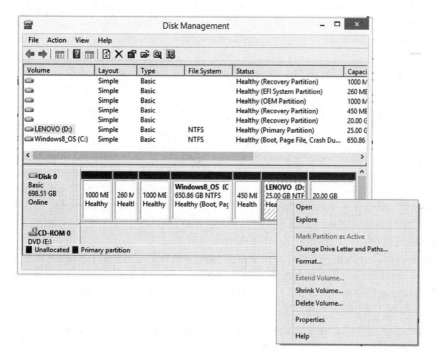

ADDING DRIVES

When removable drives are added, the Windows operating system is configured, by default, to identify them and assign a drive letter. When nonremovable drives are added, you must mount them and assign a drive letter as mentioned earlier.

ADDING ARRAYS

Arrays are added to increase fault tolerance (using RAID) or performance (striping). Disk Management allows you to create and modify arrays as needed.

Diskpart

Diskpart is command-line disk management utility in Windows. It enables you to manage objects (disks, partitions, or volumes) by using scripts or direct input at a command prompt. It can perform all the functions that can be done with the Disk Management utility and quite a few that cannot be done with Disk Management. In many ways, it is an updated version of fdisk. It can be used to create and manage volumes on the drive.

Summary

In this chapter you learned about software troubleshooting, beginning with the CompTIA methodology for troubleshooting. You learned that following these eight steps can help to organize your efforts and solve issues in the least amount of time. We also covered hardware troubleshooting, which included discussing the common issues you will see and the likely causes of these issues. Finally, this chapter closed with a discussion of common software issues, their sources, and the tools you would use to deal with them.

Exam Essentials

List the eight steps in the CompTIA troubleshooting method. In order, the steps are identify the problem and determine the scope; establish a theory of probable cause; test the theory to determine cause; establish a plan of action to resolve the problem and notify impacted users; implement the solution or escalate as appropriate; verify full system functionality and if applicable implement preventative measures; perform a root cause analysis, and document findings, actions; and outcomes throughout the process.

Identify common hardware issues, their causes, and solutions. Describe common hardware issues, among them failed POST, overheating, memory failure, onboard component failure, processor failure, incorrect boot sequence, expansion card failure, operating system not found, drive failure, power supply failure, and I/O failure.

Identify common software issues, their causes, and solutions. Describe common software issues, among them user unable to logon, user cannot access resources, memory leak, BSOD / stop, OS boot failure, driver issues, runaway process, cannot mount drive, cannot write to system log, slow OS performance, patch update failure, service failure, hangs on shut down, user cannot print.

Review Questions

You can find the answers in the Appendix.

1. Which of the following steps in the CompTIA troubleshooting method come last?

    A. Verify full system functionality and, if applicable, implement preventative measures.

    B. Document findings, actions, and outcomes throughout the process.

    C. Identifying the problem and determining the scope.

    D. Perform a root cause analysis.

2. Which of the following actions should be taken before making changes during troubleshooting?

    A. Reboot the computer in safe mode.

    B. Perform a backup.

    C. Notify the user.

    D. Disable the anti-malware.

3. Which of the following statements is true with regard to troubleshooting?

    A. Make one change at a time.

    B. If multiple users are involved, the source is likely their local computers.

    C. You should always try to replicate the issue in the production environment.

    D. Always assume the cabling is good.

4. Which of the following events causes chip creep?

    A. High humidity

    B. Overheating

    C. Dropping the device

    D. Power surges

5. Replacing slots covers helps to prevent which event?

    A. Corrosion

    B. Overheating

    C. Theft

    D. EMI

6. Which of the following is frequently the source of the error message `Data_Bus_Error` ?

    A. Motherboard

    B. Memory

    C. CPU

    D. Hard drive

7. What is typically the solution if an integrated component does badly?

   A. Replace the component.

   B. Replace the socket.

   C. Replace the motherboard.

   D. Disable the component.

8. Which of the following is *not* a source of slow hard drive performance?

   A. Fragmentation

   B. Lack of memory

   C. Improper data cables

   D. Excessive interrupts

9. Which of the following starts by using a preselected minimal set of drivers and startup programs?

   A. Clean boot

   B. Safe mode

   C. Diagnostic boot

   D. Core mode

10. Which if the following is designed to replace the BIOS?

   A. EEPROM

   B. UEFI

   C. BCD

   D. GUID

11. Which if the following does not need to be matched correctly?

   A. Multiple CPUs

   B. Multiple memory modules

   C. Multiple network cards

   D. Multiple power supplies

12. Which of the following is true of server backplanes?

   A. They can be a single point of failure.

   B. They provide data and control signal connectors for the CPU.

   C. Backplane failures are common.

   D. You should implement redundant backplanes.

13. How should you use compressed air inside the case?

   A. Long sustained bursts.

   B. Short bursts.

   C. Hold the can 12 inches away from the system.

   D. Hold the can upside down.

14. What should the humidity be in the server room?

    A. 30 percent

    B. 40 percent

    C. 50 percent

    D. 60 percent

15. What can be the result of low humidity?

    A. Corrosion

    B. ESD

    C. RFI

    D. EMI

16. Which of the following is a short-term voltage drop?

    A. Blackout

    B. Surge

    C. Brownout

    D. Sag

17. Which of the following is used to test a power supply?

    A. POST card

    B. Toner probe

    C. Multimeter

    D. ESD strap

18. Which of the following could *not* be reason why a user cannot logon?

    A. User error typing the password

    B. Unauthorized user

    C. Incorrect password

    D. Spyware

19. Which if the following occurs when an application is issued some memory to use and does not return the memory?

    A. Kernel panic

    B. BSOD

    C. Memory leak

    D. Mantrap

20. Which command ensures the system files are all intact?

    A. sfc/scannow

    B. Bootrec/RebuildBcd

    C. BOOTREC/FIXBOOT

    D. BOOTREC/FIXMBR

Chapter

11

Troubleshooting Connectivity Issues

COMPTIA SERVER+ EXAM OBJECTIVES COVERED IN THIS CHAPTER:

✓ **7.4 Given a scenario, effectively diagnose network problems, selecting the appropriate tools and methods**

- Common problems (Internet connectivity failure, email failure, resource unavailable, DHCP server misconfigured, nonfunctional or unreachable, destination host unreachable, unknown host, default gateway misconfigured, failure of service provider, cannot reach by host name/FQDN)

- Causes of common problems (improper IP configuration, VLAN configuration, port security, improper subnetting, component failure, incorrect OS route tables, bad cables, firewall [misconfiguration, hardware failure, software failure], misconfigured NIC, routing/switch issues, DNS and/or DHCP failure, misconfigured hosts file, IPv4 vs. IPv6 misconfigurations)

- Networking tools (ping, tracert/traceroute, ipconfig/ifconfig, nslookup, net use/mount, route, nbtstat, netstat)

✓ **7.6 Given a scenario, effectively diagnose security issues, selecting the appropriate tools and methods**

- Common problems (file integrity issue, privilege escalation, applications will not load, can't access network file/shares, unable to open files, excessive access, excessive memory utilization)

- Causes of common problems (open ports, active services, inactive services, intrusion detection configurations, antimalware configurations, local/group policies, firewall rules, misconfigured permissions, virus infection, rogue processes/services)

- Security tools (port scanners, sniffers, cipher, checksums, telnet client, antimalware)

When users are unable to connect to the resources they need, they can't do their job. There are two main sources of connectivity problems. *Network* issues mean that a misconfigured or malfunctioning device exists somewhere between users and their resources. *Security* issues mean that a security feature is either correctly or incorrectly denying the user access to the resources. In this chapter, we'll discuss the diagnosis of both of these issues.

Diagnosing Network Problems

Users cannot access a resource if a clear and valid path in the network does not exist between their device and the device holding the resource. This means that any network connectivity issue could exist in a number of places between the two. It could be that one of the two end devices is misconfigured, or the problem could be related to one of the infrastructure devices between them (switches and routers). In this section we're going to first look at common network issues and error messages and then follow that discussion up with possible solutions. Finally, we'll look at tools that can aid you in identifying these issues.

Common Problems

As you address networking issues, you'll find a number of common problems seem to appear frequently. The users may not always describe the issues in these terms, but you will learn over time which of these issues are possible causes of their dilemma.

Resource Unavailable

Network problems, usually manifesting themselves as an inability to connect to resources, can arise from many different sources. This section discusses some common symptoms of networking issues. For many of the issues we will cover, you may find that the user simply has no connectivity. This is as good a time as any to talk about general network troubleshooting for a single device.

No Connectivity

When no connectivity can be established with the network, your troubleshooting approach should begin at the Physical layer and then proceed up the OSI model. As components at each layer are eliminated as the source of the problem, proceed to the next higher layer. A simple yet effective set of steps might be as follows:

1. Check the network cable to ensure it is the correct cable type (crossover or straight-through) and that it is functional. If in doubt, try a different cable.

2. Ensure that the NIC is functional and the TCP/IP protocol is installed and functional by pinging the loopback address (127.0.0.1 in IPv4 or ::1 in IPv6). If required, install or reinstall TCP/IP and/or replace or repair the NIC.

3. Check the local IP configuration and ensure that the IP address, subnet mask, and gateway are correct. If the default gateway can be pinged, the computer is configured correctly for its local network and the problem lies beyond the router or with the destination device. If pings to the gateway are unsuccessful, ensure that the IP configurations of the router interface and the computer are compatible and in the same subnet.

When dealing with a wireless network, ensure that the wireless card is functional. The wireless card is easily disabled with a keystroke on a laptop and should be the first thing to check. If the network uses a hidden SSID, ensure that the station in question is configured with the correct SSID.

APIPA/Link Local Addresses

Automatic Private IP Addressing (APIPA) is a TCP/IP feature Microsoft added to its operating systems. If a DHCP server cannot be found, the clients automatically assign themselves an IP address, somewhat randomly, in the 169.254.x.x range with a subnet mask of 255.255.0.0. This allows them to communicate with other hosts that have similarly configured themselves, but they will be unable to connect to the Internet or to any machines or resources that have DHCP-issued IP addresses.

If the network uses DHCP for IP configuration and the computer with the connectivity issue has an APIPA address, the problem is one of these three things:

- The DHCP server is out of IP addresses.

- The DHCP server is on the other side of a router and there is no functional DHCP relay present or no IP helper address configured on the router—all of which is to say the DHCP request is not reaching the DHCP server.

- The computer has a basic connectivity issue preventing it from connecting to the network (see the sections, "Limited connectivity, Local connectivity and Intermittent connectivity" later in this chapter.)

In Chapter 2, "Installing and Configuring Servers," you learned about a type of IPv6 address called a *link local address* that in many ways is like an APIPA address in that the device will generate one of these addresses for each interface with no intervention from a human, as is done with APIPA. The scope of the address is also the same; it is not routable and is good only on the segment where the device is located.

However, as is the case with APIPA addresses, if two devices that are connected to the same segment generate these addresses, they will be in the same network, and the two devices will be able to communicate. This is because the devices always generate the address using the same IPv6 prefix (the equivalent of a network ID in IPv4), which is fe80::/64. The reminder of the address is created by spreading the 48-bit MAC address across the last 64 bits, yielding an IPv6 address that looks like the following one:

FE80::2237:06FF:FECF:67E4/64

Limited Connectivity

In some cases, the computer has connectivity to some but not all resources. When this is the case, issues that may reside on other layers of the OSI model should come under consideration. These include the following:

Authentication Issues Does the user have the permission to access the resource?

DNS Issues You may be able to ping the entire network using IP addresses, but most access is done by name, not IP address. If you can't ping resources by name, DNS is not functional, meaning either the DNS server is down or the local machine is not configured with the correct IP address of the DNS server. If recent changes have occurred in the DNS mappings or if your connection to the destination device has recently failed because of a temporary network issue that has been solved, you may need to clear the local DNS cache using the ipconfig/flushdns command.

Remote Problem Don't forget that establishing a connection is a two-way street, and if the remote device has an issue, communication cannot occur. Always check the remote device as well. Any interconnecting device between the computer and resource, such as a switch or router, should also be checked for functionality.

Local Connectivity

When a computer can communicate only on its local network or subnet, the problem is usually one of the following:

Incorrect Subnet Mask Sometimes an incorrect mask will prevent all communication, but in some cases it results in successful connections locally but not remotely (outside the local subnet). The subnet mask value should be the same mask used on the router interface connecting to the local network.

Incorrect Default Gateway Address If the computer cannot connect to the default gateway, it will be confined to communicating with devices on the local network. This IP address should be that of the router interface connecting to the local network.

Router Problem If all users on the network are having connectivity problems, you likely have a routing issue that should be escalated to the proper administrators.

Intermittent Connectivity

When a connectivity issue comes and goes, it can be a hardware issue or a software issue. Check the following hardware components for functionality:

Network Cable A damaged cable can cause intermittent connectivity.

Network Interface Card If the NIC is not properly seated or has worked its way partially out of its slot, it can cause connections that come and go.

Interference On a wireless network, cordless phones, microwave ovens, and other wireless networks can interfere with transmissions. Also, users who stray too far from the access point can experience a signal that comes and goes.

The following are software issues that can cause intermittent connectivity:

DHCP Issues   When the DHCP server is down or out of IP addresses, the problem will not manifest itself to those users who already have an IP address until their lease expires and they need a new address. In this case, some users will be fine and others will not, and then users who were fine earlier in the day may have problems later when their IP address lease expires.

DNS Problems   If the DNS server is down or malfunctioning, it will cause problems for DNS clients who need name resolution requests answered. For users who have already connected to resources in the last hour before the outage, connectivity to those resources will still be possible until the name-to–IP address mapping is removed from the client DNS resolver cache.

IP Conflict

IP address conflicts are somewhat rare when DHCP is in use, but they can still happen. DHCP servers and clients both check for IP duplication when the DHCP client receives an IP address, but the process doesn't always work. Moreover, if someone with a statically configured IP address connects to the network with the same address as another machine, a conflict will exist.

Regardless of how the conflict occurs, it must be resolved because until it is, one or possibly both computers with the same address will not be able to network. You can determine the MAC address of the computer with which you are experiencing the conflict by using the ping command followed by the arp -a command. In Exercise 11.1 you will identify an IP address conflict.

EXERCISE 11.1

Identifying an IP Address Conflict

1.   Begin by pinging the IP address in conflict as shown in Figure 11.1.

    FIGURE 11.1   Pinging the conflicted address

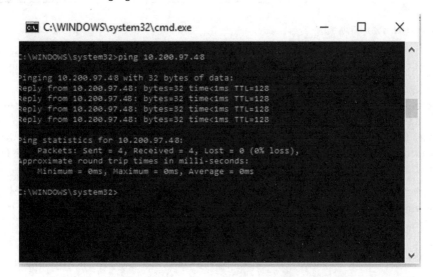

2. Now use the arp-a command to view the ARP cache where the MAC address–to–IP address mapping your computer just created will be located, as shown in Figure 11.2. As you can see in the output, the MAC address of the IP address we pinged is 18-67-b0-c3-3d-27.

FIGURE 11.2 Using arp -a to identify the MAC address

Slow Transfer Speeds

Slow transmission on the network can be caused by hardware and software issues. Some of the physical issues that can cause slow performance are as follows:

Interference Both wireless and wired networks can be affected by interference from electromagnetic interference (EMI) and radio frequency interference (RFI). EMI will degrade network performance. This can be identified by the poor performance present. Be sure to run cables around (not over) ballasts and other items that can cause EMI. RFI is a similar issue introduced by radio waves. Wireless networks suffer even more from both of these issues.

Incorrect Cabling The network can go only as fast as its weakest link. Using CAT3 cabling, for example, will only allow the device using that cable to operate at 10 Mbps even if its network cards are capable of 10 Gbps.

Malfunctioning NIC Network interface cards (NICs) can malfunction and cause a broadcast storm. These broadcast packets fill the network with traffic that slows performance for all. Use a protocol analyzer to determine the MAC address of the offending computer.

From a software standpoint, the following issues can result in less-than-ideal performance:

Router Misconfiguration   If the router is not configured correctly, it can cause slow performance because of less-than-optimal routing paths. Escalate the issue to the appropriate administrators.

Switch Misconfiguration   An improperly implemented redundant switch network can result in switching loops that cause slow performance. Escalate the issue to the appropriate administrators.

Low RF Signal

In a wireless network, the signal coming from the access point has a distance limit. With some variation by standard, this is about 300 feet. However, this distance is impacted by obstructions and interference in the area. The WLAN design should include a site survey that identifies these issues and locates access points (APs) and antenna types in such a way as to mitigate these effects.

It is also useful to know that APs and some client radios have a setting to control signal strength. It is not a normal practice to change the setting in a laptop wireless card, but it may be necessary to change the transmit level on an AP. In many cases, it is actually beneficial to reduce the transmit level of an AP in situations where it is interfering with other APs in your network or you want to limit the range of the signal to prevent it from leaving the building. This is especially true in high-density areas where several APs are collocated in the same area for increased throughput.

SSID Not Found

In an 802.11 WLAN, the service set identifier (SSID) is used as a both a network name and in some cases the magic word that allows access to the network. One of the ways you can increase the security of a WLAN (not sufficient in and of itself but a good addition to a layered approach to WLAN security) is to "hide" the SSID. This is also referred to as disabling SSID broadcast. This is done by setting the access point to *not* list the SSID in the beacon frames. These frames contain the information that is used to populate the list of available wireless networks when you "scan" for wireless networks on your wireless device.

The reason this doesn't constitute real security is that the SSID is only removed from the beacon frames, which are used by stations to locate available networks. The SSID is not removed from many other frame types, and a hacker can use a wireless sniffer to capture those frames and learn the SSID.

When the SSID is hidden, the *only* way a device can connect to the WLAN is to be configured with a profile that includes the SSID of the WLAN. While every operating system is slightly different, to do this in Windows 8.1, you follow these steps:

1.   Open the Network and Sharing Center, as shown in Figure 11.3.

2.   Select Set Up A New Connection Or Network, opening the page shown in Figure 11.4.

FIGURE 11.3 Network and Sharing Center

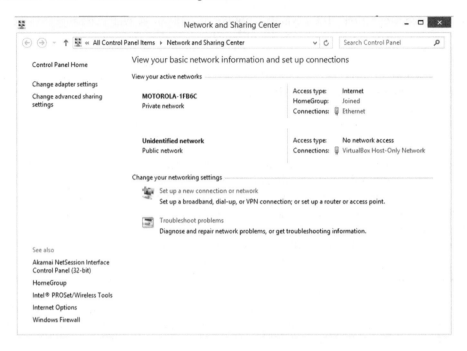

FIGURE 11.4 Set Up A New Connection Or Network

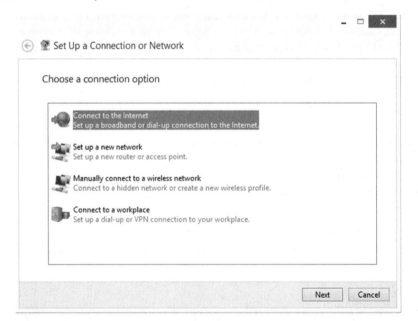

3. Select the option Manually Connect To A Wireless Network and click Next, opening the page shown in Figure 11.5.

FIGURE 11.5 Manually connecting to a wireless network

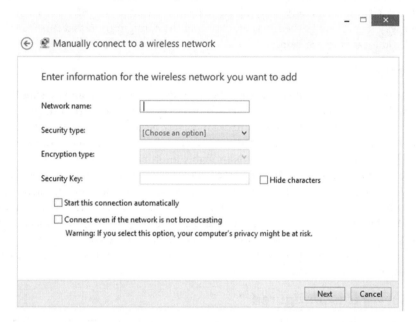

4. Complete the network name, security type, encryption type, and security key; check the box Connect Even If The Network Is Not Broadcasting; and click Next. Now the profile is complete, and you should be able to connect to the "hidden" network. To make it easier for the user, you may also want to check the box Start This Connection Automatically.

Internet Connectivity Failure

When users cannot connect to the Internet, you will hear about it and soon. This issue can have a number of sources, such as the following:

- The IP configuration of the user's computer
- The IP configuration of the user's default gateway or router
- The IP configuration of any routers that stand between the gateway and the Internet
- The DNS server
- The ISP
- The DHCP server

Each of these potential sources will yield specific clues that may indicate their involvement. Some of these clues will be covered in the sections that follow. It is always helpful to first determine the scope of the issue as that may eliminate some possibilities. If the user is the only one having the issue, then it is probably the IP configuration of that user's device (or malfunctioning hardware on the device). In that case, check for the correct IP address, subnet mask, default gateway, and DNS server address on the user's device. Don't forget to ask the user about any changes they may have made recently. Recently made changes are frequently found to be the cause of issues.

If multiple users are having this issue, it is probably an infrastructure device that stands between the users and the Internet. If you know where the affected users are located, it may help you to determine what network path these devices share to the Internet. Then you can trace your way from them to the Internet, checking the configuration and functionality of each until you locate the problem.

Email Failure

Often users will complain that the email server is down. As a technician you should learn to filter user's descriptions of issues through your deeper understanding of the network. You know that if the user can't connect to email it may be the email server, but it could also be a host of other issues as well. As always you should determine the scope of the issue first. If multiple users are having this issue, it is probably an infrastructure device that stands between the users and the email server or the email server itself. If only one user is affected, check the IP configuration of the user's device and the functionality of their email client.

Just as when addressing Internet issues, trace your way from the affected user to the email server, checking the configuration and functionality of each until you locate the problem. Keep in mind this includes both the DNS server and the DHCP server as well as the routers and switches in the path. Finally, if the path is clear it is time to check the functionality of the email server.

DHCP Server Misconfigured

As you learned earlier, if the DHCP server has an issue many users may be affected. Always ensure it has a sufficient number of IP addresses to service each scope. Also make sure that any default gateway and DNS server addresses it is issuing are correct; if they aren't, it will cause the users to be unable to leave their local subnet or perform name resolution.

Nonfunctional or Unreachable

Always keep in mind that the destination device may not be functional or it may not be reachable even though it is functioning. We'll be looking at the meaning of certain ICMP messages in a moment; they can tell you a lot, but know that although you may be able to ping the destination by both IP address and name, that doesn't mean that the service the destination is providing is working. You can determine this by attempting a Telnet connection to the IP address of the device and adding the port number of the service as shown here. In this example, the test is meant to test the functionality of HTTP:

```
telnet 192.168.5.5 80
```

If the port is open, you will see a blank screen. This will mean that the connection is successful. If it is not open, you will see this:

```
telnet 192.168.5.5 80
Connecting to 192.168.5.5 …..  could not open connection to the host on port 80:
connect failed
```

Keep in mind that this only tests connectivity to the service and does not guarantee the service is configured or functioning correctly.

Destination Host Unreachable

This is an error message you may receive when attempting to ping the destination device. This means that one of the routers along the path to destination does not have a route to the network where the device resides. It does *not* mean that the device is not on or is unavailable. That is a different message.

It will appear as a destination unreachable message (this is a group of message types that all have code numbers) with a code number of 1.

Code numbers do not appear in a destination unreachable message. However, you can use a protocol analyzer to capture one of the packets and view the code number by viewing the packet in the tool. You will do this in Exercise 11.2.

EXERCISE 11.2

Using a Sniffer to Identify the Code Number

This exercise uses Wireshark, a well-known protocol analyzer or sniffer. To get a trial version, go to www.downloadcrew.com/article/1456-wireshark.

1. If not already installed, follow the directions to install Wireshark.

2. Open Wireshark and from the opening page under the section labeled Interface List, select the interface on which you would like to capture packets. When you click on it, the capture should begin. If it doesn't, go to the Capture menu at the top of the screen and from the drop-down menu select Start Capture.

3. Open the command prompt and ping the unreachable destination to generate the ICMP messages.

4. Return to Wireshark and from the Capture menu select Stop Capture. You will have many captured packets listed, as shown in Figure 11.6.

FIGURE 11.6   Wireshark

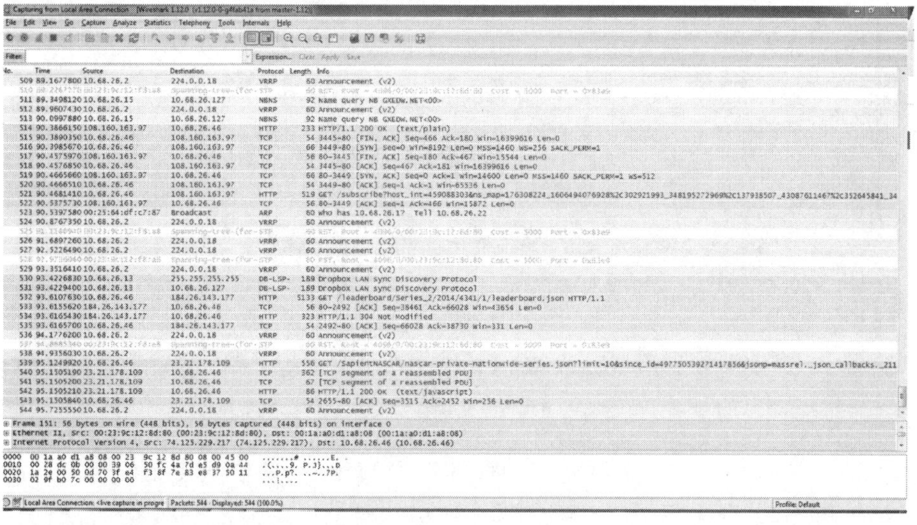

EXERCISE 11.2 *(continued)*

5. In the capture windows locate one of the ICMP packets and double-click on it. The details of that packet will appear in a pop-up. It will look something like Figure 11.7.

FIGURE 11.7 Frame details

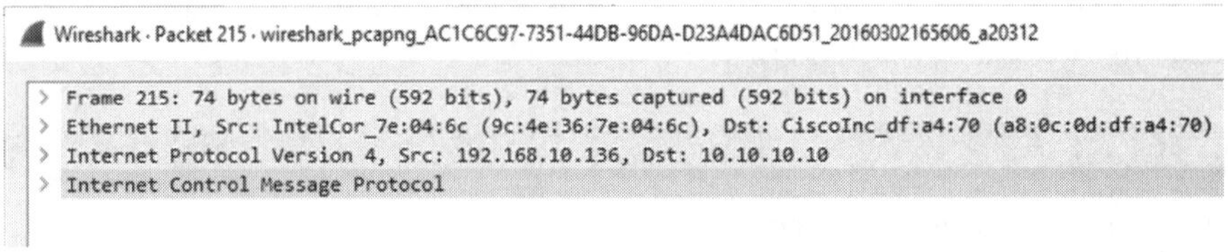

6. Expand the tree structure as shown in Figure 11.8. Under the section ICMP, you will find the type and code. In this example, the code is 3, which is Port Unreachable.

FIGURE 11.8 ICMP codes

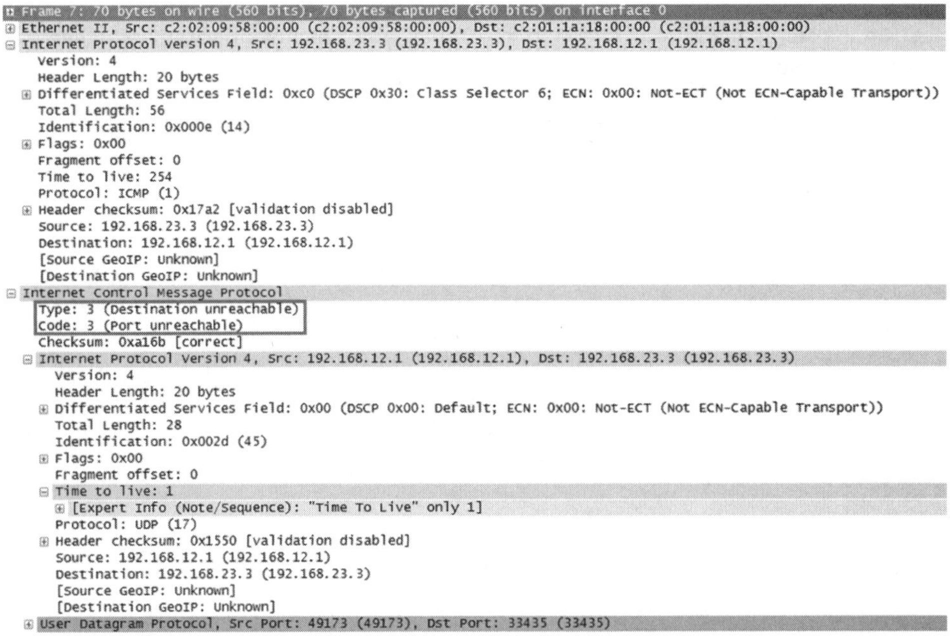

If the message comes with no source IP address, that means the message is coming from the local router (the default gateway of the sender). If it has the source IP address of the sender, then it is another router in the path. If this is the message you are getting, it's time to start looking at the routing tables of the routers or to escalate the issue if that is outside your realm.

Unknown Host

This message tells you that the host specified is not known. This message is usually generated by a router local to the destination host and usually means a bad IP address. It will appear as a destination unreachable message (this is a group of message types that all have code numbers) with a code number of 7.

Default Gateway Misconfigured

Earlier you learned that if the computer cannot connect to the default gateway, it will be confined to communicating with devices on the local network. This IP address should be that of the router interface connected to the local network. You should also ensure that the IP address of the computer is in the same network with the gateway, which means they must share the same network ID. They cannot share the same network ID unless they have the same subnet mask as well. When troubleshooting gateway issues, consider all of these factors. At the end of the day, the device must be able to ping its gateway.

Failure of Service Provider

While it is typically not the cause of Internet issues, always keep in mind that it is possible that the ISP is suffering a failure. If the entire location is suffering an inability to get to the Internet, it is time to consider this possibility. This is simple enough to verify by calling the ISP, but if you want to verify it yourself, execute a traceroute to an Internet address and then you can determine where the traffic is stopping. traceroute is a command that will be covered in "Networking Tools" later in this section, but for now, it allows you to identify the last router that was able to route the packet, thus telling you where the path ends.

Cannot Reach by Host Name/FQDN

When attempting to connect to resources by name, which is the method users employ, the connection is made to a fully qualified domain name (FQDN) in the form of *hostname .domain.com*. As you learned earlier, if this is not possible, it is a name resolution issue or a DNS issue. This means that the problem could be located in several places. Always consider those possibilities:

- The DHCP server may be issuing an incorrect DNS server address.
- The computer may be configured manually with an incorrect DNS server IP address.
- There may be a network issues preventing access to the DNS server.
- The DNS server is malfunctioning.

Causes of Common Problems

While coverage of many of the common causes of these issues is provided in each section as it applies to that issue, we'll go over them again in more detail in this section.

Improper IP Configuration

As you know already, no networking will be possible unless the IP configurations of the computers on both ends of a connection attempt are correct. This includes the following:

- IP address
- Default gateway
- Subnet mask
- DNS server

VLAN Configuration

By default, all ports in a switch are in the same Layer 2 network or the same LAN. It is possible to subdivide the switch into separate Layer 2 networks called virtual LANs, or VLANs. When we do this, we also place the devices that are in different VLANs in different Layer 3 networks as well. However, even if we assign devices in different VLANs with IP addresses in the same subnet, they will not be able to communicate because they are also separated at Layer 2.

VLANs can also span switches, meaning that devices connected to different switches can be in the same VLAN. When this is done, you must create special links called trunk links that permit the traffic of multiple VLANs between these switches.

This means that misconfiguration of VLANs can cause communication issues. The types of mistakes that can cause this include

- Ports assigned to an incorrect VLAN
- Devices in the same VLAN with IP addresses in different IP subnets
- VLANs that have been mistakenly disallowed from crossing a trunk link

When VLANs are in use, always consider these possible misconfigurations on the switch and escalate the problem if that is not your area of expertise.

Port Security

Another feature that is available on switches can cause connectivity issues. It is possible to use a feature called port security to prevent the attachment of unauthorized devices to the switch. The port security features allows you to

- Specify the only MAC address or addresses allowed to send traffic in the port.
- Specify the total number of MAC addresses that can transmit on the port.
- Specify an action to be taken when a violation occurs (either shut the port down or prevent transmissions by the guilty MAC address).

As you can imagine, this creates a scenario ripe for connectivity issues. Even if the port security configuration is correct, the connection of an unauthorized device to a port might shut down the port, causing an issue for a legitimate device when it is reconnected to the port. If you suspect port security, check the following:

- Is the port listed as err-disabled in the output of the show port command? If so, it must be enabled manually.

- Is the port allowing all required legitimate MAC addresses (don't forget the IP phone to which the computer may be connected)?

- Is the port allowing the required number of MAC addresses—for example, if it is only allowing one and there are two attached (IP phone and computer)?

When port security is in use, always consider these possible misconfigurations on the switch and escalate if that is not your area of expertise.

Improper Subnetting

Subnetting was covered in Chapter 8, "Networking," in the section "CIDR Notation and Subnetting," but let's cover a few key points again.

Devices that are in the same IP subnet must have an IP address and subnet mask combination that places them in the same subnet. Regardless of whether you are using default subnet masks or you are implementing CIDR (which allows nondefault mask lengths), for two devices to be in the same subnet they must share the same network portion of the IP address. This means that their IP addresses must agree in the bits covered by the mask. For example, consider these two addresses:

```
192.168.6.5/16
192.168.5.6/16
```

For these two addresses to be in the same subnet, they must agree in the first 16 bits (the number of bits in the mask). In this case, they both have 192.168 in the first two octets or 16 bits so they are in the same subnet. However, consider these changes:

```
192.168.6.5/24
192.168.5.6/24
```

Now they must agree in the first 24 bits, which they do not (192.168.5 and 192.168.6) so they are now *not* in the same subnet. Regardless of whether CIDR is in use, always consider these possible misconfigurations on the devices.

Component Failure

Yes, it's true, the network problem may not be your fault—at least it might not be a misconfiguration. Sometime components fail. If any router, switch, or firewall in the network fails or one of its components fails, there will be network issues. When this occurs, typically the effect is widespread. It will usually affect an entire subnet or an entire section of the network. These issues should be escalated as soon as they are discovered due to the scope of the issue.

Incorrect OS Route Tables

Routers route packets by consulting a routing table that the router creates by placing all directly connected (or local) networks in the table and then adding remote networks as they become known to the router. The router can learn remote networks in one of two ways: by administrators adding them manually or by learning them from other routers via a common routing protocol. As both of these methods involve human beings making configuration settings, there are always opportunities for misconfigurations.

When you have discovered that the path between two devices ends at a specific router (remember, you can determine this with the traceroute command), it is time to suspect the routing table of that router. The show ip route command can be used to identify the routes of which the router is aware. If the router is missing the route, it will never be able to forward packets to the destination network. While configuring routers is beyond the scope of this book, consider this possibility when you have identified a router where a path between two devices ends and then escalate as necessary.

Bad Cables

While technicians learn at the beginning of their careers to always check the Physical layer first, hours are sometime devoted to troubleshooting upper-layer issues to no avail when a bad cable is the culprit. Keep in mind as well that performance issues also sometimes have their roots in a damaged cable.

In some cases, a cable may function but not well. If the cable has a nick in the outside covering it allows EMI and RFI to more easily enter the cable. This "noise" damages packets and cause them to fail the integrity check when they arrive at their destination. This causes the packet to be lost for good in the case of UDP traffic, and it causes it to be retransmitted in the case of TCP traffic. The time spent sending the packet again could have been used to send new packets, so this results in a lower data rate. Always consider a damaged cable first when a server is suffering poor performance.

While it is beyond the scope of this book, if you examine the performance information on the switch port to which the server is connected you can identify when packets are being dropped due to CRC errors.

Firewall

As with other infrastructure devices such as routers and switches, when a firewall has issues, multiple users are typically affected. These issues usually are caused by one of three things.

Misconfiguration

Firewalls use rule sets that must be constructed carefully or they will not achieve their goal. In most cases, but not all, access control lists (ACLs) are used to control traffic through an interface. The list of rules is created and then applied either inbound or outbound to an interface. When a packet arrives at an interface on the firewall, the firewall starts at the top of the list of rules and starts comparing the traffic type in the packet to each rule in order. When it finds the first rule that matches the traffic type in the packet, it takes the action (either allow or deny) specified in the rule and stops reading the list. This means the order is very important.

For example, let's say our intent is to prevent a computer at 192.168.5.5/24 from sending traffic through an interface while allowing everyone else in the subnet to send traffic. We create these two rules in this order:

Permit 192.168.5.0/24

Deny 192.168.5.5/24

Can you guess what will happen? Since the devices at 192.168.5.5/24 matches both rules and the permit rule is first, the rule that we created designed to deny this traffic will never be denied. So as you can see, incorrect rule order is a common mistake.

Another common characteristic of ACLs is that (in most systems but not all) there is an implied deny all rule at the end of every ACL. You don't see it; it's automatic. This means that if the firewall goes all the way through the list and none of the rules allow the traffic, the traffic is denied. Failing to explicitly allow traffic that should be allowed is another common mistake.

Finally, you can create ACLs until you are blue in the face and if you never apply them to an interface, they never enforce anything. So failure to apply the ACL is another common mistake.

While most systems use the logic just explained, there are some systems that, rather than applying the first rule that matches, go all the way through the list and select the rule that is the *best* match. So a system that uses that logic would have been able to select the proper rule in our previous example because the second rule in the list is a better match of the sender's IP address than the first rule in the list. You must understand the logic of each system.

Hardware Failure

It is also possible that the firewall may suffer a hardware failure. This can happen regardless of whether the firewall is implemented as an appliance or as software running on a server. Any hardware issue that affects the server on which the software is installed will affect the firewall function. Likewise, any hardware issues with interfaces, memory, or CPU on an appliance will affect the hardware appliance as well.

Software Failure

Software failures can also occur either in the firewall software running on a server or with the firmware or operating system running in an appliance. In many cases, these failures can be avoided by maintaining all patches to the firewall software and firmware as it becomes available. Although these failures are always possible, a more likely threat is a misconfiguration of the software, as discussed earlier.

Misconfigured NIC

Most technicians don't think much about the settings on a NIC; they just plug it in and if it works they are satisfied. A misconfigured NIC, like a damaged cable, may work but not work well if its duplex and speed settings do not match those of the switch port to which it is connected. Although most network cards supposedly "autosense" the setting on the other end and set themselves to match, this function requires a negotiation process that can fail, and when it does the two ends may default to a mismatch.

Just as a damaged cable causes damaged packets that fail the integrity check and must be transmitted again, a speed or duplex mismatch causes packet collisions, which also cause packets to be re-sent and lower throughput. This is another behavior you can detect by reviewing errors occurring on the switchport.

Routing/Switch Issues

Routing and switch issues like firewall issues will typically affect multiple users. This is not a book on routers and switches, but you should be able to connect certain errors with certain devices. You've already learned that if a router has no route in its table to a destination network, it will be unable to send traffic to that network. That will result in a destination unreachable message when you attempt to ping that destination. Here are several messages that indicate a lack of a route or a security issue:

- Destination unreachable with a source address (and a code number of 0): A router in the path other than the local route has no route to that network.

- Destination unreachable with no source address (with a code number of 0): The local router has no route to the network.

- Destination unreachable (with a code number of 9 or 10); The source device is not permitted to send to that network (code 9) or to that device (code 10). This message indicates an ACL is prohibiting the traffic.

Switch issues will only affect those devices attached to the switch unless there are VLANs spanning switches; then the effect may be more widespread. Most issues with switches concern switch port security misconfigurations or speed and duplex mismatches, but problems can also occur when trunk links are misconfigured between switches. While the default setting is to allow the traffic of all VLANs across a trunk link, it is possible to disallow certain VLANs. Obviously a mistake when configuring that setting could cause issues. Always consider that possibility when intra-VLAN issues are occurring.

DNS and/or DHCP Failure

DNS and DHCP failures will affect multiple users and the damage will depend on several factors. Let's start with DHCP.

Most issues with DHCP result in computers being unable to obtain an IP configuration. That manifests itself to the user as an inability to connect to anything, which may result in all sorts of misdiagnoses by the user (the email server is down, the web server is down...). This can be caused by

- The DHCP server is out of IP addresses.

- The computer is unable to reach the DHCP server.

- The DHCP server is down.

The first problem is simple enough to solve: add more IP addresses. The second can occur if the computer is located in a different subnet from the DHCP server and *relay agents* are not in use. Since DHCP clients locate the DHCP server with a broadcast packet, they must be in the same subnet or the server will never hear the broadcast. Relay agents can be applied to the router interfaces, and then the router interface can relay these packets to the server. In their absence, an inability to connect will occur. One of the symptoms of this condition is that the device will have a self-generated IP address. If the device is Windows and it is running IPv4, the address will have 169 in the first octet.

DNS issues will also be widespread. Users will be unable to locate resources by name. To them, this issue will appear to be the same as an issue with DHCP in that they can't connect to anything. So you may get some of the same user misdiagnoses. You can easily determine which it is by pinging the destination by name and by IP address. If you can ping by IP address but not by name, the issue is DNS.

Misconfigured Hosts File

Most systems rely on DNS for name resolution, but it is not the only method a system can use. Windows and Linux systems have a file called Hosts that can be populated manually with IP address–to-name mappings. The downside to this is the static nature of the file— that is, any changes have to be made manually. This file is always located at `C:\Windows\System32\drivers\etc\hosts`. If this file is misconfigured, it will result in an inability to connect to the destination. To make matters worse, this file is the first place the device looks before it attempts DNS, so if there is an entry in the file for the name, it never uses DNS!

Finally, some forms of malware edit the Hosts file and add entries. So even if you are not aware that anyone has ever edited this file, it is still something to check since malware can add entries.

IPv4 vs. IPv6 Misconfigurations

IPv6 is the new version of IP that uses 128-bit IP addresses rather than 32-bit, as in IPv4. Many technicians are still learning IPv6, and it is an area ripe for misconfiguration.

IPv6 offers a number of improvements, the most notable of which is its ability to handle growth in public networks. IPv6's 128-bit addressing scheme allows for a huge number of possible addresses: 340,282,366,920,938,463,463,374,607,431,768,211,456.

Table 11.1 compares IPv4 to IPv6.

TABLE 11.1 IPv4 vs. IPv6

Feature	IPv4	IPv6
Loopback address	127.0.0.1	0:0:0:0:0:0:0:1 (::1)
Private ranges	10.0.0.0/8 172.16.0.0/12 192.168.0.0/24	FC00:/7
Autoconfigured addresses	169.254.0.0/16	FE80::

 In IPv6 addresses, repeating zeroes can be left out so that colons next to each other in the address indicate one or more sets of zeroes for that section.

One common mistake is to configure two ends of a link such that they are not in the same subnet. In IPv6, the number of bits in the prefix is given after the address, as shown here:

aaaa.bbbb.cccc.dddd.0000.0000.0000.0000 /64

This means that the prefix is 64 bits long, or aaaaa.bbbbb.ccccc.ddddd. Therefore, for two IP addresses to be in the same network, the address must be the same across the first 64 bits.

Networking Tools

A number of command-line tools are available to help you diagnose network issues, some of which we have already referred to. You should understand how these tools work and in which situations they may help you gather useful diagnostic data.

ping

The ping command makes use of the ICMP protocol to test connectivity between two devices. ping is one of the most useful commands in the TCP/IP protocol. It sends a series of packets to another system, which in turn sends a response. The ping command can be extremely useful for troubleshooting problems with remote hosts.

The ping command indicates whether the host can be reached and how long it took for the host to send a return packet. On a LAN, the time is indicated as less than 10 milliseconds.

Across WAN links, however, this value can be much greater. When the -a parameter is included, the command will also attempt to resolve the hostname associated with the IP address. Figure 11.9 shows an example of a successful ping.

FIGURE 11.9   The ping command

```
C:\Users\tmcmillan>ping 10.88.2.103

Pinging 10.88.2.103 with 32 bytes of data:
Reply from 10.88.2.103: bytes=32 time<1ms TTL=128
Reply from 10.88.2.103: bytes=32 time<1ms TTL=128
Reply from 10.88.2.103: bytes=32 time<1ms TTL=128
Reply from 10.88.2.103: bytes=32 time<1ms TTL=128

Ping statistics for 10.88.2.103:
    Packets: Sent = 4, Received = 4, Lost = 0 (0% loss),
Approximate round trip times in milli-seconds:
    Minimum = 0ms, Maximum = 0ms, Average = 0ms
```

tracert/traceroute

The tracert command (called traceroute in Linux and Unix) is used to trace the path of a packet through the network. Its best use is in determining exactly where in the network the packet is being dropped. It will show each hop (router) the packet crosses and how long it takes to do so. Figure 11.10 shows a partial display of a traced route to www.msn.com.

FIGURE 11.10   Using tracert

```
Microsoft Windows [Version 10.0.10586]
(c) 2015 Microsoft Corporation. All rights reserved.

C:\WINDOWS\system32>tracert www.nascar.com

Tracing route to a1269.w7.akamai.net [8.18.43.66]
over a maximum of 30 hops:

  1  2273 ms    <1 ms    <1 ms  10.200.97.1
  2     1 ms    <1 ms    <1 ms  rrcs-24-199-211-193.midsouth.biz.rr.com [24.199.211.193]
  3     1 ms    12 ms     1 ms  70.62.94.106
  4     1 ms     1 ms     1 ms  70.62.94.66
  5     1 ms     1 ms     1 ms  24.27.255.238
  6     7 ms     7 ms     7 ms  ten2-0-0.rlghncrdc-pe-rtr01.southeast.rr.com [24.93.73.78]
  7     7 ms     8 ms     7 ms  ten2-0-0.gnboncsg-p-rtr01.southeast.rr.com [24.93.73.37]
  8    21 ms     7 ms     7 ms  ten2-0-0.gnboncsg-pe-rtr01.southeast.rr.com [24.93.73.74]
  9     7 ms    22 ms     7 ms  ten2-0-0.chrlncsa-p-rtr01.southeast.rr.com [24.93.73.33]
 10    21 ms    11 ms    11 ms  24.93.67.100
 11    16 ms    20 ms    15 ms  bu-ether44.atlngamq46w-bcr00.tbone.rr.com [107.14.19.46]
 12    15 ms    12 ms    12 ms  0.ae1.pr0.atl20.tbone.rr.com [66.109.6.177]
 13    13 ms    12 ms    12 ms  216.156.108.45.ptr.us.xo.net [216.156.108.45]
 14    55 ms    26 ms    26 ms  207.88.13.48.ptr.us.xo.net [207.88.13.48]
 15    31 ms    36 ms    28 ms  te-11-4-0.rar3.washington-dc.us.xo.net [207.88.12.201]
 16    26 ms    26 ms    26 ms  207.88.12.132.ptr.us.xo.net [207.88.12.132]
 17    26 ms    26 ms    29 ms  207.88.14.191.ptr.us.xo.net [207.88.14.191]
 18    26 ms    25 ms    25 ms  be3013.ccr41.iad02.atlas.cogentco.com [154.54.9.5]
 19    26 ms    26 ms    26 ms  be2657.ccr42.dca01.atlas.cogentco.com [154.54.31.109]
 20    37 ms    30 ms    26 ms  be2113.ccr42.atl01.atlas.cogentco.com [154.54.24.222]
 21    25 ms    26 ms    25 ms  be2848.ccr41.atl04.atlas.cogentco.com [154.54.6.118]
 22    31 ms    25 ms    25 ms  38.122.47.42
 23    25 ms    25 ms    25 ms  8.18.43.66

Trace complete.

C:\WINDOWS\system32>
```

ipconfig/ifconfig

The `ipconfig` command is used to view the IP configuration of a device and, when combined with certain switches or parameters, can be used to release and renew the lease of an IP address obtained from a DHCP server and to flush the DNS resolver cache. Its most common use is to view the current configuration. Figure 11.11 shows its execution with the `/all` switch, which results in a display of a wealth of information about the IP configuration.

FIGURE 11.11 Using `ipconfig`

```
C:\Users\tmcmillan>ipconfig/all

Windows IP Configuration

        Host Name . . . . . . . . . . . . : tmcmillan
        Primary Dns Suffix  . . . . . . . : alpha.kaplaninc.com
        Node Type . . . . . . . . . . . . : Hybrid
        IP Routing Enabled. . . . . . . . : No
        WINS Proxy Enabled. . . . . . . . : No
        DNS Suffix Search List. . . . . . : alpha.kaplaninc.com
                                            kaplaninc.com

Ethernet adapter Local Area Connection:

        Connection-specific DNS Suffix  . : alpha.kaplaninc.com
        Description . . . . . . . . . . . : Broadcom NetXtreme 57xx Gigabit Controlle
r
        Physical Address. . . . . . . . . : 00-1A-A0-E1-95-AB
        DHCP Enabled. . . . . . . . . . . : Yes
        Autoconfiguration Enabled . . . . : Yes
        Link-local IPv6 Address . . . . . : fe80::ada3:8b73:a66e:6bc0%10(Preferred)
        IPv4 Address. . . . . . . . . . . : 10.88.2.103(Preferred)
        Subnet Mask . . . . . . . . . . . : 255.255.254.0
        Lease Obtained. . . . . . . . . . : Monday, January 30, 2012 9:38:37 AM
        Lease Expires . . . . . . . . . . : Tuesday, January 31, 2012 9:38:37 AM
        Default Gateway . . . . . . . . . : 10.88.2.6
        DHCP Server . . . . . . . . . . . : 10.88.10.48
        DHCPv6 IAID . . . . . . . . . . . : 234887840
        DHCPv6 Client DUID. . . . . . . . : 00-01-00-01-14-EE-0F-98-00-1A-A0-E1-95-AB

        DNS Servers . . . . . . . . . . . : 10.88.10.48
                                            10.75.139.18
        NetBIOS over Tcpip. . . . . . . . : Enabled
```

`ipconfig` can be used to release and renew a configuration obtained from a DHCP server by issuing first the `ipconfig/release` command, followed by the `ipconfig/renew` command.

It is also helpful to know that when you have just corrected a configuration error (such as an IP address) on a destination device, you should ensure that the device registers its new IP address with the DNS server by executing the `ipconfig/registerdns` command.

It may also be necessary to clear incorrect IP address–to-hostname mappings that may still exist on the devices that were attempting to access the destination device. This can be done by executing the `ipconfig/flushdns` command.

If you are using a Linux or Unix system, the command is not `ipconfig` but `ifconfig`. Figure 11.12 shows an example of the command and its output. The `ifconfig` command with the `-a` option shows all network interface information, even if the network interface is down.

FIGURE 11.12 ifconfig

```
linux@fedora11:~
[linux@fedora11 ~]$ ifconfig -a
eth2      Link encap:Ethernet  HWaddr 00:0C:29:61:B2:D8
          inet addr:192.168.228.130  Bcast:192.168.228.255  Mask:255.255.255.0
          inet6 addr: fe80::20c:29ff:fe61:b2d8/64 Scope:Link
          UP BROADCAST RUNNING MULTICAST  MTU:1500  Metric:1
          RX packets:1115 errors:0 dropped:0 overruns:0 frame:0
          TX packets:764 errors:0 dropped:0 overruns:0 carrier:0
          collisions:0 txqueuelen:1000
          RX bytes:101820 (99.4 KiB)  TX bytes:102769 (100.3 KiB)
          Interrupt:19 Base address:0x2000

[linux@fedora11 ~]$
```

nslookup

The nslookup command is a command-line administrative tool for testing and troubleshooting DNS servers. It can be run in two modes: interactive and noninteractive. Noninteractive mode is useful when only a single piece of data needs to be returned; interactive allows you to query for either an IP address for a name or a name for an IP address without leaving nslookup mode. The command syntax is as follows:

nslookup [-option] [hostname] [server]

To enter interactive mode, simply type nslookup. When you do, by default it will identify the IP address and name of the DNS server that the local machine is configured to use, if any, and then will go to the > prompt. At this prompt, you can type either an IP address or a name, and the system will attempt to resolve the IP address to a name or the name to an IP address.

```
C:\> nslookup
   Default Server:  nameserver1.domain.com
   Address:  10.0.0.1
   >
```

The following are other queries that can be run that may prove helpful when you are troubleshooting name resolution issues:

- Looking up different data types in the database (such as Microsoft records)
- Querying directly from another name server (different from the one the local device is configured to use)
- Performing a zone transfer

net use/mount

The net command is one of the most powerful on the Windows-based network, as illustrated by net use. The options that can be used with the command differ slightly based on the Windows operating system you are using; you can view a full list by typing **net /?**.

The net use command is used on Windows-based clients to connect or disconnect from shared resources. You can see what is currently shared by typing **net use** without any other parameters, as shown in Figure 11.13.

FIGURE 11.13   Typing net use lets you see what is currently shared.

```
C:\Users\tmcmillan>net use
New connections will be remembered.


Status       Local      Remote                     Network
-------------------------------------------------------------------------------
OK           G:         \\srat1060\groups             Microsoft Windows Network
OK           M:         \\srat1060\pstpickup\tmcmillan
                                                      Microsoft Windows Network
OK           P:         \\srat1060\personal\tmcmillan
                                                      Microsoft Windows Network
OK           Z:         \\10.88.2.132\fun             Microsoft Windows Network
The command completed successfully.
```

The mount command serves to attach the filesystem found on some device to the filesystem in Linux and Unix. The standard form of the mount command is

```
mount -t type device destination_dir
```

where *type* represents the type of device, *device* represents the device, and *destination_dir* represents the directory you want to mount. In the following example, a CD-ROM is mounted and the -o ro parameter indicates it should be mounted with read-only access. The iso9660 identifies the device as a CD-ROM.

```
# mount -t iso9660 -o ro /dev/cdrom /mnt
```

route

The route command can be used in both Linux and Windows to view and edit the routing table on computers. To view the routing table in Linux, use the route command like this:

```
$ route
Kernel IP routing table
Destination     Gateway         Genmask         Flags Metric Ref    Use Iface
192.168.1.0     *               255.255.255.0   U     0      0        0 eth0
```

The output shows that the device is aware of one network (the one to which it is connected).

In Windows, the command requires the print keyword, as shown here:

```
C:\WINDOWS\system32>route print
===========================================================================
Interface List
 18...9c 4e 36 7e 04 6d ......Microsoft Wi-Fi Direct Virtual Adapter
  6...0a 00 27 00 00 00 ......VirtualBox Host-Only Ethernet Adapter
 10...08 9e 01 36 53 73 ......Realtek PCIe FE Family Controller
 14...9c 4e 36 7e 04 6c ......Intel(R) Centrino(R) Wireless-N 2200
 12...e0 06 e6 be cc 7b ......Bluetooth Device (Personal Area Network)
  1...........................Software Loopback Interface 1
  7...00 00 00 00 00 00 00 e0 Microsoft ISATAP Adapter
 17...00 00 00 00 00 00 00 e0 Teredo Tunneling Pseudo-Interface
  5...00 00 00 00 00 00 00 e0 Microsoft ISATAP Adapter #9
===========================================================================

IPv4 Route Table
===========================================================================
Active Routes:
Network Destination        Netmask          Gateway       Interface  Metric
          0.0.0.0          0.0.0.0      192.168.0.1      192.168.0.6     20
        127.0.0.0        255.0.0.0         On-link         127.0.0.1    306
        127.0.0.1  255.255.255.255         On-link         127.0.0.1    306
  127.255.255.255  255.255.255.255         On-link         127.0.0.1    306
      192.168.0.0    255.255.255.0         On-link       192.168.0.6    276
      192.168.0.6  255.255.255.255         On-link       192.168.0.6    276
    192.168.0.255  255.255.255.255         On-link       192.168.0.6    276
     192.168.56.0    255.255.255.0         On-link      192.168.56.1    266
     192.168.56.1  255.255.255.255         On-link      192.168.56.1    266
   192.168.56.255  255.255.255.255         On-link      192.168.56.1    266
        224.0.0.0        240.0.0.0         On-link         127.0.0.1    306
        224.0.0.0        240.0.0.0         On-link      192.168.56.1    266
        224.0.0.0        240.0.0.0         On-link       192.168.0.6    276
  255.255.255.255  255.255.255.255         On-link         127.0.0.1    306
  255.255.255.255  255.255.255.255         On-link      192.168.56.1    266
  255.255.255.255  255.255.255.255         On-link       192.168.0.6    276
===========================================================================
Persistent Routes:
  None

IPv6 Route Table
===========================================================================
```

```
Active Routes:
 If Metric Network Destination        Gateway
 17    306 ::/0                        On-link
  1    306 ::1/128                     On-link
 17    306 2001::/32                   On-link
 17    306 2001:0:5ef5:79fb:30be:34ca:cd75:ec40/128
                                       On-link
  6    266 fe80::/64                   On-link
 10    276 fe80::/64                   On-link
 17    306 fe80::/64                   On-link
 17    306 fe80::30be:34ca:cd75:ec40/128
                                       On-link
  6    266 fe80::a1f4:3886:392:d218/128
                                       On-link
 10    276 fe80::f098:57fb:c0d7:5e65/128
                                       On-link
  1    306 ff00::/8                    On-link
  6    266 ff00::/8                    On-link
 17    306 ff00::/8                    On-link
 10    276 ff00::/8                    On-link
===========================================================================
Persistent Routes:
  None
```

This output lists both the IPv4 and IPv6 routing tables as well as a list of the interfaces. Use the route and route print commands to determine if a device has a route to its default gateway. A route of this type is called the default route, and in Windows it's listed as a destination network of 0.0.0.0 with a mask of 0.0.0.0.

nbtstat

Microsoft networks use an interface called Network Basic Input/Output System (NetBIOS) to resolve workstation names with IP addresses. The nbtstat command can be used to view NetBIOS information. In Figure 11.14 it has been executed with the -n switch, which will display the NetBIOS names that are currently known to the local machine. In this case, this local machine is aware only of its own NetBIOS names.

FIGURE 11.14   Using nbtstat

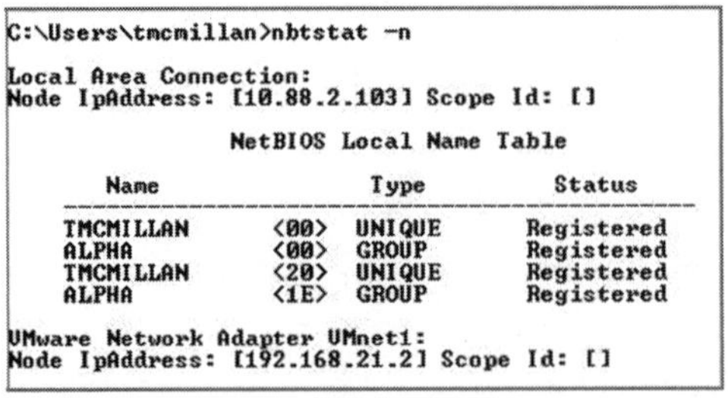

```
C:\Users\tmcmillan>nbtstat -n

Local Area Connection:
Node IpAddress: [10.88.2.103] Scope Id: []

               NetBIOS Local Name Table

        Name              Type         Status
     ---------------------------------------------
     TMCMILLAN     <00>  UNIQUE      Registered
     ALPHA         <00>  GROUP       Registered
     TMCMILLAN     <20>  UNIQUE      Registered
     ALPHA         <1E>  GROUP       Registered

VMware Network Adapter VMnet1:
Node IpAddress: [192.168.21.2] Scope Id: []
```

netstat

The netstat (network status) command is used to see what ports are listening on the TCP/IP-based system. The -a option is used to show all ports, and /? is used to show what other options are available (the options differ based on the operating system you are using). When executed with no switches, the command displays the current connections, as shown in Figure 11.15.

FIGURE 11.15   Using netstat

```
C:\Users\tmcmillan>netstat

Active Connections

  Proto  Local Address          Foreign Address        State
  TCP    10.88.2.103:51273      64.94.18.154:https     ESTABLISHED
  TCP    10.88.2.103:51525      srat1060:microsoft-ds  ESTABLISHED
  TCP    10.88.2.103:51529      gmonsalvatge:microsoft-ds  ESTABLISHED
  TCP    10.88.2.103:51573      sjc-not18:http         ESTABLISHED
  TCP    10.88.2.103:51716      schexv02:2785          ESTABLISHED
  TCP    10.88.2.103:51720      schvoip01:epmap        ESTABLISHED
  TCP    10.88.2.103:51721      schvoip01:1297         ESTABLISHED
  TCP    10.88.2.103:51722      schvoip01:1299         ESTABLISHED
  TCP    10.88.2.103:51824      69.31.116.27:http      CLOSE_WAIT
  TCP    10.88.2.103:51965      dcalpsch2:1026         ESTABLISHED
  TCP    10.88.2.103:53865      cs219p3:5050           ESTABLISHED
  TCP    10.88.2.103:53871      sip109:http            ESTABLISHED
  TCP    10.88.2.103:62522      ord08s08-in-f22:https  ESTABLISHED
  TCP    10.88.2.103:62567      ord08s08-in-f22:https  CLOSE_WAIT
  TCP    10.88.2.103:62682      by2msg3010613:http     ESTABLISHED
  TCP    10.88.2.103:63554      baymsg1020213:msnp     ESTABLISHED
  TCP    10.88.2.103:63770      v-client-2b:https      CLOSE_WAIT
  TCP    10.88.2.103:63771      ec2-174-129-205-197:https  CLOSE_WAIT
  TCP    10.88.2.103:63772      v-client-2b:https      CLOSE_WAIT
  TCP    10.88.2.103:63773      65.55.121.231:http     ESTABLISHED
  TCP    10.88.2.103:63774      168.75.207.20:http     ESTABLISHED
  TCP    10.88.2.103:63777      65.55.17.30:http       ESTABLISHED
  TCP    10.88.2.103:63779      70.37.131.11:http      ESTABLISHED
  TCP    10.88.2.103:63781      65.124.174.56:http     ESTABLISHED
  TCP    10.88.2.103:63788      69.31.76.41:http       ESTABLISHED
  TCP    10.88.2.103:63791      207.46.140.46:http     ESTABLISHED
  TCP    10.88.2.103:63792      64.4.21.39:http        ESTABLISHED
  TCP    127.0.0.1:2002         tmcmillan:51543        ESTABLISHED
  TCP    127.0.0.1:19872        tmcmillan:51571        ESTABLISHED
  TCP    127.0.0.1:51543        tmcmillan:2002         ESTABLISHED
  TCP    127.0.0.1:51549        tmcmillan:51550        ESTABLISHED
  TCP    127.0.0.1:51550        tmcmillan:51549        ESTABLISHED
  TCP    127.0.0.1:51571        tmcmillan:19872        ESTABLISHED
  TCP    127.0.0.1:53869        tmcmillan:53870        ESTABLISHED
  TCP    127.0.0.1:53870        tmcmillan:53869        ESTABLISHED
  TCP    127.0.0.1:63557        tmcmillan:63574        ESTABLISHED
  TCP    127.0.0.1:63574        tmcmillan:63557        ESTABLISHED

C:\Users\tmcmillan>
```

Diagnosing Security Issues

While many connectivity problems are rooted in network issues, others are caused by security features and functions. The end result is the same—the user cannot connect to a resource—but the symptoms are somewhat different. Next, we'll look at diagnosing security issues that cause connectivity issues and other more general security concerns.

Common Problems

Just as certain hardware and software issues seem to happen more often than others, there will be some security issues that are commonplace as well. Many of these are the result of human error in configuration, and others are the result of poorly configured or poorly written applications. In this section, we'll look at some common security issues.

File Integrity Issue

When files become altered either through corruption or unauthorized access, we say that the integrity of the file has been compromised. When system files are altered (sometimes through the actions of malware), it can cause operating system errors and crashes. In the "Security Tools" section, we'll look at some ways to maintain the integrity of both system files and other critical files that need protection.

Privilege Escalation

When any user is able to attain additional rights and permissions, we say that privilege escalation has occurred. In most cases, this occurs as a result of the user obtaining the login information for a privileged account, logging in as that user, and making use of those additional rights and permissions. If the compromised action is an administrator or root account, the situation becomes worse because then the user may be able to clear the security log and hide their tracks. In the "Causes of Common Problems" section, we'll talk about how this occurs and what can be done to minimize the likelihood of this happening.

Applications Will Not Load

Another possible symptom of a malware infection is the crashing of applications. While this will occur from time to time for other reasons, when it is occurring repeatedly you should suspect malware. When the application that is crashing is your antivirus software, this is an even stronger indication of malware, as disabling or damaging your antivirus protection is the first thing that some types of malware attempt to do.

It is also a possibility that if your organization makes use of software restriction policies, the user may be trying to run a disallowed application. In that case, you should ensure that the software restriction policies that are controlling the user are correct.

Finally, it is always possible that the application is simply corrupted. In that case, try removing and reinstalling the application.

Can't Access Network File/Shares

Although network issues should be ruled out first, in some cases network file and share permissions may be preventing a user from accessing a share or file. In Windows, you must always consider the effects of multiple permissions users may have as a result of permissions applied to their account and those applied to any groups they may be in. You should have a clear understanding of how these permissions work together. In the "Causes of Common Problems" section, we'll review how Windows permissions work.

Unable to Open Files

When files will not open on a machine, there is always the possibility that the file permissions are the cause, but there can be other reasons. If the user lacks the application required to open the file, it will not open. This often occurs when users receive an email attachment in a file format for which they do have the proper application. They may or may not know how to locate and install the application, even if the application is free. If a software restriction policy is preventing the installation of the proper application, the user may have to get assistance and permission to read the document.

Excessive Access

Over time as users change jobs, get promoted, and move from one department to another, something called permission creep occurs. This means that while they have attained new permissions as the result of the new job, the old permission that applied to the previous position are not removed as they should be. This can be prevented by performing a formal permission review at the time of the application of the new permissions and also at regular intervals thereafter.

Excessive Memory Utilization

When memory utilization goes up without a corresponding *known* increase in work-load, it is usually an indication of malware. It makes complete sense if you think about it. The memory is being used by *something* and in this case it is the malware. Any instance of excessive memory utilization should be investigated to see if malware is the issue. Otherwise, you could have a faulty application that needs to be patched or replaced.

Causes of Common Problems

It may be hard to determine, but every issue has a cause. Although it is sometimes tempting to adopt a quick workaround to get things moving (and in some cases that may be the best approach), you should always attempt to determine the root cause. Otherwise, the issue could keep returning. In this section, we'll look at some causes that are worthy of consideration because they are common. We'll also cover common security weaknesses that you should be aware of.

Open Ports

One of the guiding principles of security is to disable all services that are not needed and to close the port of any services not in use. Hackers know common attacks that utilize common port numbers. In most cases, maintaining patches and updates prevents hackers from taking advantage of open ports, but not always. In the "Security Tools" section, we'll talk about how you can use the same tools the hackers do to discover these open ports.

Active Services

While on the surface the presence of active services might appear to be a good thing, in some cases it is not. Following the same principle we followed with respect to open ports, any services or applications that are not required on a device should be disabled. The reason for this is that most services and applications have been compromised at some point. If all patches are applied, these compromises are usually addressed, but any that are not required should be disabled to be safe.

Inactive Services

When required services are inactive, it's a problem. Sometimes when the system is started you receive a message that tells you a service failed to start. When that occurs, use the event log to determine the service that failed. Then, to interact with the service, access the Administrative Tools section of Control Panel and choose Services. This starts up the Services console. You can right-click any service and choose to start, stop, pause, resume, or restart it. You can also double-click the service to access its properties and configure such things as the startup type, dependencies, and other variables.

If the service refuses to start, it could be that a service on which it depends will not start. To determine what services must be running for the problem service to start, select the Dependencies tab of the service's Properties dialog box, as shown in Figure 11.16.

FIGURE 11.16 Service dependencies

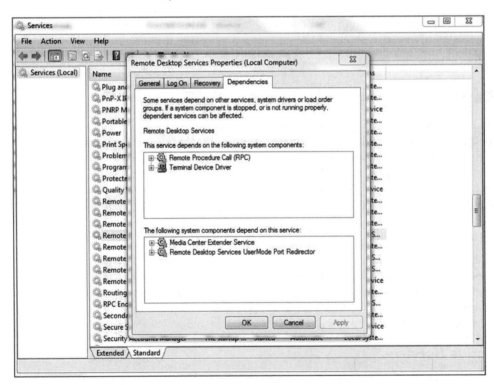

In the figure you can see that the Remote Desktop service depends on both the RPC and the Terminal Device Driver services to function. Try starting these services first. In some cases, you may need to trace the dependencies up several levels to get things going.

Intrusion Detection Configurations

An intrusion detection system (IDS) is a system responsible for detecting unauthorized access or attacks. It can verify, itemize, and characterize threats from outside and inside the network. Most IDSs are programmed to react in certain ways in specific situations. Event notification and alerts are crucial to IDSs as these devices do not respond to or prevent attacks. These notifications and alerts inform administrators and security professionals when and where attacks are detected. The most common way to classify an IDS is based on its information source: network based or host based.

The most common IDS, a network-based IDS (NIDS), monitors network traffic on a local network segment. To monitor traffic on the network segment, the network interface card (NIC) must be operating in promiscuous mode. An NIDS can monitor only the network traffic. It cannot monitor any internal activity that occurs within a system, such as an attack against a system that is carried out by logging on to the system's local terminal. An NIDS is affected by a switched network because generally an NIDS monitors only a single network segment.

When these devices are misconfigured, the result will not be what you desire. Anyone supporting these should be trained in configuring and supporting them. Even when they are configured correctly, there can be errors. A *false positive* occurs when an event is identified as a threat when it is not. A *false negative* is even worse; it occurs when a threatening event is *not* identified. As you see, configuring these can be tricky and requires expert knowledge.

Antimalware Configurations

Most issues that occur with antimalware configurations result in an inability to update either the malware definitions or the malware engine. Both should be updated regularly, preferable on an automatic basis, which almost all enterprise products support. Missing updates are one of the biggest causes of malware outbreaks in a network. Although some threats (called zero-day threats) will occur before the vendor has developed a solution, outbreaks that occur due to missing updates should be viewed as a failure of your processes. You should develop procedures to ensure that updates occur.

Local/Group Policies

When Group Policies are used to control security in an enterprise, an incomplete understanding of how Group Policies operate can result in actions being allowed that should not be allowed and actions being prevented that should not be prevented. Active Directory, the directory service used in Windows, has a hierarchal structure and policy settings are inherited from one level to another in a specific way. When a machine starts up and is applying Group Policies, it applies them in this order:

- Domain
- OU
- Local

This means that policies on the local machine will overrule any at the OU level and any at the OU level will overrule any from the domain level. Further complicating this is the fact the user may have one set of policies applied while their computer may have another. So the system is ripe for misconfiguration by someone with an incomplete understanding of the inheritance process.

Fortunately, there is a tool that can help identity why a particular policy is not being applied to a device or user. The gpresult command is used to show the Resultant Set of Policy (RSoP) report/values for a remote user and computer. Bear in mind that configuration settings occur at any number of places. Often one of the big unknowns is which set of configuration settings takes precedence and which is overridden. With gpresult, it is possible to ascertain which settings apply. An example of the output is shown in Figure 11.17.

FIGURE 11.17 gpresult

Firewall Rules

When firewall rules are misconfigured, not only can it cause network connectivity issues, it can also create serious security issues. You learned earlier that the order of the rules in an ACL are sometimes critical to the proper operation of the ACL. This is another area where an incomplete understanding of the logic used by a particular firewall product can have disastrous and far-reaching results. Only technicians who have been trained in that product should be allowed to manage these ACLs.

Misconfigured Permissions

Earlier you learned that incomplete understanding of the inheritance of Group Policies can result in the policies either not being applied or being applied incorrectly. Because filesystem permissions also use inheritance, an opportunity also exists for issues with permissions. Most of the confusion when it comes to permissions involves the inheritance process, the interaction of various permissions that a user may have as a result of being a member of groups that may also have permissions, and the fact that there are two systems at work—the NTFS security system and the Share security system. NTFS and share permissions were covered in the section "Permissions" in Chapter 7, "Securing Server Data and Network Access."

Allow vs. Deny

By default, the determination of NTFS permissions is based on the cumulative NTFS permissions for a user. Rights can be assigned to users based on group membership and individually; the only time permissions do not accumulate is when the Deny permission is invoked.

When NTFS permissions and share permissions come in conflict, the system will compare the combined NTFS permissions to the combined share permissions. The system will apply the most restrictive of these two.

Virus Infection

Sometimes despite all efforts a virus outbreak may occur. Even if you maintain all updates, the system will not be able to recognize or mitigate a zero-day attack. When this does occur, you should take certain steps to contain and eliminate the issue.

Recognize   Learn to recognize how a system reacts to malware.

Quarantine   Prevent malware from propagating.

Search and Destroy   Remove malware from infected systems.

Remediate   Return the system to normal after the malware is gone.

Educate   Train users to prevent malware outbreaks.

Rogue Processes/Services

Earlier you learned how a runaway process or service can consume all of the resources of a device, causing it to "lock up" or operate slowly. You can use the Task Manager tool to identify the guilty process and the `taskkill` command to end it.

Task Manager lets you shut down nonresponsive applications selectively in all Windows versions. In current versions of Windows, it can do so much more: Task Manager allows you to see which processes and applications are using the most system resources, view network usage, see connected users, and so on. To display Task Manager, press Ctrl+Alt+Del and click the Task Manager button to display it. You can also right-click on an empty spot in the Taskbar and choose it from the pop-up menu that appears.

 To get to the Task Manager directly in any of the Windows versions, you can press Ctrl+Shift+Esc.

The Task Manager tool in Windows Server 2012 R2 is shown in Figure 11.18. If you find that you cannot locate the process, it could be caused by malware which frequently "hides" from Task Manager. Always consider this as a possibility and scan for malware.

FIGURE 11.18 Task Manager

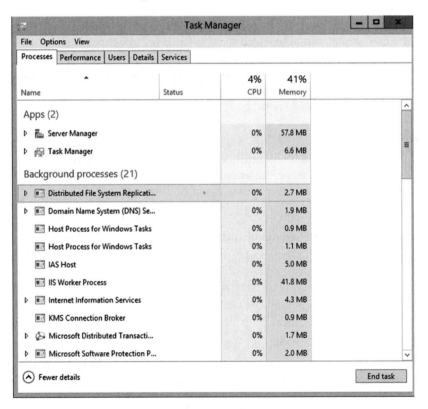

Security Tools

Just as you have many networking tools available to troubleshoot network connectivity issues, you also have an impressive set available to you for security issues. These tools allow you to gain the same visibility a hacker might have so you can make any required changes to maintain a secure network. In this section, we'll survey the most common of these tools.

Port Scanners

Internet Control Message Protocol (ICMP) messages can be used to scan a network for open ports. Open ports indicate services that may be running and listening on a device that may be susceptible to attack. An ICMP, or port scanning, attack basically pings every address and port number combination and keeps track of which ports are open on each device as the pings are answered by open ports with listening services and not answered by closed ports. One of the most widely used port scanners is Network Mapper (Nmap), a free and open source utility for network discovery and security auditing. Figure 11.19 shows the output of a scan using Zenmap, an Nmap security scanner GUI. Starting in line 12 of the output shown in this figure, you can see that the device at 10.68.26.11 has seven ports open:

```
Discovered open port 139/tcp on 10.68.26.11
```

FIGURE 11.19 Zenmap

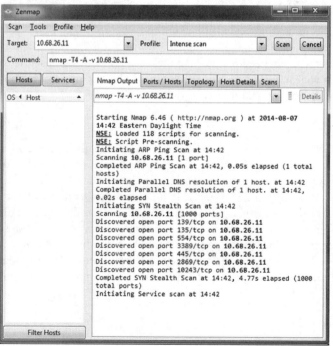

Figure 11.20 shows output from the command-line version of Nmap. You can see in this figure that a ping scan of an entire network just completed. From it you can see that the computer at 172.16.153.242 has three ports open: 23, 443, and 8443. However, the computer at 172.16.153.253 has no open ports. The term *filtered* in the output means that the ports are not open. To obtain this output, the command Nmap 172.16.153.0/23 was executed, instructing the scan to include all computers in the 172.16.153.0/23 network.

FIGURE 11.20   Nmap command line

```
Nmap scan report for 172.16.153.242
Host is up (0.00s latency).
Not shown: 997 closed ports
PORT      STATE SERVICE
23/tcp    open  telnet
443/tcp   open  https
8443/tcp  open  https-alt

Nmap scan report for 172.16.153.253
Host is up (0.00s latency).
Not shown: 996 closed ports
PORT      STATE    SERVICE
2001/tcp  filtered dc
4001/tcp  filtered newoak
6001/tcp  filtered X11:1
9001/tcp  filtered tor-orport

Nmap scan report for 172.16.153.254
Host is up (0.016s latency).
All 1000 scanned ports on 172.16.153.254 are filtered

Nmap done: 512 IP addresses (51 hosts up) scanned in 348.80 seconds

C:\WINDOWS\system32>
```

In a scenario where you need to determine what applications and services are running on the devices in your network, a port scanner would be appropriate. It also allows you to identify any open ports that should not be open.

Sniffers

Sniffing is the process of capturing packets for analysis; sniffing used maliciously is referred to as *eavesdropping*. Sniffing occurs when an attacker attaches or inserts a device or software into the communication medium to collect all the information transmitted over the medium. Sniffers, called *protocol analyzers*, collect raw packets from the network; both legitimate security professionals and attackers use them. The fact that a sniffer does what it does without transmitting any data to the network is an advantage when the tool is being used legitimately and a disadvantage when it is being used against you (because you cannot tell you are being sniffed). Organizations should monitor and limit the use of sniffers. To protect against their use, encrypt all traffic on the network.

One of the most widely used sniffers is Wireshark. It captures raw packets off the interface on which it is configured and allows you to examine each packet. If the data is unencrypted, you will be able to read the data. Figure 11.21 shows an example of Wireshark in use.

FIGURE 11.21   Wireshark

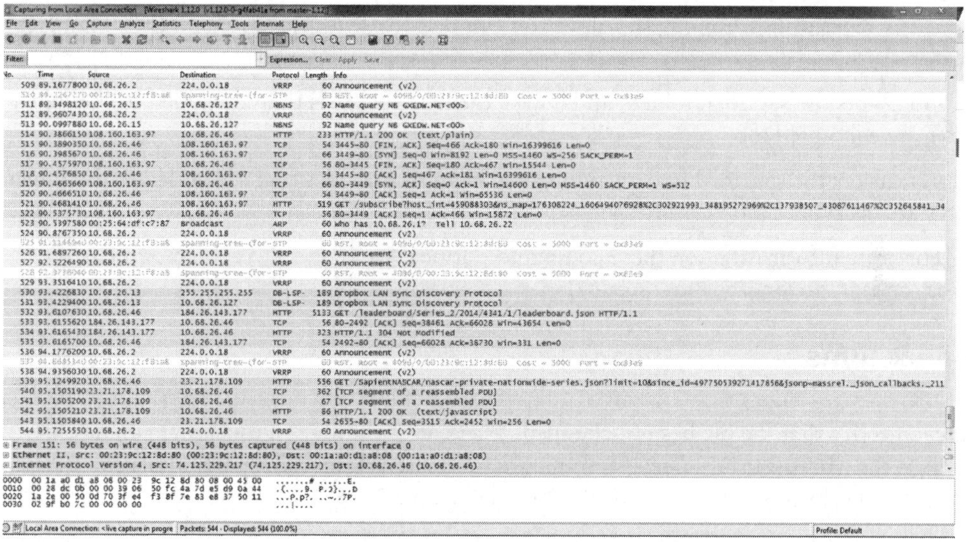

In the output shown in Figure 11.21, each line represents a packet captured on the network. You can see the source IP address, the destination IP address, the protocol in use, and the information in the packet. For example, line 511 shows a packet from 10.68.26.15 to 10.68.16.127, which is a NetBIOS name resolution query. Line 521 shows an HTTP packet from 10.68.26.46 to a server at 108.160.163.97. Just after that, you can see that the server sending an acknowledgment back. To try to read the packet, you would click on the single packet. If the data were clear text, you would be able to read and analyze it. So you can see how an attacker could acquire credentials and other sensitive information.

Protocol analyzers can be of help whenever you need to see what is really happening on your network. For example, say you have a security policy that says certain types of traffic should be encrypted. But you are not sure that everyone is complying with this policy.

By capturing and viewing the raw packets on the network, you would be able to determine whether they are.

Cipher

Cipher is a Windows command-line utility that can be used to view and alter the encryption of files on an NTFS partition. Run with no parameters, it will display the encryption state of the current folder and any file contained within it. That allows you to verify that sensitive files are encrypted as they should be. It is a very powerful tool, however, that can do many more things. Among the tasks you can perform with this tool and the parameters required are

/e Encrypts the specified folders and marks them so that files that are added to the folder later are encrypted too.

/d Decrypts the specified folders and marks them so that files that are added to the folder later are decrypted too.

For more information, on these command options, see `https://technet.microsoft` `.com/en-us/library/bb490878.aspx`.

Checksums

Checksums are values that can be calculated based on the contents of a file that can be used later to verify that the file has not changed. There are a number of tools that can do this, such as the Microsoft File Checksum Integrity Verifier. Many third-party tools can be used to create checksums that can be verified at a later time.

Telnet Client

Although a Telnet client comes on every Windows machine, the client is not installed by default. It is a handy tool to have because it allows you to connect to a device at the command line and work at the command line. You should know, however, that Telnet transmits in clear text so you would not want to use it to perform any sensitive operations (like changing a password). In Exercise 11.3 you will install the Telnet client in a Windows 10 computer.

EXERCISE 11.3

Installing the Telnet Client

1. Right-click the Start menu and select Programs And Features.

2. In the Programs And Features window, select Turn Windows Features On Or Off, as shown in Figure 11.22.

3. In the Turn Windows Features On Or Off page, scroll down until you see the Telnet client, as shown in Figure 11.23.

FIGURE 11.22   Programs And Features

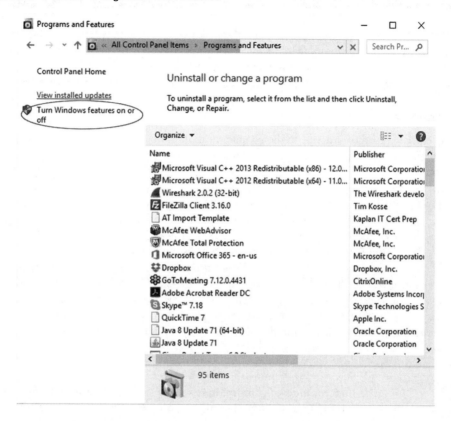

FIGURE 11.23   Turn Windows Features On Or Off

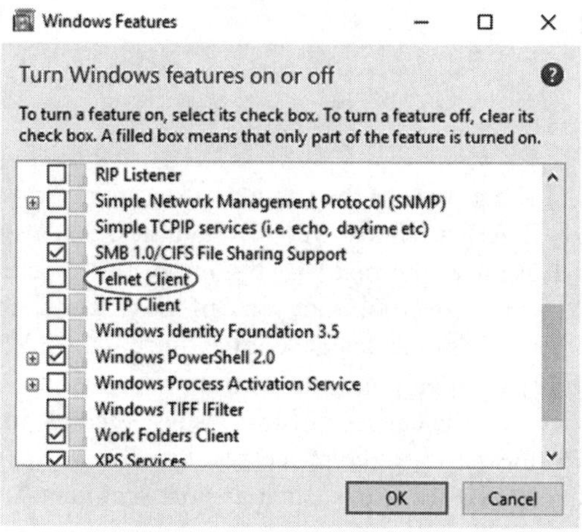

4. Check the box next to Telnet Client and then click OK. The client will be installed and you will be notified when the installation is complete. You can now use it at the command line to connect to a remote machine by its IP address.

Antimalware

The primary method of preventing the propagation of malicious code involves the use of *antimalware software*. This category includes antivirus, antispyware, and antispam software.

Antivirus software is an application that is installed on a system to protect it and to scan for viruses as well as worms and Trojan horses. Most viruses have characteristics that are common to families of virus. Antivirus software looks for these characteristics, or fingerprints, to identify and neutralize viruses before they affect you.

More than 200,000 known viruses, worms, bombs, and other malware have been defined. New ones are added all the time. Your antivirus software manufacturer will usually work hard to keep the definition database files current. The definition database file contains all the known viruses and countermeasures for a particular antivirus software product. You probably won't receive a virus that hasn't been seen by one of these companies. If you keep the virus definition database files in your software up-to-date, you probably won't be overly vulnerable to attacks.

The best method of protection is to use a layered approach. Antivirus software should be installed at the gateways, at the servers, and at the desktop. If you want to go one step further, you can use software at each location from different vendors to make sure you're covered from all angles.

Summary

In this chapter you learned about some of the common issues that prevent network connectivity, among them email failures, Internet failures, and DNS failures. You also learned many of the causes of these issues, such as misconfigured VLANs, improper subnetting, and DHCP failures. You were also exposed to some of the tools that you can use to troubleshoot these issues.

Security misconfigurations can also cause connectivity issues. You learned that this can lead to an inability to open files, applications that will not load, and privilege escalations. We also discussed the causes of these issues, such as misconfigured policies and permission, firewall rules, and rogue processes. Finally, we covered the tools you can use to troubleshoot security-related issues, such as port scanners, sniffers, and checksum tools.

Exam Essentials

Identify common connectivity issues. This includes Internet connectivity failures, email failures, a misconfigured DHCP server, destination host unreachable messages, unknown host messages, a misconfigured default gateway, failure of the service provider, and inability to reach a host by name/FQDN.

Identify common causes of connectivity issues. Describe common causes such as improper IP configuration, VLAN configuration, port security, improper subnetting, component failure, incorrect OS route tables, bad cables, firewall misconfiguration hardware failure, software failure, misconfigured NICs, routing/switch issues, DNS and/or DHCP failure, misconfigured Hosts file, and IPv4 vs. IPv6 misconfigurations.

List common tools. Tools include ping, tracert/traceroute, ipconfig/ifconfig, nslookup, net use/mount, route, nbtstat, and netstat.

Identify common security issues. These include file integrity issues, privilege escalation, applications that will not load, inability to access network file/shares, inability to open files, excessive access, and excessive memory utilization.

Identify common causes of security issues. Causes include open ports, active services, inactive services, intrusion detection configurations, antimalware configurations, local/ Group Policies, firewall rules, misconfigured permissions, virus infections, and rogue processes/services.

List common tools. Among these are port scanners, sniffers, cipher, checksums, Telnet clients, and antimalware.

Review Questions

You can find the answers in the Appendix.

1. Which of the following addresses is used to test the functionality of the NIC?
   A. 0.0.0.0
   B. 127.0.0.1
   C. 255.255.255.255
   D. 0.0.0.1

2. Which of the following features will assign a host with an address in the 169.254.x.x range with a subnet mask of 255.255.0.0?
   A. NAT
   B. DHCP
   C. APIPA
   D. SSID

3. Which of the following is the IPv6 prefix of a link local address?
   A. FE20: :/64
   B. 2001: :/64
   C. FFEE: :/64
   D. FE80: :/64

4. Which of the following commands clears the local DNS cache?
   A. ipconfig/flushdns
   B. flushdns
   C. cache/flushdns
   D. ipconfig/flush

5. Which of the following should be the same on all devices in the same subnet?
   A. IP address
   B. Subnet mask
   C. Hostname
   D. FQDN

6. Which of the following behaviors affects a WLAN but not a wired LAN?
   A. Collisions
   B. CRC failures
   C. Interference
   D. DNS issues

7. What command allows you to determine the MAC address of the computer with which you are experiencing a conflict after pinging the IP address?

    A. `ipconfig/id`

    B. `ping -i`

    C. `arp -d`

    D. `mac-id`

8. What are you hiding when you disable SSID broadcast?

    A. The MAC address of the AP

    B. The IP address of the AP

    C. The hostname of the AP

    D. The network name

9. Which of the following would not be a cause of an inability to connect to the Internet?

    A. The IP address of the computer

    B. The MAC address of the computer

    C. The default gateway address of the computer

    D. The DNS server address of the computer

10. Which of the following commands could be used to see if HTTP is working on a server?

    A. `telnet 192.168.5.5`

    B. `ping 192.168.5.5 :80`

    C. `telnet 192.168.5.65 80`

    D. `Pathping 192.168.5.5`

11. What is the code number of a destination unreachable message when it indicates the destination host is unreachable?

    A. 0

    B. 1

    C. 2

    D. 3

12. You receive a destination unreachable message with no source IP address. Where is it coming from?

    A. A remote router

    B. A remote DNS server

    C. A local DNS server

    D. The local router

13. When the default gateway address is incorrect on the router, which connections will succeed?

    A. From a local device to a remote device

    B. From a remote device to a local device

    C. From a local device to the Internet

    D. From a local device to a local device

14. Which server could be the source of an inability to connect to a local host by name?

    A. NAT server

    B. SQL server

    C. DNS server

    D. Web server

15. At what layer of the OSI model are devices in different VLANs separated?

    A. Layer 1

    B. Layer 2

    C. Layer 4

    D. Layer 7

16. Which of the following features can be used to prevent unauthorized devices from connecting to a switch?

    A. NAT

    B. Port security

    C. Portfast

    D. Cipher

17. Which of these is the default mask of a Class B network?

    A. 255.0.0.0

    B. 255.255.0.0

    C. 255.255.255.0

    D. 255.255.255.255

18. Which of the following features can administrators use to create smaller networks called subnets by manipulating the subnet mask of a larger classless or major network?

    A. NAT

    B. CIDR

    C. DHCP

    D. DNS

19. What command is used on a router to identify the routes of which the router is aware?

    A. `ip route`

    B. `show route`

    C. `route print`

    D. `show ip route`

20. Which commands are used on a router to identify the path taken to a destination network? (Choose two.)

   A. traceroute

   B. tracert

   C. ipconfig/trace

   D. trace

Chapter

12

Troubleshooting Storage Issues

COMPTIA SERVER+ EXAM OBJECTIVES COVERED IN THIS CHAPTER:

✓ **7.5 Given a scenario, effectively troubleshoot storage problems, selecting the appropriate tools and methods**

- Common problems (slow file access, OS not found, data not available, unsuccessful backup, error lights, unable to mount the device, drive not available, cannot access logical drive, data corruption, slow I/O performance, restore failure, cache failure, multiple drive failure)

- Causes of common problems (media failure, drive failure, controller failure, HBA failure, loose connector, cable problems, misconfiguration, improper termination, corrupt boot sector, corrupt file system table, array rebuild, improper disk partition, bad sectors, cache battery failure, cache turned off, insufficient space, improper RAID configuration, mismatched drives, backplane failure)

- Storage tools (partitioning tools, disk management, RAID array management, array management, system logs, net use/mount command, monitoring tools)

Since long-term storage is where all of the data resides, issues that prevent access to storage can prevent business processes from moving forward. Therefore, you should pay close attention to troubleshooting storage problems. As storage can be presented to the servers in various ways, some issues are technology specific whereas others apply to any type of storage. In this chapter, common storage problems will be discussed along with possible causes. We'll also survey various tools that can be used to deploy, manage, and troubleshoot storage systems.

Troubleshooting Storage Problems

Although experience will expose you to most of the storage issues covered in this chapter, your value to the server support team and the organization in general will be greatly enhanced by your study of and preparation to address these issues. This section will describe signs of storage issues and the potential underlying causes of these issues.

Common Problems

You may never experience some of the following issues, but there are some that will return time and again. As you gain experience addressing these more common issues, you will begin to make consistent connections between the causes and the issues. Until that time, you must rely on the application of the troubleshooting method covered in Chapter 10, "Troubleshooting Hardware and Software Issues," and a clear understanding of the common problems discussed in this section.

Slow File Access

Slow file access can have a number of causes, starting with network issues if the file is accessed across a network. Another of the potential causes of slow file access is insufficient memory. When this is the case, it causes excessive paging. Another cause can be a drive that needs to be defragmented. A fragmented drive results in it taking much longer for all the parts of a file to be located before the file will open. Other issues that cause slow performance are controller cards that need updating, improper data cables, and slower devices sharing the same cable with the hard drive in the case of local storage.

OS Not Found

When you receive the "operating system not found" message, it's usually a software error rather than a hardware error. It could be that the master boot record or the active partition cannot be located. These issues can be corrected in Windows by rebooting the computer into Recovery mode and executing one of several commands at the command line of the Recovery environment. See the "OS Boot Failure in Windows" section in Chapter 10.

In Linux and Unix, this issue can be caused by a missing GRUB/LILO. For review of the recovery process for these components, see the section "Missing GRUB/LILO" in Chapter 10.

Of course, it is still possible the issue is related to hardware. Check all the connections to the drives to ensure they are secure.

Data Not Available

A "data not available" message can be generated by an application when the application cannot access required data, because the data has either been moved or deleted by another user. The message also can occur in web-based applications such as Salesforce, where a user is unable to edit data because the data is unavailable, typically due to sharing issues. In most cases, the message is an indication of a problem with the accessing application rather than the storage itself or the network. In these cases, contact the application vendor as in many cases (such as the Salesforce example) these are known issues to the vendor and you can save a lot of time troubleshooting by using their solution.

Unsuccessful Backup

Most backup processes occur with no issues, but occasionally a backup will fail. This is a serious issue especially if it isn't discovered unit you need to restore the data. There are many reasons for unsuccessful backups. In some cases, it is because some files could not be backed up because they were moved from the original location to some other location. In Windows, when using an automatic backup if you choose to *remove unused library or folder locations* this will sometimes solve this issue. Failures can also occur in these cases:

- If your computer is off, sleeping, or hibernating.
- If the backup destination isn't available.
- If the backup destination is a network location and it's not available or your network credentials have expired.
- If the backup destination is encrypted by BitLocker, it needs to be unlocked when it's time for your scheduled backup.

Error Lights

All servers have LEDs that are used to communicate to you events and situations. These vary widely by device so a generalization is difficult. Just as an example, review the LEDs and error messages covered in Chapter 3, "Server Maintenance," in the section "Check System Health Indicators."

Unable to Mount the Device

If a device cannot be mounted, it cannot be accessed by the system. This can result from having no formatted partition or volume on the device or from filesystem corruption on the device. In Windows, you can try running Check Disk to attempt to repair any errors on the drive. Another possibility is to back up the data on the external device from a different system, format the drive again, and restore the data. This issue seems to happen most frequently when devices with NTFS partitions are introduced to Unix and Linux systems. Keep in mind that these systems do not have native support for NTFS and you must install some type of support. An example is installing `fuserfs-ntfs` in Free BSD.

Drive Not Available

The "drive not available" message indicates the local or remote drive to which you are attempting to connect cannot be reached. Although it can always be a network issue in the case of a remote drive, there can be other reasons as well.

If the drive is local, the following can be the issue:

- The hard drive data or power cable may have become unseated. Sometimes even if the cable appears to be seated fine, reseating it can have a positive effect. Also ensure that the data cable has not been reversed.

- If you just added a drive, ensure that both drives have not been set to master or slave and that the boot drive is set as master on the first channel.

- If the system uses serial ATA and you just added a drive, ensure that all of the onboard SATA ports are enabled.

- If you just added a drive, ensure that there is no conflict between the new drive and another device.

- If you receive the "No boot device available, strike F1 to retry boot, F2 for setup utility" message, it could be incorrect drive geometry (which is probably not the case if this drive has been functioning properly before), a bad CMOS battery, or an inability to locate the active partition or master boot record.

In the case of remote drives, any changes in the permissions associated with the drive may cause the problem as well.

Cannot Access Logical Drive

When a logical drive cannot be accessed, the error message could come in several forms since the issue can be from several sources. The two main issues that cause an inability to access a logical drive are corruption of the drive (bad sectors, for example) and encryption of the drive.

In Windows, if the error message says "Data error (cyclical redundancy check)," it could be either of these issues. First try turning off BitLocker on the drive. Then follow these steps:

1. Press Windows key+X, and select Control Panel.

2. Click the View By option at the top right and set it to Large Icons.

3. Click BitLocker Drive Encryption and then expand the options for the F:\ drive.

4. Click Turn Off BitLocker and check if you are able to access the drive.

If the drive is not encrypted or you still get an error message after turning off BitLocker, use Check Disk to attempt to locate and repair any bad sectors.

In cases where the operating system of a device must be reinstalled, there will sometimes be issues accessing the existing logical drives after the reinstallation of the operating system to its previous partition. If this occurs and the problem partition appears in Disk Management with a name rather than a drive letter, assign it a drive letter and that usually solves the issue. Of course, this issue can be avoided entirely by always backing up data.

In some cases, none of these methods will allow access to the drive. There are recovery tools such as Wondershare Data Recovery for Windows that may allow you to at least recover the data off the drive. In that case, you will need to delete it and re-create it, and then restore the data afterward.

Data Corruption

Data corruption is also a possibility when data is being written to and read from a drive and when data is being transferred within a system and between systems. If even a single bit in a file is altered at any time, the data will no longer pass the CRC check and will be considered by the system to be corrupted.

So how does corruption occur? There are a number of ways:

- Failure to eject external hard drives and related storage devices before disconnecting them or powering them off

- Power outages or other power-related problems

- Hardware problems or failures, including hard drive failures, bad sectors, bad RAM, and the like

- Bad programming, particularly if it results in either hard restarts or data that is saved incorrectly

- Improper shutdowns, like those caused by power outages or by performing a hard restart, pressing and holding the power button, or on Macs so equipped, the restart button

If the corrupted files are system files, the system may not even boot. If this is the case, try performing one of the system repair processes, which will check the integrity of all system files and replace any bad ones.

In Linux, you can use the `fsck` command to make a repair attempt. For example, the following command will check the sda1 partition:

```
fsck /dev/sda1
```

It is important to note that this command should *not* be used on a mounted drive. If you do so, you run the risk of damaging the filesystem and making the issue worse. If you want fsck to attempt to repair any errors it finds, add the -a or -y parameter after the command as shown here for the same partition:

```
fsck -a /dev/sda1
```

Of course, if these recovery procedures are not useful, you can restore the data from backup.

Slow I/O Performance

Slow disk access can have a number or sources, some that may surprise you. While the actual disk itself may be the problem, it can also be low memory and CPU issues that manifest themselves as slow I/O.

The root of the problem can be found by using the Linux command top. While this command doesn't work in Windows, you can create a PowerShell script that will yield the same information. First let's look at the command output in Linux shown in Figure 12.1.

FIGURE 12.1   top output

```
top - 00:23:58 up 8 min,  2 users,  load average: 0.36, 0.55, 0.28
Tasks: 118 total,   3 running, 115 sleeping,   0 stopped,   0 zombie
Cpu(s):  6.0%us,  2.0%sy,  0.0%ni, 92.0%id,  0.0%wa,  0.0%hi,  0.0%si,  0.0%
Mem:   1026436k total,   478668k used,   547768k free,    15692k buffers
Swap:  1646620k total,        0k used,  1646620k free,   216820k cached
```

In this output, you are interested in six values:

- CPU% time
- Idle time
- I/O wait time
- Swap usage
- Memory usage
- Memory cached

In this example, the values are

- CPU% time: 6%
- Idle time: 92% (a high value is good)
- I/O wait time: 0% (anything above 10% is an issue)
- Swap usage: 1646620k
- Memory usage: 478668k
- Memory cached: 218620k

The following combinations of values indicate the following issues:

- I/O wait and idle time are low: A single process (probably the application in use) is causing the issue and should be killed.

- I/O wait time is low and idle time is high: This is caused by an application or an external process the server is waiting on.

- I/O wait time is high: Check the swap usage; if high, this is probably a memory issue.

- I/O wait time is high: Check the swap usage; if low, this is probably not a memory issue. Some process is hogging the I/O.

- High memory usage: Subtract the cached memory from the used memory to get this value. If this is an anomaly, it is an offending process that must be killed. If it is constantly high, you need more memory.

So in summary, a real I/O issue is only indicated when I/O is high, use of swap is low, and use of memory is high. If you need to create a PowerShell script for this process, run this command:

```
while (1) { ps | sort -desc cpu | select -first 30; sleep -seconds 2; cls }
```

The output will be different but the same information is displayed.

Restore Failure

When data restoration fails, it is never a good thing because the only reason you ever perform this activity is to replace deleted or damaged data that you *need*. While most data recovery failures are due to human error in the data backup process (such as running multiple jobs simultaneously, failure to change tapes, or forgetting to remove a cleaning tape), some issues are beyond your control, including

- Software errors, such as scripts used to run backup operations, mount media, or perform other operations

- Resource contention during the process

- SAN or other connectivity problems

- Tape drive or media error

- Hardware errors

Although script errors are somewhat under your control, most of these issues are beyond your control. Your best defense against data recovery errors is to develop and maintain a backup procedure that includes frequent verifications of backups.

Cache Failure

During the boot process, the BIOS or UEFI of many systems will check the cache. If there is an issue with the cache, the boot process may stop or it may continue and simply disable the cache. This will impact the performance of the server if you consider the way in which the CPU uses this cache.

When this occurs, it can be either cache memory itself or it can be the motherboard to which the cache is attached. You will need to troubleshoot both—specifically

- Check to see if the cache is securely inserted into the motherboard, if that is where it is located.

- If you have added or changed any cache, investigate whether any changes should have been made to any jumpers on the board as well.

- Check to see if the cache chips get hot after the system has been on a bit. This indicates the chip may be bad, but if you replace it and the same thing occurs, it's the motherboard.

Multiple Drive Failure

When drives fail and are replaced with new drives that subsequently fail, it is always possible that you were just unlucky and got two bad drives in a row, but odds are that is not the case. Typically, something else is causing the drives to fail. In some cases, design flaws in the positioning of the drive may be causing stress that is killing the drives. For example, many laptop owners experienced this, and some theories were that the drives were positioned in such a way that pressure from the user resting their palm on the laptop was causing pressure on the read-write heads, thus damaging the drives over time.

While we are dealing with servers and not laptops, design flaws can occur. Some of the issues to consider when multiple drives have failed are

- Are all of the fans functioning?

- Is the airflow from the fans impeded in any way?

- Have you made any firmware changes that may be causing the issue?

- Is the server room or datacenter sufficiently cooled and is airflow ensured?

- Have you protected the server from electrical outages, surges, and sags?

Multiple drive failures in RAID arrays are even more vexing. If two drives fail before you attempt to rebuild the array, you will not be able to do so. This illustrates the value of using hardware RAID with hot spares so that this possibility is reduced.

Causes of Common Problems

Although we have covered many causes in the process of discussing issues, in this section we'll look at some the most common sources of component and process failures.

Media Failure

We usually think of media as CDs, DVDs, flash drives, and the like, but sometimes an error message will refer to a "media test failure." In this case, it may be referring to this type of media, but it can also be referring to the hard drive or to an ability to boot to a network. In most cases, the message is indicating an ability to locate boot files, and you'll see this message early in the boot process.

Ensure that the boot order is set correctly in the BIOS. If that is not the issue, attempt to run any hardware diagnostics that may be available to you from the server vendor. Reseating the drive cables may also solve the issue. In some devices this will occur if the boot order is set with Network Boot at the top of the list and there are no boot files on the network.

Drive Failure

Every drive is going to fail—it's just a matter of when. Frequent backups are the first line of defense, but sometimes even when your backup plan is sound, a drive fails that contains critical data that has not yet been committed to backup. If you locate this type of data in a fault-tolerant RAID array, your recovery options increase. You still have the data on the other drive in RAID 1, or in the case of RAID 5, you have the parity information required to re-create the data.

When all else fails, data recovery specialists may be able to get the data off the failed drive. They do this by opening the drive in a clean room and reading the data from the exposed platters with special equipment. In cases where the issue is electronics, they may replace the circuit board and attempt to start the drive. Whatever method they use will be costly.

Controller Failure

In hardware RAID implementations, the RAID process is managed by a controller. If the RAID server has only one controller, this is a serious single point of failure. If it fails, you may not be able to recover the data on any of the drives. Many technicians put too much faith in RAID and become lax in preforming backups, which exacerbates the situation when it occurs. Some systems allow for a backup of the RAID configuration, which can mitigate this single point of failure.

HBA Failure

Host bus adapters (HBA) are installed into expansion slots in a server and are used to allow the server to communicate on internal or external networks using technologies such as SCSI, Fibre Channel, and SATA. These networks are typically populated with storage devices.

When an HBA fails, it prevents the server from being able to communicate with the storage network and thus the storage devices. An HBA failure can cause a number of the scenarios we have discussed in which a storage device is unreachable and should always be considered as a possibility in a server that uses HBAs.

Whenever you suspect an HBA failure, you should first check the cables and reseat the adapter in its slot. One of the best mitigations for HBA failure is to implement redundant HBAs providing multiple paths to the storage network. Keep in mind that while a dual port HBA may provide another path to the network, if the HBA fails it's still a single point of failure.

Loose Connectors

In any of the situations we have covered where connections are involved, the connectors should always be checked. Even if the connection appears to be solid, disconnect it and reconnect it to be sure. Every technician can tell a story about a connection that appeared secure as could be but failed to work until this was done. So always check connections to HBAs, controllers, NICs, and other physical interfaces.

Cable Problems

The same approach you take with connectors should be taken with cables. Remember, just because a cable works doesn't mean it is working well. Issues such as cuts in the outer cover and stressed connectors can cause the cable to allow noise into the cable (RFI, EMI) that causes packets to be damaged or corrupted. This leads to retransmissions and lower throughout. Also keep in mind that you should always check the Physical layer first before attempting to troubleshoot issues higher in the OSI model.

Misconfiguration

In many cases, issues are caused by human error when configuring the hardware or software involved in a process. In some cases, this results from an incomplete understanding of the configuration process; in others, it is simply the result of human error. If the configuration of the device or software has recently been changed, misconfiguration should be a prime suspect. On the other hand, if there have been no changes for some time, it is less likely that misconfiguration is the cause.

When there are multiple configuration settings that can be the cause of an error, follow some structured plan to approach it. For example, start at the device and then work your way toward the destination, checking the settings of each device or piece of software that takes part in the communication process.

Improper Termination

Some networks require each end of the network to be terminated. SCSI network-attached storage is an example. SCSI is a bus topology that requires that each end have a terminator. Typically, termination issues occur when a device is added or removed from the bus and a terminator is left somewhere that is *not* one of the ends of the bus. Keep in mind that some older SCSI devices set the terminator using jumpers on the storage device. Also, you should carefully review the documentation to ensure you have the right type of terminator. Some systems use a passive terminator, whereas others that use Low Voltage Differential (LVD) mode will require active terminators.

Corrupted Boot Sector

Booting problems can occur with corruption of the boot files or missing components. Common error messages include an invalid boot disk, inaccessible boot drive, a missing NTLDR file, or the BOOTMGR is missing.

When the boot sector is corrupted, the system is unable to locate the operating system. In Windows you have several options to remedy this situation. In Exercise 12.1 you will perform a system repair.

EXERCISE 12.1

Repairing the System in Windows Server 2012 R2

1.   Insert the installation DVD or USB and boot Windows Server 2012 R2 from it.

2. On the Windows Setup page, specify Language To Install, Time And Currency For-mat, and Keyboard Or Input Method, and click Next.

3. Click Repair Your Computer.

4. Click Troubleshoot and then click Advanced Options.

5. Click Command Prompt and type the following commands (press Enter after each command):

   ```
   Bootrec /fixmbr
   Bootrec /fixboot
   Bootrec /rebuildbcd
   ```

6. Restart the computer. Check if you're able to boot now.

In Linux, a common tool that is used to repair a boot sector is GRUB. You will recover using this tool in Exercise 12.2.

EXERCISE 12.2

Restoring Linux's Boot Sector with GRUB

1. Start Linux from the Ubuntu Live CD, and open a Terminal window.

2. To get to a GRUB prompt, type

   ```
   sudo grub
   ```

3. Type

   ```
   find /boot/grub/stage1
   ```

   You will be shown the location of Stage1, such as (hd0,4). (If more than one Stage1 is located, choose one.)

4. Type

   ```
   root (hd?,?)
   ```

   where ?,? is the location just found.

5. Type

   ```
   setup (hd0)
   ```

6. Type

   ```
   quit
   exit
   ```

7. Open Partition Editor and right-click the partition where GRUB is set up, usually (hd0).

Select Manage Flags and make sure the Boot flag is checked for this partition.

8. Exit and restart. Remove the CD when it pops out.

When you reboot, you will have the GRUB boot loader menu at startup.

Corrupted File System Table

The fstab file (File System Table) is used by Linux operating systems to mount partitions on boot. The following messages may be displayed at boot time if the /etc/fstab file is missing or corrupted:

```
WARNING: Couldn't open /etc/fstab: No such file or direcctory
WARNING: bad format on line # of /etc/fstab
```

This prevents some or all filesystems from being mounted successfully. If you have a backup of fstab you can restore it. To restore a missing or corrupted /etc/fstab file

1. Log in under Maintenance Mode.

2. Remount the root filesystem in read-write mode (an ext3 type root filesystem is assumed in this example; modify as appropriate):

```
# mount -t ext3 -o remount,rw /dev/vx/dsk/rootvol /
```

3. Restore the /etc/fstab file from a recent backup, or correct its contents by editing the file.

4. Reboot the system.

Array Rebuild

Sometimes, the term *array rebuild* refers to the process of the redundancy regeneration in RAID5. In this case we're talking about a degraded RAID array, one that has failed to rebuild for one reason or another. In cases where the rebuild must be done manually (which means no hot spare), if drives are not connected back in the correct position it can cause a failed rebuild.

To prevent this from occurring, follow these procedures when performing a manual rebuild:

▪ Clearly label the disks as you remove them and note the corresponding port.

▪ Identify, remove, and similarly label the faulty drive.

▪ The drives should be placed back in the reversed order of failures (failures, not removals).

▪ If you are replacing a failed drive, ensure that it and the other drives are connected to the original port numbers.

Improper Disk Partition

Partitions can get corrupted or damaged due to a number of reasons. Among these are

- Virus attack
- Installation of defective software
- Instant shutdown or power failure

There are a number of commercial partition tools that you can use, such as Partition Magic, to repair damaged partitions. Before you use one of these commercial tools, you might want to use one of the system tools available to you. One of these is chkdsk (Check Disk). You will use chkdsk in Exercise 12.3 to identify and repair disk issues that may be part of the partition issue.

EXERCISE 12.3

Checking the Disk in Windows Server 2012 R2

1. Insert the installation DVD or USB and boot Windows Server 2012 R2 from it.

2. On the Windows Setup page, specify Language To Install, Time And Currency Format, and Keyboard Or Input Method, and click Next.

3. Click Repair Your Computer.

4. Click Troubleshoot and then click Advanced Options.

5. Click Command Prompt and type the following command:

   chkdsk /p

   If after the test completes, the message "One or more errors detected on the volume" appears, then proceed to step 6. If no errors are reported, then your drive cannot be repaired using chkdsk.

6. Type

   chkdsk /r

   When the repair process completes and you are returned to the command prompt, check to see if the repair worked by typing

   chkdsk /p

   If no errors are reported, the repair worked. Check to see if this solved the partition issue.

Bad Sectors

When sectors on a hard drive go bad, many filesystems can mark the sector as bad so that it is not used again. You can also identify bad sectors using tools such as Check Disk on

Microsoft systems, or badblocks on Unix-like systems. Bad sectors are one of the issues that the procedure you performed in Exercise 12.3 is designed to locate and repair (repair in this case meaning moving the data to a good sector and marking the old sector as bad).

badblocks has several different modes that enable you to detect bad sectors in Linux. One of those is destructive to the data and should be used only on new drives and not ones where you have data. The nondestructive method creates a backup of the original content of a sector before testing with a single random pattern and then restores the content from the backup. The command you want to run and an example of the output are shown here:

```
# badblocks -nsv /dev/<device>
Checking for bad blocks in non-destructive read-write mode
From block 0 to 488386583
Checking for bad blocks (non-destructive read-write test)
Testing with random pattern: done
Pass completed, 0 bad blocks found. (0/0/0 errors)
```

Cache Battery Failure

RAID arrays often use caching to improve performance. A battery-backed cache is one that can maintain the data in the cache during a power outage, preventing the loss of data still residing in the cache at the moment of the power failure. When this battery fails, it can cause the loss of data.

To change the battery, you must first put the battery in an error state. You can do so after powering on the device and using the tools provided with the operating system to force the battery into the error state. Even if you think that process went well, do *not* remove the battery if the Cache Present LED is flashing because that indicates data is still present in the cache. When the light is out, you can remove the cover and replace the battery. Use the tools to start the write cache again.

Cache Turned Off

Several methods are available that a server can use to cache information that it is preparing to send to long-term storage. The most beneficial to performance is a method called write-back cache. In this method, write I/O is directed to cache and completion is immediately confirmed to the host. This results in low latency and high throughput for write-intensive applications, but there is data availability exposure risk because the only copy of the written data is in cache.

When the cache is turned off, you lose all of those performance benefits. Cache can be enabled in both the operating system and in the storage software. While it must be done in both places, typically when you set it in the storage software it will be reflected in the settings in Windows as well, but it's always worth checking. In Windows Server 2012 R2 this is done in the properties of the RAID volume in Device Manager, as shown in Figure 12.2.

FIGURE 12.2   Enabling write-back cache in Windows

Insufficient Space

In some cases, you receive an error message from the storage system that there is insufficient space in the cache. For example:

```
WARNING: Failure to reserve space on any cache data file storage location.
 Failure has occurred '@1%d'times since last warning.
```

or:

```
1006006 Failed to bring block into the memory. Data cache is too small. Please
 increase the data cache size.
```

You can use the storage software to increase the cache available to the system. This may require adding more memory as well. The procedures for doing that are in the documentation that came with the software.

Improper RAID Configuration

Most RAID misconfigurations involve a misunderstanding of the requirements and benefits of each type. Each has a minimum number of drives required, and each provides advantages and disadvantages that must be clearly understood or expectations will not be met. The common types of RAID and the requirements and benefits of each were covered in Chapter 5, "Identifying Capacity and Fault Tolerance Requirements," in the section "RAID Levels and Performance Considerations."

Mismatched Drives

When choosing drives for a RAID array, the best choice is to buy the same models from the same manufacturer with the same speed, size, and other characteristics. However, if you search for "mismatched drives," you will find many forums where experienced technicians are saying, "I know all the drives should be the same but they just aren't." Budgets and the real world sometimes interfere with best practices.

Although it is possible to use mismatched drives, you should have a clear understanding of the implications of each type of mismatch. The only requirement set in stone is that they be of the same architecture.

A speed mismatch will simply mean that the fastest drive will have to wait for the slower drives to finish writing in cases where data is being written to multiple drives. This is why it is sometimes said that it "dumbs down" the faster drives. A size mismatch will simply mean that the largest volume on any drive can be no larger than the smallest drive in the array. That results in some wasted drive space.

Backplane Failure

In Chapter 1, "Server Hardware," you learned about backplanes. You learned that the backplane provides a connection point for the blade servers in the blade enclosure. Some backplanes are constructed with slots on both sides, and in that case they are located in the middle of the enclosure and are called midplanes. They can host drives as well as servers in storage devices.

When a backplane fails, it affects all the drives that connect to it. Luckily backplane failures are much less likely than drive failures, so you should always suspect a drive failure first. Blade systems and rack servers typically come with several management tools you can use to identify the failing part.

If you confirm that the backplane is bad and must be replaced, ensure that you follow the directions in the documentation to the letter. Each system will have its own unique quirks and "gotchas" to avoid. Read through the entire operation before you start! Otherwise you could make your situation much worse.

Storage Tools

There are a number of common tools that can be used to monitor, configure, and trouble-shoot storage and storage issues. We will survey some of these tools in this section. Keep in mind that there will probably be vendor-specific tools that come with the server or with the storage hardware that may provide more functionality because the tools were written specifically for the server or storage device.

Partitioning Tools

Partitioning tools are used to divide the storage media into sections called partitions or volumes. Some of these have GUIs and others operate from the command line. While there are many, many commercial and free software products that can do this, you can also use tools built into the operating system.

In Windows Server 2012 R2 the diskpart command lets you manage storage from the command line. Although there are GUI tools that you can use (covered in the next section), there is almost always more functionality with the command-line tool. diskpart enables you to manage objects (disks, partitions, or volumes) by using scripts or direct input at a command prompt. It can perform all the functions that can be done with the

Disk Management utility and quite a few that cannot be done with Disk Management. In many ways, it is an updated version of fdisk. It can be used to create and manage volumes on the drive.

An example of one of the things you can do with diskpart is initializing a disk. Initializing a disk makes it available to the disk management system, and in most cases, the drive will not show up until you do this. Once the drive has been connected or installed, you should initialize it. You can do so at the command using diskpart or by using the Disk Management tool. Keep in mind that initialization will wipe out the drive! To use diskpart to perform the initialization on 2TB drives and smaller

1. Open the Start menu, type **diskpart**, and press Enter.

2. Type **list disk**, and press Enter.

3. Type **select disk** *X* (where X is the number your drive shows up as), and press Enter.

4. Type **clean**, and press Enter.

5. Type **create partition primary**, and press Enter.

6. Type **format quick fs=ntfs**, and press Enter.

7. Type **assign**, and press Enter.

8. Type **exit**, and press Enter.

To use diskpart to perform the initialization on drives that are 2 TB drives and larger

1. Open the Start menu, type **diskpart**, and press Enter.

2. Type **list disk**, and press Enter.

3. Type **select disk** *X* (where X is the number your drive shows up as), and press Enter.

4. Type **clean**, and press Enter.

5. Type **convert gpt**, and press Enter.

6. Type **create partition primary**, and press Enter.

7. Type **format quick fs=ntfs**, and press Enter.

8. Type **assign**, and press Enter.

9. Type **exit**, and press Enter.

fdisk

Although the fdisk command is no longer used in Windows Server 2012 R2, it is still the tool used on Linux to manage partitions. The sudo fdisk -l command lists the partitions on the system. To make any changes to a disks partitioning, you must enter command mode for that device. That means you need to know how the system refers to that device, which can be found in the output of the fdisk -l command.

For example, in the output in Figure 12.3, the name of the first listed device is dev/sda.

FIGURE 12.3   Using fdisk

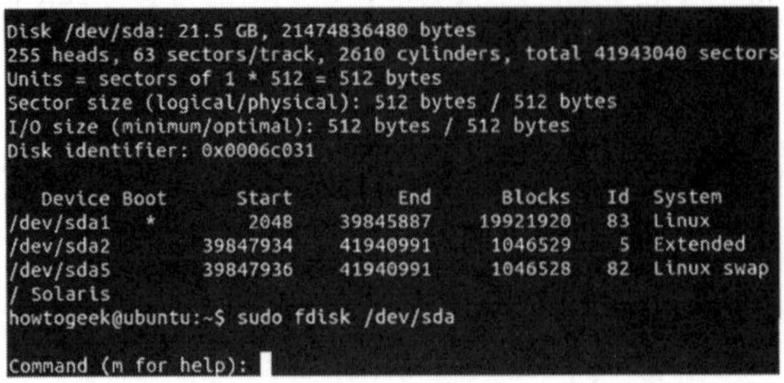

Therefore, to enter the mode required to manage it, type

sudo fdisk /dev/sda

In command mode, you use single-letter commands to specify actions. At the following prompt, you can type **m** to list the actions and their letters.

Command (type m for help)

If you do so, you will get the output shown in Figure 12.4.

FIGURE 12.4   Actions menu

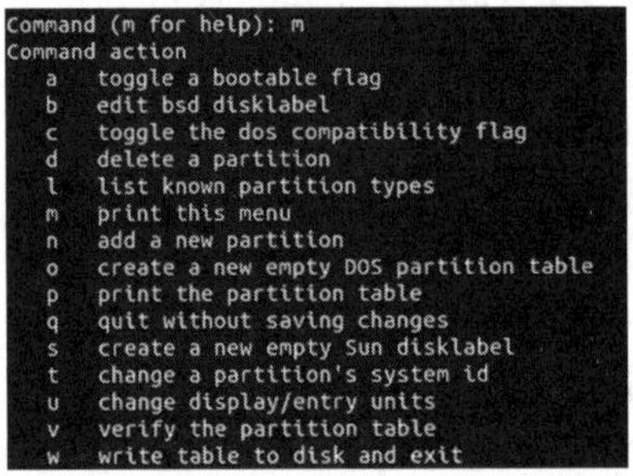

As you can see, you can create and delete partitions from this menu using **n** and **d**, respectively.

Disk Management

To access Disk Management, open Control Panel and double-click Administrative Tools. Then double-click Computer Management. Finally, double-click Disk Management.

The Disk Management screen lets you view a host of information regarding all the drives installed in your system, including CD-ROM and DVD drives. The list of devices in the top portion of the screen shows you additional information for each partition on each drive, such as the filesystem used, status, free space, and so on. If you right-click a partition in either area, you can perform a variety of functions, such as formatting the partition and changing the name and drive letter assignment. For additional options and information, you can also access the properties of a partition by right-clicking it and selecting Properties.

Once the disk is formatted, the next building block is the directory structure, in which you divide the partition into logical locations for storing data. Whether these storage units are called directories or folders is a matter of semantics—they tend to be called *folders* when viewed in the graphical user interface (GUI) and *directories* when viewed from the command line.

Drive Status

The status of a drive can have a number of variables associated with it (System, Boot, and so on) but what really matters is whether it falls into the category of *healthy* or *unhealthy*. As the title implies, if it is healthy, it is properly working, and if it is unhealthy, you need to attend to it and correct problems. In Figure 12.5 you can see in the Status column of Disk Management that all drives are Healthy.

FIGURE 12.5   Status in Disk Management

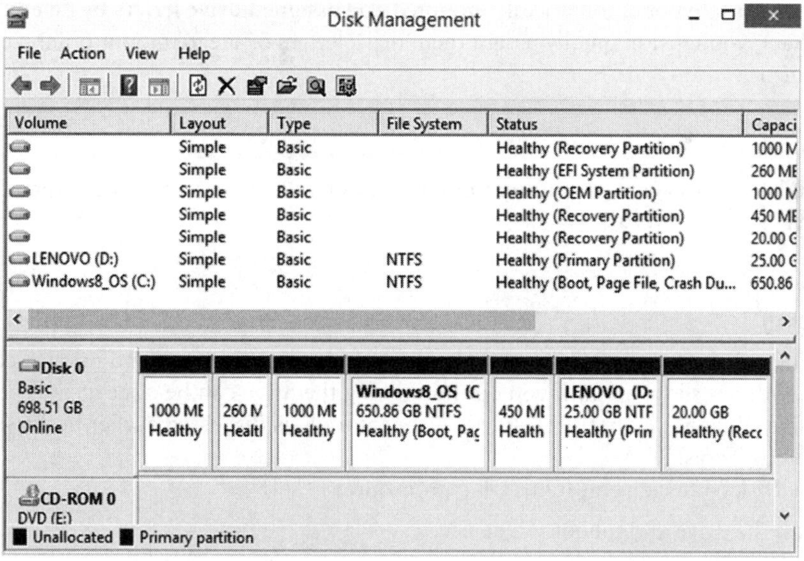

Table 12.1 lists some of the most common states and their resolution. You can find a complete list of status states that are possible and require action at http://technet .microsoft.com/en-us/library/cc771775.aspx.

TABLE 12.1   Disk states

State	Resolution
Foreign	Import the disk.
Not initialized	Initialize the disk.
Unreadable	Rescan the disk or restart the server.
Online (errors)	Reactivate the disk.
Offline	Check cables and controller, and then reactivate.
Missing	Check cables and controller, and then reactivate.

Mounting

Drives must be mounted before they can be used. In Windows, most removable media (flash drives, CDs, and so forth) are recognized when attached and mounted. Volumes on basic disks, however, are not automatically mounted and assigned drive letters by default. To mount them, you must manually assign them drive letters or create mount points in Disk Management.

You can also mount from the command line using either diskpart or mountvol.

Initializing

Initializing a disk makes it available to the disk management system, and in most cases the drive will not show up until you do. Initializing the drive can be done at the command using diskpart or in the Disk Management tool, as discussed earlier in the section, "Partitioning Tools."

To use Disk Management, follow this procedure:

1. Install the drive and reboot the device.

2. In the search line, type **Disk Management** and press Enter. With the drive connected, you will get the pop-up box shown in Figure 12.6.

3. Choose either MBR or GPT, and click OK.

   If you didn't get the pop-up, then right-click and select to initialize the newly added drive under where it displays the disk number, as shown in Figure 12.7.

FIGURE 12.6 Initialize Disk pop-up

Initialize Disk   ✕

You must initialize a disk before Logical Disk Manager can access it.

Select disks:

☑ Disk 1

Use the following partition style for the selected disks:

◉ MBR (Master Boot Record)
○ GPT (GUID Partition Table)

Note: The GPT partition style is not recognized by all previous versions of Windows. It is recommended for disks larger than 2TB, or disks used on Itanium-based computers.

[OK]   [Cancel]

FIGURE 12.7 Initializing a disk

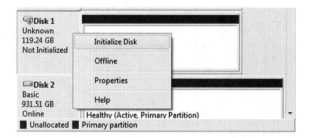

⟳**Disk 1**
Unknown
119.24 GB
Not Initialized

| Initialize Disk |
| Offline |
| Properties |
| Help |

▭**Disk 2**
Basic
931.51 GB
Online | Healthy (Active, Primary Partition)
■ Unallocated ■ Primary partition

Extending Partitions

It is possible to add more space to partitions (and logical drives) by extending them into unallocated space. This is done in Disk Management by right-clicking and choosing Extend or by using the diskpart command.

Shrinking or splitting Partitions

Just as you can extend a partition, you can also reduce the size of it. While generically known as splitting the partition, the menu option in Disk Management is Shrink. By shrinking an existing partition, you are creating another with unallocated space that can then be used for other purposes. You can only shrink basic volumes that use the NTFS filesystem (and space exists) or that do not have a filesystem.

It is also possible to shrink a volume from its size at creation. To do so in Disk Management, access the volume in question, right-click the volume, and select Shrink Volume, as shown in Figure 12.8.

This will open another box that will allows you to control how much you want to shrink the volume, as shown in Figure 12.9.

FIGURE 12.8   Shrink Volume

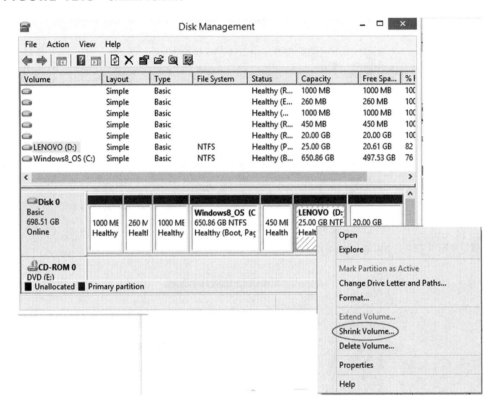

FIGURE 12.9   Setting the volume size

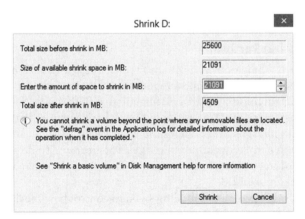

Assigning/Changing Drive Letters

Mounting drives and assigning drive letters are two tasks that go hand in hand. When you mount a drive, you typically assign it a drive letter in order to be able to access it. Right-click on a volume in Disk Management to see the Change Drive Letter And Paths option shown in Figure 12.10.

FIGURE 12.10   Change Drive Letter And Paths

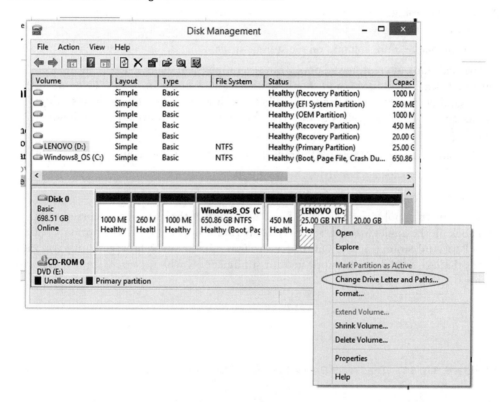

Adding Drives

When removable drives are added, the Windows operating system is configured, by default, to identify them and assign a drive letter. When nonremovable drives are added, you must mount them and assign a drive letter, as mentioned earlier.

Adding Arrays

Arrays are added to increase fault tolerance (using RAID) or performance (striping). Disk Management allows you to create and modify arrays as needed.

Storage Spaces

Configuring storage spaces is a fault tolerance and capacity expansion technique that can be used as an alternative to the techniques described in the section on dynamic volume types. It enables you to virtualize storage by grouping industry-standard disks into storage pools, and then creating virtual disks called storage spaces from the available capacity in the storage pools. This means from a high level that you have three tasks to use storage spaces:

1. Create a storage pool, which is a collection of physical disks.

2. From the storage pool, create a storage space, which can also be thought of as a virtual disk.

3. Create one or more volumes on the storage space.

First let's look at creating the pool from several physical disks. Each of the disks must be at least 4 GB in size and should not have any volumes in them. The number of disks required depends on the type of resiliency you want to provide to the resulting storage space. Resiliency refers to the type of fault tolerance desired. Use the following guidelines:

▪ For simple resiliency (no fault tolerance), only a single disk is required for the pool.

▪ For mirror resiliency, two drives are required.

▪ For parity resiliency (think RAID5), three drives are required.

To create the pool, access Control Panel using any of the methods discussed so far and click on the applet Storage Spaces. On the resulting page, select the option Create A New Pool And Storage Space. On the Select Drives To Create A Storage Pool page, the drives that are available and supported for storage pools will appear, as shown in Figure 12.11.

FIGURE 12.11   The Select Drives To Create A Storage Pool page

In this case, only one drive is eligible, so we can only create a simple type of pool. Check the drive and click the Create Pool button at the bottom of the page. On the next page, assign the space a name, select a drive letter, choose the filesystem (NTFS or REFS), and specify the resiliency type (in this case we can only select simple) and the size of the pool.

ReFS
Resilient File System (ReFS) is a Microsoft filesystem that maximizes data availability. It protects against the damage caused by many common errors. To read more about this filesystem, which was introduced with Windows Server 2012, see
https://msdn.microsoft.com/en-us/library/windows/desktop/hh848060%28v=vs.85%29.aspx?f=255&MSPPError=-2147217396.

In Figure 12.12 we have set the pool as Myspace, with a drive letter of F, an NTFS filesystem, simple resiliency, and a maximum size of 100 GB. When we click Create Storage Space, the space will be created. Be aware that any data on the physical drive will be erased in this process.

FIGURE 12.12   Creating a storage space

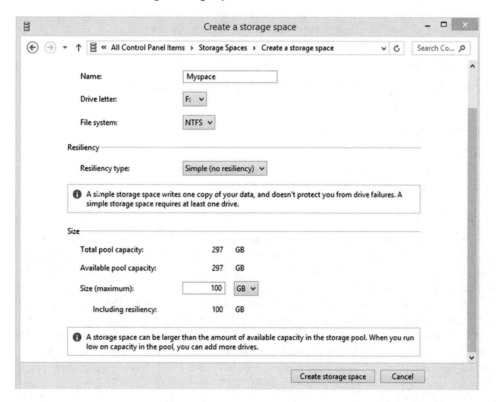

When the process is finished, the new space will appear on the Manage Storage Spaces page. Now we have a pool and a space derived from the pool. The last step is to create a volume in the storage space. If you now access Disk Management, you will see a new virtual disk called Myspace. It will be a basic disk, but you can convert it to dynamic by right-clicking it and selecting Convert To Dynamic Disk. This will allow you to shrink or delete the existing volume if you desire.

RAID Array Management

The tool used to manage a RAID array depends on whether it is software or hardware RAID. If it is software RAID (which is highly unlikely on a server), you will manage it with the tools in the operating system. If it is hardware RAID, you will use the tools available with the system, which you can sometimes access by rebooting and selecting the RAID tool from the initial menu. In other cases, GUI tools may be provided that allow you to create and manage the array.

For a review of managing hardware RAID from the initial menu at bootup, see the section on "RAID Setup" in Chapter 2, "Installing and Configuring Servers."

Array Management

Some servers and storage solutions include array management software, but you can also buy it from commercial vendors. This software is specifically designed to make creating, troubleshooting, and managing storage arrays of various types easier.

Some of the features that may be available with this type of software are

- A single interface to use across many arrays
- Interactive service and maintenance reminders and information
- Proactive remote monitoring with alerts
- Management from anywhere
- Automated best practices

An example of the interface of an array manager is shown in Figure 12.13, which is the welcome page of the HP Array Configuration Utility.

System Logs

The system logs of the server are always a good source of information on storage issues. There are typically log files for different components, such as a security log, an application log, or a system log. These file can be used to troubleshoot operating system issues, and events related to this are usually in the System log.

If the enterprise is large, you may want to have all of the devices send their logs to a central server, where they can be stored and analyzed. In Windows these logs can be viewed, filtered, and saved using a tool called Event Viewer. This utility provides information about what's been going on system-wise to help you troubleshoot problems. Event Viewer shows warnings, error messages, and records of things happening successfully. You can access it through Computer Management, or you can access it directly from Administrative Tools in Control Panel.

FIGURE 12.13 HP Array Configuration Utility

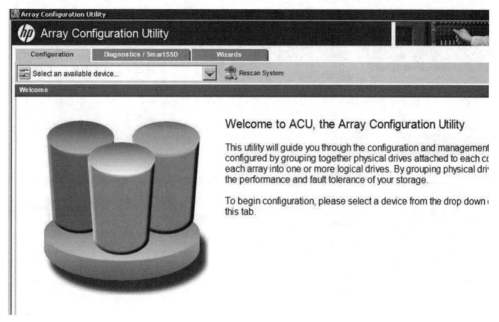

In Linux, the log file that contains general and system-related messages like any you would be interested in for storage issues is located here:

`/var/log/messages`

There are also log files for the storage device if it is an appliance and for any array management software you have in use.

net use/mount Commands

You will use the net use and mount commands frequently when working with storage to mount a device so that it is accessible. To share that device with others, use the net use command to connect them. For a review of these commands, see "Networking Tools" in Chapter 11, "Troubleshooting Connectivity Issues."

Monitoring Tools

Many servers and storage devices come with monitoring tools, and others can be used from within a storage array manager. For example, in Figure 12.14, you can see that the Solarwinds Storage Manager has several monitors (or logs) available in the menus tree on the left side of the console.

FIGURE 12.14 Solarwinds Storage Manager

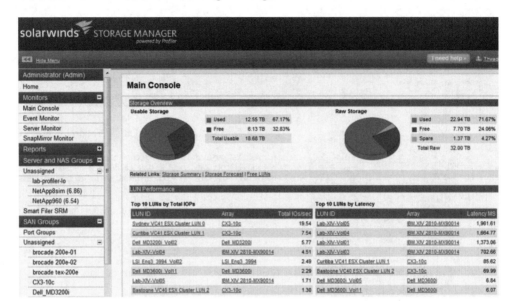

Servers will also have performance monitoring tools you can use. In Windows you can use Performance Monitor, which differs a bit between versions but has the same purpose throughout: to display performance counters. While lumped under one heading, two tools are available—System Monitor and Performance Logs And Alerts. System Monitor will show the performance counters in graphical format. The Performance Logs And Alerts utility will collect the counter information and then send it to a console (such as the one in front of admins so they can be aware of the problem) or event log.

Summary

In this chapter you learned about common issues that can plague storage system—issues such as slow file access, data corruption, slow I/O performance, and drive failures. This included a discussion of error lights, restoration failures, and cache issues.

You also learned the cause of many of these issues, including but not limited to hardware issues such as media failures, drive failures, controller failures, and HBA failures. We also looked at misconfiguration issues such as improper termination, having the cache turned off, improper RAID configuration, and mismatched drives.

Finally, you learned about the tools that can be used to manage and diagnose storage system, such as partitioning tools, RAID array management, array management software, system logs, and monitoring tools.

Exam Essentials

Identify common storage issues.   These issues include slow file access, OS not found, data not available, unsuccessful backups, error lights, inability to mount the device, drive not available, cannot access logical drive, data corruption, slow I/O performance, restore failure, cache failure, and multiple drive failure.

Describe common causes of storage issues.   Describe common causes of storage problems, such as media failures, drive failures, controller failures, HBA failures, loose connectors, cable problems, misconfiguration, improper termination, corrupted boot sector, corrupted filesystem table, array rebuild, improper disk partition, bad sectors, cache battery failure, cache turned off, insufficient space, improper RAID configuration, mismatched drives, and backplane failure.

List common tools.   Understand the use of tools such as partitioning tools, disk management, RAID array management software, array management software, system logs, net use/mount commands, and monitoring tools.

Review Questions

You can find the answers in the Appendix.

1. In Linux, which of the following can cause an inability to locate the operating system?

    A. Missing NTLDR

    B. Missing GRUB

    C. Missing Bootmgr

    D. Missing boot.ini

2. You receive the error message "Data error (cyclical redundancy check)" when attempting to access a logical drive. Which of the following is not a possible cause of this message?

    A. Corruption of the drive.

    B. Bad sectors.

    C. The drive is encrypted.

    D. The drive is not formatted.

3. What command can be used to attempt a repair of the dda drive in Linux?

    A. fsck -a /dev/dda

    B. fdisk -s /dev/dda

    C. fsck /dev/dda

    D. fdisk /dev/dda

4. Which of the following commands in Linux can be used to diagnose a memory issue?

    A. fsck

    B. top

    C. grub

    D. grep

5. Which of the following combinations of factors indicates an I/O issue?

    A. I/O is low, use of swap is low, and use of memory is high

    B. I/O is high, use of swap is high, and use of memory is high

    C. I/O is high, use of swap is low, and use of memory is low

    D. I/O is high, use of swap is low, and use of memory is high

6. Which of the following is the most common cause of backup failures?

    A. Tape drive failure

    B. Human error

    C. Software errors

    D. SAN issues

7. Which of the following is a single point of failure?

  A. Two single port HBAs

  B. One double port HBA

  C. Two double port HBAs

  D. Two triple port HBAs

8. Which of the following issues can be caused by a cable with a cut in the outer covering?

  A. Crosstalk

  B. EMI

  C. Collisions

  D. Poor performance

9. Which of the following will result from an L2 cache failure?

  A. Increased performance

  B. Increased use of swap

  C. Degraded performance

  D. Depleted drive space

10. What type of terminator is used with SCSI drives operating in LVD mode?

  A. Static

  B. Dynamic

  C. Active

  D. Passive

11. What file is used by Linux to mount partitions on boot?

  A. fstab

  B. grub

  C. lilo

  D. remount

12. Which of the following is *not* a best practice when manually rebuilding RAID arrays?

  A. Clearly label the disks as you remove them and note the corresponding port.

  B. Identify, remove, and similarly label the faulty drive.

  C. The drives should be placed back in the reversed order of removals.

  D. If you are replacing a failed drive, ensure that it and the other drives are connected to the original port numbers.

13. What command can be used in Linux to detect bad sectors?

  A. fschk

  B. badblocks

  C. fstab

  D. grub

14. Which of the following *must* match when adding drives to a set of existing drives?

    A.　Speed

    B.　Capacity

    C.　Architecture

    D.　Vendor

15. What command is used to connect users to shared drives?

    A.　`net share`

    B.　`net use`

    C.　`mount`

    D.　`dmap`

16. Which of the following is used to manage storage in Windows Server 2012 R2 at the command line?

    A.　`fdisk`

    B.　`format`

    C.　`diskpart`

    D.　`fstab`

17. Which of the following commands lists the partitions in a Linux system?

    A.　`sudo fdisk -l`

    B.　`sudo fdisk /dev`

    C.　`fstab -a`

    D.　`sudo fstab -a`

18. Which of the following tools cannot be used to mount a volume on a basic disk in Windows Server 2012 R2?

    A.　`mountvol`

    B.　`diskpart`

    C.　Disk Management

    D.　`fdisk`

19. Which of the following is conceptually like a virtual disk?

    A.　Witness

    B.　Basic disk

    C.　Page file

    D.　Storage space

20. In Linux the log file that contains general and system-related messages like any you would be interested in for storage issues is located where?

    A.　`/var/messages`

    B.　`/var/log`

    C.　`/log/messages`

    D.　`/var/log/messages`

Appendix

Answers to Review Questions

Chapter 1: Server Hardware

1. A. When we use the term *form factor* when discussing any computing device or component, we are talking about its size, appearance, or dimensions. It is typically used to differentiate one physical implementation of the same device or component from another. In the case of servers, we are talking about the size and dimensions of the enclosure in which the server exists.

2. B. Rail kits, when implemented, allow you to slide the server out of the rack for maintenance.

3. C. Each U is 1.75 inches (4.445 cm) high.

4. D. This technology consists of a server chassis housing multiple thin, modular circuit boards, known as server blades. Each blade (or card) contains processors, memory, integrated network controllers, and other input/output (I/O) ports.

5. A. The Level 1 cache, also known as the L1 or front-side cache, holds data that is waiting to enter the CPU. On modern systems, the L1 cache is built into the CPU.

6. B. The internal speed may be the same as the motherboard's speed (the external or bus speed), but it's more likely to be a multiple of it. For example, a CPU may have an internal speed of 1.3 GHz but an external speed of 133 MHz. That means for every tick of the system crystal's clock, the CPU has 10 internal ticks of its own clock.

7. C. When monitoring CPU performance, the following are common metrics and their meanings:
   - User time—the time the CPU was busy executing code in user space
   - System time—the time the CPU was busy executing code in kernel space
   - Idle time—the time the CPU was not busy; measures unused CPU capacity
   - Steal time (virtualized hardware) —the time the operating system wanted to execute but was not allowed to by the hypervisor, because it was not the CPU's turn for a time

8. D. When CPUs undergo revisions, the revisions are called stepping levels. When a manufacturer invests money to do a stepping, that means they have found bugs in the logic or have made improvements to the design that allow for faster processing.

9. A. ARM requires fewer resources than either x86 or the x64. In that regard they are suitable for tablets, smartphones, and other smaller devices.

10. B. The primary benefit of DDR3 over DDR2 is that it transfers data at twice the rate of DDR2 (eight times the speed of its internal memory arrays), enabling higher bandwidth or peak data rates.

11. True.

12. A. When installing the memory, install the same size modules in the same bank. If you do not, the modules will not operate in dual-channel mode. This will impair the performance of the bank.

13. A. Memory timing measures the performance of RAM and is composed of four components:

- CAS Latency—the time to access an address column if the correct row is already open
- Row Address to Column Address Delay—the time to read the first bit of memory without an active row
- Row Precharge Time—the time to access an address column if the wrong row is open
- Row Active Time—the time needed to internally refresh a row

14. A, D. You can mix speeds and manufacturers but not form factors or types.

15. B. PCI-eXtended (PCI-X) is a double-wide version of the 32-bit PCI local bus. It runs at up to four times the clock speed, achieving higher bandwidth, but otherwise uses the same protocol and a similar electrical implementation.

16. A. An auto-MDIX card is capable of detecting what type of device is on the other end and changing the use of the wire pairs accordingly. For example, normally a PC connected to another PC requires a crossover cable, but if both ends can perform this sensing, that is not required.

17. D. Many servers attach to storage networks and may run converged network adapters (CNA), which acts both as a host bus adapter (HBA) for the SAN and as the network card for the server.

18. A, C. There are two main approaches to this: dual-drive hybrid and solid-state hybrid.

19. B. 1U and 2U systems, which are 1.75″ and 3.5″, respectively.

20. B. UEFI provides faster startup and resuming from hibernation times.

Chapter 2: Installing and Configuring Servers

1. C. Some of the enhancements this new interface provides are

- Better security by helping to protect the preboot process against bootkit attacks
- Faster startup and resuming from hibernation times
- Support for drives larger than 2.2 TB
- Support for modern, 64-bit firmware device drivers that the system can use to address more than 17.2 billion GB of memory during startup
- Capability to use BIOS with UEFI hardware

2. A. RAID 0 is also known as disk striping. This is RAID that doesn't provide fault tolerance. Data is written across multiple drives, so one drive can be reading or writing while the next drive's read/write head is moving. This makes for faster data access. However, if any one of the drives fails, all content is lost.

3. B. Introduced by Microsoft along with Windows NT (and available on all Windows Server operating systems), NTFS is a much more advanced filesystem in almost every way than all versions of the FAT filesystem.

4. B. The Zettabyte filesystem (ZFS) was developed by Sun Microsystems. It is part of Sun's Solaris operating system and is thus available on both SPARC and x86-based systems, but it's also an open source project.

5. C. Today's operating systems support the use of swap files. These are files located on the hard drive that are used to temporarily hold items moved from memory when there is a shortage of memory required for a particular function.

6. D. Although a good idea, ensuring the server has sufficient processing power is not a part of hardening the system as it does nothing to reduce the attack surface.

7. A. You can use third-party monitoring tools or you can rely on some that are built into the system, such as the Performance Monitor tool in Server 2012 R2. This tool can be used to take snapshots over a period of time as well so you get a feel for the rise and fall of the workload on the server.

8. B. The swap file is often called the pagefile.

9. C. With Windows servers, set the pagefile to 1.5 times the RAM.

10. A. Windows Deployment Services in Server 2012 R2 can be used to create and deploy images.

11. B. The Preboot Execution Environment (PXE) is an industry-standard client-server interface that allows networked computers that are not yet loaded with an operating system to be configured and booted remotely by an administrator.

12. C. When working with servers locally—that is, standing in the same room with the server—one of the most common ways technicians connect to the server is through a KVM. A keyboard, video, and mouse (KVM) device allows you to plug multiple PCs (usually servers) into the device and to switch easily back and forth from system to system using the same mouse, monitor, and keyboard.

13. A. Integrated Lights-Out, or iLO, is a proprietary embedded server management technology from Hewlett-Packard that provides out-of-band management facilities.

14. B. Developed by Microsoft, Remote Desktop Protocol (RDP) allows you to connect to remote computers and run programs on them. When you use RDP, you see the desktop of the computer you've signed into on your screen.

15. B. Dell Remote Access Controller, or DRAC, is an interface card from Dell that provides out-of-band management facilities. The iDRAC refers to a version of these interface cards that is integrated on the motherboard of the server.

16. A. Virtual Network Computing (VNC) is a graphical desktop sharing system that uses the RFB protocol to remotely control another computer.

17. B. If you don't need access to the graphical interface and you just want to connect to a server to operate at the command line, you have two options: Telnet and SSH. While Telnet works just fine, it transmits all of the data in cleartext, which obviously would be a security issue. Therefore, the connection tool of choice has become Secure Shell (SSH).

18. C. Type I hypervisor (or native, bare-metal) runs directly on the host's hardware. A Type II hypervisor runs within a conventional operating system. VMware Workstation and Virtual-Box exemplify Type II hypervisors.

19. C. Values such as Low, Normal, High, and Custom (using VMware as an example) are compared to the sum of all shares of all VMs on the server. Therefore, they define the relative percentage each VM can use.

20. B. RAID 1 is also known as disk mirroring. This is a method of producing fault tolerance by writing all data simultaneously to two separate drives.

Chapter 3: Server Maintenance

1. A. Web servers are used to provide access to information to users connecting to the server using a web browser, which is the client part of the application. It uses the HTTP protocol as its transfer mechanism.

2. C. The CPU is the component that is stressed on an application server since it is doing all of the processing on behalf of the clients. Multicore and multiple processors are advisable.

3. C. A directory server is one that accepts and verifies the credentials of users. Typically it not only authenticates them but also provides them with access to resources using single sign-on.

4. C. DHCP servers are used to automate the process of providing an IP configuration to devices in the network. These servers respond to broadcast-based requests for a configuration by offering an IP address, subnet mask, and default gateway to the DHCP client.

5. D. Network Time Protocol (NTP) servers are used as a time source by the devices in the network. This service ensures that log entries that are time stamped can be properly interpreted and that digital certificates, which depend heavily on time, continue to function correctly.

6. A. DNS servers resolve device and domain names (website names) to IP addresses, and vice versa.

7. A. Device drivers are the software stubs that allow devices to communicate with the operating system. Drivers are used for interacting with printers, monitors, network cards, sound cards, and just about every type of hardware attached to the server.

8. C. One of the metrics that is used in planning both SLAs and IT operations in general is mean time to repair (MTTR). This value describes the average length of time it takes a vendor to repair a device or component.

9. **A.** When monitoring resources, you select performance counters that represent aspects of the workload the resource is undergoing.

10. **D.** The four are disk, CPU, memory, and NIC or network.

11. **A.** Processor\% Processor Time is the percentage of time the CPU spends executing a non-idle thread. This should not be over 85 percent.

12. **C.** Memory\Available Mbytes is the amount of physical memory, in megabytes, available for running processes. If this is less than 5 percent, you need more memory.

13. **B.** IOPS (Input/Output Operations per Second, pronounced eye-ops) is a common disk metric that describes how fast the disk subsystem is able to read and write to the drive. The higher this value, the better.

14. **C.** Servers have backplanes that abut the drives and make a connection with the drive so no cables are required. These can go bad and sometimes need replacing.

15. **B.** A soft reboot is better for the system and allows the proper shutdown of all running applications and services. But it requires that you be logged in as either administrator or root and that the server be in a responsive state.

16. **A.** In load balancing, a frontend device or service receives work requests and allocates the requests to a number of backend servers. This type of fault tolerance is recommended for applications that do not have a long-running in-memory state or frequently updated data.

17. **C.** End of life can mean a couple of different things. From the vendor perspective, it probably means that they no longer provide support for a product.

18. **B.** Print servers need lots of memory to hold the print jobs waiting in the print queue. The exact amount will depend on the number of users assigned to the printers being managed by this print server.

19. **B.** Mail servers run email server software and use SMTP to send and receive email on behalf of users who possess mailboxes on the server.

20. **D.** RAID 5 can recover from a single disk failure, and it can read multiple drives, thus increasing performance.

Chapter 4: Storage Technologies

1. **C.** One of the key features of DAS is that there is no network connection standing between the server and the storage, as is the case with SAN and NAS.

2. **A.** On the contrary, a NAS has higher latency and lower reliability than a SAN.

3. **A.** Network-attached storage, as the name implies, consists of storage devices that are attached to the network and not attached locally to the server or servers that may be accessing the NAS. Although the storage may not be attached locally to the server, it is reachable via the TCP/IP network.

4. D. While sharing is made easier by the fact that the SAN is not connected directly to any network or server, a SAN is expensive, doesn't use Ethernet, and doesn't allow you to leverage legacy investments in non-fiber technologies.

5. B. In a classic SAN, devices communicate using the Fibre Channel protocol over a fiber network of storage devices typically connected to a Fibre Channel switch. This means that any servers that will be directly connected to this fiber network must have a host bus adapter (HBA) installed that can communicate on the fiber network.

6. B. HBAs have World Wide Names (WWNs) that identify them, much like MAC addresses.

7. A. Zones are divisions of the storage created for performance and/or security reasons.

8. A. A logical unit number (LUN) identifies a device addressed by the SCSI protocol or protocols that encapsulate SCSI, such as Fibre Channel or iSCSI.

9. B. Internet Small Computer Systems Interface (iSCSI) is an IP-based networking storage standard method of encapsulating SCSI commands (which are used with storage area networks) within IP packets. This allows the use of the same network for storage as is used for the balance of the network.

10. D. On the contrary, iSCSI is susceptible to network congestion.

11. A. Fibre Channel over Ethernet (FCoE) encapsulates Fibre Channel traffic within Ethernet frames much as iSCSI encapsulates SCSI commands in IP packets. However, unlike iSCSI, it does not use IP at all.

12. C. The acronym JBOD refers to "just a bunch of disks." The disks in this "bunch of disks" are independent of one another, unlike disks that participate in a RAID arrangement of some sort. While the data may be striped across the disks, no fault tolerance is provided.

13. C. The Linear Tape Open (LTO) drives have been through a number of generations, the latest of which, LTO-6, has a maximum capacity of 2.5 TB.

14. B. A tape library is a storage device that contains multiple tape drives. It also contains a number of slots to hold tape cartridges and a barcode reader that is used to identify the cartridges. Finally, it typically contains a robotic method for loading the tapes.

15. B. Revolutions per minute (RPM) is a value that indicates how fast the drive spins. This is a value with meaning only for hard disk drives. SSDs do not spin at all.

16. A. Input/Output Operations per Second (IOPS), or in-outs per second, is a value that describes how fast the drive can read and write to the disk.

17. C. Seek time is the time it takes for the actuator arm to arrive at the proper location where the read or write will occur.

18. D. Latency is a measure of the time it takes the platter to spin the disk around so the actuator arm is over the proper section. Latency is largely a function of the RPMs since a faster spinning disk will arrive at the desired location faster than a slower disk.

19. C. A hot-swap disk is one that can be changed without shutting down the server. In some cases, while the server may be left on, the software in the server may need to be disconnected from the disk being changed and then reconnected after the swap is done. Lower-end SCSI devices may be of this type, which is also called cold pluggable.

20. B. Serial attached SCSI (SAS) is a type of SCSI that uses serial operation rather than parallel as the original SCSI did.

Chapter 5: Identifying Capacity and Fault Tolerance Requirements

1. C. When the hard disk manufacturer advertises a 120 GB hard drive, they are selling you 120,000,000,000 bytes. Windows divides this number by what it considers a GB (1073741824) and reports the hard disk size as:

120000000000 (bytes)/1073741824 (bytes per GB) = 111.8 GB

2. D. Be aware that when you do this to files and folders that are frequently accessed, you will be placing a load on the CPU of the server because it decompresses the file to make it available and then compresses it again when it is saved.

3. B. One of the things that you can do in Windows to mitigate the amount of space used by constant updates is to manage a folder called the component store. This folder, called windows\winsxs, contains all the files that are required for a Windows installation.

4. B. Managing log files can be done at the command line using the following command, which inserts the name of the log file and the maximum size in bytes:

wevtutil sl <LogName> /ms:<MaxSizeInBytes>

5. B. Manually performing a disk cleanup will allow you to get rid of these files (and many other useless files as well), but if you would like to create a batch file, you can automate the process.

6. A. RAID 0, also known as disk striping, provides no fault tolerance.

7. B. RAID 1 is also known as disk mirroring. This is a method of producing fault tolerance by writing all data simultaneously to two separate drives.

8. D. A minimum of three drives is required. RAID 5 uses $1/n$ (n = the number of drives in the array) for parity information (for example, one third of the space in a three-drive array), and only $1 - (1/n)$ is available for data. So if three 250 GB drives are used in the array (for a total of 750 GB), 500 GB will be the available drive space.

9. B. A minimum of three drives is required.

10. C. One disadvantage in using RAID 6 is that each set of parities must be calculated separately, which slows write performance.

11. B. The advantages of using software RAID are

- Lower cost
- The ability to implement disk duplexing

12. B. The ability to implement disk duplexing is an advantage of software RAID, not hardware RAID.

13. C. Since this is effectively a mirrored stripe set and a stripe set gets 100 percent use of the drive without mirroring, this array will provide half of the total drive space in the array as available drive space.

14. C. Disk duplexing is the use of separate controller cards for each disk when implementing disk mirroring (RAID 1), thus providing fault tolerance at both the disk level and the disk controller level, protecting against both a single disk failure and a single controller card failure.

15. A. SATA is the slowest and least expensive of the options with a maximum cable length of 1 meter (3 feet).

16. C. While Fibre Channel is the fastest and provides the longest allowable cable length, it is the most costly.

17. D. The faster the RPM, the faster the disk access will be.

18. A. Mixing any of the following drive specifications in the same array will result in the entire array using the least capable specification (also called "dumbing down" the array):

- Slowest speed (performance)
- Smallest size
- Smallest buffer

19. B. If you are using SATA disks, hot swapping is inherently supported due to the pin layout.

20. C. A cold spare is one that is attached to the system and available but cannot replace the bad disk without administrator intervention and in some cases a reboot.

Chapter 6: Securing the Server

1. C. While passwords and usernames are examples of something you know and a retina scan is an example of something you are, possessing a smart card is an example of something you have.

2. A. A mantrap is a series of two doors with a small room between them. The user is authenticated at the first door and then allowed into the room. At that point additional verification will occur (such as a guard visually identifying the person) and then the user is allowed through the second door.

3. B. The tags can be of two types: passive and active. Active tags have batteries whereas passive tags receive their energy from the reader when the reader interrogates the device. As you would expect, the passive tags are cheaper but have a range of only a few meters and the active tags are more expensive but can transmit up to a hundred meters.

4. A. Biometric devices use physical characteristics to identify the user. Such devices are becoming more common in the business environment. Biometric systems include hand scanners, retinal scanners, and soon, possibly, DNA scanners.

5. B. Security guards offer the most flexibility in reacting to whatever occurs. Guards can use discriminating judgment based on the situation, which automated systems cannot do. This makes guards an excellent addition to the layers of security you should be trying to create.

6. A. With respect to fire, first understand that no safe is fireproof. Many are fire resistant and will protect a document from being destroyed, which occurs at a much higher temperature than many of the other items (such as backup tapes and CDs) can tolerate without damage. For these reasons, items such as backup tapes should be stored offsite.

7. D. Assigning a BIOS password is considered a physical hardening technique.

8. B. When discussing network security, an endpoint is any point of entry into the network. A typical example of an endpoint is a laptop connected to the network with a remote access connection. Therefore, the process of providing endpoint security is the process of ensuring that every endpoint (including servers) has been secured in the same way in which you would secure the network gateway.

9. D. A host-based system is installed on the device (for purposes of our discussion, a server) and the system focuses solely on identifying attacks on that device only. This is in contrast to a network-based system, which monitors all traffic that goes through it looking for signs of attack on any machine in the network.

10. A. For your Windows servers, an excellent tool is the Microsoft Baseline Security Analyzer (MBSA). This tool can identify missing security patches, weak passwords and other security issues that are specific to installed products.

11. B. While important, implementing strong authentication is a form of digital security.

12. B. Many NICs are capable of a function called Wake on LAN (WOL). This allows the device to be started up from the network by sending a special packet to the NIC (which is not ever actually off).

13. C. The runtime is the amount of time that a UPS can provide power at a given power level. This means you can't really evaluate this metric without knowing the amount of load you will be placing on the UPS.

14. A. Capacity is the maximum amount of power a UPS can supply at any moment in time. So if it has a capacity of 650 volt amperes (VA) and you attempt to pull 800 VA from the UPS, it will shut itself down.

15. C. Putting a UPS in bypass mode removes the UPS from between the device and the wall output conceptually, without disconnecting it.

16. B. A power distribution unit (PDU) is a device that looks much like a simple power strip with multiple outlets, but depending on the model, a PDU can be much more than that. Some are large freestanding devices. Some of the features these devices can provide besides multiple outlets are

- Power conditioning (evening out sags and surges)
- Surge protection
- Environmental monitoring
- Case alarms

17. C. The National Electric Code, which is published by the National Fire Protection Association, requires that the continuous current drawn from a branch circuit does not exceed 80 percent of the circuit's maximum rating. Therefore, PDUs have a maximum input value and a de-rated value. The de-rated value will be 80 percent of the maximum input value. So a PDU with a maximum value of 30 amps will have a de-rated value of 24 amps.

18. D. It's unlikely, but there may be a point in time in which all your devices require what's called maximum power at the same time. Multiplying total wattage by 0.67 gives you a truer idea of what a spike could be. Then divide the result by 1000 to establish the kilowatt (kW) load level of the anticipated critical load.

19. D. The lowest static voltage transfer that you can feel is around 3,000 volts (it doesn't electrocute you because there is extremely little current). A static transfer that you can see is at least 10,000 volts! However, a component can be damaged with as little as 300 volts.

20. A. At one time, fire suppression systems used Halon gas, which works well by suppressing combustion through a chemical reaction. However, these systems are no longer used because they have been found to damage the ozone layer.

Chapter 7: Securing Server Data and Network Access

1. A. The proxy firewall can also offer web caching, should the same request be made again, and can increase the efficiency of data delivery.

2. C. The proxy function can occur at either the application level or the circuit level. Application-level proxy functions read the individual commands of the protocols that are being served. This type of server is advanced and must know the rules and capabilities of the protocol used.

3. A. In stateful inspection (or stateful packet filtering), records are kept using a state table that tracks every communications channel.

4. C. On Linux-based systems, a common host-based firewall is iptables, replacing a previous package called ipchains. It has the ability to accept or drop packets.

5. A. This rule set blocks all incoming traffic sourced from the 192.168.0.0/24 network, which is from 192.168.0.1–192.168.0.255.

6. A. It is not possible to specify a minimum number of MAC addresses allowed on a port.

7. B. The IEEE 802.1x security standard describes a method of centralizing the authentication, authorization, and accounting of users who connect either locally or remotely to the network. It is sometimes called port-based access control because in an 802.1x architecture, the user's port to the network is not opened until the process is complete.

8. C. The role of the authentication server can be performed by a Remote Authentication Dial-in User Service (RADIUS) or a Terminal Access Controller Access Control System+ (TACACS+) server. Both of these server types centralize the authentication process on behalf of the multiple authenticators.

9. C. The role of the authenticator can be performed by a wide variety of network access devices, including remote access servers (both dial-up and VPN), switches, and wireless access points. The role of the authentication server can be performed by a RADIUS or TACACS+ server.

10. D. If traffic matches a rule, the action specified by the rule will be applied, and no other rules will be read.

11. B. Lightweight Directory Access Protocol (LDAP) is a protocol that provides a mechanism to access and query directory services systems.

12. D. To provide encryption, the data is encrypted with the receiver's public key, which results in cipher text that only his private key can decrypt.

13. A. SSL is related to a PKI in that a certificate is required on the server end and optionally can be used on the client end of an SSL communication.

14. C. In VPN operations, tunneling protocols wrap around or encapsulate the original packet when this process occurs. PPTP will encrypt the result using Microsoft Point-to-Point Encryption (MPPE).

15. D. Authentication Header (AH) provides authentication and integrity, but not confidentiality.

16. A. The Security Parameter Index (SPI) is a type of table that tracks the different SAs used and ensures that a device uses the appropriate SA to communicate with another device. Each device has its own SPI.

17. A. One of the challenges with IPsec is how to generate an encryption key for the session (each session key is unique). Internet Key Exchange (IKE) is the key exchange method that is most commonly used by IPsec. IKE with IPsec provides authentication and key exchange.

18. B. Devices in different VLANs usually have IP addresses in different IP subnets. However, even if they have IP addresses in the same subnet, communication cannot occur without routing—if they reside in different VLANs—because VLANs separate devices at Layer 2, or the Data Link layer, of the OSI model.

19. C. Switch ports can be set to use a protocol called Dynamic Trunking Protocol (DTP) to negotiate the formation of a trunk link. If an access port is left configured to use DTP, it is possible for a hacker to set their interface to spoof a switch and use DTP to create a trunk link. If this occurs, the hacker can capture traffic from all VLANs. To prevent this, disable DTP on all switch ports.

20. C. Personally identifiable information (PII)—information that can be used to identify an employee or customer and perhaps steal their identity—should only be located in secure zones and never in the DMZ or the extranet or in public clouds.

Chapter 8: Networking

1. C. In IPv6 the loopback address is all zeroes in every hextet except the last. Closing up the first seven hextets with a double colon results in ::, and the one in the last hextet results in ::1 after omitting the leading zeroes in the last hextet.

2. B. When autoconfiguration is used, the first hextet will always be FE80::. The rest of the address will be derived from the MAC address of the device.

3. B. Using CIDR, administrators can create smaller networks called subnets by manipulating the subnet mask of a larger classless or major network ID. This allows you to create a subnet that is much closer in size to what you need, thus wasting fewer IP addresses and increasing performance in each subnet.

4. D. The Class B range of private IP addresses is from 172.16.0.0 to 172.31.255.255.

5. D. Automatic Private IP Addressing (APIPA) is a TCP/IP feature Microsoft added to their operating systems. If a DHCP server cannot be found and the clients are configured to obtain IP addresses automatically, the clients automatically assign themselves an IP address, somewhat randomly, in the 169.254.*x.x* range with a subnet mask of 255.255.0.0.

6. A. In IPv6, there is a type of address called a link local address that in many ways is like an APIPA address in that the device will generate one of these addresses for each interface with no intervention from a human, as is done with APIPA. The devices always generate the address using the same IPv6 prefix (the equivalent of a network ID in IPv4), which is FE80::/64. The reminder of the address is created by spreading the 48-bit MAC address across the last 64 bits.

7. A. Fully qualified domain names (FQDN) identify the host and the location of the hostname in the DNS namespace of the organization. It consists of at least two parts and perhaps more. All FQDNs will have a hostname and a domain name.

8. B. In many instances, users make references to unqualified hostnames when accessing resources. When this occurs, DNS needs to know how to handle these unqualified domain names. It is possible to configure a list of domain names called "suffixes" for the DNS to append to unqualified hostnames and the order in which they should be tried.

9. A. In a Linux environment, creating a DNS suffix search list can be done by editing a file called `resolv.conf`, which is located at `/etc/resolv.conf`.

10. B. WINS servers perform NETBIOS name resolution on behalf of WINS clients.

11. B. When EUI-64 is used, it doesn't actually change the format of the physical 48-bit MAC address. It is a method of spreading the 48-bit MAC across 64 bits so that it can be used as the last 64 bits of the 128-bit IPv6 address.

12. C. Each part of this address communicates information. The left half of the address is called the organizationally unique identifier (OUI). The right half is called the universally administered address (UAA). Together they make a globally unique MAC address.

13. A. Combining physical links can be done using proprietary methods, and there is also an IEEE standard for the process called 802.3ad, later replaced by 802.1ax-2008.

14. C. To configure Ethernet 6 to be used as a slave by a NIC team, open the `ifcfg-eth6` file and edit it as follows. In this case, the NIC team will be created and identified as bond0.

    ```
    # vi /etc/sysconfig/network-scripts/ifcfg-eth1
    DEVICE="eth1"
    TYPE=Ethernet
    ONBOOT="yes"
    BOOTPROTO="none"
    USERCTL=no
    MASTER=bond0
    SLAVE=yes
    ```

15. B. You set the speed and duplex of an interface by using the Configuration button found in the Properties window of the network card in Device Manager.

16. C. Simple Mail Transfer Protocol (SMTP) is a protocol for sending email. SMTP uses port 25 by default.

17. A. Secure File Transfer Protocol over SSH, or SFTP, is a version of FTP that is encrypted by SSH. Since it operates over an SSH session and SSH uses port 22, SFTP uses port 22.

18. B. Telnet is a protocol that functions at the Application layer of the OSI model, providing terminal-emulation capabilities. Telnet runs on port 23, but has lost favor to SSH because Telnet sends data—including passwords—in plain-text format.

19. C. If the same standard is used on each end, the cable will be a straight-through cable, and if a different standard is used on either end, it will be a crossover cable. If one end is completely reversed, it results in a rollover cable.

20. D. CAT6 transmits data at speed up to 10 Gbps, has a minimum of 250 MHz of bandwidth, and specifies cable lengths up to 100 meters (using CAT6a).

Chapter 9: Disaster Recovery

1. C. A cold site is a leased facility that contains only electrical and communications wiring, air conditioning, plumbing, and raised flooring. No communications equipment, networking hardware, or computers are installed at a cold site until it is necessary to bring the site to full operation.

2. B. When implementing disk-to-disk replication (also sometimes called storage- or array-based replication), the data is copied from the local disk on the server to either another disk on the same server or to another disk in the remote office.

3. D. While server-to-server replication is typically less costly than disk- (array-) based, it will impact the performance of the servers on which it is running.

4. C. Site to site (sometimes called network-based replication) uses Fibre Channel switches to replicate from one site to another. It is also likely the most expensive solution.

5. A. Each organizational function or system will have its own disaster recovery plan (DRP). The DRP for each function or system is created as a direct result of that function or system being identified as part of the business continuity plan (BCP).

6. C. The resulting document (business impact analysis) that is produced lists the critical and necessary business functions, their resource dependencies, and their level of criticality to the overall organization.

7. B. The archive bit is used to communicate to the backup system whether a particular file has changed since the last backup. When the archive bit is cleared (0), it communicates that the file has been backed up already and has not changed since. When the bit is on (1), it communicates that the file has changed since the last backup and should be backed up again.

8. B, D. Neither the differential nor the copy backup clears the archive bit.

9. B. While a full backup requires only one backup tape for restoration and the number of tapes required when using incremental and copy methods depends on when the failure occurs, when the differential method is used you always only need the last full backup and the last differential backup tapes to restore.

10. D. You will need the last full tape from Saturday and the incremental tapes from Sunday, Monday, Tuesday, Wednesday, and Thursday.

11. B. This type of snapshot is taken every time a user enters data or changes data, and it only includes the changed data. Although it allows for very rapid recovery from a loss of data, it requires you to have access to all previous snapshots during recovery.

12. A. Back up programs that use the Windows Volume Shadow Copy Service (VSS) can back up open files. However, you should know that when you back up open files in this manner, changes that may have been made to the file while it was open and the backup job was proceeding will *not* be present in the backup of the open file and will not be recorded until the next backup.

13. B. When the operating system is backed up, the configuration of the operating system, sometimes called the system state, is what is saved.

14. B. While younger technicians may be unfamiliar with the task of rewinding or fast-forwarding a music tape or cassette to access a particular song, it illustrates the way linear access works. A song cannot be played until the tape head (reader) is positioned over the location where that song resides. Accessing data on a tape must be done the same way.

15. A. If you create the backup using checksums (which is an option with many utilities) it will allow you to check that the data has not changed since it was made or that it has been corrupted or damaged.

16. A. The amount of time you should retain tapes or other backup media will be driven by several issues:

- Any regulations that may apply to the industry in which the company operates
- The criticality of the data
- Any company policies that may exist

17. A. In this scheme, three sets of backups are defined. Most often these three definitions are daily, weekly, and monthly.

18. C. In this scheme, the newest backup is saved to the oldest media. Although this is the simplest rotation scheme, it does not protect against data errors. If an error in data occurs, this system may result over time in all copies containing the error.

19. C. Risk of theft and vandalism is reduced when using onsite and not offsite storage.

20. A. Temperature should not exceed 110 degrees F (43 degrees C) or fall below 32 degrees (0 degrees C). Ideally it should be kept below 74 degrees F (23 degrees C).

Chapter 10: Troubleshooting Hardware and Software Issues

1. B. The steps in order are
- Identify the problem and determine the scope.
- Establish a theory of probable cause.
- Test the theory to determine cause.
- Establish a plan of action to resolve the problem and notify affected users.
- Implement the solution or escalate as appropriate.
- Verify full system functionality and, if applicable, implement preventative measures.
- Perform a root cause analysis.
- Document findings, actions, and outcomes throughout the process.

2. B. You may find yourself attempting significant changes on a server in an attempt to locate and/or solve the issue. Be sure that you do a backup before you make any changes so that all your actions can be undone, if necessary.

3. A. When you make multiple changes at a time, those changes might interact with one another and make the picture even muddier.

4. B. Chip creep—the unseating of components—is one of the more common byproducts of a cycle of overheating and cooling off the inside of the system.

5. B. Replacing slot covers is vital. Servers are designed to circulate air with slot covers in place or cards plugged into the ports. Leaving slots on the back of the computer open alters the air circulation and causes more dust to be pulled into the system.

6. B. The problem is frequently related to defective RAM, L2 RAM cache, or video RAM.

7. C. Onboard components (also called integrated components) are those that are built into the motherboard. Unfortunately, when these components fail, a replacement of the motherboard is usually required.

8. D. Excessive interrupts effect the CPU, not the disk system.

9. A. When you start the server in clean boot, it starts by using a preselected minimal set of drivers and startup programs, and because the computer starts with a minimal set of drivers, some programs may not work as you expected.

10. B. UEFI (Unified Extensible Firmware Interface) is a standard firmware interface for PCs, designed to replace BIOS.

11. C. While other items require careful matching, it is not required of network cards.

12. A. Backplanes are advantageous in that they provide data and control signal connectors for the hard drives. They also provide the interconnect for the front I/O board, power and locator buttons, and system/component status LEDs. Unfortunately, this creates a serious single point of failure because if the backplane fails, we lose communication with the servers to which it is connected.

13. B. You can remove dust and debris from inside servers with compressed air blown in short bursts. The short bursts are useful in preventing the dust from flying too far out and entering another machine, as well as in preventing the can from releasing the air in liquid form.

14. C. Maintain the relative humidity at around 50 percent.

15. B. It is a balancing act keeping humidity at the right level since low humidity causes ESD and high humidity causes moisture condensation.

16. D. A sag is a short-term voltage drop.

17. C. With one basic multimeter, you can measure voltage, current, and resistance (some will even measure temperature).

18. D. Spyware would compromise the privacy of the users browsing but would not prevent them from logging on.

19. C. Memory leaks occur when an application is issued some memory to use and does not return the memory and any temporary file to the operating system after the program no longer needs it.

20. A. To ensure the system files are all intact execute the following command at the command prompt sfc /scannow

Chapter 11: Troubleshooting Connectivity Issues

1. B. Ensure that the NIC is functional and the TCP/IP protocol is installed and functional by pinging the loopback address 127.0.0.1.

2. C. Automatic Private IP Addressing (APIPA) is a TCP/IP feature Microsoft added to its operating systems. If a DHCP server cannot be found, the clients automatically assign themselves an IP address, somewhat randomly, in the 169.254.*x.x* range with a subnet mask of 255.255.0.0.

3. D. Devices always generate the address using the same IPv6 prefix (the equivalent of a network ID in IPv4), which is fe80::/64. The reminder of the address is created by spreading the 48-bit MAC address across the last 64 bits.

4. A. If recent changes have occurred in the DNS mappings or if your connection to the destination device has recently failed because of a temporary network issue that has been solved, you may need to clear the local DNS cache using the ipconfig/flushdns command.

5. B. Sometimes an incorrect mask will prevent all communication, but in some cases it results in successful connections locally but not remotely (outside the local subnet). The subnet mask value should be the same mask used on the router interface connecting to the local network.

6. C. On a wireless network, cordless phones, microwave ovens, and other wireless networks can interfere with transmissions. Also, users who stray too far from the access point can experience a signal that comes and goes.

7. C. You can determine the MAC address of the computer with which you are experiencing the conflict by using the ping command followed by the arp -d command.

8. D. The service set identifier (SSID) is used as a both a network name and in some cases the magic word that allows access to the network.

9. B. This issue can have a number of sources, including

- The IP configuration of the user's computer
- The IP configuration of the users default gateway or router
- The IP configuration of any routers that stand between the gateway and the Internet
- The DNS server
- The ISP
- The DHCP server

10. C. You can determine this by attempting a Telnet connection to the IP address of the device and adding the port number.

11. B. It will appear as a destination unreachable message (this is a group of message types that all have code numbers) with a code number of 1.

12. D. If the message comes with no source IP address, the message is coming from the local router (the default gateway of the sender). If it has the source IP address of the sender, then it is another router in the path.

13. D. If the computers cannot connect to the default gateway (which will be the case if the gateway is incorrect), it will be confined to communicating with devices on the local network.

14. C. If this is not possible, it is a name resolution issue or a DNS issue.

15. B. Even if we assign devices in different VLANs with IP addresses in the same subnet, they will not be able to communicate because they are also separated at Layer 2.

16. B. Some of the things you can specify using this feature are the only MAC address or addresses allowed to send traffic in the port, the total number of MAC addresses that can transmit on the port, and an action to be taken when a violation occurs (either shut the port down or prevent transmissions by the guilty MAC address).

17. B. The default masks are

- 255.0.0.0
- 255.255.0.0
- 255.255.255.0

18. B. To allow for the creation of smaller networks that operate better, the concept of classless routing, or Classless Interdomain Routing (CIDR), was born.

19. D. The show ip route command can be used to identify the routes of which the router is aware.

20. A, B. The tracert command (called traceroute in Linux and Unix) is used to trace the path of a packet through the network on routers.

Chapter 12: Troubleshooting Storage Issues

1. B. In Linux and Unix, this issue can be caused by a missing GRUB/LILO.

2. D. In Windows, if the error message says "Data error (cyclical redundancy check)," it could be a result of corruption of the drive, bad sectors, or an encrypted drive.

3. A. If you want fsck to attempt to repair any errors it finds, add the -a or -y parameter after the command.

4. B. Among the issues that can be diagnosed with this command are memory issues.

5. D. A real I/O issue is only indicated when I/O is high, use of swap is low, and use of memory is high.

6. B. While most data recovery failures are due to human error in the data backup process (running multiple jobs simultaneously, failure to change tapes, forgetting to remove a cleaning tape), there are some issues that are beyond your control.

7. B. A dual port HBA may provide another path to the network, but if the HBA fails it's still a single point of failure.

8. D. Issues such as cuts in the outer cover and stressed connectors can cause the cable to allow noise into the cable (RFI, EMI) that causes packets to be damaged or corrupted.

9. C. L2 cache failure will impact the performance of the server because it will slow the processor down.

10. C. Some systems use a passive terminator, while others that use Low Voltage Differential (LVD) mode will require active terminators.

11. A. fstab (File System Table) is a file used by Linux operating systems to mount partitions on boot.

12. C. The drives should be placed back in the reversed order of failures (failures, not removals).

13. B. badblocks has several different modes that allow you to detect bad sectors in Linux.

14. C. While it is possible to use mismatched drives, you should have a clear understanding of the implications of each type of mismatch. The only requirement set in stone is that they must be of the same architecture.

15. B. The net use command is used to connect users to shared drives.

16. C. In Windows Server 2012 R2, the diskpart command is used to manage storage from the command line.

17. A. The sudo fdisk -l command lists the partitions on the system.

18. D. fdisk is not available in Windows Server 2012 R2.

19. D. Configuring storage spaces is a fault tolerance and capacity expansion technique that can be used as an alternative to the techniques described in the section on dynamic volume types. It enables you to virtualize storage by grouping industry-standard disks into storage pools, and then creating virtual disks called storage spaces from the available capacity in the storage pools.

20. D. In Linux this log file is located at /var/log/messages.

Index

Note to the Reader: Throughout this index boldfaced page numbers indicate primary discussions of a topic. Italicized page numbers indicate illustrations.

C

J–K

L